BRISTOL AND AMERICA

AN

ORDINANCE OF T[

Lords and Commons Assembled in Parliament

For the Apprehending and bringing to condigne punishment, all such
persons as shall steale, sell, buy, inveigle, purloyne, convey, or ree
any little Children. And for the strict and diligent search of all Ships
and other Vessels on the River, or at the Downes.

Die Veneris, 9 *Maii.* 1645.

Hereas the Houses of Parliament are informed, that divers p
sons doe goe up and downe the City of London, and elsewh
in a most barbarous and wicked manner steale away th
Children, It is ordered by the Lords and Commons in P
assembled, That all Officers and Ministers of Justice b
streightly charged and required to be very diligent in app
all such persons as are faulty in this kind, either in stealing
buying, inveigling, purloyning, conveying, or receiving
so stolne, and to keepe them in safe imprisonment, till t
brought to severe and exemplary punishment.

It is further ordered, That the Marshals of the Admiralty, and the Cinqu
immediately make strict and diligent search in all Ships and Vessels upon the Ri
the Downes, for all such Children, according to such directions as they have of
from the Committee of the Admiralty, and Cinque-ports.

It is farther ordered, That this Ordinance be forthwith published in Pr
claimed in the usuall manner as other Proclamations, in all parts of the City
within the Lines of communication, and in all Parishes within the Bils of mo
sently: And in all Churches and Chappels by the Ministers, within the Line of co
tion, and Bils of mortality on the next Lords day: And in all other Churches an
elsewhere respectively, the next Lords day after the receipt hereof, that it may app
World, how carefull the Parliament is to prevent such mischiefes, and how fa
detest a crime of so much villany.

Mr. Spurstow, Mr. Vassall, and Collonell Venn, (Members of the House of Com
desired to got to the Lord Major, and to acquaint him with this Order, and to ta
it may be Proclaimed presently, and Published according to the directions, on the
day.

Die Veneris, 9 *Maii.* 1645.

ORdered by the Lords and Commons assembled in Parliament, that this Ord
be forthwith Printed and published presently, and read in all Parish Churche
pels within the Line of Communication and Bills of mortality, the next Lords day
other Churches and Chappels elsewhere respectively, the next Lords day after
hereof.

J. Brown Cler. Parliamentor.

London, Printed for *John Wright* at the signe of the Kings-head in the Old-baily, May 9.

TITLE PAGE OF THE FIRST VOLUME OF THE LIST OF "SERVANTS TO
FOREIGN PLANTATIONS"

Frontispiece

BRISTOL AND AMERICA

A RECORD OF THE FIRST SETTLERS IN THE COLONIES OF NORTH AMERICA

1654—1685

Including the names with places of origin of more than 10,000 Servants to Foreign Plantations who sailed from the Port of Bristol to Virginia, Maryland, and other parts of the Atlantic coast, and also to the West Indies from 1654 to 1685. This List is compiled and published from records of the Corporation of the City of Bristol, England

With Preface by
N. DERMOTT HARDING
Keeper of the Bristol Archives

and Historical Introduction by
WM. DODGSON BOWMAN
Author of "Bristol and its Associations"

Transcribed by
R. HARGREAVES-MAWDSLEY

Baltimore
GENEALOGICAL PUBLISHING CO., INC.
1978

Originally published: London, 1929, 1931
Reprinted: Genealogical Publishing Co., Inc.
Baltimore, 1967, 1970, 1978
Library of Congress Catalogue Card Number 64-19762
International Standard Book Number 0-8063-0170-8
Made in the United States of America

CONTENTS

PREFACE

OF all English cities, Bristol stands second only to London for the wealth and variety of its archives. Though many of the earliest writings and evidences no longer exist, enough remain to form an uninterrupted record of its municipal history for nearly eight hundred years. Its ecclesiastical archives go back even earlier. Until late in the eighteenth century only London surpassed in importance this great trading centre, port, and manufacturing city. For this reason its archives have a value above their local interest. Bristol is doubly rich in the possession of notable history and the preservation of exhaustive documentary evidences.

Communal government, which developed from the constitution of the old merchant guild, had its headquarters at the Guildhall in Broad Street. Here, in a great chest, were kept most of the earliest archives of the town. The Mayor himself had custody of some, such as the latest charter and the Little Red Book of Bristol, begun in 1344 by William de Colford, Recorder, who caused " the ordinances, customs and liberties, together with certain laws, other memoranda and divers necessary things to be kept in perpetual remembrance " to be, for the first time, put down in writing, that oral tradition might have a written foundation for all time to come.

As successive kings granted new charters of liberties, as the town developed into a county and a city, its archives increased in number and variety. Adjoining the Guildhall, the Chapel of St. George, closed as a place of worship in Henry VIII's reign, became a repository for the increasing store of records. In 1552 a Council House was built in Corn Street opposite All Saints' Church and the covered walk known as the Merchants' Tolzey. A similar covered way, erected outside the new building, was called the Mayor's Tolzey, so that the Council House itself was sometimes referred to as " the Tolzey House," a name which has long since dropped into disuse.

The building was repeatedly altered and enlarged, but its site has remained that of the municipal offices to the present day. The Town Council and its committees held, and still hold, their meetings there ; the Town Clerk and City Chamberlain, now the City Treasurer, have their offices and house their departments in the same building. St. George's Chapel continued to be used as a storehouse for the oldest archives until extensions in the eighteenth century, covering the site of one of the old city churches, allowed them to be transferred to new repositories in the Council House, where they have remained ever since. There were compiled and kept the proceedings and minutes of council meetings, the books of its committees, the many series of account books, all letters and letter books, archives of the numerous ancient courts, market books, all that concerned the important charities administered by the Corporation, town dues and Mayor's dues accounts, volumes of enrolments of deeds, ordinances, apprentices, burgesses, and assize of bread, and the archives which arose under each new Act of Parliament concerning the city. There, too, were stored the great accumulation of documents ranging from royal charters and letters patent, thousands of property deeds, files of memoranda, maps and plans, to the treasurer's vouchers to account. In addition were printed reference books and, at last, printed duplicates of many of the official archives. From the first deed now extant—a royal charter dated 1188—to the books and documents in current use, the "city evidences" in the Council House are themselves a treasure of no mean value.

There have, of course, been losses and instances of destruction during that long period. Just as the shipping records at the Customs House were nearly all destroyed in the Bristol riots of 1831, tradition has it that the city archives suffered fire in 1466. If true, this would explain why comparatively few early deeds now exist. The original letter files and letter books were all destroyed prior to the end of the eighteenth century. But much that had been accounted similarly destroyed or missing has been discovered of late years safely stored away. For example, records of old city courts such as the Mayor's Court, Court of the Staple, Piepowder and Tolzey Courts, Sessions and others, have come to light, although the Record Commissioners reported in 1915 that they had probably been destroyed in the riots.

The reason for such misapprehension is simple. In 1824–7 the Council House was rebuilt and a series of rooms in the top storey were reserved for the ancient archives, those in current use being stored in strong-rooms downstairs. In 1835 the Municipal Corporations Act inaugurated new methods of local government, while subsequent Acts continually enlarged the powers and functions of the city's governing body. There were corresponding changes in its archives, followed by a rapid increase in their quantity and variety. They accumulated more and more quickly, so that it became constantly necessary to relegate new divisions of them to the larger storerooms at the top of the building. Ancient series were displaced and finally lost sight of in the accession of more recent material. Their existence was perforce forgotten as the business of the modern city grew ever more pressing.

In 1924 an Archives Department was established. As, by local custom, the Chamberlain or City Treasurer was, in practice, custodian of the ancient archives (although the Town Clerk by reason of his office was their legal guardian), the first step had to be examination of those in the Treasurer's department. A survey of the contents of strong-rooms and repositories was made in readiness for the preparation of an inventory. It became possible to piece together scattered series, to arrange documents, to follow clues and to report discoveries of unsuspected material. Most important of these was the finding of the city court books, closely followed by that of the two volumes entitled "Servants to Foreign Plantations."

At first only listing was possible, then more detailed examination could be made and evidences of how the archives were compiled could be collected as guide to their arrangement. It became clear that after the first Council House was erected, the Mayor attended there early each morning for the transaction of city business. All that transpired was hurriedly written into rough entry books by appointed clerks. Both ends of the books were used, each type of business having its allotted space. In one series, Mayor's Court actions were entered up at the beginning and Apprentices at the end ; in another, Burgesses and Assize of Bread. The hours of attendance over, these entries were sorted and fair-copied into the big separate volumes of enrolment kept in the Chamberlain's office.

After 1654 a new type of entry was added to the apprenticeships in the "Actions and Apprentices" rough entry books. In that year Council had ordained that, before embarkation, persons bound as servants for overseas were to be articled and enrolled as were the city apprentices. " Servants to Foreign Plantations " were the fair copies of this system of enrolment. They were kept with the other Apprentice and Burgess Books in the Chamberlain's office. After the last entry on the last page of the second volume the word " Finis " is written. That is under date 1679. There is no later fair copy. But in the rough entry books, interspersed among the city apprenticeships, which are always written in Latin, further English entries concerning these servants bound for overseas continue after 1679. The last one appears in February 1685, after which the enrolment ceases. The final entries are very few, probably because this type of emigration from Bristol ceased, not because the system broke down.

Unlike the city Apprentice Books whose use continued, these volumes were finished, their purpose at an end. They were quite definitely completed archives and could be stored away as such. After this had been done and the occasion of their use become a piece of long-past history, it was natural, with the passage of time, that later officials should be in ignorance of their existence. So they remained in official custody and forgotten isolation for about two hundred years. At the end of that time, just as general interest in early American history and widespread research into its sources were growing keener, their existence was discovered at the moment when their use was most evident.

It is usual to find histories repeating the statement that emigration from England might be said to have ceased from the middle of the seventeenth until towards the end of the eighteenth century. These books prove that at least ten thousand emigrants sailed from Bristol between 1654 and 1685. They came from all over the British Isles, one from Burgundy in France, and only a very few are noted as having been released. To begin with, full and most interesting particulars are given about each servant. The earliest entries in the first volume contain the date of enrolment, servant's name and place of origin, master's name, destination, term of years, and conditions of service. The place of origin is omitted in all but a very few cases after the first half of the first volume had been completed, but the names are often a clue to nationality, Welsh, Irish, and Scotch being easily distinguished from English. The varied attempts made by the city clerks to put into writing the pronunciation of certain personal and place names are themselves an interesting study. The destination is omitted in but few instances, and it is probable that in each of those it would have been the same as for the preceding entry. City apprentices were bound for seven, eight, or nine years ; these foreign servants were indentured for four or five, and their conditions of service insured, at the end of that period, receipt of land, money, or, as in Virginia, a house, an axe, a year's provision, and double apparel. The last conditions made a new settlement possible, one where the apprentice, having served his time, might establish his own home and plantation with the security of enough supplies to carry him through the first lean year.

Entry of conditions of service rapidly becomes abbreviated and is often entirely omitted. Its absence is less unfortunate than omission of the place of origin, though the latter is balanced towards the end of the first volume by the addition of the name of the ship in which each servant was to sail and of the ship's master. On page 285 in the second volume there are complete entries, including the last addition, but they are the exception. Names of ships, such as *Love's Increase* and the *Unichorne*, give interesting information as to which vessels must have been in Bristol harbour on a given date, and also what ports were served by the ships mentioned. The frequency with which each name appears gives the length of time

B

taken over the various voyages, while the number of servants allotted to each ship is some indication of its size.

This is a brief summary of a big matter, a new chapter in the history of a nation, and a new light on early colonization. Even the order in which destinations are named is a silent comment on colonial development. The first servants go out to Barbados and Virginia. Then new names appear in the following order : Nevis, St. Christopher, New England, Maryland, Antigua, Jamaica, the Leeward Islands, Montserrat, the Caribbee Islands, York River, Newfoundland, New York, and Pennsylvania. They read like a muster-roll of pioneer achievement, and the thick pages of these long-finished volumes, which tell of service long since rendered, of masters and servants whose work is over, of ships known on the seas no more, tell also another and more eloquent story. They speak of Western nations whose roots are to be found in a common and ancient soil ; they are evidence of blood relationship and close ties of kinship ; they bear silent witness to the service an English city has rendered the New World since the day when through her gates and down her waterways John Cabot sailed out to the discovery of America.

N. Dermott Harding.

James Loyd | James Loyd of Tibister in the County of Hartford yeoman bound to Richard Allen of Virginia for fowre yeeres on the usuall condicions.

Tho: Jones | Thomas Jones bound to Henry Gough of Bristoll inhabitant for fowre yeeres to serve in Barbados on ye usuall condicions.

The Tenth Day.

John Obberbury | John Overbury of Henton in the County of Hereford milwright bound to Richard Whippy of Bristoll Marind for fowre yeeres in Virginia on the usuall condicions

Katherine Davis | Katherine Davy bound to George Morris for fowre yeeres to serve on the like condicions.

Anne Braine | Anne Braine of Bristoll widdow bound to the sd George Morris for six yeeres to serve on ye like condicions.

Wm Denford | William Denford Corriniston in ye County of Devon needlmaker bound to Richard Whippy for fowre yeeres on the like condicions

A FACSIMILE PAGE (SLIGHTLY REDUCED) FROM "SERVANTS TO FOREIGN PLANTATIONS"

HISTORICAL INTRODUCTION

By Wm. Dodgson Bowman

Chapter I

BRISTOL AND AMERICA

I

FOR those who seek to know the early history of those scattered settlements along the Atlantic seaboard which grew ultimately into that vast confederate Republic the United States of America, the record of the English seaport, Bristol is one of peculiar interest and fascination.

For hundreds of years before these settlements were founded, Bristol was one of the great maritime centres of the world. She was the Venice of the West, and, excepting London, the largest and busiest port in England. Her natural position, sheltered by the gorge of the Avon, with a navigable stream running beneath her walls, marked her out as a great naval city.

To this advantage alone, Bristol owes her greatness. Kings bestowed charters on her, but they took away more than they gave. Overlords oppressed her citizens, and the castle, under whose shadow they lived, was a symbol of the tyranny that fettered their liberties. Bishop and abbot only added to the weight of their burdens.

In the course of her thousand years of history Bristol has endured much. Her shipping was pillaged and burnt by Irish sea-rovers and French and Spanish privateers. Her walls were stormed and her peaceful citizens slain by the Barons and their hirelings. In the war between King and Parliament, Bristol was besieged and captured in turn by Royalist and Roundhead. More than once the city was destroyed by fire. The Black Death and other plagues swept away her inhabitants. Famine lowered her vitality.

Yet the indomitable spirit of Bristol rose superior to all calamities. No misfortunes shook the courage of her citizens. No disaster weakened their faith. Through good and ill fortune they followed the path of destiny with unfaltering courage. They discovered continents, peopled strange lands, and settled the destinies of generations yet unborn. They planned mighty works and achieved still greater. Among the great tasks they essayed was that of discovering and exploring the mainland of North America. They also took a decisive part in the more arduous task of colonizing that primitive and inhospitable land. A century and a half were to elapse before that attempt was rewarded with even a modified success. But by that time the twin dangers of dearth and massacre had been overcome, and the colony of Virginia had a population of about 10,000 white people, including women and children. In the twenty-five years that followed, 10,000 English people sailed from the port of Bristol to take their part in colonizing Virginia, Maryland, and other New England States. A few went to the Bermudas, but the majority to Virginia. The name of each one of these settlers is given in this book. The names of these founders of American families, members of which are still living in different parts of the United States, came to light through one of those happy accidents that occur from time to time and serve to show how rich the Old Country is in ancient records. These to the historian are amongst the most precious of earthly things.

II

The present Tolzey or Council House of the Corporation of the City of Bristol is one of the show-places of the West of England. It was rebuilt almost exactly a century ago, but in late years it has become too small for the increasing numbers of municipal officials that occupy its spacious chambers.   Its top floor consisted of a number of storerooms which were fitted up as archives for the great mass of old records that the City Corporation dearly prize.   Gradually, with the passing of the years, the shelves, presses, chests, and floor-space became congested.   New additions to the stock covered the older books and papers ; and as in olden times no list of these ancient books and parchments had been kept, no one knew what treasures these archives held.

In 1925 this storey was rebuilt in order to provide more office-room, and the city records were moved to new quarters.   The old books and stained title-deeds, ledgers, and letter books were then submitted to expert examination, with the result that a rich mass of historical material was brought to light.   As the examination proceeded, discovery followed discovery.   Old letter books that had been tossed aside and lain dusty and neglected became suddenly precious, for the information they contained and the light they cast on " old forgotten far-off things." But the most important of these discoveries was that of two volumes bearing the title " Servants to Foreign Plantations."   These had been found at the back of an ancient wall-press, and evidently had not been consulted for more than two centuries.

These volumes are dated 1654–1662 and 1663–1679.   The first volume is bound in smooth brown calf, and contains, exclusive of index and title-pages, 545 folios.   The second is bound in rough calf, and has, without index, 318 folios.   On the title-page is a black-letter Parliamentary ordinance, dated May 9, 1645, in which officers and justices are ordered to be very diligent in apprehending persons concerned in kidnapping children for overseas ; and marshals of the Admiralty and Cinque Ports are ordered to make diligent search of ships and vessels to discover such.

On the next page is written an ordinance of the Bristol Common Council, from which it is evident that the instructions of the Long Parliament had gone unheeded for a period of more than nine years, for the Council ordinance is dated September 29, 1654.   This apparent indifference to the orders of Parliament is explained by the fact that at that period Bristol had its own Admiralty jurisdiction, and that the local Council had the right to exercise its own discretion in such affairs.

The Council ordinance states that in view of many complaints of kidnapping, and for the prevention of such mischief, " It is this day agreed ordained and enacted by the Maior Aldermen and Common Councell, in Common Councell assembled, that all Boyes Maides and other persons which for the future shall be transported beyond the Seas as servants shall before their going a shipboard have their Covenants or Indentures of service and apprenticeship inrolled in the Tolzey Books as other Indentures of apprenticeship are and have used to be " (Tolzey Book means Council Book).   It was further ordained that when the master of a ship carried a passenger who was not so enrolled he was to be fined £20 for each offence.   One-quarter of this fine went to the informer, the rest to the poor.   The water-bailiff of the port was empowered to make a thorough and systematic search for unindentured passengers of all ships and vessels.

The enrolment began on the following day.   The first folio has the following heading : " The enrolment of apprentices and servants as are shipped at the port of Bristol to serve in any of the foreign plantacons beginning the 29th September 1654, John Gonninge Esq. being then Maior."

The first few entries of the earlier volume give several particulars of the agreements, of which the following is typical : " The Nineth day of October 1654 inrolled as followeth, Joane Robinson of Droitwich in ye countie of Worcester, Single Woman bound to the said Richard Allen for Five years, to goe to Virginia and to have at the ende of her terme one ax, one hous, one yeeres provisions and double apparrell." The later entries are much shorter, and often give no more than the name of the ship in which the " servant " is to sail. The significance of these so-called agreements will be explained later. It is sufficient now to say that these two volumes contain the names of every settler leaving England for Virginia, Maryland, and other settlements on the Atlantic seaboard as well as for Barbadoes from September 1654 to August 1679.

III

There is no more thrilling story in world-history than that record of the exodus from the Old to the New World in the sixteenth and seventeenth centuries. It has the lights and shadows of vivid drama, its war of passions, its moments of despair, its complete and triumphant *finale*. It is a story that should be treasured in the heart of every American citizen, for it tells of the deeds of the early fathers of his country. The memory of the sufferings they endured and the unflinching courage they showed in the face of overwhelming odds can never fail, so long as generous hearts feel love and reverence for true nobility. For these men lived greatly and died heroically. Some died before their allotted task was done, and they passed—

> " Still nursing the unconquerable hope,
> Still clutching the inviolable shade."

These men, as well as those that carried the conflict to ultimate triumph, command our veneration. For their blood is the seed of the puissant nation that is still " mewing its mighty youth."

This story is briefly recited here so that the significance of what follows may be understood.

It would be presumptuous and foolish to claim for any city the distinction of being the cradle of the American people, but if the problem were seriously considered Bristol could advance more solid and valid claims to that distinction than any other city.

Bristol seamen in a Bristol ship first sighted the American sea-board, and emigrants from the port of Bristol were the first settlers in the new American colonies. In this book, which is compiled from the records of the Corporation of the City of Bristol, a list of more than 10,000 names is given of men and women who elected to begin a new life in Virginia, Maryland, and the West Indies between the years 1654 and 1685. These people came from all parts of the British Isles, and sailed from the port of Bristol. They were of all classes. Some were landed gentry, ruined by the Civil War. Others were farmers, tradesmen, mechanics, and labourers. There was also an admixture of those who were leaving the country " for the country's good."

This list forms an historical document of the first importance. It records the names and destinations of the pioneers who cleared the woods, bridged the streams, drained the swamps, and transformed that Dark Continent of primeval forests into a smiling prosperous land. These pioneers little guessed as they strove to gain sustenance from an unfriendly and alien soil that they were " building better than they knew," and that in days to come they would be held in honour as the founders of one of the world's mightiest nations. Yet so it was. Though they knew it not these forefathers of the American people were fulfilling the decrees of Destiny, and settling the future of generations of millions yet unborn. This book proclaims their fame, and perpetuates their memory.

Chapter II
THE EXPLORERS

I

THE closing years of the fifteenth century and the first twenty of the sixteenth mark one of the most momentous eras in world-history. All around were signs of revolutionary change. The discoveries by the explorers of Prince Henry the Navigator established a bond between East and West, and threw open the portals of the East to European traders and travellers. Men's minds were excited by the strange tales brought by travellers from foreign lands, and year by year new wonders were revealed that kindled the imagination and excited strange fancies and beliefs; and among these beliefs none was more widely held and more difficult to dissipate than that across the Atlantic lay China and the East Indian Spice Islands. This belief did not expire until the sixteenth century had nearly run its course.

In 1498 the Spanish Ambassador in England wrote home to his sovereign rulers, Ferdinand and Isabella : " For the last seven years the people of Bristowe [Bristol] have sent out every year two, three, or four light ships in search of the Island of Brazil and the Seven Cities."

Two years before this letter was written, a patent was granted to a Venetian resident of Bristol, John Cabot, and his three sons, Lewis, Sebastian, and Sancius. This document is of note, for it is the earliest surviving relic that connects England with America. Of the voyage undertaken on the authority of this patent, there is but the most meagre information. Never was a momentous discovery announced in more laconic terms than in that old Bristol record which states : " In the year 1497, June 24, on St. John's Day, was Newfoundland found by Bristol men in a ship called the *Matthew*."

Another account, probably published by Cabot's direction, states that at five o'clock in the morning of June 24, Cabot discovered that land which no man before that time had attempted, and named it Prima Vista. The only other record that remains is an entry in the privy purse expenses of Henry VII which runs : " £10 to hym that found the new isle." By those who clung to the delusion of the seven fabled cities, it was announced on Cabot's return from his voyage that Henry VII had " won a part of Asia without a stroke of the sword."

Of Sebastian Cabot's voyage to the coast of Labrador in 1498, Eden tells us that he persevered until " seying suche heapes of ice before hyme he was enforced to tourne his sayles and folowe the west."

After the voyages of John Cabot and his famous son Sebastian, the merchants of London and Bristol lost their enthusiasm for voyages of discovery. France settled colonists in Canada and Spain, and not content with consolidating her power in the

6

south, extended her dominions as far north as Florida. Englishmen, whose golden visions had vanished in the cold light of reality, counted their losses, and sought other avenues of activity. It was not till the age of Elizabeth that Englishmen again sought fame in adventure by sea. Frobisher, " among the famousest men of our age," as Camden calls him, made three voyages to the coast of Labrador in 1576 and following years, and ruined himself and friends in the venture.

Sir Humphrey Gilbert made a fruitless effort to form a settlement on the Atlantic coast. The expedition sent by his brother-in-law Sir Walter Raleigh was scarcely more fortunate, and the prospective settlers were driven back to their ships by the native Indians.

While the fate of Raleigh's expedition hung in the balance, the Venturers of London and Bristol co-operated in a scheme of colonization. It was proposed that London should contribute £3,000 to the expenses of this, and Bristol £1,000. Walshingham, the Elizabethan statesman, was attracted by the project. He communicated with Thomas Aldworth, the Mayor of Bristol, and proposed that the Bristol merchants should fit out two barques for the expedition. He also advised Aldworth to consult Richard Hakluyt, the author of " Navigations, Voyages, and Discoveries of the English Nation." No better counsel could have been given.

It is easy to sneer at Hakluyt, as some historians do. They tell us he believed in the north-west passage to China, and that gold and precious stones were to be found in America. Well, what if he did ? Had not every experienced seaman and explorer of that age the same convictions ?

Hakluyt had beliefs, and he preached them with the fierce fervour of a New England gospeller. He was a booster, if you will, and was tireless in his advocacy of American colonization. As Sidney said, " Your Mr. Hakluyt hath served for a very good trumpet." His famous book, published some twenty years before the Authorized Version of the English Bible, set a new standard of English prose, is one of the foundation-books of English literature. It is at once a classic and a mine of information for all interested in navigation, and has been pored over and studied by every generation of scholars for more than three hundred years.

Aldworth took Walshingham's advice. He talked over his scheme with Hakluyt, and the latter promised to meet the Bristol merchants and address them on the subject. The Bristol men approved Hakluyt's advice, and, as Aldworth says, " there was aftsoons set down by men's own hands, then present, the sum of 1,000 marks and upward, whiche sum if it should not suffice, we doubt not but otherwise to furnish out for this western discovery a ship of three score, and a bark of 40 tunne to be left in the country."

The Bristol Company sent out a small ship and a barque to America, under the command of Martin Pring. The vessels carried a light cargo of kerseys, tools, beads, caps, etc. The Atlantic was safely crossed, and Pring brought his vessels round Cape Cod into Massachusetts Bay, and found a safe anchorage in a natural harbour that was afterwards known to the world as Plymouth. The voyagers stayed on the American mainland about five weeks, and at first suffered from the unwelcome attentions of the Indians. The shipmaster, however, had brought with him two great mastiffs, " Fool " and " Gallant." Of these the natives were greatly terrified, and kept at a safe distance whenever they were in sight.

From the financial point of view the voyage was a success. On the mainland the voyagers discovered immense quantities of sassafras, which at that time was highly valued in England for its medicinal properties.

Hakluyt was anything but satisfied with the result of this voyage. He was convinced that the new lands could not be thoroughly explored by short visits, and he urged in and out of season the imperative need of colonization.

His preaching fell on receptive ears. In 1606 James I granted two patents—one to a London Company for the colonization of Southern Virginia; the other to the merchants of Bristol, Exeter, and Plymouth for the colonization of that part of Virginia lying between 38° and 45° N. The chief organizers of the latter—known as the Plymouth Company—were Chief Justice Popham and Sir Ferdinando Gorges.

Of this Plymouth Company little need be told here, though, like its London rival, it succeeded after many trials and sufferings in planting its colonists on the soil of Virginia. Its first venture ended in misfortune, as Captain Pring and his vessel were captured by the Spaniards. But this did not discourage the Company, for ship after ship followed with would-be colonists eager and ready to try their fortunes in the New World, and some hundreds were lodged in hastily devised wooden shelters along the banks of the Sagadahoc River.

These new settlers, like their friends farther south, found the task of making a home amid the swamps and forests of an uncultivated land one of almost insuperable difficulty. The glowing fancy of Raleigh had painted this unknown continent as one where " men lived after the manner of the Golden Age." The stories of the vast wealth unearthed by the Spaniards in South America, and of the plate ships laden with gold and silver, had excited their cupidity and raised their expectations to an extraordinary degree. Here, they believed, was the fabled wealth of the Indies, and they had but to seek for the treasure that lay hidden all around them. These unfounded beliefs caused death and suffering, and brought the enterprise to the verge of disaster. Here were men, face to face with famine, frittering away precious time in searching for phantom gold, which they should have devoted to augmenting their scanty food supplies. In this mad gamble for wealth many perished.

It is clear that, whatever the wishes of the Company, these earlier colonists had no intention of settling permanently in Virginia. Their homes were the rudest shelters. The wives and families of those that were married had been left in England, and they doubtless hoped to rejoin them there as soon as they discovered the precious metals with which this new El Dorado was stored. At last, after enduring much hardship and privation, they discovered the one secret of successful colonization—labour. On this, clearings were made in the forest, and land was put under the plough. As one writer of the time expressed it, " men fell to building houses and planting corn."

The original colony on the Sagadahoc River was abandoned, but many of the Bristol men settled in the peninsula of Pemmaquid and carried on an extensive commerce there. Among other men whose names figure on the list of pioneer colonists in Virginia are those of Robert Aldworth and Giles Elbridge. These were Bristol merchants who sought a footing in the new land, by appointing a business agent in the Pemmaquid country to buy and sell on their behalf. This agent must have conducted a profitable trade, for in 1632—seven years after he was appointed—Aldworth received a grant from the Council of New England of 1,200 acres, close to the Pemmaquid River, and the offer of 100 acres extra for every new emigrant he brought out. By the terms of this grant he was also bound to establish and maintain a township. What progress these Bristol men made in fulfilling these conditions we do not know. But their efforts must have been crowned with success, for a town called Bristol was founded in the Pemmaquid district, and other townships bearing the name of their native city were established in neighbouring

States. Another bond between Old and New England was forged when New Somersetshire in Maine was conceded to Sir Ferdinando Gorges, to whom allusion has already been made as one of the chief organizers of the Plymouth Company.

II

And now let us consider the fortunes of the London Company, whose patent to colonize Southern Virginia had been granted simultaneously with that of the Plymouth Company. This in the course of time proved the more important and fruitful of the two enterprises. Yet in the beginning its equipment was so modest as to promise nothing but disaster. Only three tiny ships shared this momentous adventure, the *Susan Constant* of one hundred tons, the *Godspeed* of forty tons, and the pinnace *Discovery* of but twenty tons—all of them so small that a modern traveller would feel himself worthy of war decorations if he ventured afloat in them.

Considering the equipment for it, this adventure seemed reckless to the point of foolhardiness. Yet it is on reckless and foolhardy enterprises that the empires of the world have been founded.

This attempt to colonize an unknown land touched the imagination of Londoners. Public prayers were recited in the churches; sermons on the expedition were preached; James I, in an unusually gracious mood, expressed his approval of the expedition; and Michael Drayton wrote a poem for the occasion.

On the 19th day of December 1606 the little fleet set sail. The sufferings of the emigrants began as soon as they left the safe shelter of the Thames. The weather was exceedingly stormy, even for December, and the little boats were so tossed and delayed by tempests that the poor landsmen aboard were fain to turn back. As was the way of navigators at that period, the distance of the voyage was doubled by sailing round the Canary Islands; and the voyagers did not reach Virginia until May 6, 1607. The vessels were driven into Hampton Roads by a storm, and they then sailed up a broad river which they named the James. After their long months in cramped quarters aboard ship, the men found great pleasure in being able to walk about freely on dry land; and this no doubt accounts in some measure for their raptures on first beholding their new abode. We are told that when they went ashore they found " all the ground bespread with many sweet and delicate flowers of divers colours and kinds." And they added : " Heaven and earth had never agreed better to frame a place for man's habitation."

This verdict they afterwards modified, as events will show.

The men forming that first band of colonists were not of a type that a modern emigration agent would select. The company was described by one of its members as a crowd of " poor gentlemen, tradesmen, serving men, libertines, and such like." Captain Smith bluntly expressed the opinion that a " hundred good workmen were better than a thousand such gallants."

In the rules and orders of the new colony, everything that official stupidity could contrive to secure the failure of the enterprise had been set out. The worst blunder of all was in ignoring the rights of the individual settlers, on whom the success or failure of the scheme depended. It was decreed that all the produce of the colony was to go into a common stock for five years, so that no man had the incentive which self-interest supplies for working harder than his neighbours. This, coupled with the absence of any ruling authority, led the way to anarchy and the despotism that results from it.

Scarcely had the emigrants touched Virginian soil than they were attacked by the Indians, and, as one of the colonists says : " At night, when we were going aboard, there came the savages creeping from the Hills like Beares, with their Bowes in their Mouthes, charged us very desperately, hurt Captain Gabriel Archer in both hands, and a Sayler in two places of the body very dangerous. After they had spent their arrowes, and felt the sharpness of our shot, they retired into the Woods with a great noise and so left us."

But not all the Indians were unfriendly. The chief of the Rappahannocks welcomed them and offered gifts of game and corn.

The settlers chose for the site of their township a spot naturally defended by the river on all sides, except where a ridge of sand joined the mainland. Another advantage was that the ships lying in deep water near the shore could be moored by the simple expedient of tying them to trees. But though admirably suited for defence, this peninsula—since become an island—was one of the deadliest sites for a township that could have been chosen. In a short time the poor settlers discovered that it was little better than a fever swamp, and they paid dearly for their lack of judgment in selecting it.

On this plot of ground the colonists sought such shelter as they could hastily contrive—cabins roofed with bark, and tents, while others dug out burrows in the ground.

Before they had been in Virginia a month, the stores of the settlers had almost disappeared. As there was no appointed leader, each one did what seemed to him right, and the company, which had quarrelled continually since leaving England, became, instead of an organized fraternity, a discontented rabble. The shortage of food became so acute that nothing seemed more likely than that the whole band would perish before the winter was over. " There never were Englishmen," said George Percy, brother of the Duke of Northumberland, " left in a foreign country in such misery as we were in this new discovered Virginia. Each man's daily ration was a pint of worm-eaten barley or wheat. This was made into porridge, and a small ladleful was served out to every man at meal-times.

There was always the danger of attack from Indians, and every man had to take turns in keeping watch, lying on the ground. This exposure to the germ-laden air of the malarial peninsula was as deadly as any attacks by hostile tribes could have been. Poisoned air and scanty food quickly did their work. The majority of the colonists soon became affected with swellings, dysentery, and fever. Sometimes the number of men able to bear arms was reduced to less than five. Fifty of the men died. The rest were saved from starvation by the Indians, who bartered game and corn in exchange for beads and other trinkets.

The position of the little company of settlers, now reduced to half their number, was critical and the need of a strong leader urgent. After various experimental changes, Captain John Smith was chosen as President.

John Smith was one of the most remarkable men of a remarkable age. He was an embodiment of the spirit of adventure. He had the energy of a dynamo, the alertness and cunning of an Indian hunter, and something, as his writings show, of the calm sagacity of a statesman. Withal he was in company aggressive and boastful by turns, and these qualities made him unpopular among his acquaintances.

Like many men of his age, he was much given to hard lying and fervent prayer. There can be little doubt that when telling the story of his adventures, his imagination glowed sometimes with unnatural heat. The romances with which he fed his soul in youth are not a bit more amazing than his record of his own career.

Yet whatever doubt may be cast on Smith's account of his adventures, there is no doubt whatever that he was an able and successful administrator. He was conciliatory in negotiation, prudent in council, brave in emergencies. His comments on public affairs show him to have been in advance of his time in breadth of view and insight. The story of his early adventures reads like an Arabian Nights fairytale. As a youth he fought in Flanders, after which he travelled East and was taken prisoner by the Turks. He was robbed, and shipwrecked at sea. In the presence of some ladies he fought three Infidel champions in single combat and cut off their heads. While still in the hands of the Turks a beautiful girl, Tragabigzanda, fell violently in love with him. But liberty meant more to him than the magic influence of a woman's eyes, and he escaped from captivity by killing his master with a flail. He made his way to South Russia, where once more he became an object of adoration—this time of a Russian lady named Calamata. Tiring of love's soft enchantments, he made his way to Barbary, where he had his fill of fighting and excitement. When returning to Europe in a passenger ship, a mighty storm arose. The pious pilgrims on board became panic-stricken. Looking upon Smith as a Jonah who had brought ill-luck to the ship, they threw him overboard. That was one of Smith's unlucky days. There was no friendly whale to render him assistance. This did not seriously perturb him, for he emerged triumphantly from the adventure by swimming ashore. After many similar hair-raising incidents, he began to tire of the life strenuous and turned his face homewards. But a man of Smith's temperament was constitutionally unfitted for a humdrum existence. Once more he felt the insurgent blood racing in his veins, and looked around for fresh employment. In London he heard of the proposed colonization of Virginia, and promptly offered himself as an emigrant. He was then only twenty-eight years of age, but he had crowded a lifetime of experience into his few years of manhood. Even when due allowance has been made for the exaggeration which marked all travellers' narratives at that period, enough had been left to furnish the experiences of a dozen heroes of fiction.

In Virginia, Smith found life strenuous enough to satisfy even his adventure-loving spirit. He was captured by the Indians, carried in triumph from village to village, and was about to be shot by the Indians when the lovely Pocohantes, daughter of Powhatan, threw her arms round him, and refused to move until her father promised to spare the life of the captive. How far this is true it is impossible to say, but we do know that somehow Smith contrived to secure his release. During his short tenure of the Governorship of Virginia, Smith did invaluable service for the colonists. But for him the settlers would have starved. In his voyages of discovery through the bays and rivers he kept on good terms with the Indians and brought back with him to Jamestown large stores of grain that he had persuaded the natives to sell. Instead of wasting time in searching for gold, he counselled the settlers to labour on the land. One exploit deserves special mention, though it is rarely alluded to in any story of his career—his exploration of Chesapeake Bay. In an open boat, and with no instrument but a compass, he thoroughly explored every part of this bay ; and so well and accurately was this done that the map he made of it superseded all others for a hundred and forty years.

In the spring of 1609 five hundred new colonists arrived, under the leadership of Archer and Ratcliffe, two of the original settlers, who were declared enemies of the Governor. Smith settled some of the new colonists at Nansemond, and the rest near the falls of the James River. Archer and Ratcliffe had no sooner arrived than they began to stir up trouble and intrigue with the authorities in England against Smith. After much turmoil and dissension, Smith, who had been incapacitated by an accident, was recalled to London.

Disaster followed swift on Smith's removal from the scene ; and the colonists began dimly to realize that to his influence they owed both immunity from attack and the very food they ate. Once he had departed, the Indians became openly hostile. They drove the settlers from Nansemond and the Falls of St. James. Ratcliffe, who had intrigued incessantly to get Smith banished from the colony, attempted to trade with the natives as the former Governor had done. But he was captured in an ambuscade, and tortured to death by Indian women.

Food became scarce. Soon the brood-hogs were eaten. Then the dogs followed, and finally the horses. Even rats and mice were relished, so appalling was the hunger of the starved settlers. We read that even the body of an Indian slain, and three days buried, was eaten " by the poorer sort." One among these famished men—Daniel Tucker—had a happy thought. He built a boat to catch fish in the river. The expedient, as Percy confesses, " did keep us from killing one another to eat." Some of these unfortunates vainly sought food in the wood and died of starvation, and their bodies were eaten by those who found them dead. The empty dwellings were burnt for firewood.

The colony seemed doomed to extinction. In the autumn of the previous year there were nearly five hundred colonists. In the following June but sixty emaciated wretches survived. Nothing but a miracle could save them. But the miracle happened !

The emigrants who had arrived in Virginia in the previous autumn had expected to find their leaders, Sir Thomas Gates and Sir George Somers, there when they landed. But to their surprise no tidings had reached the colony about them. These gentlemen had embarked on a vessel which became separated from the rest of the fleet and was wrecked on the shores of the Bermudas. Sir George Somers, an experienced seaman, built two pinnaces, provisioned them well, and sailed for Virginia early in 1610. They arrived when the tiny community had reached starvation point. Finding no supplies in Jamestown, Gates and Somers decided to embark the whole company in four pinnaces and sail for Newfoundland. But as they sailed down the river they met Lord De La Warr, who, with a large store of supplies, was coming to take charge of the colony. To the keen regret of some of the old settlers, they were ordered back by the new Governor.

The houses and palisades in Jamestown were repaired and strengthened, and the town cleansed. Even the little church was enlarged and decorated daily with flowers.

Lord De La Warr did not stay long in Virginia. A few months after his arrival a fresh epidemic broke out, and in the year following he forsook the settlers and sailed for England.

His successor, Sir Thomas Dale, put the colony under a military despotism, and his administration in later years was referred to as the five years of slavery. The colonists under his rule were treated a little worse than dogs, and the Governor's sole aim was to earn dividends for the Company. At the end of his term there were three hundred and twenty-six men and twenty-five women and children in Virginia. Under Dale's rule the profitable cultivation of tobacco began.

Of Captain Argall's corrupt government it is unnecessary to say anything except that he robbed everyone impartially, including the Company and settlers, and made the name of Virginia stink in the nostrils of all honest men.

The official mind is not receptive to new ideas, but a succession of bitter disasters and failures at last brought to those in charge of colonial policy some realization of the fact that any system of government which outrages elementary human rights and interests is ultimately doomed to failure. That abler men even in early Stuart times had grasped this truth is evident, as this quaint proposition shows : " A plantation can never flourish till families be planted with the respects of Wives and children fix the people on the soyle."

This by 1618 was well understood, for in that year a ship sailed to Virginia carrying ninety maids, and the Company offered special rewards to the men who should marry them. The offer of rewards was needless in that Eve-less wilderness ; not only the young and handsome, but also the old and homely, had the best of matrimonial opportunities. Shipload after shipload of these girls sailed from England, and they were eagerly courted and won by the crowds of settlers who waited their arrival at the harbour. As the number seeking wives greatly outnumbered the maids that arrived, the women were able to pick and choose. This novel form of export went on for many years, but still the demand was greater than the supply.

Until the arrival of women, the colonists were never settlers in the true sense of the word. But now, with wives by their side, they were at home, and had no inclination to leave the country. There was also a younger generation growing apace who had known no other land and would some day take over the work their fathers were now doing. And as now there were native-born white Virginians, the country could in truth be called settled, whatever its economic condition.

INTRODUCTION TO THE TRANSCRIPTIONS

By Wm. Dodgson Bowman

ITH the granting of the Charter of Liberties and the assembly of the
settlers in the church at Jamestown in 1619, all doubt of the ultimate
success of the new Dominion was at an end. But the goal of peace and
prosperity was yet afar off. Attacks by the Dutch, massacres, rebellions, and other
ills were endured before the way was made straight. But Virginia was no longer a
wilderness. With every year that passed it became a more desirable place of residence, and the settlers whose names are given in this volume and who found a home
in Virginia between the years 1654 and 1679 had every reason to be contented with
their lot.

It is now necessary to say something of these colonists. Though known officially
as " Servants of the Plantations," this name was a misnomer in the vast majority of
cases. In the earlier days of the Virginia Company, their " servants," in return for
their labours on the public land, received an allotment for themselves, and in course
of time, by working out their period of service, became landholders. After the
extinction of the Company, no change was made in the tenure of land. As before,
fifty acres were granted to every free emigrant who went out at his own charge,
and fifty more for every person whom he brought in.

For the first seven years all quit-rents were remitted, and the only condition
imposed was that out of every fifty acres occupied, three should be cultivated within
the year.

These terms were anything but onerous, and in the years following the Civil
War in England there was a rush to take advantage of them.

In the list given here there are more than 10,000 names. All of them sailed
from Bristol, and as at that time Bristol had a monopoly of the Virginian trade, this
list gives the names of practically every person who left England for Virginia, Maryland, and the West Indies. As is inevitable in any large number, these emigrants
were of all sorts and conditions of men and women. A few of them were pardoned
criminals ; a small proportion were political prisoners. There were few ages in English
history when this resource insured so constant a supply. Penruddock's rebellion
in 1655 and the Scottish rising in 1666 furnished their share of emigrants. Many
Cavaliers rescued by the Civil War sought shelter and peace in this new home in the
American Dominions.

There were also a number of children and apprentices who were kidnapped and
sold to the plantations. But the vast majority were respectable and industrious
men and women who bound themselves for a fixed term of service with the certainty
of becoming freeholders at the end of that period. Many of these prospered.
Others ultimately became overseers for the great planters. But whatever their

material condition, all found in the new land a greater measure of liberty than they had enjoyed in England.

In Virginia and Maryland as well as throughout the United States there are many who are proud to claim these early settlers as their forefathers. To be the descendants of the founders of a mighty nation is a source of legitimate pride; for these hardy pioneers who fought a mighty conflict with nature and emerged triumphant are among those the world holds in veneration.

Here are a few typical entries from the list of Servants to the Plantations :

Page 5

Alice Cowbreach of the County of Glamorgan singlewoman bound to John Young Merchant for 4 yeeres to Virginia—to have 50 acres of land.

Mary Giles of Salwarpe, spinster, bound to the said Richard Allen for five yeeres to goe to Virginia and to have at the end of the time one axe, one hous, one yeeres provisions and double apparrell.

Dec. 7, 1678.

Joane Nicholls bound to Abraham Wild for 5 yeeres in Maryland.

Aug. 27, 1675.

Benjamin Bevis bound to George Parker for 4 yeeres in Merryland.

August 1662.

Thomas Trottman, bound to Elias Trottman for 5 yeeres in Maryland.

Servants to Foreign Plantations

VOL. I, 1654-63

Transcribed by R. Hargreaves-Mawdsley

Page 1

Richard Pell (no place of residence given); destination, Barbadoes.—Thomas Ree (of Upper Warren); destination, Virginia.—George Palmer (of Taunton); destination, Virginia.—Richard ffenne (of Badminton); destination, Virginia.— Susan Selfe (of Chipnam); destination, Barbadoes.—Thomas Cletter (no place of residence given); destination, Virginia.—John Dawks (of Redermister); destination, Virginia.—Robert Cartwright (of Droitwich); destination, Virginia.

Page 2

John Jones (of Droitwich); destination, Virginia.—Charles Corbet (of Colla); destination, Virginia.—William Haiwood (of Charleton); destination, Virginia.— Susanna White (of Preston); destination, Virginia.—Joane Robinson (of Droitwich); destination, Virginia.—Margery Coles (of Beareford); destination, Virginia.—Mary Giles (of Salwarpe); destination, Virginia.—John Edward (of Lamsadder); destination, Virginia.—Morgan Thomas (of Clanspethie); destination, Virginia.—Richard Combes (of Sturton); destination, Virginia.—James Sheppard (of Kingswood); destination, Virginia.—Mary Ravenell (of Woolhope); destination, Virginia.

Page 3

John Rose (of ffarly); destination, Virginia.—Stephen Trotman (of Nibley); destination, Virginia.—Jesse Trotman (of Nibley); destination, Virginia.—William Jones (of Lanvaier); destination, Virginia.—Roger Reece (of Redwelly); destination, Virginia.—John Davis (of Berrowin); destination, Virginia.—Morgan Jones (of Trelocke); destination, Virginia.—George Jones (of Trelocke); destination, Virginia.—Henry Davis (of Lansamfroid); destination, Virginia.—George Pearse (of Hull); destination, Barbadoes.—James ffraven (of Ruarden); destination, Virginia. —John Gooding (of Abergainy); destination, Virginia.

Page 4

John Horsnet (of Bromheadrin); destination, Virginia.—John Henikir (of Ross); destination, Virginia.—Clement Everet (of Stone); destination, Virginia.— John Williams (of Cowbreach); destination, Virginia.—Evan Watkin (of Langattock); destination, Barbadoes.—Phillip Thomas (of Landavid); destination, Barbadoes.—

Lewis Williams (of Abergainy) ; destination, Barbadoes.—Ruth Phillips (of Tithring-ton) ; destination, Barbadoes.—Martin Jones (of Abergainy) ; destination, Vir-ginia.—Ann Dabdes (of Tewksbury) ; destination (no place given).—John Watkins (of Brotherden) ; destination, Barbadoes.—John Griffith (of Blackmore) ; destina-tion, Barbadoes.

Page 5
   William Norvell (of Uphill) ; destination, Barbadoes.—Lewis Bevan (of Carlion) ; destination, Virginia.—Alice Jenkins (of Cowbreach) ; destination, Virginia.—Hanna White (of Stogumber) ; destination, Virginia.—William Bowen (of Langadock) ; destination, Virginia.—William Davis (of Cardiffe) ; destination, Virginia.—Thomas Gothridge (of Northcurry) ; destination, Virginia.—Thomas Morgan (of Newport) ; destination, Virginia.—John Watkins (of Laughan) ; destina-tion, Virginia.—Joane Norman (of Ashwicke) ; destination, Nevis Island.—Jane Phelks (of Midford) ; destination, Virginia.—Susan Selfe (of Chipnam) ; destination, Virginia.

Page 6
   Welthian Morris (of Mivor) ; destination, Virginia.—Robert ffox (of Bristoll) ; destination, Virginia.—John Merriweather (of Taunton) ; destination, Barbadoes.—David Williams (of Glanaty) ; destination, Barbadoes.—David Maxall (of Glanane) ; destination, Barbadoes.—Richard Allen (of Harlington) ; destination, Barbadoes.—Michael Vowle (of Ballinure); destination, Barbadoes.—George Stephens (of Bristoll); destination, Barbadoes.—Richard Wolfe (of Herefford) ; destination, Barbadoes.—John Chilcot (of Stoey) ; destination, Barbadoes.—John Hill (of Ludford) ; destina-tion, Barbadoes.—John Lewis (of Blakemare) ; destination, Barbadoes.

Page 7
   Ann Amphlet (of Brosely) ; destination, Barbadoes.—Katharine Perry (of Brosely) ; destination, Barbadoes.—Elizabeth Llewellin (of Bristoll) ; destination, Barbadoes.—Honor Edwards (of Bristoll) ; destination, Barbadoes.—John Griffith (of Brinsop) ; destination, Barbadoes.—Thomas Kimbridge (of Pollet); destination, Barbadoes.—Prudence Leggat (of Bristoll) ; destination, Barbadoes.—Evan Ellis (of Landeliolen) ; destination, Barbadoes.—Walter Harry (of Brungwin) ; destina-tion, Barbadoes.—Thomas Morris (of Dublin) ; destination, Barbadoes.—William Philpe (of Reading) ; destination, Barbadoes.—Joseph ffreeman (of Nanton) ; destination, Nevis.

Page 8
   Edward Harry (of Lanero) ; destination, Barbadoes.—Michaell Bennet (of The Barbadoes) ; destination, Barbadoes.—Bridget Watkins (of Egget) ; destination, Barbadoes.—John Allen (of Werr) ; destination, Barbadoes.—John Smith (of London) ; destination, Barbadoes.—William Beacon (of Bathe) ; destination, Barbadoes.—Mathew Maclelen (of Orcougule) ; destination, Barbadoes.—John Luffe (of Bath) ; destination, Barbadoes.—Thomas Hembrow (of Lamport) ; destination, Barbadoes.—Edward Batsson (of Yorcombe) ; destination, Barbadoes.—John Pimple (of Somerton) ; destination, Barbadoes.—Thomas Strashly (of Taunton); destination, Barbadoes.

Page 9

John Williams (of Tregard) ; destination, Barbadoes.—Seth Williams (of Kemmis) ; destination, Barbadoes.—Benjamin Stephens (of Swainswick) ; destination, Barbadoes.—Barry Thomas (of Calcot) ; destination, Barbadoes.—Thomas Beale (of Bristoll) ; destination, Barbadoes.—Christopher Hix (of Bristoll) ; destination, Barbadoes.—Henry Stiffe (of ffishiton) ; destination, Barbadoes.—William Brownjohn (of Salisbury) ; destination, Barbadoes.—William Rinold (of Kemis) ; destination (no place given).—John Reynolds (of Wellington) ; destination, Barbadoes.—William Woodfield (of London) ; destination, Barbadoes.—Thomas Collins (of London) ; destination, Barbadoes.

Page 10

Bartholomew Jones (of Baslick) ; destination, Barbadoes.—John Davis (of Rosse) ; destination, Barbadoes.—George Wotton (of Bridgewater) ; destination, Barbadoes.—Richard Eckinfull (of Ledbury) ; destination, Barbadoes.—Morris Power (of Waterford) ; destination, Barbadoes.—Mary Clarke (of Bristoll) ; destination, Barbadoes.—Evan David (of Lanyangell) ; destination, Barbadoes.—Thomas Harris (of Raglan) ; destination, Barbadoes.—Ann Holbrooke (of Bristoll) ; destination, Barbadoes.—Humfry Ellis (of Welshpoole) ; destination, Barbadoes.—Mary Lovell (of Dimock) ; destination, Barbadoes.—Ann Olman (of Bristoll) ; destination, Barbadoes.

Page 11

Joane ffreeman (of Wister) ; destination, Barbadoes.—Elinor Cox (of Cannington) ; destination, Barbadoes.—Rachell Ley (of Kennington) ; destination, Barbadoes.—William Mountague (of Astoncling) ; destination, Barbadoes.—Henry Harris (of Bitton) ; destination, Barbadoes.—John Dickery (of Salisbury) ; destination, Barbadoes.—Nicholas Garby (of Southwarke) ; destination, St. Christopher.—Thomas Cooper (of ffroome) ; destination, Barbadoes.—Edward Godsell (of St. Phillip's in Bristol) ; destination, Barbadoes.—William Walter (of London) ; destination, Barbadoes.—ffrancis Wimball (of Wootton) ; destination, Barbadoes.—Dorathy Balle (of Salisbury) ; destination, Barbadoes.

Page 12

Robert Stary (of Axbridge) ; destination, Barbadoes.—Thomas Boy (of Belanamore) ; destination, Barbadoes.—Timothy Boy (of Belanamore) ; destination, Barbadoes.—Luke Morgan (of Kemford) ; destination, Barbadoes.—William Peters (of West Chester) ; destination, Nevis.—Richard Crabb (of Bristoll) ; destination, Barbadoes.—Isaac Palmer (of Sutton) ; destination, Barbadoes.—Richard Jones (of Worcester) ; destination, Barbadoes.—Matthew Williams (of Nulim) ; destination, Barbadoes.—William Baker (of St. John's in St. Lewis) ; destination, Barbadoes. —John Wagget (of Shepton upon Stower) ; destination, Barbadoes.—Thomas ffurnis (of Warwick) ; destination, Barbadoes.

Page 13

Richard Marler (of Coventry) ; destination, Barbadoes.—Stephen Gun (of Oxford) ; destination, Barbadoes.—Michaell Pinkney (of St. Martin's in London) ; destination, Barbadoes.—Henry Gittis (of Bathe) ; destination, Barbadoes.— John Gwilliam (of Edlain) ; destination, Barbadoes.—Hanna Leere (of Corke) ; destination, Barbadoes.—Gennet Reece (of Langattock) ; destination, Barbadoes.—

Elinor Cubis (of Corfe) ; destination, Barbadoes.—Susan Jefferis (of Winford) ; destination, Barbadoes.—Sara Peters (of Hindon) ; destination, Barbadoes.—John Pasten (of Bristoll) ; destination, Barbadoes.—Elinor Griffeth (of Worcester) ; destination, Barbadoes.

Page 14
George Edin (of Rouick) ; destination, Barbadoes.—Myles Carill (of Waterford) ; destination, Barbadoes.—John Bande (of Gloucester) ; destination, Barbadoes.—James Davis (of Kingsloe) ; destination, Virginia.—William Davis (of Kingsloe) ; destination, Virginia.—Roger Jones (of Carlion) ; destination, Virginia. —John Ruther (of Cardigan) ; destination, Barbadoes.—Phillip Jones (of Butterwood) ; destination, Virginia.—ffrancis Jones (of Butterwood) ; destination, Virginia.—Katherine Mathew (of Swanzey) ; destination, Virginia.—Morgan David (of Whichwich) ; destination, Barbadoes.—Rice Howell (of Estrodwelta) ; destination, Virginia.

Page 15
James Harris (of Langatto) ; destination, Barbadoes.—William Bennet (of Waring) ; destination, Barbadoes.—Roger Spreake (of Culliford) ; destination, Virginia.—William James (Spixen) ; destination, Barbadoes.—John Parker (no place given) ; destination, Barbadoes.—Elizabeth Barley (of Thornebury) ; destination, Barbadoes.—Judith Paifry (of Milburton) ; destination, Barbadoes.—Mary Jones (of Marlis) ; destination, Virginia.—Katharine Dimant (of Bristoll) ; destination, Virginia.—Hester Meene (of Weston-under-Poinard) ; destination, Virginia.— Dorothy ffarmer (of Gloucester) ; destination, Virginia.—Joane Howlet (of Gloucester) ; destination, Virginia.

Page 16
Edward Hilman (of Yatton) ; destination, Virginia.—Huddy Harris (of Corsham) ; destination, Barbadoes.—Ann Pits (of Porbury) ; destination, Barbadoes.— Robert Coller (of Sutton) ; destination, Virginia.—Richard Powell (of Lanwarne) ; destination, Virginia.—Mary Onion (of Tipponton) ; destination, Barbadoes.— Ann Speake (of Bristoll) ; destination, Barbadoes.—Thomas Lillicrop (of Huethick) ; destination, Virginia.—Stephen Smalman (of Wilderhope) ; destination, Barbadoes. —George Hayter (of Eston Yleris) ; destination, Barbadoes.—John Trustrome (of Dunsborne Leard) ; destination, Barbadoes.—John Sambrooke (of St. Michael's in London) ; destination, Barbadoes.

Page 17
Thomas Jones (of Lantillo Gresem) ; destination, Virginia.—William Bryan (of Lantillo Gresem) ; destination, Virginia.—William Webb (of Cremcard) ; destination, Virginia.—John Cundrick (of Westerly) ; destination, Barbadoes.— George Bonde (of Bristoll) ; destination, Barbadoes.—Ann Jones (of Bristoll) ; destination, Virginia.—Priscilla Rogers (of Lanthony) ; destination, Virginia.— William Musgrave (of Taunton) ; destination, Virginia.—Anthony Agg (of Bristoll) ; destination, Virginia.—Ann Toulson (of Gloucester) ; destination, Virginia.— Peter Whitingham (of Midlewich) ; destination, Barbadoes.—Mary Dyer (of Nantwood) ; destination, Virginia.

Page 18

Edward Streatly (of Weymouth) ; destination, Virginia.—John Rice (of Cadwelly) ; destination, Virginia.—Abigaile Grannt (of Bradford) ; destination, Barbadoes.—Jane Stroud (of Bristoll) ; destination, Virginia.—John Ross (of Bute) ; destination, Virginia.—Sara Jones (of Landaffe) ; destination, Virginia.—Margaret Williams (of Ragland) ; destination, Barbadoes.—Alice Watkins (of Penrose) ; destination, Barbadoes.—Edward Davis (of Newton) ; destination, Barbadoes.— Daniel Abbot (of Trinity in Isle of Ely) ; destination, Barbadoes.—Thomas Taylor (of Luggerdine) ; destination, Virginia.—Rebecca Davis (of Grossemount) ; destination, Virginia.

Page 19

Anne Morgan (of Rollstone) ; destination, Virginia.—Mary Jones (of Greekehowell) ; destination, Virginia.—Markes Thomas (of Greekehowell) ; destination, Virginia.—Nicholas Winston (of Bristoll) ; destination, Barbadoes.—Sarah Carter (of Bristoll) ; destination, Virginia.—James Stephens (of Abraham Chest) ; destination, Virginia.—Robert Bult (of Chelton) ; destination, Virginia.—Ann Prichard (of Greekehowell) ; destination, Virginia.—Joseph Cox (of Mangotsfield) ; destination, Virginia.—Edward Whiting (of Madston) ; destination, Virginia.—William Worgan (of Blakeney) ; destination, Virginia.—John Window (of Winsfield) ; destination, Virginia.

Page 20

Hanna Window (of Winsffield) ; destination, Virginia.—Dorathy Pegler (of Winsffield) ; destination, Virginia.—Margaret Trippick ; destination, Virginia.— George Stephens (of Bisly) ; destination, Virginia.—Edward Benny (of Bodington) ; destination, Virginia.—Elinor ffowler (of St. Andrewes) ; destination, Virginia.— Richard ffrankeland (of Clapoole) ; destination, Barbadoes.—Morgan Williams (of Newport) ; destination, Virginia.—Robert Smith (of Kingsale) ; destination, Virginia.—Robert Haker (of Balsbury) ; destination, Barbadoes.—John Noblin (of North Yarmouth) ; destination, Virginia.—Edward Mills (of Bishops Upton) ; destination, Virginia.

Page 21

Thomas Warr (of Bishops Upton) ; destination, Virginia.—Mary Jones (of Manithiselo) ; destination, Virginia.—Thomas Wally (Congreton) ; destination, Virginia.—Elizabeth Wally (of Congreton) ; destination, Virginia (released).— John Whitmore (of Dudley) ; destination, Virginia.—Susan Wits (of Cawne) ; destination, Barbadoes.—Thomas Rooke (of Nunson) ; destination, Virginia.— John Charles (of Manthusilo) ; destination, Virginia.—Elinor Harvert (of Bath) ; destination, Barbadoes.—William Avery (of Shepston uppon Stower) ; destination, Virginia.—William White (of Herefford) ; destination, Virginia.—John ffalconer (of Sherhampton) ; destination, Virginia.

Page 22

John Blast (of Newlands) ; destination, Virginia.—Elizabeth Care (of Cheltnam) ; destination, Barbadoes.—Richard Mooreton (of Bristoll) ; destination, Virginia.—James Price (of Gloucester) ; destination, Virginia.—Mary Golding (of Devizes) ; destination, Virginia.—Sidney Bailey (of Clonvaiday) ; destination, Virginia.—Thomas Jones (of Landaffe) ; destination, Virginia.—Mary Giles (of

Trevin); destination, Virginia.—Alice Stewart (of Pensford); destination, Virginia.—John Watkins (of Monmouth); destination, Virginia.—Evan Thomas (of Lanwinnellins); destination, Virginia.—John Hatten (of Bristoll); destination, Virginia.

Page 23
Thomas Hubbert (of Bristoll); destination, Virginia.—Joseph Coventry (of Hull); destination, Barbadoes.—John Waters (of Penhow); destination, Virginia. —Joane Davis (of Bristoll); destination, Virginia.—John Atkins (of Huthorne); destination, Virginia.—Morrice Evans (of Bruton); destination, Virginia.—Jane Jones (of Gloucester); destination, Virginia.—William Lade (of East Mauling); destination, Barbadoes.—William Cooke (of Hereford); destination, Barbadoes.— David Jones (of Cowbridge); destination, Virginia.—William Chambers (of Bristoll); destination, Virginia.—John Jenkins (of Clohen neare Clammell [Clonmell]); destination, Virginia.

Page 24
Arthur Skinner (of London); destination, Virginia.—Elizabeth Williams (of Bristoll); destination, Virginia.—John Bayly (of Bristoll); destination, Virginia.—John Jones (of Bristoll); destination, Virginia.—Morris Evans (of ffroome); destination, Virginia.—Sarah Jones (of Bristoll); destination, Barbadoes.— Elizabeth Stephens (no place given); destination, Barbadoes.—Elioner Johnson (of London); destination, Virginia.—Elioner Williams (no place given); destination, Virginia.—Anne Bevington (of Hasely); destination, Virginia.—Isaac Gale (of Keinton); destination, Virginia.—John Yate (of Orleton); destination, Virginia.

Page 25
John Hughs (of Carno); destination, Virginia.—David Howell (of Crickhowell); destination, Virginia.—Thomas Jones (of Crickhowell); destination, Virginia.— John Millard (of Westwood); destination, Virginia.—Markes Young (of Ile of Wayte); destination, Virginia.—Robert Sansum (of Bristoll); destination, Virginia. —John Page (of Elmester); destination, Barbadoes.—John Pugginham (of Sias Newton); destination, Barbadoes.—Mary Barnard (of Taunton); destination, Virginia.—Hugh Partridge (of Bristoll); destination, Virginia.—Hugh Ingrome (of Bristoll); destination, Virginia.—John Page (of Elmister); destination, Virginia.

Page 26
John Thomas (of Morgan); destination, Barbadoes.—Edward Hancocke (of Hancocke); destination, Virginia.—Johnes Webb (of Bristoll); destination, Virginia.—Thomas Blany (of Letton); destination, Barbadoes.—Richard Clements (of Broniard); destination, Virginia.—Elioner Edwards (of Monmouth); destination, Virginia.—Margaret Barnewell (of Bristoll); destination, Virginia.—Lawrence Asx (of Dublin); destination, Virginia.—Barbara Pattingall (of Bristoll); destination, Virginia.—Thomas Wally (of Sparrowgrave); destination, Virginia.—Elizabeth Wally (of Sparrowgrave); destination, Virginia.—John King (of Mayer); destination, Barbadoes; John Haskins (of Tewton Mendip); destination, Virginia.

Page 27
John Davis (of Wooten); destination, Barbadoes.—Peter Kilby (of Corke); destination, Virginia.—John Brisco (of Barnett); destination, Barbadoes.—Rebecca

Brisco (of Barnett) ; destination, Barbadoes.—John ffeason (of Cawson) ; destination, Barbadoes.—Andrew Vaughan (of Sandersfoote) ; destination, Barbadoes.—James Sharland (of Bradford) ; destination, Barbadoes.—Robert Hiscox (of Sutton) ; destination, Barbadoes.—Augustine Granger (of Henley) ; destination, Barbadoes.—Jenkin Jones (of Coychwich) ; destination, Barbadoes.—Edward Croswell (of Screelsby) ; destination, Barbadoes.—Evan Jones (of Amell) ; destination, Barbadoes.

Page 28

John Trenchfeild (of I. of Christophers) ; destination, Barbadoes.—Andrew Guddrige (of I. of Nevis) ; destination, Barbadoes.—William Broddrip (of Rowborow) ; destination, Barbadoes.—Thomas Blashfeild (of Langtondine) ; destination, Barbadoes.—Phillip Jenkin (of Woostoy (?)) ; destination, Barbadoes.—Gabriell Burt (of St. Stephens) ; destination, Barbadoes.—George Adams (of Long Ashton) ; destination, Barbadoes.—John Hollier (of Southams) ; destination, Barbadoes.—Alice Hale (of Bristoll) ; destination, Barbadoes.—Israell Mason (of Taunton St. John) ; destination, Barbadoes.—Joane Young (of Bristoll) ; destination, Barbadoes.—Edward Long (of Bristoll) ; destination, Barbadoes.

Page 29

John Howell (of Langarren) ; destination, Barbadoes.—David Williams (of Langorrig) ; destination, Barbadoes.—Lawrence Barton (of Lancaster) ; destination, Barbadoes.—Robert Parry (of fflintshire) ; destination, Barbadoes.—Sarah Gardener (of Cisiter) ; destination, Barbadoes.—Mary Howell (of Langarron) ; destination, Barbadoes.—Thomas Silvester (of Howcayle) ; destination, Barbadoes.—Barbara Candy (of Warmister) ; destination, Barbadoes.—Lewis William (of Erethvin) ; destination, Barbadoes.—James Hanson (of Bristoll) ; destination, Barbadoes.—Evan Edwards (of Lantrishen) ; destination, Barbadoes.—Griffith Edwards (of Lantrishen) ; destination, Barbadoes.

Page 30

Dorothie Mew (of Cardife) ; destination, Barbadoes.—John Williams (of St. ffagans) ; destination, Barbadoes.—Walter Jones (of Wenvoe) ; destination, Barbadoes.—Edward Wale (of Tyso) ; destination, Barbadoes.—James Taylor (of Northcurry) ; destination, Barbadoes.—Thomas Williams (of Ragland) ; destination, Barbadoes.—Watkin Griffen (of Eland) ; destination, Barbadoes.—Charles Richard (of Langotton) ; destination, Barbadoes.—John Edwards (of Chelten) ; destination, Barbadoes.—Katherine Waters (of Long Towne) ; destination, Barbadoes.—David Bayley (of Bristoll) ; destination, Barbadoes.—Thomas Vaughan (of St. Bridges) ; destination, Barbadoes.

Page 31

Samuel Baker (of Shornbury) ; destination, Barbadoes.—Margaret Hopkins (of Swansey) ; destination, Barbadoes.—John Knight (of Methallry) ; destination, Barbadoes.—John Powell (of Walford) ; destination, Barbadoes.—John Branghinge (of Greete Marlo) ; destination, Barbadoes.—Henry Morgan (of Abergavenney) ; destination, Barbadoes.—John Pope (of ffrome) ; destination, Barbadoes.—Henry Croutch (of Oxford) ; destination, Barbadoes.—Allen Garrett (of Milford) ; destination, Barbadoes.—Henry Nathen (of Milford) ; destination, Barbadoes.—James Vaughan (of Landilo) ; destination, Barbadoes.—Robert Millard (of Lidney) ; destination, Barbadoes.

Page 32

Christopher Gome (of Chenar) ; destination, Barbadoes.—John Oliver (of Bristoll) ; destination, Barbadoes.—Joseph Bowdon (of Wednam) ; destination, Barbadoes.—William Hingson (of Bristoll) ; destination, Barbadoes.—Mary Howell (of Langarron) ; destination, Barbadoes.—John Crosse (of Taunton) ; destination, Barbadoes.—Stephen Plaice (of Bodliscomb) ; destination, Barbadoes.—Thomas Nash (of Blodiscomb) ; destination, Barbadoes.—Richard Matthewes (of Westerly) ; destination, Barbadoes.—Thomas Jones (of Baglen) ; destination, Barbadoes.— Lewis William (of Eglush Elam) ; destination, Barbadoes.—Evan Jones (Nuport) ; destination, Barbadoes.

Page 33

Nicolas Watkins (of Uske), destination, Barbadoes.—Richard Jones (of Brecknocke) ; destination, Barbadoes.—Anne Thomas (of Bristoll) ; destination, Barbadoes. —John Cannon (of London) ; destination, Barbadoes.—Phillip Williams (of Lantreege) ; destination, Barbadoes.—David Lewis (of Goytrie) ; destination, Barbadoes.—Charlie Witch (of Northwood) ; destination, Barbadoes.—Morgan Evan (of Peekelt) ; destination, Barbadoes.—William Jones (of Mulson Dennots) ; destination, Barbadoes.—David Poskin (of Traga) ; destination, Barbadoes.—Bridget Pendry (of Langorell) ; destination, Barbadoes.—John Chick (of Bristoll) ; destination, Barbadoes.

Page 34

Elizabeth Webbe (?) (of Bristoll) ; destination, Barbadoes.—John Cox (of Swanborne) ; destination, Barbadoes.—Thomas Coulton (of Carbe) ; destination, Barbadoes.—Mary Hensly (of Borolton) ; destination, Barbadoes.—Thomas Waker (of Middlesex) ; destination, Barbadoes.—Robert Plumley (of Middlesex) ; destination, Barbadoes.—Mathew Whitesonne (of ffraunton) ; destination, Barbadoes.— ffrancis Hardidye als. Mason (of Bristoll) ; destination, Barbadoes.—Eliorner Hulett (of Rosse) ; destination, Barbadoes.—Henry Hutson (of Defford) ; destination, Barbadoes.—Walter Sennit (of Waxford) ; destination, Barbadoes.—ffrancis Thomas, (of Shrewsbury) ; destination, Barbadoes.

Page 35

Susan Morsam (of Taunton) ; destination, Barbadoes.—Margery Combe (of Crewkerne) ; destination, Barbadoes.—Margaret Thier (of Curry Evill) ; destination, Barbadoes.—Thomas Markhowell (of Shrewsbury) ; destination, Barbadoes.— Anne Starke (of Bristoll) ; destination, Barbadoes.—John Searle (of Callon) ; destination, Barbadoes.—John Mascall (of Yeardsley) ; destination, Barbadoes.—Lawrence Rogers (of Stratford-upon-Havon) ; destination, Barbadoes.—Henry Basset (of Cowbridge) ; destination, Barbadoes.—Margaret Smith (of Hereford) ; destination, Barbadoes.—Edward Wheeler (of Bristoll) ; destination, Barbadoes.—Griffith John (of Cardigan) ; destination, Barbadoes.

Page 36

Richard Axby (of London) ; destination, Barbadoes.—Thomas Jones (of Brecknocke) ; destination, Barbadoes.—Thomas Tyther (of Shirenuton) ; destination, Barbadoes.—George Browne (of Murlun) ; destination, Barbadoes.—Evan Harry (of Uske) ; destination, Barbadoes.—Meredith Hamet (of Abergainy) ; destination, Barbadoes.—Rice Morris (of Laniangell) ; destination, Barbadoes.—Richard Underhill (of Passell) ; destination, Barbadoes.—Samuell Specons (of Spaxon) ; destination, Barbadoes.—Walter Morgan (of Lanvaire) ; destination, Barbadoes.—William Gee (of Lime) ; destination, Barbadoes.—Arnell Thomas (of Glamorgan) ; destination, Barbadoes.

Page 37
Thomas Cox (of Malborough) ; destination, Barbadoes.—George Dunninge (of Hoburne) ; destination, Barbadoes.—John Garton (of Kingston-upon-Hull) ; destination, Barbadoes.—John Herrikett (of Bristoll) ; destination, Barbadoes.— Michaell Shaw (of Canterbury) ; destination, Barbadoes.—Thomas Ilicke (of Duncaton) ; destination, Barbadoes.—William Smith (of Almellin) ; destination, Barbadoes.—Lidea Thomas (of Landenny) ; destination, Barbadoes.—Esay Williams (of St. Tillary) ; destination, Barbadoes.—Humphry Cooke (of Lower Ardley) ; destination, Barbadoes.—Richard Powell (of Cornall) ; destination, Barbadoes.— John Somers (of Northorton) ; destination, Barbadoes.

Page 38
Thomas ffrie (of Winchester) ; destination, Barbadoes.—John Braine (of Thorncombe) ; destination, Virginia.—James Bishop (of Westwood) ; destination, Barbadoes.—William Hipsley (of Wrington) ; destination, Barbadoes.—Samuel Hort (of Churchill) ; destination, Barbadoes.—Roger Williams (of Cannington) ; destination (no place given).—James Bibby (of Limscombe) ; destination (no place given).—Vallentine Jones (of Hedborough) ; destination, Virginia.—ffrancis Morgan (of Persknott) ; destination, Virginia.—Anthony Shore (of Sutlenshany) ; destination, Virginia.—Richard James (of Hartford) ; destination, Barbadoes.—Margaret Watkins (of Brecknocke) ; destination, Barbadoes.

Page 39
Richard Kanedy (of Bristoll) ; destination, Barbadoes.—Susan Twaites (of Wells) ; destination, Barbadoes.—Bartholomew Roberts (of Pembrooke) ; destination, Virginia.—Rice James (of Marris) ; destination, Virginia.—Susan Pitman (of Wells) ; destination, Virginia.—Thomas Williams (of Carmarthen) ; destination, Barbadoes. —Anthony Locke (of Wrington) ; destination, Barbadoes.—Margaret Jones (of Bristoll) ; destination, Barbadoes.—Charles Sewell (of Somerby) ; destination, Virginia.—Edmund Waters (Gwarnesney) ; destination, Barbadoes.—Thomas Rice (of Shirenewton) ; destination, Barbadoes.—Edmund Williams (of Grange of Trulliske) ; destination, Barbadoes.

Page 40
Edward Rich (of Dragnell) ; destination, Virginia.—Hugh Travericke (of Waterford) ; destination, Virginia.—William Bevan (of Tagarth) ; destination, Virginia.—Joane Warden (of Bristoll) ; destination, Virginia.—Margaret Price (of Wike) ; destination, Virginia.—William Hobson (of Maukhas) ; destination, Barbadoes.—John Gilbert (of Bristoll) ; destination, Barbadoes.—William Slade (of Roseash) ; destination, Barbadoes.—Robert Hull (of South Stoake) ; destination, Barbadoes.—Elioner Lewis (of Cardigan) ; destination, Barbadoes.—Tobias Bartlett (of Westwood) ; destination, Barbadoes.—Jane Bowen (of Bristoll) ; destination, Virginia.

Page 41
    Anne Williams (of Cowbridge); destination, Barbadoes.—Richard Hoskin
(of Crowly); destination, Barbadoes.—Owen Vaughan (of Landavilo); destination,
Barbadoes.—Anne Bellinger (of Gloucester); destination, Barbadoes.—John Jones
(of Brecknocke); destination, Virginia.—Maudlin Williams (of Hereford); destination, Virginia.—John Lewis (of Westerly); destination, Virginia.—Henry Jones
(of Bridgwater); destination, Virginia.—Richard Lane (of Combe); destination,
Barbadoes.—Thomas Burges (of Eaton); destination, Barbadoes.—William Sey-
mour (of St. Margaret Stratton); destination, Barbadoes.—Elizabeth Willis (of
Bridgwater); destination, Virginia.

Page 42
    William Thomas (of Cardife); destination, Virginia.—Joane Jones (of Hereford);
destination, Virginia.—Elioner Hale (of Bristoll); destination, Barbadoes.—
Elizabeth Kenner (of St. John's, Bristoll); destination, Barbadoes.—Richard Powell
(of Westbury); destination, Virginia.—Thomas Morris (of Langum); destination,
Barbadoes.—Oliver Williams (of Clifford); destination, Barbadoes.—Phillip Watts
(of Glamorgan); destination, Virginia.—William Cornabee (of Alderbridge);
destination, Virginia.—William ffinell (of Staverton); destination, Virginia.—
Dorothie Davis (of Landoveny); destination, Virginia.—John Drinkwater (of
Rudden); destination, Barbadoes.

Page 43
    George Williams (of Bristoll); destination, Virginia.—William Tucker (of
Gly); destination, Virginia.—Joane Sturges (of Bristoll); destination, Virginia.—
Thomas Club (of Congresbury); destination, Virginia.—John Champin (of Bemister);
destination, Virginia.—Abraham Evans; destination, Virginia.—William ffowler;
destination, Virginia.—James ffowler; destination, Virginia.—Elizabeth Grim (of
Cheltnam); destination, Virginia.—Richard Adams (of Winscombe); destination,
Virginia.—John Harris (of Newlam); destination, Virginia.—William Price (of
Wintney); destination, Virginia.

Page 44
    Elizabeth Ireson; destination, Virginia.—Elizabeth Williams; destination,
Virginia.—Grigory Knellin (of Hannam); destination, Barbadoes.—Giles Daby (*sic*)
(of Whitmaster); destination, Barbadoes.—Matthew Argile (of Limbricke); destination, Barbadoes.—Joseph Newman (of Winset); destination, Virginia.—Hugh
Hobbs (of Bristoll); destination, Virginia.—Mary Renols (of Worcester); destination, Virginia.—Dorothy Williams (of Preston); destination, Virginia.—ffrancis
Howell (of Newman); destination, Virginia.—Thomas Brotherhood (of Bristoll);
destination, Virginia.—Thomas Wheeler (of Compton); destination, Virginia.

Page 45
    William Taylor (of Bedminster); destination, Virginia.—William Breame (of
Slifford); destination, Barbadoes.—Alexander Watts (of London); destination,
Virginia.—Henry Morgan (of Bristoll); destination, Virginia.—David Thomas (of
Lanover); destination, Virginia.—William Lewis (of Abergainy); destination,
Virginia.—Joane Henton (of Tickenham); destination, Virginia.—Thomas Somers

(of Norridge [Norwich]) ; destination, Virginia.—Lettice Pasler (of Eely) ; destination, Barbadoes.—John Lewis (of Bristoll) ; destination, Barbadoes.—Howell Jones (of Bristoll) ; destination, Barbadoes.—Robert Hanrenne (of Bristoll) ; destination, Barbadoes.

Page 46

John Jones (of Peterstone) ; destination, Virginia.—Elizabeth Harris (of Taunton Deane) ; destination, Virginia.—John Bullocke (of Sheffeild) ; destination, Virginia. —John Hitchens (of Bristoll) ; destination, Virginia.—Stephen Elliott (of Bristoll) ; destination, Virginia.—Thomas Meredith (of Langum) ; destination, Virginia.— Ann ffurlong (of Crewkerne Pill) ; destination, Virginia.—Joane Powell (of Hereford) ; destination, Virginia.—Thomas Lewis (of Carmarthen) ; destination, Virginia.—Elioner Rennolds (of Bristoll) ; destination, Virginia.—David Lewis (of Bristoll) ; destination, Virginia.—George Rendall (of Bristoll) ; destination, Barbadoes.

Page 47

William Archer (of Monmouth) ; destination, Barbadoes.—Andrew Jones (of Evercridge) ; destination, Barbadoes.—Martha Reynolds (of Bristoll) ; destination, Barbadoes.—Edward Dike (of Hopesay) ; destination, Virginia.—ffrancis Darling (of Brainsgrove) ; destination, Virginia.—Thomas Davis (of Penarth) ; destination, Virginia.—Richard Kidley (Trawen) ; destination, Virginia.—John Worgan (of Covert) ; destination, Virginia.—Nicholas Kitchen (of Keef) ; destination, Barbadoes.—Stephen Price (of Chepstow) ; destination, Barbadoes.—ffrances Bartholemew (of Hamersmith) ; destination, Barbadoes.—Phillip Stephens (of Swansleed) ; destination, Virginia.

Page 48

William Brown (of Nutchitter) ; destination, Virginia.—William Crannell (of Sneeds) ; destination, Virginia.—John Scallier (of Armschurch) ; destination, Virginia.—John Davis (of Brecknocke) ; destination, Virginia.—Henry Williams (of Cardiffe) ; destination, Virginia.—Thomas Coles (of Marticke) ; destination, Virginia.—Elizabeth Berrill (of Twinney) ; destination, Virginia.—Mary Barrett (of Stresham) ; destination, Virginia.—Alice Stephens (of Gloucester) ; destination, Barbadoes.—Hannah Shepherd (of Gloucester) ; destination, Barbadoes.—Elizabeth Edwards (of Taunton) ; destination, Barbadoes.—Thomas Smith (of Taunton) ; destination, Barbadoes.

Page 49

Margarett Jones (of Wedburne) ; destination, Barbadoes.—John Payne (of Marticke) ; destination, Virginia.—Elizabeth Roberts (of Yeaston) ; destination, Virginia.—Thomas Davis (of Bristoll) ; destination, Virginia.—Marmaduke Cole (of Berraton) ; destination, Virginia.—John Barrett (of Bristoll) ; destination, Virginia.—John Loreing (of Bristoll) ; destination, Virginia.—Thomas Hayden (of Uphill) ; destination, Virginia.—Thomas Jones (of Bristoll) ; destination, Virginia.—Henry Scammell (of Dunnett) ; destination, Virginia.—James Taplin (of ffokland) ; destination, Barbadoes.—Roger Hill (of St. Ausly) ; destination, Barbadoes.

Page 50

Richard Groves (of St. Eowsley) ; destination, Virginia.—Silas Love (St. Georges) ; destination, Barbadoes.—Jane Painter (of Bristoll) ; destination, Barbadoes.—Richard Rallens (Bathe) ; destination, Barbadoes.—John George (of Bristoll) ; destination, Barbadoes.—Elizabeth Pitslow (of Pistlow) ; destination, Barbadoes.—John Niblett (of Malsbury) ; destination, Virginia.—Robert Evans (of Brathe [?]) ; destination, Barbadoes.—Judith Sheppard (of Bristoll) ; destination, Barbadoes.—Richard Harris (of Brean Down) ; destination, Barbadoes.—John Long (of Henton) ; destination, Virginia.—Phillip Chapwell (of Martly) ; destination, Virginia.

Page 51

Mary Wood (of Llandafe) ; destination (no place given).—George Gilbes (of Barnestable) ; destination (no place given).—Thomas Pace (of Bathe) ; destination (no place given).—Walter Phillips (of Bristoll) ; destination, Virginia.— Lawrence Adams (of Taunton) ; destination, Barbadoes.—ffrancis Burcombe (of Barton Regis) ; destination, Virginia.—Symon Millard (of Hartfordwest) ; destination, Virginia.—John Collins (of Hutton) ; destination, Virginia.—William Read (of Tooke) ; destination, Virginia.—Mary Lawrence (of Rowberow) ; destination, Virginia.—ffrancis Williams (of Hereford) ; destination, Virginia.—Robert Thomas (of Stogunmer) ; destination, Virginia.

Page 52

Henry Watkin (of Talgat) ; destination, Virginia.—Samuel Galer (of Yarmouth); destination, Barbadoes.—Thomas Water (of London) ; destination, Virginia.— Mary Rogers (of Timbey) ; destination, Virginia.—Anne Lewis (of Newport) ; destination, Virginia.—John Gardener (of Withood) ; destination, Virginia.— William Waters (of Lanvaire), destination, Virginia.—Nicholas Thomas (of Boiceslon [?]) ; destination, Virginia.—Sarah Heading (of Bristoll) ; destination, Barbadoes.—Richard Moore (of Pidlein) ; destination, Virginia.—ffrancis Day (of Brockley) ; destination, Barbadoes.—John Perry (of Preston) ; destination, Barbadoes.

Page 53

Howell Bowen (of Klincorne) ; destination, Barbadoes.—Paul Earle (of Wooten Underedge) ; destination, Barbadoes.—Mozes John (of Basset) ; destination, Barbadoes.—Morgan William (of Laniangell) ; destination, Virginia.—William Knell (of Evangape) ; destination, Virginia.—John Roberts (of Milford) ; destination, Barbadoes.—Joseph Morse (of Thornbury) ; destination, Virginia.—Edward Davis (of Manganbricke) ; destination, Virginia.—Margarett Jones (of Duzley) ; destination, Barbadoes.—Arabella Wilferemerit (of St. Martin's in the Mide) ; destination, Barbadoes.—Amy Turner (of Winchester) ; destination, Virginia.— William Rickets (of Newbury) ; destination (no place given).

Page 54

Sarah Jones (of Gloucester) ; destination, Barbadoes.—Elizabeth Gilbert (of Bristoll) ; destination, Barbadoes.—John Richards (of St. Nicholas, co. Glamorgan) ; destination, Virginia.—Thomas Davis (of Cardife) ; destination, Virginia.—Richard Hinder (of The Breene) ; destination, Barbadoes.—Emanuell Rogers (of Bartlishe) ;

destination, Virginia.—Anne Roger (of Bartlishe); destination, Virginia.—John Lewis (of Bristoll); destination, Barbadoes.—Thomas Gabey (of Broomyard); destination, Virginia.—John Wilson (of St. Giles, co. Stafford); destination, Barbadoes.—Katherine Earle (of Wells); destination, Barbadoes.—Grace Jones (of Bristoll); destination, Barbadoes.

Page 55

Edward Phips (of Powderlatch); destination, Barbadoes.—Walter Warren (of Shipham); destination, Barbadoes.—Rebecca James (of Bedminster), destination, Virginia.—Henry Saunders (of Bedminster); destination, Virginia.—Robert Lewis (of St. Tauthen); destination, Virginia.—Thomas Cotton (of Woolerd); destination, Barbadoes.—John Pindar (of Todgaster); destination, Virginia.— Anthony Dusebury (of Londonderry); destination, Virginia.—Joane Bonnunare (of Torher); destination, Virginia.—John Starns (of Comongarden); destination, Barbadoes.—John Davis (of Tewksbury); destination, Virginia.—Edward Dyer (of Tewksbury); destination, Virginia.

Page 56

John Lewis (of Bristoll); destination, Barbadoes.—Margaret Jones (of Carlion); destination, Virginia.—Thomas Morse (of Spuriton); destination, Virginia.— William Vaughan (of Bristoll); destination, Virginia.—Thomas Allen (of Bridgwater); destination, Virginia.—John Knill (of New Rodner); destination, Virginia. —John Robbins (of Cothislow); destination, Virginia.—Edward Webb (of Brignoler); destination, Virginia.—Silverton Hurley (of Biknell); destination, Virginia. —William Davis (of Old Cleeve); destination, Virginia.—Susanna Hill (of Matlebury); destination, Virginia.—Jeremiah Dikeson (of Bristoll); destination, Barbadoes.

Page 57

William Powell (of Landilo); destination, Barbadoes.—John Jones (of Horton); destination, Barbadoes.—Samuell Downton (of Brockton); destination, Barbadoes. —Katherine Langley (of Barrow); destination, Barbadoes.—Thompson Young (of Scantford); destination, Barbadoes.—Joan Phillips (of Scantford); destination, Barbadoes.—John Lloyde (of St. Martins, co. Salop); destination, Barbadoes.— Susanna Bowen (of Lizzorra); destination, Barbadoes.—Dorothy Roberts (of Carmarthen); destination, Barbadoes.—Mary Johnson (of Peterborough); destination, Barbadoes.—Robert Slitch (of Berrow); destination, Barbadoes.—Katherine Garvis (of Newchurch); destination, Barbadoes.

Page 58

William Edwards (of Lanihangell); destination, Barbadoes.—John Sorrill (of Slego); destination, Barbadoes.—Amy Gaull (of Borton); destination, Barbadoes. —William Morgan (of Northpetherton); destination, Barbadoes.—John Bedow (of Chepstow); destination, Barbadoes.—Walter Evans (of Bristoll); destination, Barbadoes.—John Date (of Kilfeild); destination, Barbadoes.—Thomas Snaylum (of Weeke); destination, Barbadoes.—John Blackway (of Pauntly); destination, Barbadoes.—John Williams (of Bristoll); destination, Barbadoes.—William Merricke (of Callicott); destination, Barbadoes.—William King (of Thornbury); destination, Barbadoes.

Page 59

Morgan Evans (of Abergavenny) ; destination, Barbadoes.—Alice Wetly (of Norledge) ; destination, Barbadoes.—Henry Andrewes (of Carmarthen) ; destination, Barbadoes.—Robert Shelverdine (of Carnarvon) ; destination, Barbadoes.— William Start (of Langford) ; destination, Barbadoes.—Robert Bolls (of Tulteel) ; destination, Barbadoes.—Edward Thomas (of St. John Evangelist, co. Brecknocke); destination, Barbadoes.—William Charles (of Parnew) ; destination, Barbadoes.— Jennet Rogers (of Bristoll) ; destination, Barbadoes.—Elizabeth Griffen (of Bristoll) ; destination, Barbadoes.—John Curtis (of Salop, co. Wilts) ; destination, Barbadoes. —Jenkin Williams (of Aberdare) ; destination, Barbadoes.

Page 60

Thomas Butler (of Winney) ; destination, Barbadoes.—Richard Scarlett (of Carlion) ; destination, Barbadoes.—Richard Bradford (of Exeter) ; destination, Barbadoes.—Thomas Watkins (of Langanger) ; destination, Barbadoes.—John Williams (of Landelavour) ; destination, Barbadoes.—Daniell Smith (of Kingswood) ; destination, Barbadoes.—Henry Lelam (of St. Edmondsbury) ; destination, Barbadoes.—Edmund Jones (of Goldclift) ; destination, Barbadoes.—Morgan Williams (of Newchurch) ; destination, Barbadoes.—John Gosse (of Wells) ; destination, Barbadoes.—Thomas Johnson (of Taunton) ; destination, Barbadoes.—George Rogers (of Doddington) ; destination, Barbadoes.

Page 61

Edward Davis (of Ossestrie [Oswestry]) ; destination, Barbadoes.—Thomas Phillips (of Newcastle, co. Carmarthen) ; destination, Barbadoes.—John Little (of Cosham) ; destination (no place given).—William Gill (of Shorncombe) ; destination (no place given).—Henry Thomas (of Kingsaile) ; destination, Barbadoes. —Elizabeth Collins (of Bristoll) ; destination, Barbadoes.—Winifret Roberts (of Bristoll) ; destination, Barbadoes.—Philip Jones (of Cardiffe) ; destination, Barbadoes.—Howell Aphowell (of Mallpus) ; destination, Barbadoes.—James Crosse (of Kingspeare) ; destination, Barbadoes.—William Webb (of Thornebury) ; destination, Barbadoes.—William Clarke (of Buckland) ; destination (no place given).— John Weekes (of Bow, co. Devon) ; destination (no place given).

Page 62

William Price (of ——, co. Hereford) ; destination, Barbadoes.—Christian Sheppard (of Redwick) ; destination, Barbadoes.—Margaret Williams (of Swansy) ; destination, Barbadoes.—Richard ffleetwood (of Chipnam) ; destination, Barbadoes. —John Bragg (of Chirrick) ; destination, Barbadoes.—Nicholas Sparrow (of Gormoania Winnington) ; destination, Barbadoes.—William Giles (of Nash) ; destination, Barbadoes.—Nathaniell Jobsons (of Axbury) ; destination, Barbadoes.— David Phillips (of Langunney) ; destination, Barbadoes.—Elizabeth Wretry (of Backwell) ; destination, Barbadoes.—Richard Hall (of Bristoll) ; destination, Barbadoes.—Roger Williams (of Lantrissen) ; destination, Barbadoes.—Lewes Hughes (of Cary) ; destination, Barbadoes.

Page 63

Griffith William (of Cadwelly) ; destination, Barbadoes.—Lewis Rich (of Cadwelly) ; destination, Barbadoes.—John Duncombe (of St. Toolyes) ; destination, Barbadoes.—Ann Allen (of Bristoll) ; destination, Barbadoes.—Margery Rogers (of Penhow) ; destination, Barbadoes.—Richard Dorton ; destination, Barbadoes.—

Richard Roe ; destination, Barbadoes.—Mathew Harrison ; destination, Barbadoes. —Edward Loyd ; destination, Barbadoes.—Thomas Perret ; destination, Barbadoes.—Margaret Alders ; destination, Barbadoes.—Sarah Jenkins (of Lawrence Weston) ; destination, Barbadoes.

Page 64
George Oke (of Moreton) ; destination, Barbadoes.—Henry Duning ; destination (no place given).—Margaret ffude (of Slinter) ; destination (no place given). —John ffrye (of Madley) ; destination (no place given).—John Hancock (of Reddinge) ; destination (no place given).—William Thomas ; destination (no place given).—Elizabeth Browne (of Morlinck) ; destination (no place given).—Thomas Tyler (of Shrewsbury) ; destination (no place given).—Margaret Pilsher (of Shrewsbury) ; destination (no place given).—Margaret Aston (of Bullhelley) ; destination, (no place given).—Thomas Collins ; destination (no place given).—Richard Ricket (of Litle Haddum) ; destination (no place given).

Page 65
Nicholas Higgins (of Blackhorton) ; destination (no place given).—John Lilly (of Worcester) ; destination (no place given).—Johan Knight (of Crokernpill) ; destination (no place given).—Mary Jones (of Carwent) ; destination (no place given).—Grace Collins (of Bristoll) ; destination (no place given).—William Watkins (of Longely) ; destination, (no place given).—William Sutton (of Elmly Castle) ; destination (no place given).—Elinor Sutton (of Elmly Castle) ; destination (no place given).—John Cornish (of Taunton) ; destination (no place given).—Edward Burgess (of Bristoll) ; destination (no place given).—William Edwards (of Tartlin) ; destination (no place given).—James Rutter (of Bone, co. Essex) ; destination (no place given).

Page 66
Cecilly Rosser (of Bashuk) ; destination (no place given).—Margery Giles (of Bristoll) ; destination (no place given).—Thomas Prior (of Trewbridge) ; destination (no place given).—Henry Hart (of Bristoll) ; destination (no place given).— George Tailer (of Cane) ; destination (no place given).—Nicholas Stone (of Landilp) ; destination (no place given).—Richard Thomas (of Trodeciock) ; destination (no place given).—Davy Thomas (of Cary Parris) ; destination (no place given).— William Jones (of Bast Church) ; destination (no place given).—William Jones (of Carleane) ; destination (no place given).—David Morgan (of Traveane) ; destination (no place given).—Ralph Milman (of Shebeare) ; destination (no place given). —Richard London (of Chedington) ; destination (no place given).

Page 67
Thomas Williams (of Cardiffe) ; destination (no place given).—Morgan Edward (of Lanhenock) ; destination (no place given).—Alice Johnson (of Lutoft) ; destination (no place given).—Thomas Williams (of Sully) ; destination (no place given).— Margery Williams (of Nuport) ; destination (no place given).—Mary Williams (of Lanvallteage) ; destination (no place given).—Johan Hooper (of Sandford) ; destination (no place given).—John Hughes (of Newport) ; destination (no place given). —Patience Tutchin (of Sondton) ; destination (no place given).—Owen Thomas (of Canarthy) ; destination (no place given).—Evan Bassett (of Cambridge) ; destination (no place given).—Richard Sheppard (of ffroone Selwood) ; destination (no place given).

Page 68

Walter Williams (of Longenny) ; destination (no place given).—Arthur Jones (of Atchon Bridge) ; destination (no place given).—Samuell Baker (of Thornbury) ; destination (no place given).—Mary Marmion (of Bristoll) ; destination (no place given).—Anthony Sevior (of Wells) ; destination (no place given).—Reece Jones (of Beltowes) ; destination (no place given).—John Bishop (of Didlebury) ; destination, Barbadoes.—Lawrence Darby (of Tromford) ; destination, Barbadoes.— John Mortire (of Branford) ; destination, Barbadoes.—Henry Swelling (of Trowbridge) ; destination, Barbadoes.—Richard Hillman (of Trewbridge) ; destination, Barbadoes.—Hanna Evans (of Hampton Reade) ; destination, Barbadoes.—Johan Willes (of Abergavenney) ; destination, Barbadoes.—Henry Swelling (of Trowbridge) ; destination, Barbadoes.—Richard Hilman ; destination, Barbadoes.

Page 69

John Draper (of Bristoll) ; destination, Barbadoes.—Thomas Millard (of North Yarmouth) ; destination, Barbadoes.—John Merritheape (of Tewxbury) ; destination, Barbadoes.—John Thomas (of New Church) ; destination, Barbadoes.— Marrine Vallaro (of London) ; destination, Barbadoes.—Robert Hull (of South Stoke) ; destination, Barbadoes.—William Dudstone (of Herreford) ; destination, Barbadoes.—Edward Barnet (of Herreford) ; destination, Barbadoes.—Alice Hibbert (of Westdowne) ; destination, Barbadoes.—Herbert Jones (of Lankengall) ; destination, Barbadoes.—Pearce Smith (of Manningford) ; destination, Barbadoes.— Miles Davy (of Glamorgan) ; destination, Barbadoes.—Thomas Bidle (of Shasbury) ; destination, Barbadoes.

Page 70

Griffith Jenken (of Glamorgan) ; destination, Barbadoes.—Joan Widowes (of Newbery) ; destination, Barbadoes.—Judith Ruthry (of Bristoll) ; destination, Barbadoes.—William Powell (of Bedwelthy) ; destination, Barbadoes.—David Jenkin (of Mutchnet) ; destination, Barbadoes.—Elizabeth Tison (of London) ; destination, Barbadoes.—John Powell (of Bristoll) ; destination, Barbadoes.— William Sander (of Cornwell) ; destination, Barbadoes.—Samuel Jennigs (*sic*) (of Bruton) ; destination, Barbadoes.—William Matthewes (of Lanmillow) ; destination, Barbadoes.—George Ball (of Rosse) ; destination, Barbadoes.—William Phillips (of Bristoll) ; destination, Barbadoes.

Page 71

Elizabeth Willis (of Gloucester) ; destination, Barbadoes.—Thomas Williams ; destination, Barbadoes.—ffranciss Jones (of Winscombe) ; destination, Barbadoes.— Lettice Davis (of Landilo) ; destination, Barbadoes.—William Davis (of Landonstarke) ; destination, Barbadoes.—Walter Jones (of Carleant) ; destination, Barbadoes.—Jacob Gilboard (of Bath) ; destination, Barbadoes.—Arthur Davis (of Mineyard) ; destination, Barbadoes.—Anne Jones (of Munmouth) ; destination, Barbadoes.—Mary Langford ; destination, Barbadoes.—Richard Hughes (of Dehay) ; destination, Barbadoes.—Margaret Ball (of Bristoll) ; destination, Barbadoes.— Hugh Rogers (of Ireland) ; destination, Barbadoes.

Page 72

Margaret Saye (of Bawnton) ; destination, Barbadoes.—Susan Britten (of Bawnton) ; destination, Barbadoes.—John Parry ; destination, Barbadoes.—Johan Harper (of Mineyard) ; destination, Barbadoes.—George Richards (of Munmouth) ;

destination, Barbadoes.—Lawrence Devenish ; destination, Barbadoes.—Griggory Hennis (of Eater) ; destination, Barbadoes.—Anne Hardige (of Yaton) ; destination, Barbadoes.—Matthew Williams ; destination, Barbadoes.—David Jones ; destination, Barbadoes.—Edward Jacob (of Burwood) ; destination, Barbadoes.—Margery Jacob ; destination, Barbadoes.

Page 73

Owen Thomas (of Bristoll) ; destination, Barbadoes.—John Jones ; destination, Barbadoes.—Dorathy Martine (of Bristoll) ; destination, Barbadoes.—James Warren (of Kingswarth) ; destination, Barbadoes.—John ffloyd (of Landenny) ; destination, Barbadoes.—Lewis Williams (of Lannangell) ; destination, Barbadoes.—Elizabeth Williams ; destination, Barbadoes.—Robert Bennett (of Wilton) ; destination, Barbadoes.—Hugh Evans ; destination, Barbadoes.—William Samuell (of Landivellour) ; destination, Barbadoes.—Jane Smith (of Langrofen) ; destination, Barbadoes.—Griffith William ; destination, Barbadoes.

Page 74

William Bozwell (of Sutton) ; destination, Virginia.—Everard Roberts ; destination (no place given).—Davy Thomas ; destination (no place given).—George Perry ; destination (no place given).—Margaret Ball ; destination (no place given). —Henry Perie ; destination (no place given).—John Davis ; destination (no place given).—William Pattison ; destination (no place given).—Margaret Thomas ; destination, Barbadoes.—Joane Williams ; destination (no place given).—Thomas Smith ; destination (no place given).—Judith Rutherow ; destination (no place given).

Page 75

Edward Poddy ; destination (no place given).—Edward Addams ; destination (no place given).—John Munded (?) (of Chernuton) ; destination, Virginia.—Hugh Brangwell (of Exeter) ; destination, Virginia.—Phillip Jones (of Weeke) ; destination (no place given).—Elizabeth Martine (of Evill) ; destination (no place given). —Edith Palmer (of Exeter) ; destination (no place given).—Phillip Cooth ; destination (no place given) ; Katherine Palmore ; destination (no place given).—Edward Addams ; destination (no place given).—Christopher Clarke ; destination (no place given).—Edward Bayley (of London) ; destination (no place given).

Page 76

John Ansbrewer (of Cardiffe) ; destination (no place given).—George Allen (of Taunton) ; destination, Virginia.—John Braine (of Thorncombe) ; destination, Barbadoes.—Katharine Davis ; destination, Virginia.—Sarah Colley (of Newland) ; destination, Barbadoes.—Johan End (of Wooton Underedge) ; destination, Barbadoes.—Mary Awborne (of Gloucester) ; destination, Barbadoes.—Anne Nethway (of Gloucester) ; destination, Barbadoes.—David Jones ; destination, Barbadoes.— Katherine Nott ; destination (no place given).—Henry Jones ; destination (no place given).—Henry Lewes (of Cowbridge) ; destination (no place given).

Page 77

Phillip David (of Cowbridge) ; destination (no place given).—Jonas Jones ; destination (no place given).—Mary Evies ; destination (no place given).—John Bowles ; destination (no place given).—John George ; destination, Virginia.— Sarah Lorgan ; destination, Virginia.—Thomas Jones ; destination, Virginia.—

D

Thomas Geter ; destination, Virginia.—Elizabeth Hiscox ; destination, Virginia.—Ann Austines ; destination, Barbadoes.—John Thomas ; destination, Barbadoes.—Thomas Williams ; destination, Barbadoes.

Page 78
John Cory ; destination, Barbadoes.—Richard Kemer (of Bristol) ; destination, Barbadoes.—George Russell ; destination, Barbadoes.—Trustrom Peirce ; destination, Barbadoes.—John Reece ; destination, Barbadoes.—Anne Williams ; destination (no place given).—Mary Williams ; destination (no place given).—Edward Evans ; destination (no place given).—George Stephens ; destination (no place given).—William Prosser ; destination, Virginia.—Jonathan Cole ; destination, Virginia.—Mary Thomas ; destination, Virginia.—Robert Thomas ; destination, Virginia.

Page 79
Elizabeth Jones ; destination, Virginia.—Anne Jones ; destination, Virginia.—William Morgan ; destination, Virginia.—William Addams ; destination, New England.—Elizabeth ffeare ; destination, Virginia.—Susan Barnerd ; destination, Virginia.—Thomas Smith (of Warmister) ; destination, Barbadoes.—Ann Nethway ; destination, Virginia.—Mary Osbourne ; destination, Virginia.—Robert Hancock ; destination, Barbadoes.—Jesper Easter ; destination, Virginia.—John Rose ; destination, Barbadoes.

Page 80
Thomas Davis ; destination, Virginia.—Richard Jenkins ; destination, Barbadoes.—Thomas Symons ; destination, Barbadoes.—Jeremy Price ; destination, Barbadoes.—Daniell Jones ; destination, Barbadoes.—Robert Wilson ; destination, Barbadoes.—William Some ; destination, Virginia.—John Thomas ; destination, Virginia.—Elizabeth Allen ; destination, Barbadoes.—Mary Williams ; destination, Barbadoes.—Cecilly Culme ; destination, Barbadoes.

Page 81
Aaron Dodge (of Exeter) ; destination, Virginia.—Elizabeth Coradine (of Butley) ; destination, Barbadoes.—George Edwards (of Christchurch, co. Monmouth) ; destination, Virginia.—William Evans als. Reece (of Cardiffe) ; destination, Barbadoes.—Humphry Jenings ; destination, Virginia.—William Morgan (of Pembrooke) ; destination, Virginia.—John England (of Bristoll) ; destination, Barbadoes.—Thomas England ; destination (no place given).—Mary Gough (of Bristoll) ; destination (no place given).—Thomas Morgan (of Thornbury) ; destination, Barbadoes.—Thomas Jones (of Breton) ; destination, Barbadoes.—James Litle ; destination, Barbadoes.

Page 82
John Pope ; destination, Barbadoes.—John Thomas (of Coychurch) ; destination, Barbadoes.—Tobitha Watlis (of Bristoll) ; destination, Barbadoes.—Elizabeth Cobb (of Kingswarth) ; destination, Barbadoes.—Elizabeth Gidings (of Ushant, co. Wilts) ; destination, Virginia.—Margery England (of Taunton) ; destination, Virginia.—Anne Davis (of Trethedim) ; destination, Barbadoes.—Richard Silvester ; destination, Virginia.—James Richards ; destination (no place given).—William Bullock ; destination (no place given).—William Davis (of Whitland) ; destination, Barbadoes.—Ann North ; destination, Virginia.

Page 83

Richard Jenkins ; destination, Virginia.—Edmund Nicholas (of Landilo) ; destination, Virginia.—Alice Jennigs (*sic*) (of Barkly) ; destination, Virginia.—Richard Davis (of Cheshire) ; destination, Barbadoes.—James Edwards ; destination, Virginia.—Roger Ingrum (of Worle) ; destination, Virginia.—Sego Boell ; destination, Virginia.—Christopher Stephens ; destination, Virginia.—Oliver Morse ; destination, Barbadoes.—Mary Greene ; destination, Virginia.—Mary Beckenford ; destination, Virginia.—Anne Howell ; destination, Virginia.

Page 84

Elizabeth Hickman ; destination, Virginia.—Sarah Happton ; destination, Virginia.—Rice Thomas ; destination, Barbadoes.—William Wainright ; destination, Barbadoes.—Thomas Davis ; destination, Barbadoes.—Alice Evans ; destination, Barbadoes.—Jane James ; destination, Barbadoes.—Samuell Bromley (of Woocester) ; destination, Barbadoes.—Thomas Browne ; destination, Barbadoes.— Elizabeth Emson (of Winscombe) ; destination, Virginia.—Ann Ceco (of Winscombe) ; destination, Virginia.—Robert Cotten (of Winscombe) ; destination, Virginia.

Page 85

Luke Manson (of Winscombe) ; destination, Virginia.—Richard Davies (of Grinson) ; destination, Virginia. Margaret Partlut (of Munckton) ; destination, Virginia.—William Rice (of Bristoll) ; destination, Virginia.—John Hyett (of Bockford) ; destination, Virginia.—Richard ffavell (of Bristoll) ; destination, Barbadoes. —Edward Greene ; destination, Barbadoes.—Richard Mason ; destination, Barbadoes.—Charles Mason ; destination, Barbadoes.—James Mason ; destination, Barbadoes.—Joane Davis (of St. Georges, co. Somerset) ; destination, Virginia.— Anne Davie (of Carmarthen) ; destination, Virginia.

Page 86

Mary Cooper (of Bristoll) ; destination, Virginia.—John Ingrum (of Bristoll) ; destination, Virginia.—Richard Younge (of Tritall) ; destination, Virginia.—Edward Humphris (of Ludlow) ; destination, Virginia.—Joan Jones (of Landogger) ; destination, Virginia.—Anne Jones (of fforest of Deane) ; destination, Virginia.— Richard ffluellin (of St. Andrews, co. Glamorgan) ; destination, Virginia.—Welthian Thomas (of Carlian) ; destination, Virginia.—Thomas Pritchard (of Longoven) ; destination, Virginia.—Morgan Price ; destination, Virginia.—Anthony ffrims (of Querne) ; destination, Virginia.—John Parsons (of Bristoll) ; destination, Virginia.

Page 89 (sic)

John Parsons ; destination, Virginia.—John Andrewes ; destination, Barbadoes.—Gerrard Lewes ; destination, Virginia.—Calib Harris (of Henton) ; destination, Barbadoes.—Deborah Catchmad (of Wiston) ; destination, Virginia.—George Catchmad ; destination, Virginia.—James Loyd (of Tibister) ; destination, Virginia. —Thomas Jones ; destination, Barbadoes.—John Overbury (of Henton) ; destination, Virginia.—Katherne (*sic*) Davy ; destination, Virginia.—Anne Braine (of Bristoll) ; destination, Virginia.—William Denford (of Torrinston) ; destination, Virginia.

Page 90
Richard Haines (of Mavom) ; destination, Virginia.—John Cooke (of Camsham) ; destination, Virginia.—Elizabeth Hewlett (of Ross) ; destination, Virginia.— William Edmunds ; destination, Virginia.—Phillip Evans ; destination, Virginia.— Jane Leonard Merrick (*sic*) (of Nambash) ; destination, Barbadoes.—William Cooper, destination, Barbadoes.—Howell Jones ; destination, Barbadoes.—Robert Ridnot (of Possett) ; destination, Barbadoes.—George Pegler (of Durzley) ; destination, Barbadoes.—John Green (of froome) ; destination, Nevis.—William Williams ; destination (no place given).

Page 91
John Weare (of Bristoll) ; destination, St. Christopher.—William Moore (of Little Hunton) ; destination, Barbadoes.—Dorathy Roberts (of Carmarthen) ; destination, Barbadoes.—Thomas Symons (of Chepstow) ; destination, Barbadoes. —Thomas Bradman (of Congersbury) ; destination, Barbadoes.—John Smith ; destination, Barbadoes.—Robert Smith (of Shencriffe) ; destination, Barbadoes.— Elizabeth Pritchard ; destination (no place given).—Thomas Champion ; destination (no place given).—Richard Haydon ; destination (no place given).—Elinor George ; destination (no place given).—Cibell Powell ; destination (no place given).

Page 92
Henry Greene (of Bromsbury) ; destination (no place given).—Richard Hadduck ; destination (no place given).—Daniell Vaughan (of Shrewsbury) ; destination (no place given).—Walter Symons (of Cornewall) ; destination (no place given). —Charles Jenkins ; destination (no place given).—Thomas Williams (of Arlingam) ; destination (no place given).—John Jenkins (of Pile) ; destination (no place given). —Humphrey Drew (of Colmton) ; destination (no place given).—John Harris (of Bristoll) ; destination, Barbadoes.—Davy Evan (of Sanboy) ; destination, Barbadoes.—Richard Clarke (of Kingson) ; destination, Barbadoes.—Lawrence Hellicar (of Axford) ; destination (no place given).

Page 93
Robert Gifford (of Kennore) ; destination (no place given).—John Hancock (of Elberton) ; destination (no place given).—William Carpenter (of Southmolten) ; destination (no place given).—Johan Roper (of Burneham) ; destination (no place given).—John Hopkins (of Barkly) ; destination (no place given).—John Roberts (of Bristoll) ; destination (no place given).—Mary Collins (of Bristoll) ; destination (no place given).—Elizabeth Taylor ; destination (no place given).—Thomas Beddard ; destination (no place given).—William Mathewes ; destination (no place given).—Thomas Butler (of Plimouth) ; destination (no place given).—Joice Hamlin (of Artum) ; destination, Virginia.

Page 94
Thomas Berry (of Newent) ; destination, Barbadoes.—Thomas ffrancis (of Parshire) ; destination, Virginia.—David Mathewes (of Wilson) ; destination, Barbadoes.—Joseph Davis (of Langhorne) ; destination, Barbadoes.—Joan Pecock (of Hannum) ; destination, Barbadoes.—Morgan Jones (of Munmouth) ; destination, Barbadoes.—Tega Kegan (of Bristoll) ; destination, Barbadoes.— George Andrew ; destination, Barbadoes.—John White ; destination, Barbadoes.— James Hudson ; destination, Barbadoes.—John Rogers ; destination, Barbadoes. —Mary Davis ; destination, Barbadoes.

Page 95

Mary Vaughan ; destination, Barbadoes.—Gwinna Wealch ; destination, Barbadoes.—Debora Johnson ; destination, Barbadoes.—William Hughes ; destination, Barbadoes.—William Boone; destination (no place given).—Jenkin Jones; destination, Barbadoes.—William Littleford ; destination (no place given).—Richard Rowland ; destination (no place given).—Anne Thomas (of Newport) ; destination (no place given).—Charles Watkins (of Newport) ; destination, Barbadoes.—John Price ; destination, Virginia.—Margaret Legg (of Bristoll) ; destination, Barbadoes.

Page 96

Henry Lloyd (of Cary) ; destination, Barbadoes.—John Alise (of Bristoll) ; destination, Virginia.—Thomas Briggs (of Malborne) ; destination, Barbadoes.— Thomas Reynolds (of Dudley) ; destination, Barbadoes.—Thomas George ; destination, Barbadoes.—Bridgett ffloyd (of Pembroke) ; destination, Barbadoes.—William Nutt ; destination, Barbadoes.—Susan Norvill (of Uphill) ; destination, Barbadoes. —Josias Jones (of Shrewsbury) ; destination, Barbadoes.—Nicholas Willen (of Tenby) ; destination, Barbadoes.—Elinor Harris (of Chepstow) ; destination, Barbadoes.—George Kelly (of Barnestaple) ; destination, Barbadoes.

Page 97

Thomas Stephens (of Cornewell) ; destination, Barbadoes.—Henry Martin ; destination, Virginia.—William Morris ; destination, Barbadoes.—Jenkin Evans ; destination, Barbadoes.—Phillice Short (of Redwick) ; destination (no place given). —Thomas Parker (of Bristoll) ; destination (no place given).—Charles Huntington (of Bristoll) ; destination (no place given).—John Turkey (of Clackford) ; destination, Virginia.—Rowland Wathon (of Nangle) ; destination, Barbadoes.—John Williams (of Sullock) ; destination, Barbadoes.—Henry Godby (of Trowbridge) ; destination, Barbadoes.—Nathaniell Pascoe ; destination, Barbadoes.

Page 98

Mary West (of Bristoll) ; destination, Barbadoes.—William Briant (of Bridgwater) ; destination, Barbadoes.—Thomas Davis (of Landolivour) ; destination, Virginia.—ffrancis Wale (of Bridgwater) ; destination, Barbadoes.—Elizabeth Williams ; destination, Barbadoes.—Elizabeth Smith ; destination, Barbadoes.— John Watkins (of Munmouth) ; destination, Barbadoes.—Jane Darrow (of Shrewsbury) ; destination, Barbadoes.—William Wade (of Saint ffaggons) ; destination, Barbadoes.—Ann Morgan (of Barsliche) ; destination, Barbadoes.—John Blackworth (of ffishfroome) ; destination, Barbadoes.—William Gibsin (of Bristoll) ; destination, Barbadoes.

Page 99

William Howell (of Stoke) ; destination, Barbadoes.—Richard Rogers (of Cherington) ; destination, Barbadoes.—John Rogers ; destination, Barbadoes.— Gabriell Ascom (of Cowfold) ; destination, Barbadoes.—Roger Williams (of Bristoll) ; destination, Barbadoes.—Noell Shem (of Burgundoy in France) ; destination, Barbadoes.—Daniell Brian (of Carlion) ; destination, Barbadoes.—Wilthian Jones (of Brecon) ; destination (no place given).—John Morice (of Balson) ; destination (no place given).—Thomas Weeks (of Newcastle) ; destination (no place given).— Thomas Harbert (of Lanvahans) ; destination (no place given).—William Brooks (of Ausly) ; destination (no place given).

Page 100

Samuell Baker (of Bartley) ; destination (no place given).—Margery Godby (of Trowbridge) ; destination (no place given).—Gabriell Crame (of London) ; destination (no place given).—Thomas Gibbin (of Axbridge) ; destination, Virginia.— John Owen (of Pembrooke) ; destination, Barbadoes.—John Kinge (of Bishopp Cannons) ; destination, Barbadoes.—Elizabeth Addams ; destination, Barbadoes. —Walter Jones (of Raglon) ; destination, Barbadoes.—John Champnes (of Bristoll) ; destination, Barbadoes.—Jane Champnes ; destination, Barbadoes.—Ann Hubbard ; destination, Barbadoes.

Page 101

George Mors (of Thornebury) ; destination, Barbadoes.—Morgan Jones (of Munmouth) ; destination, Barbadoes.—Alice Thomas (of Tenby) ; destination, Barbadoes.—John Papell ; destination, Barbadoes.—Jenkin Grayman ; destination, Barbadoes.—John Moore ; destination, Barbadoes.—William Gillett (of Martick) ; destination (no place given).—Edward White (of Stow) ; destination (no place given). —John Jones ; destination (no place given).—Benjamin Butler ; destination (no place given).—William Godfry ; destination (no place given).—Evan Morgan ; destination (no place given).—David Pritchard ; destination (no place given).

Page 102

Charles Pritchard ; destination (no place given).—John Starr ; destination (no place given).—Richard Davis ; destination (no place given).—Rowland David ; destination, Virginia.—William Hopkins (of London) ; destination, Barbadoes. —Redowick Haryst ; destination, Barbadoes.—Thomas Evans (of Pensford) ; destination, Virginia.—John Page (of Gloucester) ; destination, Virginia.—Sarah Griffis (of Shrewsbury) ; destination, Virginia.—William Armitage (of Sturbridge) ; destination, Virginia.—Rebecca Thomas (of Grindam) ; destination, Virginia.— Margaret Jiner (of Esum) ; destination, Virginia.

Page 103

Rice Williams (of Brecon) ; destination, Virginia.—Mary Davis (of Clifthuniton); destination, Barbadoes.—Edward Brooke (of Compton Duning) ; destination, Barbadoes.—Morgan Davy ; destination, Barbadoes.—Ann Drayton ; destination, Barbadoes.—Henry ffale ; destination, Barbadoes.—Henry ffale ; destination (no place given).—Elizabeth Hale ; destination (no place given).—Elizabeth Cooke (of Tewksbury) ; destination (no place given).—Susan Blisse (of Bristoll) ; destination (no place given).—William Jones (of Carlion) ; destination (no place given).— Susan Amor ; destination (no place given).

Page 104

Thomas Howell (of Carlion) ; destination (no place given).—Pancell Williams (of Bristoll) ; destination (no place given).—Richard Williams ; destination (no place given).—Rice Williams (of Abergavenney) ; destination (no place given).— Thomas Butler (of Bristoll) ; destination, Nevis.—Mary Gray (of Bristoll) ; destination, Barbadoes.—Ann Saw (of Bath) ; destination, Barbadoes.—William Dando (of Longashton) ; destination, Barbadoes.—Mathew Curtis (of Wilton) ; destination, Barbadoes.—John Edwards (of Charvill) ; destination, Barbadoes.—Stephen Clement (of Killington) ; destination, Barbadoes.—Alice Vaughan (of Bristol) ; destination, Barbadoes.

Page 105

Griffin Phillips ; destination, Barbadoes.—Humphrey Susbitch ; destination, Barbadoes.—Isaac Barrington (of Draggett) ; destination, Barbadoes.—Samuell Bower (of Bath) ; destination (no place given).—Thomas Bower (of Bath) ; destination (no place given).—Walter Williams ; destination, Barbadoes.—John Andrews (of Overton) ; destination, Barbadoes.—Thomas Billington (of London) ; destination, Barbadoes.—Thomas Barker (of Cirencester) ; destination, Barbadoes.— John Morgan ; destination, Barbadoes.—Thomas Pearce ; destination, Barbadoes. —Owen Griffen (Lanraddock) ; destination, Barbadoes.

Page 106

Lewis Morgan ; destination, Barbadoes.—Jane Jones (of Kingswood) ; destination, Barbadoes.—John Scudamore (of Trobridge) ; destination (no place given).— Katharine Hampton ; destination (no place given).—ffrancis Merrick (of Tikurton) ; destination (no place given).—Ann Nurdon (of Bristoll) ; destination (no place given).—Evan Williams ; destination (no place given).—Robert Bridgood (of Washwell) ; destination, Barbadoes.—John fflower (of Munmouth) ; destination, Barbadoes.—Alice ffuller (of Widney) ; destination, Barbadoes.—Peter Griffis (of Blaynemore) ; destination, Barbadoes.—James Lewis (of flanvurmuck) ; destination, Barbadoes.

Page 107

Evan Humphry (of Lampathy) ; destination, Barbadoes.—Edward ffluellin (of St. ffaggons) ; destination, Barbadoes.—Mathew Lower (of St. Johns, co. Cornwall) ; destination, Barbadoes.—Evan Jones ; destination, Barbadoes.—John Hucker (of Streete) ; destination, Barbadoes.—Edward Dam (of Carnuton) ; destination, Barbadoes.—Thomas Williams (of Lanhangell) ; destination, Barbadoes.—John Price (of Galy) ; destination, Barbadoes.—Richard Stanley (of Cardigan) ; destination, Barbadoes.—William Williams (of Causon) ; destination, Barbadoes.—William Moate ; destination, Barbadoes.—William Grimes ; destination, Barbadoes.

Page 108

Thomas Harris ; destination, Barbadoes.—Richard Moadly ; destination, Barbadoes.—William Thomas ; destination, Barbadoes.—Thomas Nicholls (of Lanhangell) ; destination, Barbadoes.—Richard Jones ; destination (no place given). —Bonadventure Joseph (of Tewxbury) ; destination (no place given).—Thomas Morgan ; destination (no place given).—Rowland Watkins ; destination (no place given).—Ann Masy (of Swansy) ; destination (no place given).—George Chambers (of Ratliffe) ; destination (no place given).—Edward Phelps (of Stroudwater) ; destination (no place given).—John Timbrell (of Okesey) ; destination, Barbadoes.

Page 110 (*sic*)

George Kelly ; Barbadoes.—ffrancis Jenkin ; destination (no place given).— Thomas Griffith (of Langandagerne) ; destination (no place given).—Thomas Prosser (of London) ; destination (no place given).—Stephen Pester (of Tiverton) ; destination (no place given).—James Easter ; destination (no place given).—Thomas Owen ; destination (no place given).—Jane Symons (of Bristoll) ; destination (no place given).—Margaret Jones (of Cardiffe); destination (no place given).—Prudence Evans ; destination (no place given).—Rebecca Mumford ; destination (no place given).—Elizabeth Manning ; destination (no place given).

Page 111

John Addams (of Woocester) ; destination (no place given).—William Addams ; destination (no place given).—Elizabeth Davis ; destination (no place given).— David Jones (of Clantarry) ; destination (no place given).—Lewes Jones (of Langarduck) ; destination (no place given).—Christopher Reaven ; destination (no place given).—Phillip Ricketts (of Dilton) ; destination (no place given).—Edward Banton ; destination (no place given).—William Debdin ; destination (no place given).—Thomas Morrill (of Wocester) ; destination (no place given).—Gilbert Lews ; destination (no place given).—John Tailer ; destination (no place given).

Page 112

James Braine (of Kingdowne) ; destination (no place given).—Robert Price (of Mockos [?]) ; destination (no place given).—Johane Roberts ; destination (no place given).—David Williams ; destination (no place given).—Rice Morgan (of fforrest of Deane) ; destination (no place given).—James Chappell (of Bishopp Litchett) ; destination (no place given).—John Martyn (of Bristoll) ; destination (no place given).—William Hopkins ; destination (no place given).—Thomas Hodgins (of Kings Norton) ; destination (no place given).—John Baber (of Bristoll) ; destination (no place given).—Thomas Bagnell ; destination (no place given).—William Booker ; destination (no place given).

Page 113

William Gunter ; destination (no place given).—ffrancis Williams ; destination (no place given).—Robert Penford (of Ivelchester) ; destination (no place given). —Humphrey Lary ; destination (no place given).—Richard Axford ; destination (no place given).—Rice Morgan (of Narbuth) ; destination (no place given).— Nicholas Hawkins ; destination, Barbadoes.—Thomas Andrews ; destination, Barbadoes.—Thomas Tomlinson ; destination, Barbadoes.—Margaret Thomas ; destination, Barbadoes.—William Saunders ; destination, Barbadoes.—Jeffery Braynon ; destination (no place given).

Page 114

Abell Lavington (of Westbury) ; destination (no place given).—Edward ffrancis (of Clanour) ; destination (no place given).—Henry Robert (of Trillims) ; destination (no place given).—Richard Massinger (of Cricklett) ; destination (no place given).—David Southerland (of Kellkenye [Kilkenny]) ; destination (no place given).—Michaell Otty (of Kings Cramby) ; destination (no place given).—William Jones ; destination (no place given).—Edward Trach (of Ely, co. Glamorgan) ; destination (no place given).—John Smabridge ; destination (no place given).— David Lewis ; destination (no place given).—Samuell Stockwell ; destination (no place given).—Edward Griffis (of Shrewsbury) ; destination (no place given).

Page 115

James ffollend (of Kary) ; destination (no place given).—James Agriston (of Whitney) ; destination (no place given).—William Watken (of Thornebury) ; destination (no place given).—Lawrence Cornich (of Habin) ; destination (no place given).—Edward Mathews (of Lavington) ; destination (no place given).—Mary Thomas ; destination (no place given).—Mary John ; destination (no place given).— Andrew Evans ; destination (no place given).—Deborah Minchin (of Lutton) ; destination (no place given).—James Maxfield ; destination (no place given).—Ann Smith ; destination (no place given).—Margery Crumpe ; destination (no place given).

Page 116

Thomas Tompson (of York) ; destination (no place given).—Thomas Rogers (of Telbury) ; destination (no place given).—Charles Jones ; destination (no place given).—David Edwards (of Brecon) ; destination, Barbadoes.—Thomas Seye ; destination, Barbadoes.—John Grannt (of Holt) ; destination (no place given).—Thomas Morgan (of Trigluck) ; destination (no place given).—Richard Rice (of Pill) ; destination (no place given).—Dennis Martin ; destination (no place given). —Thomas Bevin (of Thornebury) ; destination (no place given).—David Jones ; destination (no place given).—Miles Walter (of Penterr) ; destination (no place given).

Page 117

Grace Bevan (of Bristoll) ; destination (no place given).—Morrice William (of Carmarthen) ; destination (no place given).—Dorathy James ; destination (no place given).—Jennett ffowler ; destination (no place given).—William Jacques (of Alderton) ; destination (no place given).—Thomas Jacques ; destination (no place given).—ffrancis Loveridge ; destination (no place given).—George Bartlett ; destination (no place given).—William Willsheere ; destination (no place given).— William Edwards ; destination (no place given).—Richard Perrebridge (of Sedford) ; destination (no place given).—Sibell Loyd ; destination (no place given).

Page 118

Jasper Harris (of Bristoll) ; destination (no place given).—Margery·Lluellin ; destination (no place given).—Jonas Leonard ; destination (no place given).—Elizabeth ·Blaque (of Gloucester) ; destination (no place given).—John Mathews (of Wapping) ; destination, Barbadoes.—Isaac Chapman ; destination (no place given). —Jeremy Smith (of Ipswich) ; destination (no place given).—Thomas Meredith (of Old Radnor) ; destination (no place given).—Roger Millard (of Old Radnor) ; destination (no place given).—Susan Williams ; destination (no place given).—ffrancis Skidmore (of Trowbridge) ; destination (no place given).—Elizabeth Kaile (of Milton Alley) ; destination (no place given).

Page 119

John Davis ; destination (no place given).—William Cole ; destination (no place given).—Richard Arnold ; destination (no place given).—Hugh·Rice (of Lan-rillia) ; destination (no place given).—John ffloyd (of St. Davids) ; destination (no place given).—John James ; destination (no place given).—Humphrey Bullary (of Witcombe) ; destination (no place given).—Ann Jones (of Bristoll) ; destination (no place given).—Mary ffincombe ; destination (no place given).—Margaret Williams ; destination (no place given).—Margaret Thomas ; destination (no place given).—Arculus Davis (of Shepton·Mallett) ; destination (no place given).

Page 120

Mathew Phillips ; destination (no place given).—Thomas Jones ; destination (no place given).—Henry Addams ; destination (no place given).—Edmund·Allen ; destination (no place given).—Thomas Lewis (of Lanelton) ; destination (no place given).—Edward Griffen ; destination (no place given).—Margaret fferiz (of Cane) ; destination (no place given).—Joane Tompkins ; destination (no place given).— William Walter (of Bristoll) ; destination (no place given).—Katherine Winsor ; destination (no place given).—Mary Griffen ; destination (no place given).—Evan Harris (of Cardiffe) ; destination (no place given).

Page 121

Margaret Roberts ; destination (no place given).—Walter Lewis ; destination (no place given).—John Mathews ; destination (no place given).—Robert Duckett (of Swansy) ; destination (no place given).—Thomas House (of Bath) ; destination (no place given).—Thomas Gibbins (of Gloucester) ; destination (no place given). —Deborah Harris (of Bristoll) ; destination (no place given).—Reynold Langford ; destination (no place given).—Henry Jones ; destination (no place given).—Daniell Moorly ; destination (no place given).—Thomas Reece (Michaell Deane) ; destination (no place given).—Thomas Player (of Bristoll) ; destination (no place given).

Page 122

Thomasin Smith (of Woottonunderedge) ; destination (no place given).— George Hainsworth (of Kitlington) ; destination (no place given).—Robert Henry (of Londonderry) ; destination (no place given).—Richard Jenings (of Hutton) ; destination (no place given).—James Addams (of Kent) ; destination (no place given). —Anne Keene (of Bristoll) ; destination (no place given).—William Good (of Mangersbury) ; destination (no place given).—John Brooks (of Droytwitch) ; destination (no place given).—Thomas Langford (of Netherbury) ; destination, New England.—Martha White (of Michaell Deane) ; destination, New England.— William Jenkins (of Ragland) ; destination, New England.—Paule Medcalfe (of St. Dunstone, London) ; destination, New England.

Page 123

Nicholas Powell (of Saint Peters, co. Hereford) ; destination, New England.— John Martin (of Tedbury) ; destination, New England.—Thomas Hyom (of Southam) ; destination (no place given).—Hannah Morgan (of Abergavenny) ; destination (no place given).—George Boulton (of Bradford) ; destination (no place given).—Elinor Jones ; destination (no place given).—Thomas Jones (of Churchill) ; destination (no place given).—Robert Aishworth (of Titherington) ; destination (no place given).—James Mebry ; destination (no place given).—Blainch Humphris ; destination (no place given).—Mary Collins ; destination (no place given).—Mary Williams ; destination (no place given).

Page 124

Anne Treavis ; destination (no place given).—Anne Davis (of London) ; destination (no place given).—Thomas Richard (of Blewmares [Beaumaris]) ; destination (no place given).—Thomas Hall ; destination (no place given).—William Watts ; destination (no place given).—Philip Watkins ; destination (no place given).—Peter Ireton (of Blackfriars) ; destination (no place given).—Darby Deare ; destination (no place given).—John Gardner ; destination (no place given).—Daniel Davis ; destination (no place given).—Charles Belonger ; destination (no place given).—William Smith (of Grigory Stoke) ; destination (no place given).

Page 125

Charles Young ; destination (no place given).—Elizabeth Prier (of Bridgwater) ; destination (no place given).—Henry Carr (of Bristoll) ; destination (no place given). —Davy Roberts (of Milford) ; destination (no place given).—Margaret Vaughan ; destination (no place given).—Davy Bevan ; destination (no place given).—James Wall (Northpetherton) ; destination (no place given).—Joane Heney (of Box) ; destination (no place given).—John Lucas (of Warminster) ; destination (no place given).—Margery Morgan; destination (no place given).—William Champion; destination (no place given).—Simon Coop (of ffroome); destination (no place given).

Page 126

Richard Harris (of Islippe); destination (no place given).—Mary Read (of All Holland); destination (no place given).—Millier Jones (of Cosly); destination (no place given).—Mary Mainsbridge (of St. Johns, Winchester); destination (no place given).—Roger Silcocke (of Sondton); destination (no place given).—Martha Smith (of Bristoll); destination (no place given).—George Thomas (of Cowbridge); destination (no place given).—William Hayford (of Burford); destination (no place given).—John Brace; destination (no place given).—James fflower; destination (no place given).—Thomas Prosser; destination (no place given).—Hugh Davis; destination (no place given).

Page 127

John Bowen; destination (no place given).—Abigell Pharesint; destination (no place given).—Katharine Morrice; destination (no place given).—Elizabeth Morgan; destination (no place given).—Robert Humphris (of Chedder); destination (no place given).—Thomas Jones (of Clansford); destination (no place given). —Phillip Watkins; destination (no place given).—Richard Ridby (of Liddin); destination (no place given).—Robert Clarke (of Liddin); destination (no place given).—Edward Brooks (of Nueberry); destination (no place given).—Jane Hall (of Munmouth); destination (no place given).—Robert Pharns (of Midford); destination (no place given).

Page 128

John Cadell (of Bristoll); destination, Barbadoes.—Andrew Gritly (of Taunton); destination, Barbadoes.—Joseph Moore (of Dundry); destination (no place given). —Andrew Bedow (of Cainsham); destination (no place given).—Morgan Cony; destination (no place given).—Edmund Davy; destination (no place given).—Mary Patton (of Dunster); destination (no place given).—Mathias Jones (of Abergainey); destination (no place given).—Jane Harris (of Tennett); destination (no place given).—Richard Cooper (of ffroome Sellwood); destination (no place given).— William Jones (of Cardiffe); destination (no place given).—Thomas Phillipps (of Brecon); destination (no place given).

Page 129

Ephraim Rogers (of Dorchester); destination (no place given).—Anne Parker (of Wooky); destination (no place given).—Henry Druce (of ffroome Sellwood); destination (no place given).—John Allin (of Worster); destination (no place given).— Robert Pritchard (of Worster); destination (no place given).—John Clarke (of Worster); destination (no place given).—Howell Whitehall (of Worster); destination (no place given).—John Callowhill (of Worster); destination (no place given).— George Jelph (of Gloucester); destination (no place given).—John Niblett (of Montonfarly); destination (no place given).—John Cary (of Munster); destination (no place given).—Thomas Williams (of Langue); destination (no place given).

Page 130

Thomas Evans; destination (no place given).—Morgan Jenkin; destination (no place given).—John Herne (of Sherbourne); destination (no place given).—

Nathaniell Berrell; destination (no place given).—James Harris (of Wocester); destination (no place given).—James Rogers; destination (no place given).—William Dee; destination (no place given).—Susan Williams (of Bandon Bridge); destination (no place given).—John Escutt; destination (no place given).—Lawrence Tharpe; destination, Barbadoes.—Jane Jenkins; destination, Barbadoes.—Robert Driver; destination, Barbadoes.

Page 131
Edward Price; destination (no place given).—Thomas Barnes (of Westbury); destination (no place given).—Richard George; destination (no place given).—Thomas Roberts; destination (no place given).—William Elmes (of Sondton); destination (no place given).—ffrancis Williams; destination (no place given).—Joseph Owen (of Bristoll); destination, Virginia.—William Williams; destination, Virginia.—William Petty; destination, Barbadoes.—William Thomas; destination, Barbadoes.—Thomas Philpott; destination, Barbadoes.—James Powell (of Walterstone); destination, Barbadoes.

Page 132
Roger Rosewell; destination (no place given).—Robert Jones; destination (no place given).—John ffowles (of Bristoll); destination (no place given).—Amy Powell; destination (no place given).—Richard Wells; destination (no place given).—Edward Wells; destination (no place given).—Margaret Bruster (of Dovebridge); destination, Virginia.—Planch (*sic*) James (of Kemmis); destination, Barbadoes.—Morgan Lewis (of Greate Landilo); destination, Virginia.—Thomas Evans (of Lanure); destination, Barbadoes.—Mary Arton; destination, Barbadoes.

Page 133
Henry Alley (of St. Clements, London); destination, Barbadoes.—Robert Dory; destination, Barbadoes.—Mary Lewis (of Cardigan); destination, Barbadoes.—Water (*sic*) Davy; destination, Barbadoes.—Thomas ffoster; destination, Barbadoes.—Samuell Manning (of St. Martin's, London); destination, Virginia.—John Gardener (of Bristoll); destination, Barbadoes.—William Poskins (of Lanarth); destination, Barbadoes.—John Dike (of Winshcombe); destination, Barbadoes.—Elizabeth Loyd (of Worcester); destination, Barbadoes.—Sallomon Evans (of Landoshilio); destination, Barbadoes.

Page 134
Evan Thomas (of Bristoll); destination, Barbadoes.—Thomas Jenkins; destination, Barbadoes.—David Evasts; destination, Barbadoes.—John Chitterbake (of Gloucester); destination, Virginia.—James Edwards (of Ely, co. Glamorgan); destination, Barbadoes.—William ffarmer (of Garway); destination, Virginia.—Jane Hanny; destination, Barbadoes.—Elizabeth Griffen; destination, Barbadoes.—Richard Edwards (of Berne); destination, Barbadoes.—Thomas Mathew (of Henbury); destination, Barbadoes.—Morgan Davis; destination, Barbadoes.

Page 135
Thomas Stephens (of Worcester); destination, Barbadoes.—William Powell (of Brecknock); destination, Barbadoes.—Phillip Vercoe (of Island of Barbadoes); destination, Barbadoes.—Jenkin Thomas (of Swansey); destination, Virginia.—Henry Jones (of Landethin); destination, Virginia.—William Thomas (of co. Mon-

mouth) ; destination, Virginia.—Ralph Coleman (of Bedminster) ; destination, Barbadoes.—Mary [blank] ; destination, Barbadoes.—Nathaniell Herne (of Netherbury) ; destination, Virginia.—William Honny Burns (of Banton) ; destination, Virginia.—William Jones ; destination, Barbadoes.—William Clarke (of Runford) ; destination, Virginia.

Page 136
　　Edward Say ; destination, Barbadoes.—Henry Stafford ; destination, Barbadoes.—Evan Phillips ; destination, Barbadoes.—Anne Corney (of Cosham) ; destination, Barbadoes.—Reece Hopkin (of Carmarthen) ; destination, Barbadoes. —Nicholas Browne ; destination, Barbadoes.—John Browne ; destination, Barbadoes. —John Owen ; destination, Virginia.—Guy Moore ; destination, Barbadoes.— Elizabeth Light ; destination, Barbadoes.—Elizabeth Light ; destination, Barbadoes.—Thomas Price ; destination, Barbadoes.

Page 137
　　William Lancy ; destination, Barbadoes.—Theophilus Kinge ; destination, Barbadoes.—William Brown ; destination, Barbadoes.—Samuell Williams (of Lanloird) ; destination, Virginia.—Mary Stafford (of St. Maries, co. Gloucester) ; destination, Virginia.—Elizabeth Dennis ; destination, Barbadoes.—Walter Williams ; destination, Virginia.—Walliam Awbry (of Brecknock) ; destination, Virginia.— Elizabeth Church ; destination, Barbadoes.—Robert Church ; destination (no place given).—Gabriell Church ; destination (no place given).—William Griffis ; destination (no place given).

Page 138
　　Thomas Harrts ; destination, Virginia.—Margaret Rose ; destination, Barbadoes.—Edward Evans ; destination, Barbadoes.—Walter Price ; destination, Barbadoes.—Anthony Lawrence ; destination, Barbadoes.—Edward Skidinore ; destination, Barbadoes.—John Taylor ; destination, Virginia.—Judith Whitinge ; destination, Barbadoes.—James Binnbom ; destination, Virginia.—Evan Jones ; destination, Barbadoes.—Robert Cinson ; destination, Barbadoes.—Samuell Vaughan ; destination, Barbadoes.

Page 139
　　John Seger ; destination, Barbadoes.—Mary Philpett ; destination, Virginia.— Jonathan Drake ; destination, Virginia.—John Watts ; destination, Virginia.—Mary Thomas ; destination, Barbadoes.—Sibell Jones ; destination (no place given).— Edmund Rogers ; destination, Virginia.—John Woodward ; destination, Virginia. —Phillip Watkins ; destination, Barbadoes.—Elizabeth Hayward ; destination, Virginia.—Robert Hughes ; destination, Barbadoes.—Lewes Haskins ; destination, Barbadoes.

Page 140
　　John Kinge ; destination, Virginia.—Peter Owen ; destination, Virginia.— ffrancis Whittock ; destination, Virginia.—Walter Walker (of Newtowne) ; destination, Virginia.—Joane Weight ; destination, Barbadoes.—John Harris ; destination, Barbadoes.—George Gray ; destination, Virginia.—Siscock West (of Bristoll) ; destination, Virginia.—Simon Wrentmore ; destination, Virginia.—Margaret Waters ; destination, Virginia.—John Thomas ; destination, Virginia.—Richard Griffen (of Bristoll) ; destination, Barbadoes.

Page 141

Elisabeth Jones (of Woester) ; destination, Virginia.—Daniell Sawman ; destination, Virginia.—John fflower (of Bristoll) ; destination, Virginia.—John Lewis (of Dursley) ; destination, Barbadoes.—Arthur Noeton (of London) ; destination, Virginia.—David Webb (of Shirehampton) ; destination, Virginia.—John Davis (of Swanly) ; destination, Barbadoes.—ffrancis Bristow (of Westerly) ; destination, Barbadoes.—Margerett Arnold (of Westbury) ; destination, Barbadoes.—John Martin (of Bristoll) ; destination, Virginia.—Margeret Lewis (of Abergavenny) ; destination, Virginia.—Susan King (of Bristoll) ; destination, Barbadoes.

Page 142

John Martyn (of Abergavenny) ; destination, Virginia.—Bridgett Lewis (of Abergavenny) ; destination, Virginia.—Jane Richards ; destination, Barbadoes.— Thomas Church (of Bristoll) ; destination, Barbadoes.—George Diton (of Corke) ; destination, Virginia.—John Browne (of fframpton Cotterell) ; destination, Virginia.—John Browne (of ffishenton) ; destination, Virginia.—Robert Minson (of Bristol) ; destination, Virginia.—Luellin Jones (of Bristoll) ; destination, Virginia. —Moses Hardidge (of Westbury) ; destination, Virginia.—Joseph Dyer (of Wells) ; destination, Virginia.—Elizabeth Warner ; destination, Virginia.

Page 143

ffrancis Mosse (of Monmouth) ; destination, Virginia.—John Shaw ; destination, Virginia.—John Coward ; destination, Virginia.—Lawrance Gringer ; destination, Virginia.—Margeret Jones (of Chepstow) ; destination, Barbadoes.—Elisabeth Dennis ; destination, Virginia.—John Mays ; destination, Virginia.—Thomas Edwards (of Quickenny) ; destination, Virginia.—Richard Phelps ; destination, Virginia.—Ann Powell ; destination, Virginia.—Elizabeth Yeamone ; destination, Virginia.—David Hughes (of Bristoll) ; destination, Barbadoes.

Page 144

David Miller ; destination, Virginia.—Giles Marden (of Gloucester) ; destination, Barbadoes.—John Robins (of Lempster) ; destination, Virginia.—Mary Millard ; destination, Virginia.—William Bird ; destination, Virginia.—Ann Hall ; destination, Barbadoes.—Thomas Mathews ; destination, Barbadoes.—Henry Davis ; destination, Barbadoes.—Hugh Cavenagh ; destination, Virginia.—Stephen West ; destination, Virginia.—Richard Symons ; destination, Virginia.—ffrancis Parsons ; destination, Virginia.

Page 145

Thomas Bargnor ; destination, Virginia.—Margeret Nicholas (of Cardiff) ; destination, Virginia.—Elinor Davidge ; destination, Virginia.—Bridgett Turner ; destination, Barbadoes.—Sibill Heale ; destination, Barbadoes.—Phillip Jones ; destination, Barbadoes.—William Alford ; destination, Virginia.—William Boulton ; destination, Virginia.—John Watkins ; destination, Virginia.—Jonas Williams ; destination, Virginia.—Charles Rigby ; destination, Virginia.—William Turner (of Wedmore) ; destination, Barbadoes.

Page 146

Michaell Hopkin (of Newman) ; destination, Barbadoes.—Margery Lane ; destination, Barbadoes.—Barnard Bond ; destination, Virginia.—Robert Vannor ;

destination, Virginia.—Richard Tayler (of Woester) ; destination, Virginia.—James Smout (of Bricknell) ; destination, Virginia.—Grissett Lewis ; destination, Barbadoes.—Joane Smith ; destination, Virginia.—Elisabeth Lewis ; destination, Virginia.—Elizabeth Powell ; destination, Virginia.—Charles Thomas (of Usqe) ; destination, Barbadoes.—Philip Thomas ; destination, Barbadoes.

Page 147
Susan Baker ; destination, Virginia.—John Crooke ; destination, Virginia.— Anne Bowles ; destination, Virginia.—William Lugg ; destination, Virginia.— John Treavett ; destination, Virginia.—Katherine Williams ; destination, Virginia. —Richard Nash ; destination, Barbadoes.—William Ward ; destination, Virginia. —Tobias Kibble ; destination, Virginia.—Margerett Turner ; destination, Virginia. —Elisabeth Hobson ; destination, Virginia.—Ann Lydea ; destination, Virginia.

Page 148
George Edwards (of Woester) ; destination, Virginia.—Charles Edwards ; destination (no place given).—Walter Kidney (of Bitton) ; destination (no place given).—John Crooke ; destination (no place given).—John Sikes (of Teddrington) ; destination (no place given).—Edward Jones ; destination (no place given).—Howell Jones ; destination (no place given).—James Mockland ; destination (no place given).—David Howell ; destination (no place given).—Alexander Lawry (of Dumfries) ; destination (no place given).—Edward Moody (of Salisbury) ; destination (no place given).—James Eastbound ; destination (no place given).

Page 149
Thomas Tucker (of Gloucester) ; destination (no place given).—Richard Drake (of Bristoll) ; destination (no place given).—Thompson Drake ; destination (no place given).—Mary Drake ; destination (no place given).—John Drake ; destination (no place given).—Thomas Drake ; destination (no place given).—William Morton ; destination (no place given).—Oliver Lewis (of Ludlow) ; destination, Barbadoes.—Robert Copnell ; destination, Virginia.—Thomas Watkins (of Nuport) ; destination, Virginia.—Mary Prosser (of Heriford) ; destination, Virginia.—Alice Streeton (of Bristoll) ; destination, Virginia.

Page 150
Miles Jones (of Hereford) ; destination, Barbadoes.—Roger Spittle ; destination, Barbadoes.—Robert Spittle ; destination, Barbadoes.—Elizabeth Cooper ; destination, Barbadoes.—William Davis (of Monmouth) ; destination, Virginia.—John Deelieth ; destination, Virginia.—George Teage (of Wartery) ; destination, Virginia.—Margaret Rodwell ; destination, Virginia.—Thomas Arne (of Lancaster) ; destination, Virginia.—Robert Cory ; destination, Virginia.—Susan Ballin (of Bristoll) ; destination, Barbadoes.

Page 151
William Stokes ; destination, Barbadoes.—Robert Jackson ; destination, Virginia.—fferdinand Bishop ; destination, Barbadoes.—John Hooke (of Almonsbury) ; destination, Virginia.—John Richman (of Emsbury) ; destination, Virginia. —William Sutton (of Lurgessor) ; destination, Virginia.—Richard Philpott ; destination, Virginia.—Grace Ricketts (of Emsbury) ; destination, Virginia.—Alice

Ricketts (of Lurgessor); destination, Virginia.—Grace Ricketts; destination, Virginia.—Margerett Phillpot (of Emsbury); destination, Virginia.—William Marchant (of Warmester); destination, Virginia.

Page 152

Herbert Richardson; destination, Barbadoes.—Elizabeth Roberts (of Bridgen); destination, Virginia.—William Douth (of Bristoll); destination, Virginia.—Ann Williams (of Langenne); destination, Virginia.—Elisabeth Wolfe (of London); destination, Barbadoes.—Elinor Boyer (of Kiderminster); destination, Virginia.— Richard ffloyd (of Montgomery); destination, Virginia.—Katherine Johnes; destination, Virginia.—Thomas Griffeth; destination, Virginia.—Paul Medcalfe; destination, Virginia.—Elisabeth Machen (of Bartly); destination, Nevis.—Ann Jones (of Apledore); destination, Virginia.

Page 153

Michaell Everett (of Bristoll); destination (no place given).—John Balsh (of Ilchester); destination (no place given).—John Curtis (of Ilchester); destination (no place given).—William Garbett (of Bridgnorth); destination, Barbadoes.— John Andrews (of Marsfield); destination, Barbadoes.—Bridgett Jones (of Bristoll); destination, Virginia.—Richard Moore (of Willington); destination, Barbadoes.— Lettice Brewster (of Bristoll); destination, Virginia.—Nathaniel Pill (of Stroudwater); destination, Virginia.—David Evans (of St. Eallins); destination, Virginia. —Walter Williams (of Staubridge); destination, Virginia.—Lishon Thomas (of Lanridia); destination, Virginia.

Page 154

John Mascall; destination, Virginia.—John Bolteir; destination, Virginia.— Walter Cory (of Bristoll); destination, Virginia.—Joane Cory; destination, Virginia.—William White; destination, Virginia.—Stephen Bridle; destination, Virginia.—Richard Harford (of Bristoll); destination, Virginia.—John Bilson (of Bradford); destination, Virginia.—Elinor Sabrin (of Uphaiven); destination, Virginia.—John Ashby; destination, Virginia.—Thomas Lewis (of Bristoll); destination, Virginia.—John Lydiat (of Winston); destination, Barbadoes.

Page 155

Sarah Roberts (of Purlion); destination, Virginia.—Thomas Evans; destination, Virginia.—William Trasier; destination, Virginia.—William Gary (of Norridge); destination, Virginia.—Henry Evill (of Milburne); destination, Barbadoes.—David Smith (of Mangersfeild); destination, Barbadoes.—Joane Hurd (of Bristoll); destination, Barbadoes.—Elisabeth Shere (of Bristoll); destination, Barbadoes.—Susan Spenser (of Penmarke); destination, Virginia.—Thomas Whitmish (of Wilton); destination, Barbadoes.—John Baker (of Wincanton); destination, Barbadoes.—Margarett Lewis (of Karmarden [Carmarthen ?]); destination, Barbadoes.

Page 156

Robert Ayleworth (of Titherington); destination, Barbadoes.—Thomas Jones (of Churchill); destination, Barbadoes.—Thomas Bramble (of Bath); destination, Barbadoes.—Isaac James; destination, Barbadoes.—Thomas Rees; destination, Barbadoes.—Thomas Phillips; destination, Barbadoes.—Susan Thomas; destination, Barbadoes.—James Cruster; destination, Barbadoes.—Morgan James; destination, Barbadoes.—Mary Jones; destination, Barbadoes.—James Davis (of Cardife); destination, Barbadoes.—John Vaughan (of Chewstook); destination, Barbadoes.

Page 157

William Evans (of Aberquilly); destination, Barbadoes.—Marstry Lewis; destination, Barbadoes.—John Watkins (of Bristoll); destination, Virginia.—William Morgan (of Landaff); destination, Barbadoes.—William Millard; destination, Nevis.—John Card; destination, Nevis.—Richard Rouch (of Tisbury); destination, Nevis.—Richard Avare; destination, Nevis.—Nicholas Harding; destination, Nevis.—John Harding (of Meer); destination, Nevis.—William Bird (of Ashband); destination, Nevis.—William Roods (of Marticke); destination, Nevis.

Page 158

Robert Tenham (of Porten); destination, Virginia.—Thomas Wallis; destination, Virginia.—David Morgan (of Lowerddford); destination, Barbadoes.—John Homes (of Anger); destination (no place given).—John Duck (of Anger); destination (no place given).—William Davis (of Anger); destination (no place given).—Abigail Hayes; destination, Barbadoes.—ffrancis Brewer; destination, Barbadoes.—Margerett Homes; destination, Barbadoes.—Katherine Williams; destination, Barbadoes.—Edmund Williams; destination, Barbadoes.—James Jones; destination, Barbadoes.

Page 159

Susan Lewis (of Notely); destination, Nevis.—Alice Howell (of Wells); destination, Nevis.—Griffen John (of Talbon); destination, Nevis.—Sanders Jones; destination, Nevis.—Roger Kerkinn (of Yateon); destination, Virginia.—Walter Kidney (of Bitton); destination, St. Christopher.—Robert Hart; destination, Barbadoes.—Thomas Johnson (of Henly); destination, Virginia.—Darkas Smart (of Bristoll); destination, St. Christopher.—William Saw (?) (of Eddington); destination, Barbadoes.—William Burkey (of Henly); destination, Barbadoes.—Thomas Dabney (of Smithfeild); destination, Barbadoes.—Sabella ffrance (of Lydney); destination, Barbadoes.

Page 160

John Cruse (of Huddmore Miltons); destination, Barbadoes.—Katherine Morgan (of Swansey); destination, Barbadoes.—Margaret Cory (of Bristoll); destination, Barbadoes.—John Whitehouse (of Kilmister); destination, Barbadoes.—John Young (of Milton); destination, Barbadoes.—Henry Osdill (of Henton); destination, Barbadoes.—Elisabeth Dibbins (of ffroome); destination, Barbadoes.—Elisabeth Whitehouse (of Kilmister); destination, Barbadoes.—Richard Phillis (of Kilmister); destination, Barbadoes.—William Whitehouse (of Nailsey); destination, Barbadoes.—Elisabeth Court; destination, Barbadoes.

Page 161

Richard Shatford; destination, Nevis.—William Cooper; destination, Barbadoes.—William Smith (of Trawbridge); destination, Barbadoes.—Margeret Phillips (of Garway); destination, St. Christopher.—David Townsend; destination,

E

Barbadoes.—Elisabeth Dunn ; destination, Barbadoes.—John Wade (of Monmouth) ; destination, Barbadoes.—Thomas Long ; destination, Barbadoes.—Edward Richards ; destination, Barbadoes.—John Card (of Gillengam) ; destination, Nevis. —Edmund Green (of Gillengam) ; destination, Nevis.—Daniell Wilson (of Talbat) ; destination, Nevis.

Page 162
    Joseph Arson (of Bristoll) ; destination, Barbadoes.—Thomas Bird ; destination, Nevis.—George Cozner (of Trowbridge) ; destination, Nevis.—Ann ffoller (of ffrome Sellwood) ; destination, Nevis.—John Long (of Heishon) ; destination, Nevis.—Elizabeth Munday (of Bristoll) ; destination, Nevis.—Richard Hill (of Woodbridge) ; destination, Barbadoes.—Robert ffeild (of Woodbridge) ; destination, Barbadoes.—Morgan Jones (of Landlarnon) ; destination, Barbadoes.— Samuell Jones (of Bisguard) ; destination, Nevis.—John Smith (of Bristoll) ; destination, Barbadoes.—Bernard Jones (of Bristoll) ; destination, St. Christopher.— Rebecca Waites (of Andover) ; destination, St. Christopher.

Page 163
    William Skinner (of Devizes) ; destination, Barbadoes.—Peter Stower (of Crockeem Pill) ; destination, Barbadoes.—William Bernerd ; destination (no place given).—George Lane (of Hunsum) ; destination, Barbadoes.—Edmund Pater (of Monmouth) ; destination, Virginia.—Thomas Green (of ffrome) ; destination, Barbadoes.—Andrew Rakes ; destination, Barbadoes.—Walter Beard (of Standish) ; destination, St. Christopher.—Thomas Allohy (of St. Giles Holburne) ; destination, Barbadoes.—James Baker (of Barkely) ; destination, Barbadoes.—Richard Arsnis (of Stroudwater) ; destination, Barbadoes.—Samuel Bullocke (of Pensford) ; destination, Nevis.—Mary Edwards (of Bristoll) ; destination, St. Christopher.

Page 164
    Susan Hill (of Bristoll) ; destination, Nevis.—William Grange (of London) ; destination, Barbadoes.—John Parker (of Woppy) ; destination, Barbadoes.—Margeret Thorne (of Wells) ; destination, Barbadoes.—William Talbut (of Ambursly) ; destination, Barbadoes.—Joice Burnell (of Stapleton) ; destination, Barbadoes.— Joice Williams (of Bristoll) ; destination, Barbadoes.—James Mayell ; destination, Barbadoes.—Susan Humphreys (of Wells) ; destination, Barbadoes.—Thomas Parker (of Wopley) ; destination, Nevis.—William Buckley (of Ashborne) ; destination, Barbadoes.—Nathaniel Suttin (of Easton) ; destination, Barbadoes.

Page 165
    William Biggs (of Mashfeild) ; destination, Barbadoes.—Evan Harris (of Harford) ; destination, Barbadoes.—James Jones (of Abergavenny) ; destination, Barbadoes.—Robert Commeeshall (of Whitchurch) ; destination, Nevis.—Thomas Jordan (of Abergavenny) ; destination, St. Christopher.—Richard Hughes (of Uske) ; destination, St. Christopher.—Charles Jones ; destination, St. Christopher.—William Davis (of Badway) ; destination, St. Christopher.—Cleare Loe (of Bristoll) ; destination, St. Christopher.—Edward George (of Cardith) ; destination, Barbadoes.— Elizabeth Denson (of Bodnes) ; destination, Barbadoes.—Joane Roberts (of Bristoll) ; destination, Barbadoes.

Page 166

Daniell Inon (of Aberhund) ; destination, Barbadoes.—William Withers (of Devizes) ; destination, Barbadoes.—John Janes (*sic*) (of Landethllo) ; destination, Barbadoes.—Hercules Dobell (of Thornecomb) ; destination, Barbadoes.—Roger Prosser (of Whitney) ; destination, Barbadoes.—Barbara Wallis (of Gloucester) ; destination, Barbadoes.—Elizabeth Jenkins (of Usqe) ; destination, Barbadoes.— Maudlin Jones (of Abergavenny) ; destination, St. Christopher.—Ann Williams (of Lannacherow) ; destination, St. Christopher.—Edward Lee (of Shrosbury) ; destination, Barbadoes.—Thomas Davis (of Shrosbury) ; destination, Barbadoes.—William Sharp (of Rogister [Rochester]) ; destination, Barbadoes.

Page 167

Edward Wilkins (of Newport) ; destination, Barbadoes.—John Comleis (of Bath) ; destination, Barbadoes.—Gennett Hughes (of Bristoll) ; destination, Barbadoes.—John Melten (of Rumsey) ; destination, Barbadoes.—Elizabeth Rackley (of Bridgwater) ; destination, Barbadoes.—Margerett Sheppard (of Barton Regis) ; destination, Barbadoes.—Stephen Cooke ; destination, St. Christopher.—Elizabeth Beaton (of Bath) ; destination, Barbadoes.—John Smith (of Lidney) ; destination, Barbadoes.—Reece Bowen (of Dishert) ; destination, Barbadoes.—James Lord (of Harditch) ; destination, Barbadoes.—William Morgan (of Lanover) ; destination, Barbadoes.

Page 168

Ann Proaly (of Lantover) ; destination, St. Christopher.—Richard Thomas (of Lanvoe) ; destination, Barbadoes.—Thomas Giles (of Mutchmaryne) ; destination, Barbadoes.—William Sands ; destination, Barbadoes.—Joane Hall (of Martly) ; destination, Barbadoes.—Elizabeth Kelly (of Temby) ; destination, Barbadoes.— Ambrose Bissïcke (of Bristol) ; destination, Barbadoes.—Arthur Tirribby (of St. Eeth) ; destination, Barbadoes.—Lewis Browne (of Whitchurch) ; destination, Barbadoes.— Mathew ffowler (of Whitney) ; destination, Barbadoes.—John Mascall (of Walton) ; destination, Barbadoes.—William Griffeth (of Abergavenny) ; destination, Barbadoes.

Page 169

William Kingscott (of Banwell) ; destination, Barbadoes.—John Rider (of Bristoll) ; destination, Barbadoes.—Sarah Morgan (of Cardiffe) ; destination, Barbadoes.—Elizabeth Packer (of Gloucester) ; destination, Barbadoes.—William Slade (of Sherburne) ; destination, Barbadoes.—Mary Davis ; destination, Barbadoes.—David Price (of Langimond) ; destination, Barbadoes.—John Jones (of Cardiff) ; destination, Barbadoes.—James Cogin (of Bristleton) ; destination, Barbadoes. —Edward Cole (of Crambert) ; destination, Barbadoes.—Edward Wills (of ffisherton) ; destination, Barbadoes.—Mary Waytes ; destination, Barbadoes.

Page 170

Elizabeth Smith (of Harnam) ; destination, Barbadoes.—Constant Ember ; destination, Barbadoes.—Elizabeth [blank] ; destination, Barbadoes.—Giles ffees (of Twexbury) ; destination, Barbadoes.—Alis Davis (of Heriford) ; destination, Barbadoes.—David Jones (of Welshpoole) ; destination, Virginia.—Nicholas Noyes (of Hatherdin) ; destination, Barbadoes.—Moses Jones (of St. Bride's, co. Monmouth) ; destination, Barbadoes.—John Harris ; destination, Barbadoes.—Henry Reynold (of St. Mellens) ; destination, Barbadoes.—Theophilis King (of Nailsworth) ; destination, Barbadoes.—Richard Green (of Nath-Puddle) ; destination, Barbadoes.

Page 171

William Lovell (of Wedmore) ; destination, Barbadoes.—John Norris (of Bristoll) ; destination, Barbadoes.—Thomas Deed (of Bristoll) ; destination, Barbadoes. —David Edwards (of Penterk) ; destination, Barbadoes.—Priscilla Pidding (of Tainton) ; destination, Barbadoes.—Thomas Dangerfeild ; destination, Barbadoes.— Lettis Harbart (of Bristoll) ; destination, Barbadoes.—Richard Jones (of Lahannith) ; destination, Barbadoes.—John Morris (of Cilson) ; destination, Barbadoes.—Elisabeth Morris ; destination, Barbadoes.—Peter Taylor (of Rainfor) ; destination, Barbadoes.—Eliza Williams (of Newport) ; destination, Barbadoes.

Page 172

George Boylan (of Bristoll) ; destination, Barbadoes.—Jeremiah Cunningsby (of Worcester) ; destination, Virginia.—William Comb (of Atterly) ; destination, Barbadoes.—Henry Stroud (of Bloxford) ; destination, Barbadoes.—Peteridge Powell (of Landishen) ; destination, Virginia.—ffrancis Clarke (of Kingsale) ; destination, Virginia.—Daniell Wyatt (of Horrell) ; destination, Barbadoes.—Alexander Hurly (of Bitton) ; destination, Barbadoes.—David Gibbs (of Henbury) ; destination, Barbadoes.—Susan Giles (of Ly) ; destination, Barbadoes.—Thomas Stary (of Weltham) ; destination, Barbadoes.—Edward Swanbrow ; destination, Virginia.

Page 173

Jeremy Mew ; destination, Barbadoes.—Joseph Dorkett (of co. Gloucester) ; destination, Barbadoes.—Ann Green (of Rosse) ; destination, Barbadoes.—Thomas Baker ; destination, Barbadoes.—William Bower (of Miniyard) ; destination, Barbadoes.—Lewis Markham (of St. ffagons) ; destination, Barbadoes.—William Lansford (of Neston) ; destination, Virginia.—Henry Hicks (of Titherington) ; destination, Virginia.—Peace Lloyd (of Bristoll) ; destination, Virginia.—John Dixson (of Pennarke) ; destination (no place given).—William Dixson ; destination (no place given).—Henry Davis (of Neath) ; destination (no place given).

Page 174

Blanch Mathewes ; destination (no place given).—Elisabeth Thomas (of Cardiffe) ; destination (no place given).—Robert Parsons (of Bingham) ; destination (no place given).—Thomas Smith (of ffroome) ; destination (no place given).— Joane Price (of Bristoll) ; destination, Virginia.—John Leatch (of St. Tavernes) ; destination, Barbadoes.—Nicholas Dugresse (of Bristoll) ; destination, Virginia.— Davis Jones (of Weshpool [*sic*]) ; destination, Virginia.—Martha Everard ; destination, Virginia.—Robert Mason (of Hanly) ; destination, Barbadoes.—George Barrett (of Bristoll) ; destination, Nevis.—Elisa Beeke (of Bristoll) ; destination, Barbadoes.

Page 175

James Maddox (of Eaton) ; destination, Barbadoes.—Ann Nurse (of Gloucester) ; destination, Barbadoes.—Henry Davis (of Bristoll) ; destination, Virginia.—James Griffith (of Cardihan) ; destination, Virginia.—Thomas Davis (of Yeaton) ; destination, Barbadoes.—Edward Kent (of Kemsay) ; destination, Virginia.—Thomas Dunn (of Chosen) ; destination, Virginia.—Joseph Dunn (of Chosen) ; destination, Virginia.—James Broomecroft ; destination, Barbadoes.—Elisabeth Jones (of Bashcke [?]) ; destination, Barbadoes.—Edward Davis (of Lanford) ; destination, Barbadoes.—William Arlingam (of Berwick upon Tweed) ; destination, Virginia.

Page 176

William Collins (of Tidenam) ; destination, Virginia.—David Jenkins (of Swansey) ; destination, Barbadoes.—Thomas Henton (of Bristoll) ; destination, Virginia. —John Willis (of ffrancksome) ; destination, Barbadoes.—ffrances Taylor ; destination, Virginia.—William Cooke (of Baesly) ; destination, Virginia.—John Henly (of Bradford, co. Wilts) ; destination, Virginia.—Henry Whiten (of Highworth) ; destination, Barbadoes.—Ursulla Batt (of Cambridge) ; destination, Barbadoes.— John Williams (of Landoe) ; destination, Barbadoes.—John Reach (of Backwell) ; destination, Virginia.—Sarah Wasborow (of Westbury) ; destination, Barbadoes.

Page 177

Howell Hart (of Dosely) ; destination, Barbadoes.—Thomas Wills (of Exeter) ; destination, Virginia.—James Studgy (of ffroome) ; destination, Barbadoes.—John Harkett ; destination, Barbadoes.—William Mew ; destination, Barbadoes.—Henry Carpenter ; destination, Barbadoes.—Thomas Pope ; destination, Barbadoes.— Purnell Ritty (of Milsonne) ; destination, Barbadoes.—Michaell Clarke (of Newton) ; destination, Barbadoes.—John Jones (of Starkfeild) ; destination, Virginia.—John Morgan (of Cardiffe) ; destination, Barbadoes.—William Darby ; destination, Barbadoes.

Page 178

Mary Ball (of Rosse) ; destination, Barbadoes.—Charles Day (of Portishead) ; destination, Barbadoes.—Daniell Pritchard (of Kentchurch) ; destination, Virginia. —William Bolton (of Nantwich) ; destination, Barbadoes.—Nicholas Hagley (of Taunton) ; destination, Barbadoes.—Daniell Hawkins (of Cheltenham) ; destination, (no place given).—Margeret Williams (of Lanhenock) ; destination, Virginia.— Richard Gardner ; destination, Barbadoes.—Thomas Short (of Shepton Mallet) ; destination, Virginia.—Thomas English ; destination, Barbadoes.—William Jones (of Bristoll) ; destination, Barbadoes.—Richard Sarton (co. of Sussex) ; destination, Virginia.

Page 179

William Davis ; destination, Barbadoes.—George Adlum (of Westbury) ; destination, Barbadoes.—John Wyat (of Bedminster) ; destination, Barbadoes.— ffrancis Morgan ; destination, Barbadoes.—John Bessent (of Wootten Bassutt) ; destination, Barbadoes.—Joane Wall (of Croft) ; destination, Barbadoes.—Roger Lambert (of Horton) ; destination, Virginia.—Evan William (of Lambeder [Lampeter]) ; destination, Barbadoes.—Thomas Hartland (of Coller) ; destination, Barbadoes.—Thomas Kingman (of ffroome) ; destination, Barbadoes.—Thomas Richards ; destination, Barbadoes.—Evan Debry ; destination, Virginia.

Page 180

Thomas Baskerly ; destination, Virginia.—William Millard (of Nettleton) ; destination, Barbadoes.—William ffarly ; destination, Barbadoes.—William Pitman (of Gloucester) ; destination, Barbadoes.—Thomas Roberts (of Gloucester) ; destination, Barbadoes.—Thomas Morgan (of Malmsbury) ; destination, Barbadoes.— John Jones (of Gloucester) ; destination, Barbadoes.—Phillip Morgan (of St. Georges) ; destination, Barbadoes.—Henry Thomas ; destination, Barbadoes.—ffrancis Thomas (of Salisbury) ; destination, Barbadoes.—Walter Henry ; destination, Barbadoes.— Susan Pickford (of Warmister) ; destination, Barbadoes.

Page 181

John Venicot (of Bridgwater) ; destination, Barbadoes.—Valentine Nowell (of Buthry) ; destination, Barbadoes.—Morgan Watkins (of Munmouth) ; destination, Virginia.—Elizabeth George ; destination, Barbadoes.—Edward ffoster (of Winterburne) ; destination, Barbadoes.—Edward James ; destination (no place given).— Abell Powell ; destination (no place given).—Susan Pillurne (of Weyburne) ; destination (no place given).—Peter Weight ; destination, Maryland.—Thomas Lew ; destination, Barbadoes.—Bartholomew Jones ; destination (no place given).—George Wisel (of Thornebury) ; destination (no place given).

Page 182

Mary Morgan ; destination (no place given).—William Carpenter ; destination, Virginia.—Mary Morgan ; destination, Virginia.—James Williamson ; destination, Virginia.—Christopher Devalgara ; destination, Virginia.—William Light ; destination, Virginia.—William Crumhall ; destination, Virginia.—Richard Brewer ; destination, Virginia.—Edward West ; destination, Virginia.—Walter Reynold ; destination, Virginia.—William Hasell ; destination, Virginia.—William Grindall ; destination, Barbadoes.

Page 183

Richard Abbon ; destination (no place given).—Ann Maine (of Bursett) ; destination, Barbadoes.—Ann Williams (of Magor) ; destination, Barbadoes.—Robert Twiford (of Bradford) ; destination, Barbadoes.—William Day (of Misely) ; destination, Barbadoes.—Richard Bull ; destination, Barbadoes.—John Tompson ; destination, Virginia.—Elizabeth Whitney (of Earsly) ; destination, Virginia.—Thomas Stinchcom (of Tortery) ; destination, Barbadoes.—John Cooper (of Winterbourne) ; destination, Barbadoes.—Edward Pavy (of Salisbury) ; destination, Barbadoes.

Page 184

Thomas Litman (of Sheppon Mallett) ; destination, Barbadoes.—Joane Beare ; destination, Barbadoes.—ffrancis Hales (of Salisbury) ; destination (no place given).—Katherine Roberts ; destination (no place given).—Hanny Haint (of Ottingham) ; destination (no place given).—Elizabeth Hunt ; destination (no place given).—Susan Allen (of Arkall) ; destination, Nevis.—Robert Cadwallett ; destination, Nevis.—Thomas Corett (of New Sarum) ; destination, Barbadoes.— Henry Noble (of ffroome) ; destination, Barbadoes.—Lewis Jones (of Newchurch) ; destination, Barbadoes.—Daniell Godfussell (of London) ; destination, Barbadoes.

Page 185

Henry Oateway (of Bedminster) ; destination, Barbadoes.—Henry Hichings ; destination, Barbadoes.—John Howell ; destination, Barbadoes.—Robert Deapery ; destination (no place given).—Strangwayes Bradshew (of London) ; destination (no place given).—Benjamin Hassard (of Tidneham) ; destination (no place given).— John Pearse ; destination (no place given).—Ann Church ; destination (no place given).—Richard Bussett (of Buringham) ; destination (no place given.)—James Snow (of Sherton) ; destination (no place given).—James Burton ; destination (no place given).—Morgan Williams (of Usque) ; destination (no place given).

Page 186

Walter Williams (of Usque) ; destination (no place given).—Thomas Baskerfield ; destination (no place given).—William Vickaer ; destination (no place given).—

William Buckler; destination (no place given).—Thomas Hennell (of Bradford); destination (no place given).—Samuell Churchill (of Hamersmith); destination (no place given).—Thomas Berrell (of Worsall); destination (no place given).— Hugh Jones; destination (no place given).—Ann Williams; destination (no place given).—John Right (of Bewdly); destination (no place given).—Humphrey Davis (of Cardigan); destination (no place given).—Egredian Bumfree (of Shrewsbury); destination (no place given).

Page 187

Thomas. Edwards; destination (no place given).—Ann Sherly (of Bursott); destination (no place given).—Richard Getcome (of Sandford); destination (no place given).—John Gutler (of Bramsgrove); destination (no place given).— Robert Muck (of Locksford); destination (no place given).—Bartholomew Hore (of Waterford); destination (no place given).—Thomas Birch (of Taunton); destination (no place given).—Edward Hopkin (of Swansey); destination (no place given).—Thomas Morgan (of Cardiffe); destination (no place given).—Joane Robinson (of Camell); destination (no place given).—Ann Williams (of Abergavenny); destination (no place given).—Lewis Richards (of St. Beevills); destination, Barbadoes.

Page 188

John Davis (of Beammage); destination, Barbadoes.—Thomas Mace (of Compton); destination, Barbadoes.—Thomas Parker (of Shepmallet); destination, Barbadoes.—John Thomas (of Newland); destination, Barbadoes.—Richard Prosser (of Whitchurch); destination, Barbadoes.—Arthur Gum (of Axswick); destination, Barbadoes.—Jane Saunders (of Bristoll); destination, Barbadoes.—Ruth Porter (of Ciciter); destination, Barbadoes.—James Pinniat (of Lacock); destination, Barbadoes.—Thomas Morris (of Petcombe); destination, Barbadoes.—Rose Shipney (of Winterborn); destination, Barbadoes.—James Limbey (of Benton); destination, Barbadoes.

Page 189

Margeret Butler (of Benton); destination, Barbadoes.—Sarah Clarke (of Benton); destination, Barbadoes.—Thomas Edwards; destination, Barbadoes.— Mary Hartgood (of Bristoll); destination, Barbadoes.—Abraham Harris (of Sherborne); destination, Barbadoes.—William Howell; destination, Barbadoes.— Elisabeth Pritchard; destination, Barbadoes.—Daniell Garland (of Thornebury); destination, Barbadoes.—Richard Hughes (of Carwent); destination, Barbadoes.— Thomas Probat (of Nonnington); destination, Barbadoes.—John Bennett (of Aule); destination, Barbadoes.

Page 190

James Palmer (of ffarrington); destination, Barbadoes.—Lewis Davis; destination, Barbadoes.—Howell Jenkins (of Pantage); destination, Barbadoes.—Elinor Ellis (of St. Jones); destination, Barbadoes.—Robert Kerswell (of Milesbourough); destination, Barbadoes.—Robert Neale (of Luckington); destination (no place given).—Margaret Dawning (of Phillips Norton); destination, Barbadoes.— Elizabeth Reeve (of Bristoll); destination, Barbadoes.—Thomas Oxford (of Thornebury); destination, Barbadoes.—Richard Baker; destination (no place given).— John Alford; destination (no place given).—David Williams (of Abergavenny); destination (no place given).

Page 191

Abraham ffookes (of Bradford) ; destination (no place given).—Edward Boane (of Durley) ; destination (no place given).—Lewes Tudor ; destination (no place given).—David Watkins (of Brecknock) ; destination (no place given).—Anne Williams (of Landins) ; destination (no place given).—John Hotchins (of Whem) ; destination (no place given).—Richard Hatcher (of Lockera) ; destination (no place given).—Nicholas Whitchurch (of Roade) ; destination (no place given).—Margeret Phillips (of Langsbaits) ; destination (no place given).—Roger Doggett (of Porbery) ; destination (no place given).—Edward Pretty (of Maulinsbury [Malmesbury]) ; destination (no place given).—Thomas Ingram (of Limouth [Lynmouth]) ; destination (no place given).—John Thomas (of Thundaivle [Llandilo]) ; destination (no place given).

Page 192

Samuell Veizy (of Canne) ; destination (no place given).—John Lockstone (of Wickwarr) ; destination (no place given).—Margery Lockston ; destination (no place given).—Richard Danby (of Cam); destination (no place given).—Bartholomew Browne (of London) ; destination (no place given).—James Jones (of ffarington) ; destination (no place given).—William Morgan (of Millford) ; destination (no place given).—Henry Harris (of Rushford) ; destination, Barbadoes.—Charles Denham (of Shadwell) ; destination, Barbadoes.—Margery Denham ; destination (no place given).—Richard Teage (of Rosemary Lane, London) ; destination (no place given).—Richard Millard (of Nettleton) ; destination (no place given).

Page 193

Henry ffurrs (of Silverton) ; destination (no place given).—Katherine Jones ; destination (no place given).—John Whopper ; destination (no place given).—John Lewes (of Newport) ; destination (no place given).—James Corckle (of Kenardington) ; destination (no place given).—Joane Gough (of Michell Deane) ; destination (no place given).—Roger Carraway (of Lacock) ; destination (no place given).—Thomas Jones (of Rosse) ; destination, Barbadoes.—Samuell Newington (of Greenage) ; destination, Barbadoes.—William Progers (of Cannedy) ; destination, Barbadoes.—George Bowen (of Lambida [Lampeter ?]) ; destination, Barbadoes.—Dorothy Taylor (of Devizes) ; destination, Barbadoes.—Elizabeth Mason (of Winsham) ; destination, Barbadoes.

Page 194

Edith Bagwell (of Winsham) ; destination, Barbadoes.—Thomas Morris (of Meeruck) ; destination, Barbadoes.—William Milton (of Bruton) ; destination, Barbadoes.—John Jones (of Bruton) ; destination, Barbadoes.—Tobias Bassett (of Bruton) ; destination, Barbadoes.—Randall Jones (of Shitnar) ; destination, Barbadoes.—Mary Hawkins (of Nuport) ; destination, Barbadoes.—Hugh Hughes (of Nuport) ; destination, Barbadoes.—Margery Cullimor (of Nuport) ; destination, Barbadoes.—Mary Tanner ; destination, Barbadoes.—Robert Redwood ; destination, Barbadoes.—Mary Gardners (of Bromyard) ; destination, Barbadoes.

Page 195

John Evans (of Roade) ; destination, Barbadoes.—Sarah Cruse (of Roade) ; destination, Barbadoes.—William Holbin (of Bitton) ; destination, Barbadoes.—

Mary Acreman (of Bristoll) ; destination, Barbadoes.—Edmund Painter (of Woosted-comber) ; destination, Barbadoes.—Thomas Nash ; destination, Barbadoes.—Mary Davis ; destination, Barbadoes.—Morgan Williams ; destination, Barbadoes.—John Reileigh (of Worcester) ; destination, Barbadoes.—Thomas Hacock ; destination, Barbadoes.—Thomas Ashby (of Hoppon) ; destination, Barbadoes.—Nicholas Stoke ; destination, Barbadoes.

Page 196
    Roger Roany (of Cherrell) ; destination, Barbadoes.—Martha Taylor (of Ros) ; destination, Barbadoes.—Richard Russell (of Phillips Norton) ; destination, Barbadoes.—Richard Bowden (of Torrington) ; destination, Barbadoes.—Rebecca Wilcox ; destination (no place given).—Mary Richards (of Hilmarken) ; destination (no place given).—James Morgan (of Lanorth) ; destination, Barbadoes.—Henry Morgan (of Lanorth) ; destination, Barbadoes.—William Cockerell ; destination, Barbadoes.—John Norfolke ; destination, Barbadoes.—John Williams (of Dublin) ; destination, Barbadoes.—Richard Barker (of Milburne) ; destination, Barbadoes.

Page 197
    Suzan Ashby (of Roade) ; destination, Barbadoes.—George King (of Bridg-water) ; destination, Barbadoes.—Thomas More (of Lester) ; destination, Barbadoes.—Maurice Pitman (of Bruton) ; destination, Barbadoes.—Cornelius Travanian (of Titheford) ; destination, Barbadoes.—William Addison (of Bristoll) ; destination, Barbadoes.—William Hawcott (of Coventry) ; destination, Barbadoes.—Mary Manster (of Kingswood) ; destination, Barbadoes.—Sarah Atkins (of Kingswood) ; destination, Barbadoes.—John Cadewell (of Ciciter) ; destination, Barbadoes.—William Hudson (of Shippon) ; destination, Barbadoes.—Henry Hobson (of Thornbury) ; destination, Barbadoes.

Page 198
    ffortunatus Hobson als. Clarke (of Thornbury) ; destination, Barbadoes.—William Matthewes (of Swansey) ; destination, Barbadoes.—Griffith Williams (of Canarvan[shire]) ; destination, Barbadoes.—John Webley (of Hereford) ; destination, Barbadoes.—Anne Morgan (of Bristoll) ; destination, Barbadoes.—Richard Lee ; destination, Barbadoes.—Gartrey Wey (of Bristoll) ; destination, Barbadoes.—Joseph Buggis (of Gillingham, co. Gloucs.) ; destination, Barbadoes.—William Probart (of Maudley) ; destination, Barbadoes.—John Hunt (of Ickeford) ; destination, Barbadoes.—John ffoy (of Bedminster) ; destination, Barbadoes.—Rice Powell (of Brecknock) ; destination, Barbadoes.

Page 199
    Richard Bishop (of Walton) ; destination, Barbadoes.—Gregory Grumall (of Norfolk[shire]) ; destination, Barbadoes.—Nathaniel Hitchins (of Horseley) ; destination, Barbadoes.—Humphry Chick (of Bartley) ; destination, Barbadoes.—Owen David (of Lambatherne) ; destination, Barbadoes.—Mary Hollier (of Bristoll) ; destination, Barbadoes.—Andrew Morgan (of Usk) ; destination, Barbadoes.—Phillip Bennett (of Clannis) ; destination, Barbadoes.—Richard Knight (of Bartley) ; destination, Virginia.—Thomas Teall (of Charlton) ; destination, Virginia.—John Crews (of Bricksham) ; destination, Barbadoes.—James Barker (of Lidney) ; destination, Barbadoes.

Page 200
    John Jones (of Bristoll) ; destination, Barbadoes.—Anthony Michen (of Taunton) ; destination, Barbadoes.—Matthew Abbotts (of Porberry) ; destination, Barbadoes.—William Jones (of Nuport) ; destination, Barbadoes.—William Turner (of Walton, co. Hants) ; destination, Barbadoes.—Nicholas Turner (of Walton, co. Hants.) ; destination, Barbadoes.—William Morgan (of Lanelly) ; destination, Barbadoes.—Richard Pew (of Heriford) ; destination, Barbadoes.—Andrew Mercer (of Heriford) ; destination, Barbadoes.—Darby Murfey (of Corke) ; destination, Barbadoes.—Arthur Morgan (of Bristoll) ; destination, Barbadoes.—Henry Williams (of Lameplard) ; destination, Virginia.

Page 201
    George Smith (of High Ester) ; destination, Barbadoes.—Humphrey Owen (of Hawksbury) ; destination, Barbadoes.—Giles Chandler (of London) ; destination, Barbadoes.—Edward Scott (of Devizes) ; destination, Barbadoes.—Thomas Edgerley (of London) ; destination, Barbadoes.—Mary Tustin (of Sphager) ; destination, Barbadoes.—Anne Wood (of Stroud) ; destination, Barbadoes.—John Pike (of Easthartry) ; destination, Barbadoes.—William Bowell (of Brecknock) ; destination, Barbadoes.—Samuell Williams (of Westbury) ; destination, Barbadoes.—John Phillips (of Brecknock) ; destination, Virginia.—David Morce (of Brecknock) ; destination, Virginia.

Page 202
    Thomas Garburt (of Bristoll) ; destination, Virginia.—Richard Stevenson (of St. Giles, London) ; destination, Barbadoes.—John Wiltshire (of Chewstoke) ; destination, Virginia.—Thomas Watley (of Wootenunderidge) ; destination, Virginia.—Phillip Comerton (of Washford, Ireland) ; destination, Virginia.—ffrancis Watkins (of Henbury) ; destination, Virginia.—William Lewes (of Crudwell) ; destination, Virginia.—ffrancis Williams (of Burrey) ; destination, Virginia.—John Baff (of Cummerford) ; destination, Barbadoes.—William Hutchins (of Lostock) ; destination, Virginia.—John Sims (of Lostock) ; destination, Barbadoes.—Thomas Biggs (of Upton) ; destination, Barbadoes.

Page 203
    Elizabeth Johns (of Carmarthen[shire]) ; destination, Barbadoes.—John Wesson (of Bastchurch) ; destination, Barbadoes.—Joseph Buggs (of Gillingham) ; destination, Barbadoes.—Thomas Cloud (of Carvan) ; destination, Barbadoes.—John Battell ; destination, Barbadoes.—David James (of Lanabrin) ; destination, Barbadoes.—Giles Skimble (of Shippen Warrington) ; destination, Virginia.—Anne Coward (of Longashton) ; destination, Barbadoes.—Thomas Shoyle (of Culkenny) ; destination, Virginia.—William Beames (of Mangottsfeild) ; destination, Nevis.—William Jones (of Brecknock[shire]) ; destination, Virginia.—Richard Vinson (of Sherbourne) ; destination, Barbadoes.

Page 304 (*sic*)
    Robert Jervis (of Nuberry) ; destination, Virginia.—Robert White (of Nuberry) ; destination, Virginia.—John Lee (of Nuberry) ; destination, Virginia.—Anne Vaughan (of Worcester) ; destination, Virginia.—Martha Biford (of Herriford) ; destination, Barbadoes.—Ann ffloyd (of Bristoll) ; destination, Virginia.—Ann Rosser (of Bristoll) ; destination, Virginia.—John Bush (of Shaston) ; destination,

Virginia.—Henry Williams (of Birtch); destination, Barbadoes.—Jane Steale (of Worcester); destination (no place given).—William Scarlet (of Bristoll); destination, Barbadoes.—Thomas Richards (of London); destination, Barbadoes.

Page 305
Rowland Samuell (of Cardiff); destination, Barbadoes.—Margarett Terrey (of Cardiff); destination, Barbadoes.—Prescilla Kent (of Nuberry); destination, Virginia.—Elizabeth Miles (of Hamsteed); destination, Virginia.—John Windever (of Nuberry); destination, Virginia.—Dorothy Jones (of Harvest West); destination, Virginia.—Mary Morrice (of Cardiff); destination, Barbadoes.—John Ellison (of Box); destination, Virginia.—John Pavy (of Box); destination, Virginia.—Alice Hurne (of Bartley); destination, Virginia.—Joane Smith (of Bristoll); destination, Barbadoes.—Ann Westbury (of Bristoll); destination, Barbadoes.—Joshua Burt (of Montague); destination, Barbadoes.

Page 306
Ann Matthews (of Montague); destination, Barbadoes.—Hugh Silly (of Codmith); destination, Barbadoes.—John ffletcher (of ffarne); destination, Virginia.—Nathaniell Butt (of Mansbury); destination, Virginia.—John Knight (of Mulberr); destination, Barbadoes.—Elizabeth ffarrington (of Colchester); destination, Virginia.—John ffoolke (of Milbourne); destination, Barbadoes.—Peter Windar (of Kingsale); destination, Barbadoes.—Gabriell Thomas (of Bear); destination, Barbadoes.—Mary Evans (of Ludlow); destination, Virginia.—William Thomas (of Monmouth[shire]); destination, Virginia.—Sarah Hayward; destination, Virginia.

Page 307
Ann ffuller (of Sanford); destination, Virginia.—John Mills (of Upholdree); destination, Virginia.—Robert Crocker (of Currible); destination, Virginia.—James Densby (of Holcomb); destination, Virginia.—Edward Lugg (of Wolleton); destination, Virginia.—Mary Scadein (of Hermick); destination, Virginia.—Robert Reeves; destination, Virginia.—Robert Everet (of Bishopstorford); destination, Virginia.—ffrancis Chandler (of Bishopstorford); destination, Virginia.—Thomas Button (of Bishopstorford); destination, Virginia.—Sarah Smith (of Bishopstorford); destination, Virginia.—Richard Addams (of London); destination, Virginia.

Page 308
John Evans (of Bristoll); destination, Virginia.—Edward Besford (of Holbiton); destination, Virginia.—William Cherry (of Luston); destination, Virginia.—Richard Price (of Luston); destination, Virginia.—Joane Howell (of Landelavow); destination, Virginia.—Elinor Sense (of Trowbridge); destination, Virginia.—Robert Baily (of Barkeley); destination, Virginia.—Richard Howell (of Shasbury); destination, Virginia.—Thomas Churcher (of Eston); destination, Barbadoes.—Leonard Reis (of Stroud); destination, Virginia.—John Plerfit (of Padstow); destination, Barbadoes.—James Dedicott (of Bedminster); destination, Virginia.

Page 309
John Vicary (of Haverton); destination, Barbadoes.—John Waltar (of Iston); destination, Virginia.—Mary Davis (of Lidney); destination, Virginia.—Robert England (of Bristoll); destination, Virginia.—John Baker (of Berrington); destination, Virginia.—Evan Thomas (Glamorgan[shire]); destination, Virginia.—Thomas

Watkins (of Sadbury); destination, Virginia.—Sarah Hedges (of Chewmagna); destination, Virginia.—John Bowten (Homes Chappell); destination, Barbadoes.— Thomas Price (of Staunton); destination, Virginia.—John Yeo (of Smithfeild in London); destination, Virginia.—Edward Spicer (of Canterbury); destination, Virginia.

Page 310

Edward Hemming (of Bristoll); destination, Virginia.—Nicholas Sprackling (of Dorset[shire]); destination, Virginia.—John Beck and Katherine Beck; destination, Virginia.—Grace Puncher (of Dorset[shire]); destination, Barbadoes.— Deborah Ludwell (of Wells); destination, Barbadoes.—John Galley (of ffisherton Anger); destination, Barbadoes.—Mary House (of Wells); destination, Virginia. —Elizabeth Springer (of Usk); destination, Barbadoes.—Edward William Reynolds and Walter William Reynolds (of Kemis); destination, Barbadoes.—John Dion; destination, Barbadoes.—John Weurin (of Wells); destination, Virginia.—Thomas Mason (of Winstanton); destination, Nevis.

Page 311

George Simkins (of Woodspring); destination, Virginia.—Henry Lurton (of Woodspring); destination, Virginia.—Evan Jones (of Landopia); destination, Barbadoes.—Mary Davis (of Lidney); destination, Barbadoes.—Britwood Child (of Bristoll); destination, Virginia.—Ann Moore (of Portishead); destination, Virginia.—Henry Woobourne (of Maston); destination, Virginia.—Summer Adams (of Long Towne); destination, Virginia.—John Stallard; destination, Virginia.—Baldwin Harris (of Ody); destination, Virginia.—John Ellis (of Chadgeley); destination, Barbadoes.—Robert Spyer (of Landover); destination, Barbadoes.

Page 312

Ruth Atkins (of Bedminster); destination, Barbadoes.—Mary ffletcher (of Bristoll); destination, Barbadoes.—Margery Miles (of Bristoll); destination, Barbadoes.—John Bullock (of Taunton); destination, Virginia.—Lukin Botteler (of Scovest); destination, Barbadoes.—Richard Clements (of ffisherton Anger); destination, Barbadoes.—William King (of ffisherton Anger); destination, Barbadoes.—Dorothy ffrench (of ffisherton Anger); destination, Barbadoes.—Waltar fferis (of ffisherton Anger); destination, Barbadoes.—John Burton (of ffisherton Anger); destination, Barbadoes. William Gater (of Heether); destination, Virginia.

Page 313

Mary Creede; destination, Virginia.—Margaret Bainutt (of Barkley); destination, Virginia.—Thomas Silke (of Harbourne); destination, Nevis.—Anthony Bridges (of Mintie); destination, Virginia.—John Church (of Bristoll); destination, Barbadoes.—Thomas Neale (of Bristoll); destination (no place given).—Elizabeth Royall; destination, Virginia.—Richard Sore (of Chew Magna); destination, Virginia.—Ann Thomas (of Trillick); destination, Virginia.—William Willett (of Munmouth); destination, Virginia.—Thomas Gally (of Sallbridge); destination, Virginia.—Ralph Hunt (of Eastpenard); destination, Virginia.

Page 314

William Scutt (of Cheslebury); destination, Virginia.—Richard Tappet (of Burfordly); destination, Virginia.—Richard Wood (of Evill); destination, Virginia. —Suzan Pointer (of ffroome); destination, Virginia.—Mary Sprackling (of Tallow);

destination, Virginia.—Christian Sprackling (of Tallow); destination, Virginia.—ffrancis Earle (of Thornbury); destination, Virginia.—Maudlin Jones (of Munmouth); destination, Virginia.—Sarah Scuse (of Porberry); destination, Virginia.—Lewes Brian (of Bitton); destination, Virginia.—Robert Brian (of Bitton); destination, Virginia.—John Ballard (of Bitton); destination, Virginia.

Page 315
John ffailey (of Cornwall); destination, Virginia.—Ann Gibbon (of Crie); destination, Virginia.—Elizabeth Greene (of Mathan); destination, Nevis.—William Davis (of Shrewsbury); destination, Nevis.—William Hubbert (of Biston); destination, Nevis.—William Head (of Box); destination, Nevis.—Margaret Beazur (of Box); destination, Nevis.—George Hardick; destination, Virginia.—Elizabeth Thomas (of Carmarthen); destination, Virginia.—Richard Beazar (of Box); destination, Virginia.—Thomas Jenkins (of Winny); destination, Virginia.—Simon Ash (of Authrington); destination, Virginia.

Page 316
Thomas Werring (of Wells); destination, Virginia.—Richard Jones (of Taunton); destination, Virginia.—Thomas Bigg (of Gloucester); destination, Virginia.—Jonas Williams; destination, Virginia.—Robert Britt (of Bath); destination, Barbadoes.—Mary Brit (of Bath); destination, Barbadoes.—William Goldsmith (of Wappin in London); destination, Barbadoes.—Joane Hobbin (of Barton Regis); destination, Virginia.—John Allen (of Lacock); destination, Virginia.—Elizabeth Davis (of Lacock); destination, Barbadoes.—John James (of Laventon); destination, Virginia.—William Pollard (of Card [?]); destination, Virginia.

Page 317
Daniell Grigg (of Yarmouth); destination, Virginia.—Suzan Blannch (of St. Anns); destination, Virginia.—Ann Stannton (of Bristoll); destination, Virginia.—George Powell (of Stafford); destination, Virginia.—Waltar Jones (of Pembridge); destination, Virginia.—John Boulton (of Bitton); destination, Virginia.—George Davis (of Bristoll); destination, Virginia.—William Winter (of Exeter); destination, Virginia.—Edward Tucker (of Mangotsfeild); destination, Virginia.—Mary May; destination, Virginia.—John Pearcy (of Bollescum); destination, Virginia.—Joseph Bishop (of Bristoll); destination, Virginia.

Page 318
Ester James (of Bristoll); destination, Virginia.—Evan Lewes (of Lantrshen); destination, Virginia.—Mary Osbourne (of Charlton); destination, Virginia.—John Toby (of Tociter); destination, Barbadoes.—Robert Hancock (of Strawbridge); destination, Barbadoes.—Elizabeth Garnell (of Greenidge [Greenwich]); destination, Barbadoes.—Elizabeth Moone (of Bristoll); destination, Barbadoes.—William Morrice (of Usque); destination, Barbadoes.—Barbara ffuller (of Bristol); destination, Barbadoes.—John Gwin (of Bristoll); destination, Barbadoes.—Edmund Morgan; destination, Barbadoes.—John Bussle (of Wilton); destination, Barbadoes.

Page 319
Henry Eley (of Bristoll); destination, Barbadoes.—John Davis (of Trowbridge); destination, Barbadoes.—Nicholas Williams (of Landenny); destination,

Barbadoes.—John Waters (of Landenny) ; destination, Barbadoes.—Thomas Waters (of Langoome) ; destination, Barbadoes.—Roger Waters (of Langenny) ; destination, Barbadoes.—Margery Hellier (of Chippenham) ; destination, Barbadoes.—Jeptha Parker (of Midsumer Norton) ; destination, Virginia.—Robert Legg (of Wells) ; destination, Virginia.—Mathew Bendle (of Wells) ; destination, Virginia.—Elizabeth Councell (of Wells) ; destination, Virginia.—John Biddlestone (of Brookworth) ; destination, Barbadoes.

Page 320
Thomas Parker (of Shipton Mallett) ; destination, Virginia.—Thomas Hix (of Crumwell) ; destination, Virginia.—William Phillips (of Crumwell) ; destination, Virginia.—Nathan Pike (of Crumwell) ; destination, Virginia.—Katherine Williams (of Nauntwest) ; destination, Virginia.—Ann Jones (of Nauntwest) ; destination, Virginia.—Elinor James (of Nauntwest) ; destination, Virginia.—Edward Moore (of London) ; destination, Barbadoes.—Katherine Jones (of Bath) ; destination, Barbadoes.—Ann Eaton (of Westbury) ; destination, Barbadoes.—Garrard Greene (of Shrewsbury) ; destination, Virginia.—Richard Oatly (of Shrewsbury) ; destination, Virginia.

Page 321
Ann Buske (of Shrewsbury) ; destination, Virginia.—ffrancis Phipps (of Shrewsbury) ; destination, Virginia.—Robert Higgins (of Shrewsbury) ; destination, Virginia.—Dorothy Greene (of Shrewsbury) ; destination, Virginia.—ffrancis Oatly (of Shrewsbury) ; destination, Virginia.—ffrancis Crisp (of Shrewsbury) ; destination, Virginia.—Suzanna Moore (of Shrewsbury) ; destination, Virginia.—William Cowley (of ffrankly) ; destination, Virginia.—Elinor Davis (of New Towne) ; destination, Virginia.—Elinor Matthews (of New Towne) ; destination, Virginia.—Jane Evans (of Shrewsbury) ; destination, Virginia.—Ann Norris (of Shrewsbury) ; destination, Virginia.

Page 322
Sarah Lovell (of Bristoll) ; destination, Barbadoes.—Mary Worin (of Wells) ; destination, Virginia.—Evan Jones (of Panteage) ; destination, Barbadoes.— Roger Evans (of Lanover) ; destination, Virginia.—Thomas Taylor (of Wendy) ; destination, Virginia.—John Atkins (of Phillips Norton) ; destination, Barbadoes.— William Minton (of London) ; destination, Barbadoes.—Morgan Thomas (of Glamorgan[shire]) ; destination, Barbadoes.—Elizabeth Egaranton (of Burtford) ; destination, Barbadoes.—Grace Hiat (of Shepton Mallett) ; destination, Barbadoes. —Sarah Hedges (of Wallington) ; destination, Barbadoes.—Alice Cox (of Bristoll) ; destination, Barbadoes.

Page 323
Humphry Edwards (of Shrewsbury) ; destination (no place given).—John Humphry (of Crutchffryers in London) ; destination (no place given).—Walter Watkins (of Tidnam) ; destination, Virginia.—Thomas ffinden (of Alsford) ; destination, Barbadoes.—Thomas Holme (of Bristoll) ; destination, Barbadoes.—Ann Shin (of Westerleigh) ; destination, Barbadoes.—Suzan Sannsbury (of Westbury) ; destination, Barbadoes.—Elias Homber (of Ilchester) ; destination (no place given). —William Morgan (of Langattooke) ; destination, Barbadoes.—Phillip Roberts (of Newchurch) ; destination, Barbadoes.—Griffith Phillips (of Landenavore) ; destination, Barbadoes.—Ann Jayne (of Bristoll) ; destination, Barbadoes.

Page 324

Elizabeth Bradshaw (of Shepton Mallet) ; destination, Barbadoes.—Elizabeth Smith ; destination, Barbadoes.—Morgan Rice ; destination, Barbadoes.—David Jones ; destination, Barbadoes.—Andrew William ffrancis (of Trevethen) ; destination, Barbadoes.—John Gibson (of Westminster, London) ; destination, Barbadoes. —Job fflavell (of Allchurch) ; destination, Barbadoes.—John Thomas (of Cardiff) ; destination, Barbadoes.—James Edwards (of Traleage) ; destination, Barbadoes.— Phillip Edmunds (of Langoven) ; destination, Barbadoes.—Robert Drabell (of Ilchester) ; destination, Virginia.—Joane Holbrooke ; destination, Barbadoes.— Jane Hughes (of Langemill) ; destination, Barbadoes.

Page 325

Thomas Bushell (of Arton) ; destination, Barbadoes.—John Rogers (of Wickwarr) ; destination, Barbadoes.—Ann Watkins ; destination, Barbadoes.— Roger Lawrance (of Chepstow) ; destination, Barbadoes.—Stephen Webb (of Woolford) ; destination, Barbadoes.—John Overton (of Bath Eston) ; destination, Virginia,—Thomas Hopcott (of Cheltnam) ; destination, Virginia.—William English (of Marlbrough) ; destination, Virginia.—Joseph Saunders (of Puckle Church) ; destination, Virginia.—Alice Jones (of Abergainy) ; destination, Virginia.—John Hill (of Long Hope) ; destination, Virginia.—John Shatford (of Bath) ; destination, Virginia.

Page 326

Alexander ffry (of Mamesbury) ; destination, Virginia.—Jane Eles ; destination, Virginia.—Phillip Blisson (of Kingswood) ; destination, Virginia.—Charity Gayle (of Ilchester) ; destination, Virginia.—Sarah Gardner (of Ilchester) ; destination, Virginia.—Thomas Beza (of London) ; destination, Virginia.—Jonas Bricker (of London) ; destination, Barbadoes.—William Burt (of Milbourne) ; destination, Barbadoes.—Jorgan Jinkin (of Cardiff) ; destination, Barbadoes.—John Rodman ; destination, Barbadoes.—Thomas Mapas ; destination, Barbadoes.—Benjamin Ellis ; destination, Barbadoes.

Page 327

John Taylor ; destination, Barbadoes.—Mary Bevan (of Bristoll) ; destination, Barbadoes.—John Grosse (of Devon[shire]) ; destination, Barbadoes.—Abraham Edwards (of Bath) ; destination, Barbadoes.—Phillip Morgan (of Bristoll) ; destination, Barbadoes.—William Lane (of Glastonbury) ; destination, Barbadoes.— James Thomas (of Lanover) ; destination, Barbadoes.—Elizabeth Phillips (of Lanover) ; destination, Barbadoes.—James Williams ; destination, Barbadoes.— Mary Jeffers (of Gloucester) ; destination, Barbadoes.—William Clarke (of Woodborough) ; destination, Barbadoes.—Ann Prichard (of Rayland) ; destination, Virginia.

Page 328

Robert Andrewes (of Worcester) ; destination, Virginia.—Thomas Heming (of Worcester) ; destination, Virginia.—Mary Lewes (of St. Tavernes) ; destination, Virginia.—Ann Edwards (of Treleague) ; destination, Virginia.—Giles Griffin (of Ledbury) ; destination, Virginia.—William Griffin (of Ledbury) ; destination,

Virginia.—Edward fflicker (of Miltome) ; destination, Barbadoes.—John Crib (of Ashton) ; destination, Barbadoes.—Richard Morgan (of Chipnam) ; destination, Barbadoes.—Mary Richards (of Pentleene) ; destination, Barbadoes.—John Browne (of Rochester) ; destination, Barbadoes.—John Mason (of Rochester) ; destination, Barbadoes.

Page 329

John Morgan ; destination, Barbadoes.—Peter Taylor (of Barkley) ; destination, Barbadoes.—James Edwards ; destination, Barbadoes.—Robert Goodwin (of Long Lode) ; destination, Barbadoes.—John Wadds (of Bristoll) ; destination, Barbadoes.—John Peepe (of Estcombe) ; destination, Barbadoes.—Roger Loyd (of Chard) ; destination, Barbadoes.—William Jones (of Barkly) ; destination, Barbadoes.—William Price ; destination (no place given).—Richard Sandford (of Heriford) ; destination (no place given).—Henry Organ (of fframpton upon Severne) ; destination (no place given).—William Ellis (of Ledbury) ; destination, (no place given).

Page 330

John Bowle (of Stroud) ; destination, Virginia.—Elinor Vaughan (of Herriford) ; destination, Barbadoes.—Katherine Meade (of Bradford) ; destination, Barbadoes.— Hester Sage (of Bristoll) ; destination, Barbadoes.—John Wind (of Chard) ; destination, Barbadoes.—William Lydoll (of Bristoll) ; destination, Barbadoes.—Elizabeth Roynon (of London) ; destination, Barbadoes.—William Powell (of Brecknock) ; destination, Barbadoes.—Charles Swanton (of Bruton) ; destination, Barbadoes.— Brian Jillet and William Jillet (of Tidnall Hall) ; destination, Barbadoes.—Phillip Blisson (of Kingswood, Wilts) ; destination, Barbadoes.—Elizabeth House and Hester House (of Wells) ; destination, Barbadoes.

Page 331

Henry ffreestone (of Hindin) ; destination, Barbadoes.—Thomas Robines (of Sherbourne) ; destination, Barbadoes.—Thomas Porch (of Wover) ; destination, Barbadoes.—Richard Lewes ; destination, Barbadoes.—Richard fford (of Westbury) ; destination, Barbadoes.—James Pinniatt ; destination, Virginia.—John Myoll (of Taunton) ; destination, Virginia.—Thomas Pruatt (of Salisbury) ; destination, Virginia.—John Barry (of Corke) ; destination, Virginia.—William Griffen (of Langippy) ; destination, Virginia.—Thomas Browne (of Walmister) ; destination, Virginia.—Evan James (of Nuport) ; destination, Virginia.

Page 332

George Clarke (of Salisbury) ; destination, Virginia.—Thomas Tillin (of Minty) ; destination, Virginia.—John Reynolds (of Borbidge) ; destination, Virginia.— Peter Edwards (of St. Cleeves) ; destination, Virginia.—William Daby (*sic*) (of Wheatneherst) ; destination, Virginia.—James Gisbourne (of Stroud) ; destination, Virginia.—Elinor Jenings (of Hempsteed) ; destination, Virginia.—John Nash (of Bristoll) ; destination, Virginia.—Peter Tomlinson ; destination, Barbadoes.— Thomas Turner (of Hungerford) ; destination, Barbadoes.—Peter Trebilcock (of Saint Culme) ; destination, Barbadoes.—Andrew Morgan (of Hughlas) ; destination, Barbadoes.

Page 333

James Rogers (of Aust) ; destination, Barbadoes.—John Browne (of Hull, co. Wilts) ; destination, Barbadoes.—Rowland Hill (of Dursley) ; destination, Barbadoes. —William North (of Burbidge) ; destination, Virginia.—John Piper (of Gredbed) ; destination, Virginia.—Thomas Colecombe (of Preston, co. Hereford) ; destination, Barbadoes.—David Jones (of Goldcliffe) ; destination, Barbadoes.—Anne Mathewes (of Bristoll) ; destination, Barbadoes.—Ann Keator (of Heriford) ; destination, Barbadoes.—Holliberry Munn (of Heriford) ; destination, Barbadoes.—Daniell Godsafe (of London) ; destination, Barbadoes.—Mary Gibbons (of Heriford) ; destination, Virginia.

Page 334

Bridget Tiverton (of Winscombe) ; destination, Virginia.—Richard Brooke ; destination, Virginia.—Thomas Lewes (of Newton) ; destination, Barbadoes.— Henry Maddocks (of Micheldeane) ; destination, Virginia.—William Hayes (of Heriford) ; destination, Virginia.—William Williams (of Heriford) ; destination, Virginia.—Mary Parsons ; destination, Virginia.—Thomas Adams (of Wells) ; destination, Virginia.—Edward Hill (of Taunton) ; destination, Virginia.—Joane Webb (of Bath) ; destination, Virginia.—Thomas Creed (of Wolverton) ; destination, Virginia.—Thomas Crew (of fframpton) ; destination, Virginia.

Page 335

John Stone (of Okey) ; destination, Virginia.—Henry Smith (of Drayton) ; destination, Barbadoes.—John Cozens (of Wooten) ; destination, Virginia.— Robert Watson (of Nothumberland) ; destination, Virginia.—Grace Griffith (of Amoram) ; destination, Virginia.—Richard Roe (of Wells) ; destination, Barbadoes. —Richard Patten (of Arlingham) ; destination, Barbadoes.—Martha Mason (of Medstone) ; destination, Barbadoes.—John Phillips ; destination, Barbadoes.— William Browne (of Chipnam) ; destination, Barbadoes.—Richard Baker (of Thornbury) ; destination, Virginia.—John Bradford (of Arlingham) ; destination, Virginia.

Page 336

John Griffith (of Lanvigah) ; destination, Virginia.—Henry King ; destination, Virginia.—Mary Callis (of Blaydon) ; destination, Virginia.—Mathew Sinett (of Harvordwest) ; destination, Virginia.—William Stephens (of Kingswood) ; destination, Virginia.—Nathaniell Browne (of Matcomb) ; destination, Virginia.—David Jinkins (of Cardigan) ; destination, Virginia.—Inon Thomas (of Cardigan) ; destination, Virginia.—Thomas Cooper (of Banwell) ; destination, Virginia.—Nicholas Pulsford (of Kitsford) ; destination, Virginia.—Thomas Boutcher (of Dursley) ; destination, Virginia.—William Pash (of Dunsban) ; destination, Virginia.

Page 337

Robert Reynolds (of Burbidge) ; destination, Virginia.—William Blake (of Burbidge) ; destination, Virginia.—John Chillcott (of Stogumber) ; destination, Virginia.—John Waters (of Dorchester) ; destination, Barbadoes.—Thomas Lugg (of Lidney) ; destination (no place given).—Edith Williams (of Shasbury) ; destination (no place given).—Grace ffullerton (of Carmarthen) ; destination, (no place given).—Katherine ffrancis (of London) ; destination (no place given).—William West (of Shasbury) ; destination (no place given).—Joane Coward (of Dorsester) ; destination (no place given).—Thomas Elliott (of Hetchbury) ; destination (no place given).—Thomas Markes (of Lamfy) ; destination (no place given).

F

Page 338
   Henry Markes (of Lamfy) ; destination (no place given).—Henry Lewes (of Chepstow) ; destination (no place given).—Henry Small (of Ledbury) ; destination (no place given).—Robert Nicholas (of Skenfreth) ; destination (no place given).— Morgan Evan (of Aberda) ; destination (no place given).—Jane Steevens (of Salisbury) ; destination (no place given).—Mary Nott (of Salisbury) ; destination (no place given).—Mary Tippery (of Salisbury) ; destination (no place given).—Sicely Poore (of Salisbury) ; destination (no place given).—William Weekes (of Salisbury) ; destination (no place given).—Symon Tufton (of Salisbury) ; destination (no place given).—Richard Sims (of Salisbury) ; destination (no place given).

Page 339
   John Spicer (of Salisbury) ; destination (no place given).—William Austen (of Salisbury) ; destination (no place given).—John Cherry (of Salisbury) ; destination (no place given).—Andrew Baron (of Salisbury) ; destination (no place given).— Andrew Pride (of Salisbury) ; destination (no place given).—Robert Miller (of Salisbury) ; destination (no place given).—William Carter (of Salisbury) ; destination (no place given).—John Cunscome (of Salisbury) ; destination (no place given).— Evan Jones (of Salisbury) ; destination (no place given).—Henry Pavier (of Salisbury) ; destination (no place given).—John Lewes (of Clangoe) (no place given). —Sarah Grigory (of Worcester) ; destination (no place given).

Page 340
   Elizabeth Martin (of Micheldeane) ; destination (no place given).—John James (of Staunton) ; destination (no place given).—Margerett Thomas (of Bristoll) ; destination (no place given).—William Minty (of Polsteed) ; destination (no place given).—Anne Hawkins (of Bridg Yate) ; destination (no place given).—Hester Shepheard (of Sadbury) ; destination (no place given).—Daveris Jones (of Wesson) ; destination (no place given).—Edmund Davis (of Stoke, co. Somerset) ; destination (no place given).—John Brook (of Martick) ; destination (no place given).—William Orbell (of Gifford) ; destination (no place given).—John Greene (of Bristoll) ; destination (no place given).—Stephen Gawen (of Westbury) ; destination (no place given).

Page 341
   Thomas Clarke (of Hyham) ; destination (no place given).—John Phillips (of Lanveigher) ; destination (no place given).—Thomas Morgan (of Lanveigher) ; destination (no place given).—William Jones (of Lanveigher) ; destination (no place given).—William Norcott (of Chilton) ; destination (no place given).—John Smith (of Kilmanum) ; destination (no place given).—Anne Deane (of Nuberry) ; destination (no place given).—Mary Blackmore (of Wincaunton) ; destination (no place given).—John Thorneton (of Rochester) ; destination (no place given).— Howell Havard (of Lanveigher) ; destination (no place given).—Richard Mogear (of Shasbury) ; destination (no place given).—Elizabeth Bedford (of London) ; destination (no place given).

Page 342
   Elizabeth Miles (of Trowbridge) ; destination (no place given).—Christofer Rivell (of Trowbridge) ; destination (no place given).—Robert Rogers (of Shrews-

bury); destination (no place given).—Benjamin Morris; destination (no place given).—John Witte (of Ros); destination (no place given).—Richard Hudman (of Worcester); destination (no place given).—Henry House (of Bristoll); destination (no place given).—Phillip Linrin (of London); destination (no place given).— Ann Smeads (of Bristoll); destination (no place given).—Joseph Powell (of Peboth); destination (no place given).—Joane Power (of Heriford); destination (no place given).—Evan Davis; destination (no place given).

Page 343
     William Rowberry; destination (no place given).—Benjamin Maudlin (of Wedgbury); destination (no place given).—William Burrus (of Sandicilla); destination (no place given).—Henry Jones (of Bristoll); destination (no place given).— John Powne (of Arsshut); destination (no place given).—George Norton (of Emshut); destination (no place given).—William Hill (of Charlton); destination (no place given).—William Smart (of Bristoll); destination (no place given).— Thomas Collins (of Bridgwater); destination (no place given).—Josias Court (of Bitton); destination (no place given).—Mary Deane (of Lidney); destination (no place given).—Thomas Hilman (of ffroome); destination (no place given).

Page 344
     Richard Hilman (of ffroome); destination (no place given).—Evan Davis; destination (no place given).—John Evans; destination (no place given).—Reis Prigar (of Newton); destination (no place given).—William Phillips (of Newton); destination (no place given).—Thomas Gelly (of Newton); destination (no place given).—Ann Bidle (of Stannton); destination (no place given).—Richard Whelply (of Devizees); destination (no place given).—Randolph Holmarke (of Nantwich); destination (no place given).—Margery ffollutt (of ffroome); destination (no place given).—Thomas Sweet (of Wedmore); destination (no place given).—Elizabeth Say (of Arberton); destination (no place given).

Page 345
     Mary Bayly (of Maiden Bradley); destination (no place given).—John Butcher (of Rumnick); destination (no place given).—John Brian (of Bristoll); destination (no place given).—John Lazy (of Barton Regis); destination (no place given).— Jennet Roberts (of Carmarthen); destination, Barbadoes.—John Price (of Whitney); destination, Nevis.—William Jones (of Whitney); destination (no place given).— John Phillips (of Pembridge); destination (no place given).—Richard Rickett (of Pembridge); destination (no place given).—Roger Gurling (of Kingscaple); destination (no place given).—Thomas Watkins (of Madly); destination (no place given).—Jonathan Gittens (of Kineton); destination (no place given).

Page 346
     Thomas Barnard (of Woolhope); destination (no place given).—William Dyke (of Woolhope); destination (no place given).—James Wheeler (of Woolhope); destination (no place given).—Anthony Wheeler (of Woolhope); destination (no place given).—Richard Peters (of Woolhope); destination (no place given).—Richard Boone; destination (no place given).—Edward Blundell (of Katherine Colemans, London); destination (no place given).—Peter Bond (of White Chappell, London); destination (no place given).—John Smith (of White Chappell, London); destina-

tion (no place given).—James Kelleby (of New Sarum) ; destination (no place given). —Ann Williams ; destination (no place given).—Mathew Penry (of New Sarum) ; destination (no place given).

Page 347

Katherine ffell (of New Sarum) ; destination (no place given).—Adria Jones (of New Sarum) ; destination (no place given).—Suzan Spencer ; destination, Barbadoes.—Thomas Chainy (of Speene) ; destination, Barbadoes.—George Worly (of Bristol) ; destination, Barbadoes.—John Wild (of Cambridge) ; destination, Barbadoes.—William Clarke (of Salisbury) ; destination, Barbadoes.—John Brereton (of Michel Deane) ; destination, Barbadoes.—John Smith (of Poulton) ; destination, Barbadoes.—Ann Davis (of Worcester) ; destination, Barbadoes.—Ann Roch (of Worcester) ; destination, Barbadoes.—Elizaneth Holder (of Heriford) ; destination, Barbadoes.

Page 348

Robert Wilshire (of Woolverton) ; destination, Barbadoes.—William Edmunds (of Combcarvan) ; destination, Barbadoes.—John Rumsey ; destination, Barbadoes. —Sarah Webb (of Avenell) ; destination, Barbadoes.—Jane Smith (of Wooten) ; destination, Barbadoes.—Katherine Manington (of Wooten) ; destination, Barbadoes. —Elizabeth Johncy (of Heriford) ; destination, Barbadoes.—John Nibs (of Bristol) ; destination, Barbadoes.—David Jenkins (of Cardigan) ; destination, Barbadoes.— John Shepherd (of Roe) ; destination, Barbadoes.—John Stillett (of Winterbourne) ; destination, Barbadoes.—Hannah Beck ; destination, Barbadoes.

Page 349

David Jinkins ; destination, Barbadoes.—Thomas Nicholls (of Wooten) ; destination, Barbadoes.—Jon Streete (of Wooten) ; destination, Barbadoes.—John Davis ; destination, Barbadoes.—Ronert Gribble ; destination, Barbadoes.—William Selfe (of Bradly) ; destination, Barbadoes.—Stephen Woobourne (of ffroome) ; destination, Barbadoes.—John Edwards (of Westbury) ; destination, Barbadoes.— William Bayly (of Ciciter) ; destination, Barbadoes.—Elizabeth Bayly and Alice Bayly ; destination, Barbadoes.—Robert Ellmworth ; destination, Barbadoes.— John Wolfe (of Barton) ; destination, Barbadoes.

Page 350

Hannah Jenings ; destination, Barbadoes.—James Nibs (of Bristoll) ; destination, Barbadoes.—Edmund Brewer (of Lockin) ; destination, Barbadoes.—Edward Blundell (of London) ; destination (no place given).—John Draper (of Buckfostley) ; destination (no place given).—John Smith (of Stoke) ; destination (no place given). —Sarah Arey (of Wooten) ; destination (no place given).—Mary Teague (of Bath) ; destination (no place given).—Martha Ducy (of Dulsford) ; destination (no place given).—David Morgan (of Cowbridge) ; destination (no place given).—James Jones (of Penorva) ; destination (no place given).—Thurstone Thomas ; destination (no place given).

Page 351

John Ward ; destination (no place given).—Alice Tompson ; destination (no place given).—John Apperley (of Heriford) ; destination, Barbadoes.—Phillip Powell (of Langira) ; destination (no place given).—James Pugh (of Lambaddarne) ;

destination (no place given).—Elizabeth Baker (of Michel Deane) ; destination (no place given).—John Merrick (of Heriford) ; destination (no place given).—Elizabeth Apperley (of Heriford) ; destination (no place given).—John Horne (of Norfolke) ; destination (no place given).—Griffith Morgan (of Lantarnack) ; destination (no place given).—Gilbert Williams (of Heriford) ; destination (no place given).— Sarah Swift (of Heriford) ; destination (no place given).

Page 352

Roger Garnons (of Grismond) ; destination (no place given).—John Morgan (of Carlian) ; destination (no place given).—Richard Hookey ; destination (no place given).—John Randall (of Gloucester) ; destination (no place given).—Anne Beatch (of Lamster) ; destination (no place given).—Robert Cooke ; destination (no place given).—Magdalen Davis ; destination (no place given).—Samuell Wilcott (of Plimouth) ; destination (no place given).—Barbarah Reece ; destination (no place given).—William Tucker (of Tiverton) ; destination (no place given).— John Carpenter (of Standish) ; destination (no place given).—Elinor Nicholas (of Compton Chamberlaine) ; destination (no place given).

Page 353

Richard Lewes (of Brecknock) ; destination (no place given).—John Collins (of Painswick) ; destination, Barbadoes.—Katherine Nash ; destination, Barbadoes. —Elizabeth Goodinough (of Phillips Norton) ; destination, Barbadoes.—Richard Spilman (of Newent) ; destination, Barbadoes.—William Hampton (of Bristoll) ; destination, Barbadoes.—Warren White ; destination, Barbadoes.—James Reynolds (of Devizes) ; destination, Barbadoes.—Roger House (of Westbury) ; destination, Barbadoes.—John Giles (of Westbury) ; destination, Barbadoes.—William Crew (of fframpton) ; destination, Barbadoes.—John Clutterbuck (of Bartley) ; destination, Barbadoes.

Page 354

Richard Knight ; destination, Barbadoes.—John Knight ; destination, Barbadoes.—Margaret Powell ; destination, Barbadoes.—John Owen ; destination, Barbadoes.—John Kiffe ; destination, Barbadoes.—John Toomouth ; destination, Barbadoes.—Richard Stimson ; destination, Barbadoes.—Mary Teague ; destination, Barbadoes.—Elinor Phillips (of Wells) ; destination, Barbadoes.—Darby Poyniard ; destination, Barbadoes.—ffrancis Gregory ; destination, Barbadoes.— William Russell (of Exeter) ; destination, Barbadoes.

Page 355

Roger Kelsey (of Reading) ; destination, Barbadoes.—John Willing (of St. Niett) ; destination, Barbadoes.—Jane ffletcher ; destination, Barbadoes.—Andrew Hobbs (of Middlesex) ; destination, Barbadoes.—ffrancis Berman ; destination, Barbadoes.—Hannah Jones (of Swansey) ; destination, Barbadoes.—David Williams (of Periterke) ; destination, Barbadoes.—Thomas Colham ; destination, Barbadoes. —Henry Norway (of Milsome) ; destination, Barbadoes.—John Luscombe (of Devonshire) ; destination, Barbadoes.—Morgan Evans ; destination, Barbadoes.

Page 356

Hannah Durnell ; destination, Barbadoes.—Robert Robins ; destination, Barbadoes.—Humfry Pitts ; destination, Nevis.—Ann Bradley ; destination, Nevis.

—Mary Thomas; destination, Nevis.—Richard Sparry; destination, Nevis.—
Joane Elysian; destination, Nevis.—Robert Harris; destination, Nevis.—Charles
Wilts (of Chepstow); destination, Barbadoes.—Thomas Plum; destination, Barbadoes.—Robert Cribb (of Bradford); destination, Barbadoes.—William Chappell
(of Sombridge); destination, Barbadoes.

Page 357

Samuell Kemer; destination, Barbadoes.—John Kinson; destination, Bar-
badoes.—George Mary; destination, Barbadoes.—Daniell Parke; destination,
Barbadoes.—Reece Jones; destination, Barbadoes.—Suzan Williams; destination,
Barbadoes.—Suzan Davis; destination, Barbadoes.—George Morgan; destination,
Barbadoes.—Giles Chin; destination, Barbadoes.—Robert Phinney (*Little John*);
destination (no place given).—Abraham Parse; destination (no place given).—George
Walker; destination (no place given).

Page 358

Paull Price (*Little John*); destination, Barbadoes.—Thomas Beresford (*Little
John*); destination, Barbadoes.—John Woods (*Little John*); destination, Barbadoes.
—Mary Atwell (*Little John*); destination, Barbadoes.—Edward Wilson (*Little
John*); destination, Barbadoes.—Luce Buckley (*Little John*); destination, Bar-
badoes.—John Miles (*Little John*); destination, Barbadoes.—Jane King (*Little
John*); destination, Barbadoes.—James Webb (*Dolphin*); destination, Barbadoes.—
Henry Jones (*Little John*); destination, Barbadoes.—Edward Williams (*Speedwell*);
destination, Barbadoes.—Jane Morgan (*Little John*); destination, Barbadoes.

Page 359

Mary Shepheard (of Keynsham, *Speedwell*); destination, Barbadoes.—David
George (*Speedwell*); destination, Barbadoes.—William Tempus (*Dolphin*); destination, Barbadoes.—John Poldenne (*Little John*); destination, Barbadoes.—Mathew
Nelme (of Henbury, *Little John*); destination, Barbadoes.—Robert Elliott; destination, Barbadoes.—Elizabeth Amer; destination, Barbadoes.—Martha Wimball;
destination, Barbadoes.—Mary Wimball; destination, Barbadoes.—Richard Chap-
perlyn (of Linham, *Little John*); destination, Barbadoes.—Mary Bruton (*Little
John*); destination, Barbadoes.—Ann Moning (*Little John*); destination, Barbadoes.

Page 360

Benadick Wooles; destination, Barbadoes.—William Howell; destination,
Barbadoes.—Wilmott Collins (of Woolleston); destination, Barbadoes.—Thomas
Jones (of Cowbridge); destination, Barbadoes.—Joseph Jones; destination, Bar-
badoes.—John Taylor; destination, Barbadoes.—William George (of Northampton,
Dolphin); destination, Barbadoes.—Ann Combes (*Dolphin*); destination, Barba-
does.—Elizabeth Phillips (*Hopewell*); destination, Barbadoes.—Joane Williams
(*Hopewell*); destination, Barbadoes.—Mary Price (*Dolphin*); destination, Barba-
does.—John Webb; destination, Barbadoes.

Page 361

Elizabeth Cooke (*Dolphin*); destination, Barbadoes.—William Howell (*Hopewell*); destination, Barbadoes.—George Daniell (*Little John*); destination, Barbadoes.—John Haden (*Little John*); destination, Barbadoes.—Margaret Rogers

(*Little John*) ; destination, Barbadoes.—William Chamberlin (*Little John*) ; destination, Barbadoes.—Richard Day (*Hopewell*) ; destination, Barbadoes.—John Jones (of Kinbar, *Hopewell*) ; destination, Barbadoes.—Richard Wait (of Brinkworth, *Hopewell*) ; destination, Barbadoes.—Daniell Norris (*Dolphin*) ; destination, Barbadoes.—Mary ffeild (*Little John*) ; destination, Barbadoes.—Mathew Way ; destination, Barbadoes.—Jane Lacy (*Little John*) ; destination, Barbadoes.

Page 362
　　Martha Meade ; destination, Barbadoes.—Thomas Doaling ; destination, Barbadoes.—John Griffith (*Hopewell*) ; destination, Barbadoes.—Anne Sommers (of Pensford, *Hopewell*) ; destination, Barbadoes.—John Waters (*Dolphin*) ; destination, Barbadoes.—Robert Morris (*Hopewell*) ; destination, Barbadoes.—Lewis Evan Morgan (*Hopewell*) ; destination (no place given).—David Williams (*Dolphin*) ; destination (no place given).—Alice Smith (*Hopewell*) ; destination, Barbadoes.— John Straytton (*Hopewell*) ; destination, Barbadoes.—Rachell Morgan (*Dolphin*) ; destination, Barbadoes.—Elinor Harfeild (of Hursley, *Dolphin*) ; destination, Barbadoes.

Page 363
　　Griffith Morgan (of Montgomery, *Dolphin*) ; destination (no place given).— William Domas (of Langost, *Dolphin*) ; destination (no place given).—Winifrett Parry (*Hopewell*) ; destination (no place given).—Thomas Myson (*Dolphin*) ; destination (no place given).—John Arnoll (of Exeter) ; destination (no place given). —James Hallie (*Dolphin*) ; destination (no place given).—Howell Windar (*Hopewell*) ; destination (no place given).—ffardinando Jenkins (*Hopewell*) ; destination (no place given).—John Turner (*Dolphin*) ; destination (no place given).—Ffrancis Haskins ; destination (no place given).—Nicholas Bernard (*Dolphin*) ; destination (no place given).—Robert Stone (of Staunton, *Dolphin*) ; destination (no place given).

Page 364
　　Samuell Newman (of Staunton, *Dolphin*) ; destination (no place given).— Jeremiah Turner (*Dolphin*) ; destination (no place given).—Thomas Haines (*Dolphin*) ; destination, Barbadoes.—Lewis Haines (*Dolphin*) ; destination, Barbadoes.—Walter Jenkin (of Abergavenny, *Dolphin*) ; destination, Barbadoes.—Suzan ffland (*Hopewell*) ; destination, Barbadoes.—George Mason (*Delight*) ; destination, Virginia.— Thomas Noodly (*Delight*) ; destination, Virginia.—Emanuell Jones ; destination, Barbadoes.—Alice Tomalin ; destination, Barbadoes.—Thomas Watkin (*Dolphin*) ; destination, Barbadoes.—Anne Newman (*Delight*) ; destination, Virginia.

Page 365
　　Sarah Newman (*Delight*) ; destination, Virginia.—Thomas Morgan ; destination, Virginia.—John Neale (of Exeter) ; destination, Virginia.—Robert Rodes (*Delight*) ; destination, Virginia.—ffrancis (*sic*) Martin (spinster) (*Hopewell*) ; destination, Barbadoes.—ffrancis Skett ; destination, Virginia.—John Wooffe (*Dolphin*) ; destination, Barbadoes.—Rowland Mathewes (*Dolphin*) ; destination, Barbadoes.— William Jones (*Dolphin*) ; destination, Barbadoes.—William Paine (*Dolphin*) ; destination, Barbadoes.—Alice ffeeme (*Hopewell*) ; destination, Barbadoes.—Thomas Booby (*Hopewell*) ; destination, Barbadoes.

Page 366
   Elizabeth Batt (*Hopewell*) ; destination, Barbadoes.—Elizabeth Saunders ; destination, Barbadoes.—Thomas Pretty (*Hopewell*) ; destination, Virginia.—John Marichurch ; destination, Barbadoes.—Thomas Chandler ; destination, Virginia. —Edward Thomas (of Bristoll) ; destination, Virginia.—Suzan George (*Dolphin*) ; destination, Barbadoes.—Jennet Watkins (*Lutus*) ; destination, Barbadoes.—Richard Hunt ; destination, Barbadoes.—William Wilkes ; destination, Virginia.—John Morgan (of Usk) ; destination, Virginia.—James Morgan ; destination, Virginia.

Page 367
   William Wilkes (of Chipenham, *Goodwill*) ; destination, Virginia.—Miles Challoner ; destination, Barbadoes.—John Monche ; destination, Virginia.— Benjamin Johnson (of London, *Seaflower*) ; destination, Barbadoes.—Thomas Owen ; destination, Barbadoes.—Thomas Amplett ; destination, Barbadoes.—Dinah Beard ; destination, Virginia.—Johanne Roberts; destination, Barbadoes.—Wilmott Roberts; destination, Barbadoes.—George Barnes (of London) ; destination, Virginia.— Margaret ffoster ; destination, Virginia.—Richard ffoster ; destination, Virginia.

Page 368
   Thomasine Evans ; destination, Barbadoes.—Mary Evans ; destination, Barbadoes.—Daniell Gavin ; destination, Virginia.—Richard Thomas (of Carlean) ; destination, Barbadoes.—Phillip Rogers ; destination, Virginia.—Mary Shorte ; destination, Virginia.—John Withecombe ; destination, Virginia.—Edward Huit (of Northampton) ; destination, Barbadoes.—William Rivus ; destination, Virginia. —William Combes (of Hallow) ; destination, Virginia.—fflorence Roberts ; destination, Barbadoes.—Christian Wickombe ; destination, Virginia.

Page 369
   Richard Barthelemy ; destination, Virginia.—Davis Preece ; destination, Virginia.—John Mills ; destination, Virginia.—Anne Williams ; destination, Virginia. —John Tiley ; destination, Virginia.—Nicholas Virgent ; destination, Virginia.— William Bewes ; destination, Virginia.—Thomas Braughing (of London) ; destination, Barbadoes.—James Punfeild ; destination, Virginia.—Peter Old ; destination, Virginia.—Edward Davis ; destination, Virginia.—William Stroud ; destination, Virginia.

Page 370
   Thomas Undrell ; destination, Virginia.—Gabriell Studdert (of London) ; destination, Virginia.—William Jones ; destination, Virginia.—John Hughes ; destination, Virginia.—Anne Summerell ; destination, Virginia.—Elizabeth Jones ; destination, Nevis.—William Cheesman ; destination, Virginia.—Andrew Pratton ; destination, Virginia.—William Simister (of Drayton) ; destination, Virginia.—Jane Hambleton ; destination, Nevis.—John Kidwillar ; destination, Nevis.—Jane Kidwillar ; destination, Nevis.

Page 371
   Alexander Tiley ; destination, Nevis.—William Williams ; destination, Virginia.—fflorence Hill ; destination, Virginia.—William Browne ; destination, Virginia.—Robert Steevens ; destination, Virginia.—Richard Cautwell ; destination,

Virginia.—Rice Croone; destination, Virginia.—William Trevert; destination, Virginia.—Edward Davis; destination, Virginia.—John Land; destination, Nevis.—John Gibbes; destination, Nevis.—Bartholomew Bevan (of Thornbury); destination, Virginia.

Page 372
Hannah Newman (of Cawne [?]); destination, Virginia.—John Councell; destination, Virginia.—John Clarke; destination, Virginia.—William Williams; destination, Virginia.—Suzan Yard (of Wells); destination, Virginia.—Thomas ffoster (of Wells); destination, Virginia.—Henry Vincen (of Wells); destination, Virginia.—John Chipper als. Crumpe; destination, Virginia.—William Chipper als. Crumpe; destination, Virginia.—Hugh Powell (of Abergainy); destination, Virginia.—John Taylor; destination, Nevis.—Richard Harris; destination, Nevis.

Page 373
Walter Saunders; destination, Nevis.—ffrancis Latimore; destination, Nevis.—Mary Hone (of Southwark); destination, Nevis.—John Carrier; destination, Nevis.—Pacis Butler; destination, Nevis.—Anne Gold; destination, Nevis.—George ffariner; destination, Virginia.—Walter Turner; destination, Virginia.—Suzannah Jones; destination, Nevis.—Evan John Thomas; destination, Virginia.—Thomas Layte; destination, Virginia.—William Goade; destination, Virginia.

Page 374
Mary Lewis; destination, Barbadoes.—Walter Phelps; destination, Virginia.—William Godby; destination, Virginia.—Alice Griffiths; destination, Virginia.—Robert Roch; destination, Virginia.—Alice Bedow; destination, Virginia.—Markes Low; destination, Virginia.—John Palmer (of Ireland); destination, Virginia.—Thomas Phillips; destination, Virginia.—David ffloyd; destination, Virginia.—Hester Boyes; destination, Virginia.—Henry Mathewes (of Atford); destination, Virginia.

Page 375
Stephen Threlfull; destination, Virginia.—William Rush; destination, Virginia.—Mary Gapper; destination, Virginia.—Nathaniell Rice (of London); destination, Virginia.—William Jones (of Chepstow); destination, Virginia.—William Bancroft; destination, Virginia.—Elinor Jeffries; destination, Virginia.—Nicholas Beale; destination, Virginia.—Mary Simons; destination, Virginia.—Mary Emery; destination, Virginia.—Elizabeth ffreeman; destination, Virginia.—William Bowle; destination, Virginia.

Page 376
Mabell Howell; destination, Barbadoes.—John Richards; destination, Barbadoes.—John Soper; destination, Barbadoes.—Richard Haukford; destination, Barbadoes.—Richard ffranklin; destination, Barbadoes.—Elizabeth Savage; destination, Maryland.—Richard Pullin; destination, Maryland.—Thomas Bayly; destination, Maryland.—Jehu Bonnet; destination, Maryland.—Joane Howell; destination, Nevis.—Henry Shoare; destination, Virginia.—Anne Wells; destination, Virginia.

Page 377

Christopher Seegrum ; destination, Virginia.—John Burt (of Montague) ; destination, Virginia.—Robert Dickers ; destina.ion, Virginia.—Thomas Dampney ; destination, Virginia.—Peter Bernard (of Ledbury) ; destination, Virginia.—Joane Bernard, wife of Peter ; destination, Virginia.—Jane King ; destination, Antigua. —Richard Hawks ; destination, Virginia.—William Wallie ; destination, Virginia.— John Lyes ; destination, Virginia.—Hester Smith ; destination, Virginia.—Anne Brian ; destination, Virginia.

Page 378

Katherine Jenkins ; destination, Virginia.—John Kinkerby ; destination, Virginia.—Mary Waters ; destination, Virginia.—Richard Berry (of Aberdare) ; destination, Virginia.—Thomas Churchyard (of Mordiford) ; destination, Virginia.— Phillip Hitchens ; destination, Virginia.—Thomas Dudsome ; destination, Virginia. —Richard Wood ; destination, Virginia.—Lewes Watkins ; destination, Virginia.— Robert Worbenton ; destination, Virginia.—Elizabeth Simons ; destination, Virginia.

Page 379

Jane Powell ; destination, Virginia.—Walven Hopton ; destination, Virginia.—Stephen Cutler ; destination, Virginia.—William Dix ; destination, Virginia.—John Wilton ; destination, Virginia.—John Combes ; destination, Virginia. —William Cawcombe ; destination, Virginia.—Richard Wyte (of Staunton) ; destination, Barbadoes.—George Pedley ; destination, Virginia.—Winifret Lewis ; destination, Nevis.—Thomas Hall (of Thornbury) ; destination, Virginia.—Thomas Nicholas ; destination, Virginia.

Page 380

Stephen Wood ; destination, Virginia.—Elizabeth Howell ; destination, Nevis. —William Smith ; destination, Virginia.—Robert Browne (of Upton) ; destination, Virginia.—Mary Callowhill ; destination, Virginia.—ffrancis (*sic*) Hill (spinster) ; destination, Virginia.—William Hathen ; destination, Virginia.—Damalos Plumly (of Wells) ; destination, Virginia.—William Muntica ; destination, Barbadoes.— Peter Palmer ; destination, Virginia.—Henry Dorrant ; destination, Virginia.— Richard White ; destination, Virginia.

Page 381

John Perrolet ; destination, Nevis.—William Byshop ; destination, Virginia. —John Butt ; destination, Virginia.—Richard Cumberly ; destination, Virginia.— Evan Jones ; destination, Barbadoes.—Sarah Bayly ; destination, Barbadoes.—John Barret ; destination, Virginia.—Robert Mathewes ; destination, Barbadoes.— William Baker ; destination, Barbadoes.—John Woolbourne ; destination, Barbadoes.—William Bryan ; destination, Virginia.—Anne Rake (of Meere) ; destination, Virginia.

Page 382

Thomas Jones ; destination, Barbadoes.—Henry Bugby ; destination, Virginia. —John Sherbourne (of Bristoll) ; destination, Virginia.—William Rogers ; destination, Virginia.—John Hobbs ; destination, Barbadoes.—Walter Boxwell ; destina-

tion, Barbadoes.—David Morgan (of Haverfordwest) ; destination, Barbadoes.—
Thomas Griffin (of Pembroke) ; destination, Nevis.—Lewis Roberts (of Cowbridge) ;
destination, Nevis.—Richard Stone (of Lincolne) ; destination, Virginia.—Israell
Williams ; destination, Barbadoes.—Elizabeth Bowen ; destination, Virginia.

Page 383
ffrancis Milner (of Sturbridge) ; destination, Barbadoes.—Mathew Hill ;
destination, Virginia.—James Hawkins ; destination, Virginia.—Edward Haskins ;
destination, Barbadoes.—Stephen Tompson ; destination, Virginia.—William Spinke
(of Yorke) ; destination, Barbadoes.—Anne fflower (of Longdon) ; destination,
Barbadoes.—Rosamond Carter (of Longdon) ; destination, Barbadoes.—Alexander
Harris ; destination, Virginia.—Jacob Eastbrooke ; destination, Barbadoes.—Richard
Smoakinn (of Clack) ; destination, Virginia.—Benjamin Seely ; destination, Virginia.

Page 384
Robert Welsh ; destination, Barbadoes.—Joane Smith ; destination, Virginia.
—John Orton ; destination, Virginia.—Thomas Mandew ; destination, Virginia.—John Edwards ; destination, Barbadoes.—Margaret Jones (of Bristoll) ;
destination, Barbadoes.—Mary Pacy ; destination, Virginia.—Hannah Churchill ;
destination, Virginia.—Mathew Bisse ; destination, Virginia.—William Cotham ;
destination, Barbadoes.—Robert Pooleman ; destination, Barbadoes.—Anthony
Mathewes ; destination, Virginia.

Page 385
Anne Russell (of Bristoll) ; destination, Virginia.—Charity Baggs (of Barnestable) ; destination, Barbadoes.—Elizabeth Baggs (of Barnestable) ; destination,
Barbadoes.—Mary Manwaring (twice) (of Chester) ; destination, Nevis and Barbadoes.—ffrancis Howlett ; destination, Virginia.—William Reane ; destination,
Virginia.—William Mathewes ; destination, Virginia.—Thomas Aust ; destination, Virginia.—Sarah George (of New Sarum) ; destination, Virginia.—John
Payne (of New Sarum) ; destination, Virginia.—Anne Luxmore (of New Sarum) ;
destination, Virginia.

Page 386
Joane ffranklin (of New Sarum) ; destination, Virginia.—Rebecca ffoenix (of
New Sarum) ; destination, Virginia.—Elizabeth Musprat (of New Sarum) ; destina-
tion, Virginia.—Margeret Waterman (of New Sarum) ; destination, Virginia.—
John Luke (of New Sarum) ; destination, Virginia.—John Byshop (of New Sarum) ;
destination, Virginia.—Richard Talbott ; destination, Virginia.—John Plott (of
Harrow on the Hill) ; destination, Nevis.—John Nicholls ; destination, Virginia.—
Edith Webb ; destination, Barbadoes.—William Buckland ; destination, Barba-
does.—Anthony Read ; destination, Barbadoes.

Page 387
Simon Wydnoll ; destination, Virginia.—Robert Parker ; destination, Barbadoes.—John Cole ; destination, Barbadoes.—Thomas Welsh (of Nuten) ; destination, Barbadoes.—John fford (of Esterton) ; destination, Barbadoes.—Thomas
Morris (of Carmarthen) ; destination, Barbadoes.—Thomas Williams (of Lan-

bandum); destination, Nevis.—Thomas Jay; destination, Barbadoes.—Robert Whitfeild; destination, Barbadoes.—Hanniball Newman; destination, Nevis.— Nicholas Harry; destination, Nevis.—John Baker (of Puddimore); destination (no place given).

Page 388

Thomas Restall (of Redmarly); destination, Barbadoes.—Mary Wingall; destination, Barbadoes.—Joyce Ockly (of Redmarly); destination, Barbadoes.— David Jones (of Brecknock); destination, Barbadoes.—Henry Mapleton (of Redin); destination, Nevis.—George Cumberlatch; destination, Nevis.—Grace Jinkins; destination, Barbadoes.—Thomas Merrick; destination (no place given).—Joane Roberts; destination (no place given).—Thomas Trigg; destination (no place given).—Henry Pick; destination, Nevis.—Thomas Marsham; destination (no place given).

Page 389

John Harry; destination, Barbadoes.—George Beardford; destination, St. Christopher.—William Jones; destination, Barbadoes.—William Richards; destination, St. Christopher.—John Bevan; destination, Barbadoes.—Suzannah Silvester; destination, Barbadoes.—John Pritchard; destination, Barbadoes.—John Derington; destination, Barbadoes.

Page 390

Marthah Harris (of Shrewsbury); destination, Barbadoes.—Richard Perkins; destination, Barbadoes.—Elizabeth Webster; destination, Barbadoes.—Jane James; destination, Nevis.—Marthah Harris (of Shrewsbury); destination, Nevis.—William Ball (of Manalton); destination, Nevis.—John Davy; destination, Nevis.—John Ellis (of Ledbury); destination, Nevis.—Marthah Windsor; destination, Nevis.— Thomas Powell (of Bridgwater); destination, Barbadoes.—Thomas Chapman (of Boston); destination, Barbadoes.—Robert Buddle (of Peterborough); destination, Barbadoes.—Thomas Potty (of Nettle); destination, Barbadoes.—Edward Paine; destination, Nevis.—Nathan Palmer (of Shethwick); destination, Nevis.—Elinor Rodin (of ffamouth); destination, Nevis.

Page 391

Elizabeth Masters (of Bath); destination, St. Christopher.—John Morrice (of Bettoes); destination, Barbadoes.—Hugh Jones; destination, Antigua.— Nicholas Cluth; destination, Nevis.—Jeremy Perton (of Wichester); destination (no place given).—Elinor Griffin (of Carmarthen); destination (no place given). —Margery Bradinore; destination, Barbadoes.—Thurloe Bourne; destination, Nevis.—Anne Burke; destination, Barbadoes.—Evan Jones; destination, Barbadoes.—Thomas Price; destination, Barbadoes.—Walter Evans; destination, St. Christopher.

Page 392

William Wyatt; destination, Barbadoes.—John Dyas; destination, Barbadoes. —John New; destination, Barbadoes.—John Holloway (of Dorset); destination, Barbadoes.—Walter Evan; destination, Nevis.—Thomas Owen (of Exeter); destination, Nevis.—John Smith (of Stoaklane); destination, Nevis.—Edward Munday and

Mary Munday; destination, Nevis.—Michaell Brimley; destination, Nevis.—Richard Carter; destination, Barbadoes.—William Thomas; destination, Barbadoes.—Peter Treble (of London); destination, Barbadoes.

Page 393

Edward Jones; destination, Nevis.—William Hopkins (of London); destination, Nevis.—Thomas Christon (of London); destination, Nevis.—Morgan Jenkin (of London); destination, Nevis.—Richard Massy; destination, Nevis.—Edward Games; destination, Nevis.—Elizabeth Rothwell; destination (no place given).—John David (of Caddoxton); destination (no place given).—Jane Boxwell; destination (no place given).—William Tucker (of Milford); destination (no place given).—Richard Shelton; destination (no place given).—Richard Duzart; destination (no place given).

Page 394

Hugh ffloyd (of Cardigan); destination (no place given).—William Child (of Bristoll); destination, Nevis.—Anne Child; destination, Nevis.—John Cox; destination, Barbadoes.—John Maury; destination, St. Christopher.—Mary Deane; destination, St. Christopher.—Jonathan Austin; destination, St. Christopher.—Sarah Wheeler; destination (no place given).—Thomas Beecher; destination (no place given).—James Coggin (of Auxbridge); destination (no place given).—William Thomas; destination (no place given).—Elizabeth Phillips; destination (no place given).

Page 395

John Baynton (of Barton Regis); destination, Barbadoes.—Edward Clinton; destination, Barbadoes.—George Pulge (of London); destination, Barbadoes.—Richard Packer; destination, Barbadoes.—John Jenings; destination, Barbadoes.—Sarah Jenkins, Mary Jones, and Winifret Thomas; destination, Barbadoes.—Peter Slaughter; destination, Nevis.—Thomas Prichard; destination, Nevis.—Jonas Evans; destination, Barbadoes.—Arnold Nicholls; destination, St. Christopher.—William Nicholls; destination, St. Christopher.—Katherine Williams; destination, St. Christopher.

Page 396

Mary Thomas; destination, St. Christopher.—John Cadle; destination, Barbadoes.—William Morgan; destination, Barbadoes.—John Morgan; destination, Barbadoes.—Mary Edmunds (of South petherton); destination, Nevis.—John Stephens (of Bristoll); destination, Nevis.—George Watts (of Kenwely); destination, Nevis.—Samuell Dreagh; destination, Barbadoes.—Richard May (of Arton); destination, Barbadoes.—Robert Cox; destination, Barbadoes.—Humphrey Bird; destination, Barbadoes.—Richard Grand (of Edenburgh); destination, St. Christopher.

Page 397

Anne Owen (of Worcester); destination, Barbadoes.—George ffletcher (of Rawling); destination, Barbadoes.—Edward Hancock (of Sedgly); destination, Barbadoes.—James Painter (of Dublin); destination, Barbadoes.—George Gibbs; destination, Barbadoes.—William Roe; destination, Barbadoes.—Sarah Tanasty;

destination, Barbadoes.—John Harris ; destination, Barbadoes.—John Tiley ; destination, Barbadoes.—Nicholas Pye (of Westbury) ; destination, Barbadoes.—William Teuxbury ; destination, Barbadoes.—John Plumer ; destination, Barbadoes.

Page 398
   John Lock (of Tidnam) ; destination, Barbadoes.—William Tompson (of Bedow) ; destination, Barbadoes.—John Smith (of Bedow) ; destination, Barbadoes.—John Smith ; destination, Nevis.—Robert Wilch ; destination, Barbadoes.—William Lytham ; destination, Barbadoes.—Andrew Jones (of Cardiff) ; destination, Barbadoes.—Richard Inge (of Eveston) ; destination, Nevis.—Clement Webber (of Beckington) ; destination, Nevis.—ffoulke Griffith (of Hansistry) ; destination (no place given).—Sarah Browning ; destination (no place given).—Edward Davis ; destination (no place given).

Page 399
   James Hughs (of Stanton) ; destination, Barbadoes.—Jane Barton ; destination, Barbadoes.—Phillip Browne ; destination, Barbadoes.—John Taylor ; destination, Barbadoes.—Joane Taylor (Russell), wife of John Taylor ; destination, Barbadoes.— Morgan Lewis and Katherine, his wife ; destination, Barbadoes.—John Dier ; destination, Nevis.—Mary Palmer ; destination, Barbadoes.—William Hix ; destination, Nevis.—Richard Cobb ; destination, Nevis.—Prudence Cobb ; destination, Nevis.—Richard Mabbott ; destination, Barbadoes.

Page 400
   Robert Astons ; destination, Barbadoes.—John Anthony ; destination, Barbadoes.—John Walthon ; destination, Barbadoes.—John Stanley ; destination, Barbadoes.—Peter Treble ; destination, Barbadoes.—Anne Bishop ; destination, Barbadoes.—Robert Thomas ; destination, Nevis.—Edward Price (of Churcham) ; destination, Nevis.—Thomas Bearnes ; destination, Nevis.—John Gough ; destination, Nevis.—William Cole ; destination, Nevis.—Thomas Mills ; destination, Nevis.

Page 401
   George Ricketts ; destination, Barbadoes.—Mary Weare ; destination, Nevis. —Richard Pegley ; destination, Nevis.—Thomas Williams ; destination, Barbadoes. —Edward Morris ; destination, Barbadoes.—John West ; destination, Barbadoes.— Elizabeth Bevan ; destination, Barbadoes.—Morris Thomas ; destination, Barbadoes.—Marthah Bowden ; destination, Barbadoes.—Robert Price (of Amely) ; destination, Barbadoes.—Mathew Vining ; destination, Barbadoes.—John Merriatt ; destination, Barbadoes.

Page 402
   John Blisse ; destination, Barbadoes.—Lewis Evans ; destination, Barbadoes.— Hugh Powell ; destination, Barbadoes.—John ffreeman ; destination, Barbadoes. —James Niblett ; destination (no place given).—John Merriweather ; destination, Barbadoes.—George Gibbs ; destination, Nevis.—Richard Cate ; destination, Nevis. —John James ; destination, Nevis.—John Morgan ; destination, Nevis.—Thomas Jones ; destination, Nevis.—Walter Rosser ; destination, Nevis.

Page 403

Thomas Grigson ; destination, Nevis.—Henry Morgan ; destination, Nevis.—
Thomas Owen ; destination, Nevis.—William Maurice ; destination, Nevis.—Amy
Harte ; destination, Nevis.—William Griffith ; destination, Nevis.—John Mattravis ;
destination, Nevis.—Alice Evans ; destination, Barbadoes.—Richard Lloyd ; destination, Barbadoes.—Elinor Jones ; destination, Barbadoes.—Richard Pickerell ;
destination, Barbadoes.—Griffith Inon ; destination, Barbadoes.

Page 404

Walter George ; destination, Barbadoes.—Thomas Mitchell (of Taunton) ;
destination, Barbadoes.—John Dolling ; destination, Barbadoes.—Richard Jones
(of Huntly) ; destination, Barbadoes.—Elizabeth Lawrence (of Ludlow) ; destination, Barbadoes.—George Barnard ; destination, Barbadoes.—James Collins ;
destination, Barbadoes.—William Rooks ; destination, St. Christopher.—Joane fford
(of Bristoll) ; destination, St. Christopher.—Richard Evans (of Carleon) ; destination, St. Christopher.—Walter Newman (of Carleon) ; destination, St. Christopher.
—Evan Thomas ; destination, St. Christopher.

Page 405

John Essington (of London) ; destination, St. Christopher.—Humphry Jones
(of Wrexum) ; destination, St. Christopher.—Richard Hale ; destination, St.
Christopher.—Thomas Swan (of Lester) ; destination, St. Christopher.—John
Gardner ; destination, Nevis.—Samuell Thatcher (of Winterford) ; destination,
Nevis.—ffrancis Thatcher (of Winterford) ; destination, Nevis.—Job Taylor ;
destination, Nevis.—John Williams ; destination, Nevis.—Gabriell Widdord ;
destination, Nevis.—Raphaell Herring ; destination, Nevis.—Thomas Bradbury
(of Bliffeild) ; destination, Nevis.

Page 406

Christofer Wood (of Blackbourne) ; destination, Nevis.—William fferrett ;
destination, Nevis.—Rowland Jones (of Shrewsbury) ; destination, Nevis.—
Margaret Bedford (of Leinster) ; destination, Nevis.—John Crocker (of Marsh) ;
destination, Nevis.—Elizabeth Evans (of Redwick) ; destination, Nevis.—Amy
Phillips ; destination, Nevis.—John Eleson (of Segrave) ; destination, Nevis.—
Daniell White ; destination, Barbadoes.—Jenkin Davis ; destination, Barbadoes.—
James Belshire ; destination, St. Christopher.

Page 407

John Hunt ; destination, Nevis.—Robert May ; destination, Nevis.—Maudlin
Wilkin ; destination, Barbadoes.—George Nicholas ; destination, Nevis.—John
Cordin ; destination, Nevis.—Richard Martin ; destination, Nevis.—Elinor Martin ;
destination, St. Christopher.—Margeret Richards ; destination, Nevis.—George
Phillips ; destination, Barbadoes.—Margeret Bricker ; destination, Nevis or
Barbadoes.

Page 408

Thomas Hall (of Ciceter) ; destination, Barbadoes.—Henry Hughes ; destination, Nevis.—Andrew Geaston ; destination, Nevis.—John Cooke (of ffroome) ;
destination, Barbadoes.—Elizabeth Ayrde ; destination, Barbadoes.—Thomas

Bevarn ; destination, Barbadoes.—John Bush ; destination, Barbadoes.—Edward Thomas ; destination, Barbadoes.—Thomas Dyer ; destination, Barbadoes.— Thomas Boules ; destination, Barbadoes.

Page 409
Thomas Weddam (of Mayfield) ; destination, Barbadoes.—Nicholas Jones ; destination, Barbadoes.—Walter Williams ; destination, Barbadoes.—John Barsday ; destination, Barbadoes.—Richard Harris (of Dursley) ; destination, Barbadoes.— Robert Hascall ; destination, Barbadoes.—Thomas Hill ; destination, Nevis.— Thomas Reece ; destination, Nevis.—William Stubly ; destination, Barbadoes.— John Court ; destination, Nevis.

Page 410
Ann Gray ; destination, Nevis.—John Baskett ; destination, Nevis.—Mathew Burford ; destination, Barbadoes.—John Phelpes ; destination, Nevis.—Margeret Wall ; destination, Barbadoes.—James Brice ; destination, Barbadoes.—George Mitchell ; destination, Nevis.—Samuell Goad ; destination, Barbadoes or Nevis.— Benjamin Rosser ; destination, Nevis.—Morgan Davis ; destination (no place given).

Page 411
Edward Wallington ; destination, Nevis.—William Watts ; destination, Nevis. —Ann Weaver ; destination, Nevis.—Julian Hood ; destination, Nevis.—David Howell ; destination, Barbadoes.—John Brice ; destination, Nevis.—John Sly ; destination (no place given).—Mary Lewis ; destination, Barbadoes.—Daniell Farell ; destination, Barbadoes.—Elinor Cox ; destination, Barbadoes or Nevis.

Page 412
Francis Yates (of Chepstow) ; destination, Barbadoes.—Robert Day ; destination, Nevis.—John Thomas ; destination, Nevis.—Samuell Watkins ; destination, Barbadoes.—Walter Newman ; destination, Nevis.—Dennis Brenan ; destination, Nevis.—Martha Applan ; destination, Nevis.—John Williams (of Watchcett) ; destination, Nevis.—Titus Morrice ; destination, Barbadoes.—Henry Winnoll ; destination, Nevis.

Page 413
William Smith ; destination, Nevis.—William Mascall ; destination, Nevis or Barbadoes.—Martha Wilson ; destination, Nevis.—William Tilly ; destination, Barbadoes.—William Tregle (of Taunton) ; destination, Nevis.—Richard Price ; destination, Barbadoes.—William Roe ; destination, Barbadoes.—William Day ; destination, Barbadoes.—Daniel Lewis ; destination, Barbadoes.

Page 414
John Reynolds ; destination, Barbadoes.—George Johnson ; destination, Barbadoes.—ffrancis Smith ; destination, Nevis.—John Ford ; destination, Nevis.— Robert Leg ; destination, Nevis.—John Turner ; destination, Nevis.—George Bordridge ; destination, Nevis.—Richard Niblett ; destination, Virginia.—David Loyd ; destination, Nevis.—John Lewis ; destination, Nevis.

Page 415
Henry Combes ; destination, Nevis.—Charles Powell ; destination, Nevis.—
Sutton Rudney ; destination, Virginia.—William Rowland ; destination, Virginia.—
Thomas Ware ; destination, Nevis.—ffrancis Smith ; destination, Nevis.—Thomas
Cadle ; destination, Nevis.—John Cudd ; destination, Nevis.—John Roberts ;
destination, Nevis.—Rowland Jones ; destination, Nevis.

Page 416
Thomas [blank] ; destination, Virginia.—Stephen Bishop ; destination, Nevis.
—Woolfry Nollard ; destination, Nevis.—Roger Williams ; destination, Nevis.—
Mary Cauthar ; destination, Nevis.—Owen Morgan ; destination, Nevis.—John
Adney ; destination, Virginia.—William Hurlocke ; destination, Nevis.—Reece
Lewis ; destination, Nevis.—Samuell Robins ; destination, Nevis.

Page 417
Ann Farding ; destination, Nevis.—Ann Farding ; destination (no place given).
—Dorothy Bowell ; destination, Nevis.—William Aufort ; destination, Nevis.—
John Edwards ; destination, Nevis.—James Hawkes ; destination, Nevis.—Edward
Lawles ; destination, Nevis.—George Hoply ; destination, Nevis.—John Skoot ;
destination, Nevis.—Elizabeth Thomas ; destination, Nevis.

Page 418
Susan Hopkins ; destination, Nevis.—William Davis ; destination, Barbadoes.
—Richard Allin ; destination, Nevis.—John Clarke ; destination, Nevis.—George
Hopley ; destination, Nevis.—Noah Lewis ; destination, Nevis.—John George ;
destination, Nevis.—ffrancis Hale ; destination, Nevis.—William Whiteing ; desti-
nation, Nevis.—Edward Pitt ; destination, Nevis.

Page 419
Lewis David ; destination, Nevis.—John Davie ; destination, Nevis.—Ann
Peice ; destination, Virginia.—John James ; destination, Barbadoes.—Richard
Vaughan ; destination, Barbadoes.—William Bate ; destination, Virginia.—Robert
Harris ; destination, Barbadoes.—John James ; destination, Barbadoes.—Anne
Bell ; destination, Virginia.—John Davis ; destination, Barbadoes.—William Castle ;
destination, Virginia.

Page 420
John Jenkins ; destination, Virginia.—Charles Gwyn ; destination, Barbadoes.
—Jane Morgan ; destination, Barbadoes.—Suzan Morgan ; destination, Barbadoes.—
Thomas Wheeler ; destination, Barbadoes.—James Olliver ; destination, Virginia.
—Elizabeth ffrancis ; destination, Nevis.—William ffluellin ; destination, Nevis.—
Phillip fflower ; destination, Virginia.—Richard Phillips ; destination, Virginia.
—Joan Sheare ; destination, Virginia.—Herbert Price ; destination, Virginia.

Page 421
William Parker ; destination, Virginia.—James Thomas ; destination, Barbadoes.—Thomas Jones (of St. Mellon) ; destination, Virginia.—Richard Jones ;
destination, Virginia.—Edward Gally ; destination, Barbadoes.—Roger Reede ;
destination, Virginia.—William Gold ; destination, Virginia.—Edward Richards ;

G

destination, Virginia.—William Jones; destination, Virginia.—William Price (of Langaust); destination, Virginia.—Phillip Charles; destination, Virginia.—Lazarys Jenkins; destination, Virginia.

Page 422
— Phillip Roberts; destination, Nevis.—Margery Chapman; destination, Virginia. John Hooper; destination, Virginia.—Dermod Dennovand; destination, Virginia. —John Prauch; destination, Nevis.—Thomas Reede; destination, Virginia.— Joseph Read; destination, Virginia.—David Stratford; destination, Nevis.— Anthony Smeede; destination, Nevis.—Walter Edwards; destination, Nevis. —Evan Jones; destination, Nevis.—Richard Morgan; destination, Nevis.

Page 423
Samuell Ascue; destination, Virginia.—David Jones; destination, Virginia.— Jenkin Thomas; destination, Nevis.—Edward Lowden; destination, Nevis.— William Halditch; destination, Virginia.—Howell Williams; destination, Virginia. —Peter Powell; destination, Virginia.—John David; destination, Virginia.— Abraham Humphry; destination, Virginia.—John Matthewes; destination, Virginia. —Reece Williams; destination, Virginia.—John James; destination, Virginia.

Page 424
Mary Thomas; destination, Virginia.—Bridget Williams, destination, Virginia. —Margeret Powell; destination, Virginia.—Edmund Hone; destination, Nevis.— John Blisse; destination, Virginia.—John Williams; destination, Virginia.—John Sparkes; destination, Nevis.—John Wheeler; destination, Nevis.—Anne Morse; destination, Virginia.—Thomas Smith; destination, Virginia.—Edward Davis; destination, Virginia.—William Wills; destination, Virginia.

Page 425
George Hancock; destination, Virginia.—Prudence Edwards; destination, Virginia.—Morgan Jenkins; destination, Virginia.—Richard Harris; destination, Virginia.—Mary Vizard; destination, Virginia.—John Peters; destination, Virginia. —Thomas More; destination, Virginia.—John Poole; destination, Virginia.—Thomas Carrier; destination, Virginia.—William Taylor; destination, Virginia.—John Taylor; destination, Virginia.—Jane Smith; destination, Virginia.

Page 426
Benjamin Johnstone; destination, Virginia.—Thomas Dukes; destination, Virginia.—Margaret Vaughan; destination, Virginia.—Edward Burristone; destination, Virginia.—Thomas Ince; destination, Virginia.—Elizabeth Holdship; destination, Virginia.—Elinor Stannton; destination, Virginia.—Anne Phillips; destination, Virginia.—Margery Austin; destination, Virginia.—Ellin Collins; destination, Virginia.—Honnor Collins; destination, Virginia.—Mary Collins; destination, Virginia.

Page 427
Thomas Middleton; destination, Virginia.—Edward Hawkins; destination, Virginia.—George Hutton; destination, Virginia.—Mary Cause; destination, Virginia.—Grace Hedges; destination, Virginia.—ffrancis Austin, destination, Vir-

ginia.—Symon Watkins; destination, Nevis.—Edward Morgan; destination, Nevis.—Anne Lewis; destination, Nevis.—William Halling; destination, Nevis.— John Taylor; destination, Nevis.—Samuell Morgan; destination, Nevis.

Page 428
Richard Hall; destination, Nevis.—John Cole; destination, Nevis.—William Bates; destination, Nevis.—Walter Tucker; destination, Nevis.—Sarah Richard; destination, Nevis.—Elizabeth Morgan; destination, Nevis.—Elizabeth Stead; destination, Nevis.—Mary Philpott; destination, Nevis.—Mary Attwell; destination, Nevis.—John Evans; destination, Nevis.—Robert Primin; destination, Nevis.—William White; destination, Nevis.

Page 429
Hopkin Howell; destination, Virginia.—Thomas Whaite; destination, Virginia. —Mary Jones; destination, Virginia.—John Wills; destination, Virginia.—John Sherry; destination, Virginia.—Robert Challacome; destination, Virginia.—Anne Clarke; destination, Virginia.—Elizabeth Abraham; destination, Virginia.—Eve Gold; destination, Virginia.—Luke Gerry; destination, Virginia.—Robert Morgan; destination, Virginia.—Charity Hayter; destination, Virginia.

Page 430
Anne England; destination, Virginia.—Henry Reynolds; destination, Virginia. —Edmund Davis; destination, Virginia.—John Purnell; destination, Virginia.— William Morgan; destination, Virginia.—William Bennett (of Stotherton); destination, Virginia.—Thomas Cartar; destination, Nevis.—[Blank]; destination, Nevis.—Mary Allin; destination, Nevis.—Henry Newman; destination, Nevis.— Nicholas Cantar; destination, Nevis.—Mary Thomas; destination, Nevis.

Page 431
George Tucker; destination, Nevis.—Nicholas Hillary; destination, Nevis.— Margeret Dowling; destination, Nevis.—[Blank]; destination, Nevis.—Joane Rowland; destination, Nevis.—Thomas ffreeman; destination, Nevis.—Venetia Boswick; destination, Nevis.—Elinor Cary; destination, Nevis.—Thomas Daw; destination, Nevis.—Alice Allin; destination, Nevis.—Anne Clarke; destination, Nevis.—William Rawlins; destination, Nevis.

Page 432
David Jones; destination, Nevis.—Daniell Long; destination, Virginia.— Martin Young; destination, Virginia.—Richard Holland; destination, Virginia.— John Bayly; destination, Virginia.—Alice Griffin; destination, Virginia.—ffrancis Gleaves; destination, Virginia.—Anne Jones; destination, Virginia.—Hannah Combe; destination, Virginia.—John Combe; destination, Virginia.—Nicholas Cary; destination, Virginia.—Walter Howell; destination, Virginia.

Page 433
Thomas Merry; destination, Virginia.—Henry Waters; destination, Nevis.— John Tainton; destination, Virginia.—Jane Rickly; destination, Virginia.—William Roberts; destination, Virginia.—Thomas Vaughan; destination, Virginia.—Sarah Baxter; destination, Virginia.—Joseph Roberts; destination, Virginia.—Evan

Davis; destination, Virginia.—George Dunne; destination, Virginia.—John Morgan; destination, Virginia.—Nicholas ffenott; destination, Virginia.

Page 435 (*sic*)
Alice Griffin; destination, Virginia.—Sarah Davis; destination, Virginia.—Joseph Thorne; destination, Virginia.—John Salter; destination, Virginia.—Thomas Gittins; destination, Virginia.—Richard Jones; destination, Virginia.—Isaac Edwards; destination, Virginia.—Margery Woods; destination, Virginia.—Joane Bakehouse; destination, Virginia.—Richard Lewis; destination, Virginia.—John Doxy; destination, Virginia.—Mary Hughes; destination, Virginia.

Page 435 (*sic*)
Anne Thomas; destination, Virginia.—Nicholas Greene; destination, Virginia.—Anne Lovett; destination, Virginia.—Jane Willis; destination, Virginia.—Mary Haines; destination, Virginia.—Emanuell Poole; destination, Virginia.—William Smith; destination, Virginia.—Thomas Crosse; destination, Virginia.—George Munding; destination, Virginia.—Onisophorus Bennet; destination, Virginia.—Robert Clarke; destination, Virginia.

Page 436
William David; destination, Virginia.—Mordecai Elbury; destination, Virginia.—Elizabeth Bayly; destination, Virginia.—John Steevens; destination, Virginia.—Marthah Morgan; destination, Virginia.—Stephen Cole; destination, Virginia.—Marke Bowen; destination, Nevis.—Elizabeth Jones; destination, Nevis.—Elinor Watts; destination, Virginia.—Isabell Jones; destination, Virginia.—Elizabeth May; destination, Virginia.—Thomas Hogin; destination, Virginia.

Page 437
Margeret Thomas; destination, Virginia.—Henry Warner; destination, Virginia.—Thomas Lampin; destination, Virginia.—Darby Daniell; destination, Virginia.—William Mann; destination, Virginia.—Genry Bradley; destination, Virginia.—Joseph Edmunds; destination, Virginia.—William Merret; destination, Virginia.—Richard Jones; destination, Virginia.—Grace Adams, destination, Virginia.—John Trotnell; destination, Virginia.—John Butler; destination, Virginia.

Page 438
Thomas Doxy; destination, Virginia.—Mary Mandler; destination, Virginia.—Ursulah Doxy; destination, Virginia.—Sarah Pargeter; destination, Virginia.—Thomas Reynolds; destination, Virginia.—John Thorne; destination, Virginia.—Edward Reeves; destination, Virginia.—Miles Jones; destination, Virginia.—Jane Merewether; destination, Virginia.—Mathew Elliott; destination, Virginia.—George Oakley; destination, Virginia.—William Butler; destination, Virginia.

Page 439
Thomas Atkins; destination, Virginia.—Anne ffrankes; destination, Virginia.—Walter Chivers; destination, Virginia.—Thomas Window; destination, Virginia.—Mary Philpott; destination, Nevis.—Thomas Arton; destination, Nevis.—Henry Williams; destination, Nevis.—Anthony Lancaster; destination, Nevis.—Joane Stephens; destination, Nevis.—William Lewis; destination, Nevis.—Isaac Whittoes; destination, Nevis.—John Markworth; destination, Nevis.

Page 440

John Harry; destination, Nevis.—Julian Wootlane; destination, Nevis.—
Eliza Butler; destination, Nevis.—Roger Harvey; destination, Nevis.—Joane
Smurden; destination, Nevis.—John Reynolds; destination, Nevis.—Cicely Poole;
destination, Virginia.—Hester Poole; destination, Virginia.—Elizabeth Puller;
destination, Virginia.—Joane Hulett; destination, Virginia.—Elinor Whaite;
destination, Virginia.—Mary Redmond; destination, Virginia.

Page 441

Sarah Waite; destination, Virginia.—John Card; destination, Virginia.—
Arthur fflavell; destination, Virginia.—Mary Whitson; destination, Virginia.—
Blanch Jones; destination, Virginia.—Abraham Somers; destination, Virginia.
—David Salisbury; destination, Virginia.—William Brickett; destination, Virginia.
—Anne Whitwood; destination, Virginia.—John Lewes; destination, Virginia.—
George Thomas; destination, Virginia.—George Betty; destination, Virginia.

Page 442

Mary ffisher; destination, Virginia.—Thomas Darby; destination, Virginia
—George Allen; destination, Virginia.—Robert Sampson, destination, Virginia.—
Anne Pilgram; destination, Virginia.—Sarah Cooke; destination, Virginia.—
Anthony Smith; destination, Virginia.—John Powell (of Esum); destination,
Virginia.—Robert Cooke (of Gloucester); destination, Virginia.—Lawrence Whit-
house; destination, Virginia.—Valentine Mously; destination, Virginia.—Robert
Salisbury; destination, Virginia.

Page 443

Joane Mockeridge; destination, Virginia.—Edward Smith; destination,
Virginia.—David Thomas; destination, Virginia.—Charles Perkes; destination,
Virginia.—John Greene; destination, Virginia.—James By; destination, Virginia.
—William Grindon; destination, Virginia.—Alice Hunt; destination, Virginia.—
Samuell Barnard; destination, Virginia.—Olliver Spiller; destination, Virginia.—
William Griffin; destination, Virginia.—John Webb; destination, Virginia.

Page 444

Sarah Shepherd; destination, Virginia.—Nicholas Davis; destination, Virginia.
—John Lymell, Robert Roe, and Thomas St. John; destination, Virginia.—Leonard
Lester; destination (no place given).—William Good; destination (no place
given).—James Garnesay; destination (no place given).—Thomas Hall; destination,
Virginia.—John James; destination, Virginia.—Rice Williams; destination, Vir-
ginia.—John Bowen; destination, Virginia.—Meredith Price; destination, Virginia.
—Thomas Williams; destination, Virginia.

Page 445

William Inon; destination, Virginia.—John Bayly; destination, Virginia.—
Anne Bishop; destination, Virginia.—John Rosewell; destination, Virginia.—Joyce
Bowen; destination, Virginia.—James Killock; destination, Virginia.—Anne
Cordin; destination, Virginia.—Elizabeth Tompson; destination, Virginia.—Mary
Barnell; destination, Virginia.—George Painton; destination, Virginia.—Easoer
Lane; destination, Barbadoes.—Samuell Amyes; destination, Virginia.

Page 446
    Joane Smeades ; destination, Virginia.—Edward Lloyster ; destination, Virginia.
—Gilbert Jones ; destination, Virginia.—Phillip Griffen ; destination, Virginia.—
John Emmett ; destination, Virginia.—Elizabeth ffrancis ; destination, Virginia.
—Joane Spender ; destination, Virginia.—Hannah Young ; destination, Virginia.—
Anne Watkins ; destination, Virginia.—Adam Bradshaw ; destination, Virginia.
—Margeret Watkins ; destination, Nevis.—Thomas Underhill ; destination,
Virginia.

Page 447
    Richard Poole ; destination, Virginia.—Thomas Morgan ; destination, Virginia.
—John Williams ; destination, Virginia.—William Cole ; destination, Virginia.—
John Butler ; destination, Virginia.—William King ; destination, Virginia.—William
Keene ; destination, Virginia.—Winifred ffeild ; destination, Virginia.—William
Williams ; destination, Virginia.—Henry Williams ; destination, Virginia.—John
Thornbury ; destination, Virginia.—Richard Bachelor ; destination, Virginia.

Page 448
    Elinor Bradnock ; destination, Virginia.—Daniell Gardner ; destination,
Virginia.—ffrancis Gallow ; destination, Virginia.—Thomas Jones ; destination,
Nevis.—John Higgs ; destination, Virginia.—Elinor Smith ; destination, Virginia.
—Edward Ilea ; destination, Virginia.—David Williams ; destination, Virginia.—
William Lewes ; destination, Virginia.—Simon Traunter ; destination, Virginia.—
Joane Angell ; destination, Virginia.—William Powell ; destination, Virginia.

Page 449
    Margeret Butler ; destination, Virginia.—Joane Jackson ; destination, Nevis.
—Richard Gettings ; destination, Nevis.—William Browne ; destination, Nevis.—
Barbaray Culme ; destination, Barbadoes.—Henry Herne ; destination, Barbadoes.
—Thomas Phillips ; destination, Nevis.—Robert Hedges ; destination, Nevis.—
Arthur Evitt ; destination, Nevis.—John Lyning ; destination, Nevis.—Mathaniell
Linley ; destination, Virginia.—Thomas Broadrish ; destination, Virginia.

Page 450
    William Church ; destination, Virginia.—Anne Reynolds ; destination, Virginia.
—Thomas Reynolds ; destination, Virginia.—Henry ffranklin ; destination, Vir-
ginia.—Ronert ffulloway ; destination, Virginia.—John Edmunds ; destination,
Virginia.—Samson Redwick ; destination, Virginia.—Wilban Gay ; destination,
Virginia.—Ann Kite ; destination, Virginia.—Walter Price ; destination, Virginia.
—Thomas Dowing ; destination, Virginia.—Edward Price ; destination, Virginia.

Page 451
    James Williams ; destination, Virginia.—Robert Pearce ; destination, Barba-
does.—Ansell Bayly ; destination, Virginia.—John Thomas ; destination, Barbadoes.
—Thomas Oxford ; destination, Virginia.—Thomas Exon ; destination, Virginia.—
Isaac Skinner ; destination, Virginia.—William Edwards ; destination, Barbadoes.
—Anne Reede ; destination, Virginia.—John Thomas ; destination, Barbadoes.—
Margeret Bitchell ; destination, Barbadoes.—William Coates ; destination, Barba-
does..

Page 452
John Shepherd; destination, Barbadoes.—Thomas Jones; destination, Barbadoes.—Welthian Taylor; destination, Barbadoes.—John Davis; destination, Barbadoes.—Joane Clements; destination, Barbadoes.—Thomas Ruse; destination (no place given).—Phillip Burrow; destination (no place given).—Andrew Powell; destination (no place given).—Robert Young; destination (no place given). —Margeret Perry; destination (no place given).—James Hooper; destination (no place given).—David Reece; destination, Barbadoes.

Page 453
John Knight; destination, Virginia.—Mary Winseley; destination, Virginia.— Elizabeth Barnet; destination, Virginia.—Elizabeth Williams; destination, Nevis. —Mary Stone; destination, Nevis.—Edmond Williams; destination, Virginia.— William Ruddur; destination, Virginia.—Jonas Harris; destination, Virginia.— William Yeamans; destination, Virginia.—Arthur Bowen; destination, Virginia. —Arthur Severne; destination, Virginia.—Anne Cooke; destination, Virginia.

Page 456 (sic)
Anne Poore; destination, Virginia.—Mary Morse; destination, Virginia.— Sarah Ayleworth; destination, Virginia.—James Pidden; destination, Virginia. —Robert Busher; destination, Nevis.—William Witwell; destination, Virginia.— James Harry; destination, Virginia.—Richard Vidler; destination, Virginia.—Anne Greenhouse; destination, Virginia.—Katherine Everley; destination, Virginia.— Thomas West; destination, Virginia.—Samuell Rooke; destination, Virginia.

Page 455
Walter Morton; destination, Virginia.—Jane Harris; destination, Virginia. —John Dimick; destination, Virginia.—David Jones; destination, Virginia.—John Colesell; destination, Virginia.—William Smith; destination, Virginia.—Richard Shipley; destination, Virginia.—William Dyer; destination, Virginia.—Herbert Roe; destination, Virginia.—Henry Jones; destination, Virginia.—Thomas Witherington; destination, Nevis.—Robert Ward; destination, Nevis.

Page 456
Robert Redmond; destination, Virginia.—Thomas Williams; destination, Virginia.—George Southerne; destination, Barbadoes.—Thomas Wooles; destination, Virginia.—Thomas Barnes; destination, Antigua.—Dorothy Harchott; destination, Antigua.—James Williams; destination, Nevis.—Thomas Lewis; destination, Nevis.—John Morgan; destination, Virginia.—ffrancis Wrenne; destination, Virginia.—Daniall Shorte; destination, Barbadoes.—John Watkins; destination, Barbadoes.

Page 457
Joane Watkins; destination, Barbadoes.—Henry Porch; destination, Barbadoes. —William Osbourne; destination, Barbadoes.—Evan Pritchard; destination, Barbadoes.—Richard Waring; destination, Barbadoes.—Samuell Clarke; destination, Barbadoes.—Robert Redditt; destination, Barbadoes.—Thomas Williams; destination, Virginia.—Thomas Haskins; destination, Virginia.—Ambrose Yorke; destination, Nevis.—William Rumsey; destination, Nevis.—Lewis Thomas; destination, Nevis.

Page 458

Roger James ; destination, Nevis.—Walter Williams ; destination, Nevis.—
David James ; destination, Nevis.—John Kinton ; destination, Nevis.—Richard
Ives ; destination, Nevis.—Phillys Jones ; destination, Nevis.—Robert Thomas ;
destination, Barbadoes.—Robert Kitta ; destination, Barbadoes.—Thomas Battin ;
destination, Barbadoes.—John Lloyd ; destination, Barbadoes.—Isaac Gregory ;
destination, Barbadoes.—John Twiford ; destination, Barbadoes.

Page 459

Edward Thomas ; destination (no place given).—William Preston ; destination
(no place given).—David Williams ; destination (no place given).—Jane Wood ;
destination (no place given).—Roger Painter ; destination (no place given).—John
Powell ; destination (no place given).—Thomas Hull ; destination, Barbadoes.—
Thomas Moyle ; destination, Barbadoes.—Edward Gill ; destination, Barbadoes.
—Charles Watts ; destination, Barbadoes.—John Banwell ; destination, Nevis.—
Henry Kirle ; destination, Nevis.

Page 460

John Rooke ; destination, Nevis.—William Wilkins ; destination, Nevis.—
Henry Clutterbooke ; destination, Nevis.—Wartuss Dangerfield ; destination,
Barbadoes.—Edward Minard ; destination, Nevis.—Humfry Williams ; destination,
Nevis.—John Williams ; destination, Nevis.—Thomas Litman ; destination, Nevis.
—Thomas Jones ; destination, Nevis.—Edward Isles ; destination, Nevis.—Richard
Lawrence ; destination, Nevis.—Hugh Holwood ; destination, Nevis.

Page 461

Thomas Yates ; destination, Virginia.—John Berry ; destination, Nevis.—
Arthur Poole ; destination, Virginia.—Roth Hughes, Henry Nicholas, and ffrancis
Hughes ; destination, Virginia.—John Broadrip ; destination, Nevis.—Joseph
Young ; destination, Nevis.—Lewes Williams ; destination, Nevis.—Thomas
Williams ; destination, Nevis.—John Trotman ; destination, Nevis.—John Cockle ;
destination, Nevis.—Ronert Boobeer ; destination, Nevis.—Arthur Morgan ;
destination, Nevis.

Page 462

William Powell ; destination, Nevis.—Judith Powell ; destination, Nevis.—
Andrew Griffin ; destination, Nevis.—Peter Langley ; destination, Virginia.
—John Jobbins ; destination, Virginia.—Richard Ball ; destination, Virginia.—
Anthony Baby ; destination, Nevis.—Peter Wethers ; destination, Nevis.—Lodwick
Tiverton ; destination, Barbadoes.—Thomas Stockman ; destination, Barbadoes.
—Morgan Williams ; destination, Barbadoes.—William Williams ; destination,
Barbadoes.

Page 463

Margery Glace ; destination, Barbadoes.—John Gough ; destination, Barbadoes.—ffrancis Harris ; destination, Barbadoes.—Samuell Adams ; destination,
Barbadoes.—Phillip Davis ; destination, Barbadoes.—Robert Nicholls ; destination,
Barbadoes.—Grace Nicholls ; destination, Barbadoes.—Richard Phelps ; destination, Nevis.—Richard Parker ; destination, Nevis.—Mary Nelme ; destination, Virginia.—John Gunne ; destination, Nevis.—Michaell Saffin ; destination, Nevis.

Page 464
John Beind; destination, Nevis.—John Abraham; destination, Nevis.—Joseph Huish; destination, Nevis.—John Bevan; destination, Nevis.—Anne Cording; destination, Barbadoes.—Jonathan Tyre; destination, Barbadoes.—Sarah Stride; destination, Barbadoes.—Richard ffox; destination, Barbadoes.—Robert Bradford; destination, Barbadoes.—Roger Williams; destination, Nevis.—Phillip Lewis; destination, Nevis.—Bartholomew Thomas; destination, Virginia.

Page 465
Mary Collins; destination, Nevis.—ffrancis Yeamans; destination, Nevis.—William Eleate; destination, Virginia.—Phillip Jones; destination, Nevis.—John Silly; destination, Barbadoes.—Humfry Harris; destination, Nevis.—Edward Perrin; destination, Virginia.—William Owen; destination, Barbadoes.—Joseph Lawrence; destination, Nevis.—Humphry Williams; destination, Nevis.—Anthony Browne; destination, Nevis.—John Sunkis; destination, Nevis.

Page 466
Cutbert Veale; destination, Nevis.—Richard Stone; destination, Nevis.—Richard Chynne; destination, Nevis.—Timothy Iles; destination, New England.—Humfry Barber; destination, New England.—Thomas Gibbon; destination, Nevis.—Mary Richards; destination, Nevis.—Edward Timewell; destination, Nevis.—Richard Beaton; destination, Nevis.—Sarah Holder; destination, Nevis.—Anne Higgs; destination, Nevis.—Thomas Monks; destination, Nevis.

Page 467
Elinor Rogers; destination, Nevis.—Thomas Davis; destination, Nevis.—Roger Davis; destination, Nevis.—Mary Butler; destination, Nevis.—William ffry; destination, Nevis.—John Robins; destination, Nevis.—Mary Channdler; destination, Nevis.—John Grime; destination, Nevis.—Christofer Jones; destination, St. Christopher.—John Nicholls; destination, Barbadoes.—John Wilkins; destination, Nevis.—Lewis Penry; destination, Nevis.

Page 468
Hester Plummer; destination, Nevis.—John Thomas; destination, Nevis.—Thomas Leonard; destination, Barbadoes.—Thomas Dicks; destination, Barbadoes.—Margery ffloyd; destination, Barbadoes.—John Pearce; destination, Barbadoes.—John Trigg; destination, Barbadoes.—Robert London; destination, Nevis.—William Gunne; destination, Nevis.—Jenkin Jones; destination, Nevis.—James Morgan; destination, Nevis.—Henry Crosby; destination, Nevis.

Page 469
Anne Warner; destination, New England.—ffortune Roberts; destination, Nevis.—Richard Phelps; destination, Nevis.—Thomas Williams; destination, Nevis.—Richard Harding; destination, Nevis.—William Watts; destination, Nevis.—Roger Edwards; destination, New England.—James ffilla; destination, Barbadoes.—John Harvy; destination, Barbadoes.—Nicholas Wrentmore; destination, Barbadoes.—John Gough; destination, New England.—Thomas James; destination, Nevis.

Page 470
James Evilly; destination, Nevis.—John Watkins; destination, Barbadoes.—
Thomas Williams; destination, Nevis.—Anne Worley; destination, Nevis.—Robert
Widowes; destination, Nevis.—Robert Powell; destination, Nevis.—Tobyas Hele;
destination, Nevis.—Thomas Clarke; destination, New England.—Mary Rogers;
destination, Barbadoes.—Elizabeth Curtis; destination, Nevis.—John Cobby;
destination, Nevis.—Richard Williams; destination, Nevis.

Page 471
Anne Williams; destination, Nevis.—James Jones; destination, Nevis.—
Richard Burridge; destination, Nevis.—Howell Meredith; destination, Nevis.
—Thomas Thorne; destination, New England.—Evan Jinkins; destination, New
England.—George Baywell; destination, New England.—Joane Gatlock; destina-
tion, New England.—Elizabeth Binner; destination, New England.—John Gatly;
destination, New England.—Thomas Brookes; destination, New England.—
George Haggat; destination, Nevis.

Page 472
Samuell Scripture; destination, Nevis.—Joane Hill; destination, Nevis.—
Thomas Jones; destination, Nevis.—Thomas Harris; destination, Jamaica.—
William Morrice; destination, Jamaica.—William Moore; destination, Jamaica.
—William Rogers; destination, New England.—Roger Greene; destination, New
England.—Rose Alston; destination, New England.—Elizabeth Meredith; destina-
tion, New England.—Richard Welton; destination, Virginia.—William Merriman;
destination, Barbadoes.

Page 473
Thomas Williams; destination, Nevis.—Simon Brimsly; destination, New
England.—Samuel Sneath; destination, Nevis.—Roger Bevan; destination,
Nevis.—fflorence Mayne; destination, Nevis.—Thomas Lewis; destination, Nevis.
—Richard Tuftin; destination, Nevis.—Elizabeth Williams; destination, Nevis.—
Jane Robins; destination, St. Christopher.—John Morgan; destination, Nevis.—
ffabyan Price; destination, Nevis.—Isaac Bowin; destination, Nevis.

Page 474
William Duke; destination, Nevis.—Phillip Watkins; destination, Nevis.—
Lawrence Sall; destination, New England.—Daniell Towne; destination, New
England.—William Jacob; destination, Nevis.—George Ashman; destination,
Barbadoes.—George Ashman; destination, Barbadoes.—William Milsome; destina-
tion, Nevis.—Elizabeth Jones; destination, Nevis.—Jane Harris; destination,
Nevis.—Michaell ffarrington; destination, Leeward Is.—Elizabeth Hammon;
destination, Nevis.

Page 475
William Hix; destination, Nevis.—Anthony Gething; destination, Nevis.—
Johannes Steevens; destination, Nevis.—Thomas Williams; destination, Nevis.—
William Bullock; destination, Nevis.—Elizabeth Merchant; destination, Nevis.
—Humfry Bullery; destination, Nevis.—Elizabeth Jenings; destination, Nevis.—
Thomas Thomas; destination, Nevis.—William Philpot; destination, Nevis.—
Thomas Berton; destination, Nevis.—Sarah Deffell; destination, Nevis.

Page 476

John White ; destination, Nevis.—Anne Smith ; destination, Nevis.—John Richards ; destination, Nevis.—James Goodinough ; destination, Nevis.—Thomas Durbin ; destination, Nevis.—Edward Hix ; destination, Nevis.—William Mibber ; destination, Nevis.—Jenkin Jones ; destination, Nevis.—Jane Jones ; destination, Nevis.—William Prosser ; destination, Nevis.—Anthony Parsons ; destination, Nevis.—Milbrow Dicks ; destination, Nevis.

Page 477

William Poole ; destination, Nevis.—Richard Evans ; destination, Nevis.—Edward Davis ; destination, Nevis.—Thomas Seconds ; destination, Jamaica.—George Collins ; destination, Nevis.—Lewellin Thomas ; destination, Nevis.—John Smith ; destination, Nevis.—William Arnoll ; destination, Nevis.—Joseph Raise ; destination, Nevis.—Robert Leydon ; destination, Nevis.—Thomas Williams ; destination, Nevis.—William Morgan ; destination, Nevis.

Page 478

John Pritchard ; destination, Nevis.—Thomas Jenkins ; destination, Nevis.—Adan Snow ; destination, Barbadoes.—William Bush ; destination, Barbadoes.—James Edmunds ; destination, Barbadoes.—Richard Hole ; destination, Nevis.—Thomas Wright ; destination, Nevis.—Paull Prichill ; destination, Nevis.—Elinor Phillips ; destination, Nevis.—Edward Harding ; destination, Nevis.—Margeret Baker ; destination, Nevis.—Johanne Perkes ; destination, Nevis.

Page 479

Katherine Bevan ; destination, Nevis.—Edmund Thomas ; destination, Nevis.—Gainer Evans ; destination, Nevis.—Thomas Roger ; destination, Jamaica.—Edward Rowland ; destination, Jamaica.—John Hetherley ; destination, Nevis.—Thomas Smith ; destination, Nevis.—Anne Martin ; destination, Nevis.—Joane Jones ; destination, Nevis.—Elizabeth Jones ; destination, Nevis.—Ralph Crow ; destination, Nevis.—Robert Baker ; destination, Nevis.

Page 480

Jenkin Jones ; destination, Nevis.—John Pennock ; destination, Nevis.—Rice Thomas ; destination, Nevis.—John Harden ; destination, Nevis.—John Tippet ; destination, Nevis.—Elizabeth Harris ; destination, Nevis.—William Dodson ; destination, Jamaica.—Joane Cooke ; destination, Jamaica.—Daniel Wood ; destination, Jamaica.—Isaac Thomas ; destination, Nevis.—Humfrey Webb ; destination, Nevis.—John Huntur ; destination, Nevis.

Page 481

John Shiviar ; destination, Nevis.—Robert Jewman ; destination, Nevis.—Elizabeth Elyer ; destination, Nevis.—Thomas Stone ; destination, Nevis.—John Gething ; destination, Barbadoes.—John Ball ; destination, Barbadoes.—Kathwey Wheton ; destination, Barbadoes.—Robert Bennet ; destination, Barbadoes.—Penelope Baker ; destination, Nevis.—Henry Williams ; destination, Barbadoes.—Daniell Somers ; destination, Nevis.—Thomas Stephens ; destination, Barbadoes.

Page 482

Katherine Thomas ; destination, Barbadoes.—Robert Hall ; destination, Virginia.—Thomas Williams ; destination, Virginia.—Isaac Amorite ; destination,

Virginia.—John Day ; destination, Virginia.—Rebecca Thomas (*Charles*) ; destination, Barbadoes.—James Guy (*Providence*) ; destination, Barbadoes.—John Saunders (*Providence*) ; destination, Barbadoes.—John Lewis (*William and Thomas*) ; destination, Jamaica.—Henry Powell (*Charles*) ; destination, Barbadoes.—Onizephorus Cornish (*Providence*) ; destination, Virginia.

Page 483
James Jones (*Charles*) ; destination, Barbadoes.—Sarah Reede (*Charles*) ; destination, Barbadoes.—Maryan Canings (*Charles*) ; destination, Barbadoes.— Mary Norris (*Charles*) ; destination, Barbadoes.—Evan Bennet (*Providence*) ; destination, Virginia.—John Channdler (*Charles*) ; destination, Barbadoes.—John Micail (*Charles*) ; destination, Virginia.—Margeret ffarly (*Charles*) ; destination, Virginia. —John Ash (*Charles*) ; destination, Virginia.—John Williams (*Huntsman*) ; destination, New England.—Humfry Robins (*Charles*) ; destination, Barbadoes.—John Eastmead (*Providence*) ; destination, Virginia.

Page 484
George Harris (*Providence*) ; destination, Virginia.—William Harris (*Charles*) ; destination, Barbadoes.—John Lambert (*Charles*) ; destination, Barbadoes.— Richard Brasie (*Charles*) ; destination, Barbadoes.—John Power (*Charles*) ; destination, Jamaica.—Evan Davis (*Charles*) ; destination, Jamaica.—John Davis (*Charles*) ; destination, Jamaica.—Lewis Jones (*Charles*) ; destination, Virginia.—Hugh Williams (*Charles*) ; destination, Barbadoes.—Prudence Yeo (*Providence*) ; destination, Virginia.—John Taylor ; destination, Virginia.

Page 485
Elizabeth Taylor (*Providence*) ; destination, Virginia.—John Williams (*Providence*) ; destination, Virginia.—John Jones (*Charles*) ; destination, Barbadoes.— William Wilkison (*sic*) (*Charles*) ; destination, Virginia.—Mary Gale ; destination, Virginia.—Cornelius Thomas (*Charles*) ; destination, Virginia.—Marke Randell (*Huntsman*) ; destination, New England.—John Thomas (*Providence*) ; destination, Virginia.—Hannah Backwell (*Charles*) ; destination, Barbadoes.—Samuell Simms ; destination, Virginia.—Elinor Pussell (*sic*) (*Charles*) ; destination, Barbadoes.— John Watkins ; destination, Barbadoes.

Page 486
George Nicholas ; destination, Barbadoes.—Thomas Huntly ; destination, Virginia.—John Nicholas ; destination, Virginia.—William ffletcher ; destination, Virginia.—Elinor Barry ; destination, Virginia.—Henry Wolfe (*Huntsman*) ; destination, New England.—Elizaneth Garrett ; destination, Virginia.—Stephen Thomas ; destination, Virginia.—Richard Lye ; destination, Virginia.—Thomas Steevens ; destination, Virginia.—Samuell Glenne ; destination, Virginia.—Anne Williams ; destination, Virginia.

Page 487
Elizaneth Lydoll ; destination, Virginia.—Hugh Richards ; destination, Virginia.—Edward Evans ; destination, Virginia.—John Leere ; destination, Virginia. —John Simons ; destination, Virginia.—Richard Gettings ; destination, Virginia.— Richard Duncombe ; destination, Virginia.—John Daby (*sic*) ; destination, Vir-

ginia.—William Edwards; destination, Virginia.—Joyce How; destination, Virginia.—Charles James; destination, Virginia.—Mathew Richards; destination, Virginia.—Elizabeth Richards; destination, Virginia.

Page 488

Anne Deane; destination, Virginia.—Adam Weaver; destination, Virginia. —Thomas Blinnar; destination, Virginia.—Alice Woodward; destination, Virginia.—Thomas Rossell; destination, Virginia.—John Evans; destination, Virginia. —John Tomalin; destination, Virginia.—Mathew Hopkins; destination, Virginia.—Mary Lewis; destination, Virginia.—Anne Wix; destination, Virginia.— Mary Jones; destination, Virginia.—Lewis Warren; destination, Virginia.

Page 489

Robert Michell; destination, Virginia.—John Webb; destination, Virginia. —James Reynolds; destination, Virginia.—Geoffrey Sommerford; destination, Virginia.—Scalam Maglockly; destination, Virginia.—Samuell Churchell (*Shipwrite* [*sic*]); destination, Virginia.—Edward Jones; destination, Virginia.—Thomas Erbury (*Rainbow*); destination, Virginia.—Thomas Robins; destination, Virginia. —Arthur Robins; destination, Virginia.—Thomas Abram; destination, Virginia.— Hugh Gardiner; destination, Virginia.

Page 490

William Bevan; destination, Virginia.—Elizabeth Carter; destination, Virginia.—Joan Sandy; destination, Virginia.—Mary Sandy; destination, Virginia.— William Sandy; destination, Virginia.—Anne Bayly; destination, Virginia.—John Catton; destination, Virginia.—John Tilman; destination, Virginia.—John Simons; destination, Virginia.—Margery Corson; destination, Virginia.—John Davies; destination, Virginia.—Reece Jones; destination, Virginia.

Page 491

John Wenlock; destination, Virginia.—Sarah Braban; destination, Virginia. —Mary Jones; destination, Virginia.—William Morse; destination, Virginia.— David Mathew; destination, Virginia.—Phillip Jones; destination, Virginia.— Richard Vaughan; destination, Virginia.—Rosser Thomas; destination, Virginia.—Hugh John; destination, Virginia.—Katherine Rice; destination, Virginia. —Richard Jones; destination, Virginia.—David Davids; destination, Virginia.

Page 492

Richard Onions; destination, Virginia.—John Goldsworthy; destination, Virginia.—John Bovy; destination, Virginia.—Mary Bath; destination, Virginia. —Richard Gold; destination, Virginia.—Ambrose Thomas; destination, Virginia.— William Nerrifeild; destination, Virginia.—Daniel Hill; destination, Virginia.—Joane Simms; destination, Virginia.—Thomas Holcombe; destination, Barbadoes.— Thomas Charles; destination, Virginia.—Rosse Itamn; destination, Virginia.

Page 493

ffrancis Bridle; destination, Virginia.—Phillip Durdoe; destination, Virginia. —John Wall; destination, Virginia.—John Privett; destination, Virginia.—William Privett; destination, Virginia.—Edward Cony; destination, Virginia.—William

Nethway; destination, Virginia.—Edward Massey; destination, Virginia.—Anne Gwynne; destination, Virginia.—Rice Powell; destination, Virginia.—Edward Moody; destination, Virginia.—Margeret Clarke; destination, Virginia.

Page 494

William Arthur; destination, Virginia.—ffrancis Yates; destination, Virginia. —Alexander Bevan; destination, Virginia.—William Rathwell; destination, Virginia.—Thomas Edwards; destination, Virginia.—Temperance Benum; destination, Virginia.—Thomas Lock; destination, Virginia.—John Thomas; destination, Virginia.—Stephen Austin; destination, Barbadoes.—Anne ffrowan; destination, Virginia.—John Estop; destination, Virginia.—William Harris; destination, Virginia.

Page 495

Johan Olins; destination, Virginia.—John Cluse; destination, Virginia.—John Kent; destination, Virginia.—Robert Penn; destination, Virginia.—Joseph Mays; destination, Virginia.—Elizabeth Cultinghorne; destination, Virginia.—Amy Watts; destination, Virginia.—Isaac Hellier; destination, Virginia.—Elizabeth Hobson (*Providence*); destination, Virginia.—Nathaniel Hancock (*Concord*); destination, Virginia.—Richard Andrewes; destination, Virginia.—Thomas Andrewes; destination, Virginia.

Page 496

Thomas Spilman; destination, Virginia.—Mary Spilman; destination, Virginia. —John Elbridge; destination, Virginia.—John Barber; destination, Virginia.— Richard Lewis; destination, Virginia.—Richard Wix; destination, Virginia.— Thomas White; destination, Virginia.—Margeret Bevun; destination, Virginia. —Jonas Phillips; destination, Virginia.—Elinor James; destination, Virginia.— Thomas Saunders; destination, Virginia.—William Saunders; destination, Virginia.

Page 497

John Davis; destination, Barbadoes.—George Vaughan; destination, Virginia. —William Tidsum; destination, Virginia.—Jane Ingleton; destination, Virginia.— John Williams; destination, Virginia.—Richard Hick; destination, Virginia.—John Decent (*Agreement*); destination, Virginia.—John Arthur; destination, Virginia. —John Dalcott; destination, Virginia.—John Jones; destination, Virginia.—John Watkins; destination, Virginia.—Elizabeth Williams; destination, Virginia.

Page 498

Isaac Wright; destination, Virginia.—Anthony Goddart; destination, Virginia. —Owen Davis; destination, Virginia.—John Vincent; destination, Virginia.—Mary Blackman; destination, Virginia.—William Cymber; destination, Virginia.—Alice Sair; destination, Virginia.—Timothy Bennet; destination, Virginia.—Thomas Day; destination, Virginia.—Edward Harris; destination, Virginia.—Mary Guntur; destination, Virginia.—William Henning; destination, Virginia.

Page 499

Walter Hodges; destination, Virginia.—Margeret Davis; destination, Virginia. —Alice Milton; destination, Virginia.—Samuell Dale; destination, Virginia.— Robert Dale; destination, Virginia.—Rachell Higgs; destination, Virginia.—Jane

Newton ; destination, Virginia.—David Hambleton ; destination, Virginia.—John Thomas ; destination, Virginia.—Elizabeth Davis ; destination, Virginia.— Margeret Winter ; destination, Virginia.—ffrances Watling ; destination, Virginia.

Page 500
John Paradice ; destination, Virginia.—John Ricketts ; destination, Virginia.— Mary Dowle ; destination, Virginia.—Joane Roberts ; destination, Virginia.—Giles Parsons ; destination, Virginia.—Nicholas Heath ; destination, Virginia.—Robert Cawley ; destination, New England.—Ralph Jenkins ; destination, Virginia.—John Newman ; destination, Virginia.—Thomas Simons ; destination, Virginia.— Elizabeth Johnson ; destination, Virginia.—Elizabeth Cooke ; destination, Virginia.

Page 501
Margaret Phillyps ; destination, Virginia.—David Abevan ; destination, Virginia.—Alice Jones ; destination, Virginia.—William Bungy ; destination, Virginia.—John Britow ; destination, Virginia.—Adrian Martin ; destination, Barbadoes.—Robert Hicks ; destination, Barbadoes.—Mathew Gibbs ; destination, Barbadoes.—John Baker ; destination, Barbadoes.—Simon Hooper ; destination, Barbadoes.—Henry Harris ; destination, Virginia.—Mary West ; destination, Virginia.

Page 502
ffrancis West ; destination, Virginia.—Richard Jones ; destination, Virginia.— John Baker ; destination, Virginia.—Thomas Baker ; destination, Virginia.—Morrice Harris ; destination, Virginia.—Edward Carter ; destination, Virginia.—William Davis ; destination, Virginia.—Henry Harris ; destination, Virginia.—James Dedicott ; destination, Virginia.—John Bareford ; destination, Virginia.—Joane Bareford ; destination, Virginia.—Thomas Hayward ; destination, Virginia.

Page 503
Alice Child ; destination, Virginia.—William Millard ; destination, Virginia.— John Grainger ; destination, Virginia.—John Carpenter ; destination, Virginia. —Marthah Hulbert ; destination, Virginia.—Nicholas Brooke ; destination, Virginia.—Rowland Morgan ; destination, Virginia.—John Williams ; destination, Virginia.—ffrancis Thomas ; destination, Virginia.—Joyce Davy ; destination, Virginia.—William Stile ; destination, Barbadoes.—Thomas Browne ; destination, Barbadoes.

Page 504
Maudlin Jones ; destination, Virginia.—Hugh Crumpton ; destination, Virginia.—Humfry Clerke ; destination, Virginia.—Anne Woodner ; destination, Virginia.—John Richards ; destination, Virginia.—Margery Bryan ; destination, Virginia.—Evan Williams ; destination, Virginia.—George Williams ; destination, Virginia.—Robert Clarke ; destination, Virginia.—Elizabeth Pinfold ; destination, Virginia.—Jane Dowting ; destination, Virginia.—Elizabeth Scripture ; destination, Virginia.

Page 505
Robert Aston ; destination, Virginia.—Peter Nicholas ; destination, Virginia. —Anne Greene ; destination, Virginia.—James Pugsley ; destination, Virginia.— Thomas Watkins ; destination, Virginia.—Ann Anderson ; destination, Virginia.

—Henry Anderson ; destination, Virginia.—Charles Cales ; destination, Virginia.—
John Charles ; destination, Virginia.—William Richards ; destination, Virginia.
—Mathew Day ; destination, Virginia.—Cisely Morgan ; destination, Virginia.

Page 506
   Mary Smith ; destination, Virginia.—William Jones ; destination, Virginia.—
James Palmer ; destination, Virginia.—John Whitecraft ; destination, Virginia.
—David Thomas ; destination, Virginia.—Thomas Jones ; destination, Virginia.—
Martin Cole ; destination, Virginia.—John Evans ; destination, Virginia.—Thomas
Randell ; destination, Virginia.—Blanch Williams ; destination, Virginia.—Enotch
Boulton ; destination, Virginia.—John Newman ; destination, Virginia.

Page 507
   Ann Jones ; destination, Virginia.—Henry Sheapard ; destination, Virginia.—
George Dawkins ; destination, Virginia.—Thomas Barden ; destination, Virginia.
—Hugh Rosser ; destination, Virginia.—Thomas Lewis ; destination, Virginia.—
Nathaniell Bero ; destination, Maryland.—Christopher Wheeler ; destination,
Virginia.—Robert Wood ; destination, Maryland.—Richard Litter ; destination,
Virginia.—Thomas Philpot ; destination, Virginia.—Mary Rose ; destination,
Virginia.

Page 508
   Rachell Brune ; destination, Virginia.—William Linton ; destination, Virginia.
—Thomas Glenton ; destination, New England.—Henry Waters ; destination,
Virginia.—William Johnson ; destination, Virginia.—Hihn Higs ; destination,
Virginia.—Howell Jones ; destination, Virginia.—Ann Horwood ; destination,
Virginia.—Richard Bowen ; destination, Virginia.—Thomas Heath ; destina-
tion, Virginia.—Robert Webber ; destination, Virginia.—Richard [blank] ; destina-
tion, Virginia.

Page 509
   William Edwards ; destination, Virginia.—Thomas Jones ; destination, Virginia.
—Margery Spencer ; destination, Virginia.—Mary Cloas ; destination, Virginia.—
Richard Vaughans ; destination, Virginia.—Tobyas Marler ; destination, Barbadoes.
—John Chard ; destination, Barbadoes.—ffrancis Jenings ; destination, New
England.—William Burreston ; destination, Virginia.—James Hamlin ; destination,
Virginia.—Ann Ward ; destination, Virginia.—Elizabeth Ward ; destination,
Virginia.

Page 510
   John Cox ; destination, Virginia.—John Powell ; destination, Virginia.—
Richard Jones ; destination, Virginia.—Susanna Wilmott ; destination, Virginia.—
Margeret Agins ; destination, Virginia.—Katherine Jones ; destination, Virginia.
—William Thomas ; destination, New England.—John ffox ; destination, Virginia.
—Ann Peccard ; destination, Maryland.—Walter Pye ; destination, Maryland.—
Richard Walter ; destination, Virginia.—Edward Ludlow ; destination, Virginia.

Page 511
   John Bennett ; destination, Virginia.—Elionor Parish ; destination, Virginia.
—Nathaniell Dibble ; destination, Virginia.—Grace Dole ; destination, Virginia.—

Simon Rench ; destination, Virginia.—Ann Giull ; destination, Virginia.—Susanna Williams ; destination, Virginia.—Rece Price ; destination, Nevis.—Henry Jones ; destination, Virginia.—John Tigy ; destination, Virginia.—William Jones ; destination, Virginia.—Silvanus Johnson ; destination, Virginia.

Page 512
John Reece ; destination, Virginia.—Ann Price ; destination, Virginia.— Thomas Roberts ; destination (no place given).—Benjamin Bowry ; destination, Virginia.—William Gouldsmith ; destination, Virginia.—Elizabeth Rucher ; destination, Virginia.—John Wotts ; destination, Virginia.—Robert Wheler ; destination, Virginia.—ffrancis Abel ; destination, Virginia.—Samuell Audry ; destination, Virginia.—Phillip Sanders ; destination, Virginia.—George Bayton ; destination, Virginia.

Page 513
David Smith ; destination, Virginia.—John Harper ; destination, Virginia.— John Bridgman ; destination, Virginia.—Thomas Bridgman ; destination, Virginia. —Henry ffarmer ; destination, Virginia.—Ann Morgan ; destination, Virginia.— Sarah George ; destination, Virginia.—Mary Genings ; destination, Virginia.— Thomas Lewis ; destination, Virginia.—Thomas Morgan ; destination, Virginia. —Roger Phillips ; destination, Virginia.—Charles Watts ; destination, Virginia.

Page 514
William ffrancis ; destination, Virginia.—Thomas Owen ; destination, Virginia. —John Harrison ; destination, Virginia.—William Harding ; destination, Virginia. —Henry Porch ; destination, Virginia.—Abigell Heale ; destination, Virginia.— Richard Prise ; destination, Virginia.—George Long ; destination, Virginia.— Thomas Baker ; destination, Barbadoes.—William Neaell ; destination, Barbadoes. —Jane Neael ; destination, Barbadoes.—Henry Butterell ; destination, Barbadoes.

Page 515
Roger Howsen ; destination, Virginia.—William Grene ; destination, Virginia. —Margeret Cowley ; destination, Virginia.—Mary Poynting ; destination, Virginia. —Edward Berry ; destination, Virginia.—Ambrose Muckelon ; destination, Virginia.—Thomas Winyod ; destination, Virginia.—John ffrance ; destination, Virginia.—Robert Hulbright ; destination, Virginia.—David Evan ; destination, Virginia.—Richard Morgan ; destination, Virginia.—Henry Smith ; destination, Virginia.

Page 516
Richard Pearce ; destination, Virginia.—William Gwilliam ; destination, Virginia.—Henry Williams ; destination, Virginia.—Anthony Williams ; destination, Virginia.—Thomas German ; destination, Maryland.—Mary ffoster ; destination, Virginia.—John Hale ; destination, Virginia.—Ambrose Knight ; destination, Virginia.—William Reston ; destination, Virginia.—George Beroe ; destination, Virginia.—William Hill ; destination, Virginia.—Humphrey Wood ; destination, Virginia.

Page 517
Morgan Morgan ; destination, Virginia.—William Kimocke ; destination, Virginia.—Thomas Gregory ; destination, Virginia.—John Monckes ; destina-

H

tion, Virginia.—ffrances Hill ; destination, Virginia.—William Puxton ; destination, Virginia.—Hanna Hawkins ; destination, Virginia.—Jane Charles ; destination, Virginia.—Thomas Harding ; destination, Virginia.—George Haward ; destination, Virginia.—Richard ffisher ; destination, Virginia.—Owen Howell ; destination, Virginia.

Page 518
John Allen ; destination, Virginia.—Edward Thomas ; destination, Virginia. —John Toopoot (?) ; destination, Virginia.—Thomas Loyde ; destination, Virginia.—William Berrow ; destination, Virginia.—Anthonie Harris ; destination, Virginia.—Richard Martin ; destination, Virginia.—William Thomas ; destination, Virginia.—Thomas Munday ; destination, Virginia.—William Deffeild ; destination, Virginia.—Elizabeth Hay ; destination, Virginia.—John Wingate ; destination, Virginia.

Page 519
Roger Lewis ; destination, Virginia.—John ffranceh ; destination, Virginia.— Thomas Rickens ; destination, Virginia.—Sarah Digbie ; destination, Virginia. —Joane West ; destination, Virginia.—Anne Bankes ; destination, Virginia.—Bridgett Lea ; destination, Virginia.—Margarett Lucy ; destination, Virginia.— ffrancis Cable ; destination, Virginia.—Henry fflag ; destination, Virginia.— George Williams ; destination, Virginia.—Anne Davis ; destination, Virginia.

Page 520
Mary Phillips ; destination, Virginia.—Jossah Willis ; destination, Barbadoes. —Mary Evans ; destination, Virginia.—Andrew Davis ; destination, Virginia.—John Lea ; destination, Virginia.—Katherine Langford ; destination, Virginia.—Margery Clarke ; destination, Virginia.—Henry Baker ; destination, Virginia.—Edward Robinson ; destination, Virginia.—John Williams ; destination, Virginia.—John Quelch ; destination, Virginia.—David Persons ; destination, Virginia.

Page 521
Gorgius Beeders ; destination, Virginia.—John Kenner ; destination, Virginia. —William Stephens ; destination, Barbadoes.—John English ; destination, Virginia.—Joyce Thomas ; destination, Virginia.—William Reyney ; destination, Virginia.—David Rogers ; destination, Virginia.—Thomas Day ; destination, Virginia.—Simon Bouker ; destination, Virginia.—ffrancis Robinson ; destination, Virginia.—John Jones ; destination, Nevis.—James Bernard ; destination, Virginia.

Page 522
Elizabeth Waller ; destination, Virginia.—Roger Cordwint ; destination, Virginia.—Robert Phibbal ; destination, Virginia.—John Drinkwater ; destination, Virginia.—John Williams ; destination, Virginia.—Thomas Cogwell ; destination, Virginia.—Elizabeth Hakens ; destination, Virginia.—William Cookny ; destination, Virginia.—Samuell Clarke ; destination, Virginia.—Thomas Jones ; destination, Virginia.—Mary Harris ; destination, Virginia.—Thomas Hitchings ; destination, Virginia.

Page 523
Robert Harding ; destination, Virginia.—John Petteridge ; destination, Virginia.—Ann Kenton ; destination, Virginia.—Joseph Cooke ; destination, Nevis.—

Henry Thomas; destination, Virginia.—Peter Nesson; destination, Virginia.—Edward Phillips; destination, Barbadoes.—James Wills; destination, Virginia.—William Woodward; destination, Virginia.—Edward Bradford; destination, Virginia.—Anthony ffranken; destination, Virginia.—Morgan Owen; destination, Virginia.

Page 524

William Underwood; destination, Virginia.—William Jones; destination, Virginia.—Thomas Atkins; destination, Virginia.—Stephen Prough; destination, Virginia.—Ann Williams; destination, Virginia.—Samuell Woodward; destination, Virginia.—John Jones; destination, Virginia.—William Hopkins; destination, Virginia.—Henry Smith; destination, Virginia.—John Meredeth; destination, Virginia.—Andrew Vaughan; destination, Virginia.—Barnabe Wells; destination, Virginia.

Page 525

Thomas Saul; destination, Virginia.—Isaac Southern; destination, Barbadoes.—ffrancis Proser; destination, Virginia.—William Gould; destination, Virginia.—Dennis Carter; destination, Virginia.—William Morgan; destination, Virginia.—Robert Williams; destination, Barbadoes.—William Hunnaball; destination, Nevis.—fflouranc Carter; destination, Virginia.—John fflyd; destination, Virginia.—Richard Setherard; destination, Virginia.—John Kempton; destination, Virginia.

Page 526

Ann Ruther; destination, Virginia.—Nicholas Brewer; destination, Virginia.—Joseph Hambidg; destination, Virginia.—David Davis; destination, Virginia.—Richard Symons; destination, Virginia.—William Gunter; destination, Barbadoes.—William James; destination, Barbadoes.—William Lisbon; destination, Barbadoes.—Elizabeth Davis; destination, Virginia.—Richard ffelton; destination, Virginia.—Alice ffelton; destination, Virginia.—James Williams; destination, Virginia.

Page 527

Mary Palmer; destination, Virginia.—Ann Davis; destination, Virginia.—Mary Shuter; destination, Virginia.—Alice ffarmir; destination, Virginia.—William Stephens; destination, Virginia.—Elizabeth ffarle; destination, Virginia.—Henry Evere; destination, Virginia.—Alice Jones; destination, Virginia.—Mary Phillips; destination, Virginia.—John Spencer; destination, Virginia.—Thomas Spencer; destination, Virginia.—Edward Bartly; destination, Virginia.

Page 528

James Morgan; destination, Virginia.—Mary Banson; destination, Virginia.—Elizabeth Smith; destination, Virginia.—Richard Williams; destination, Virginia.—William Betayh; destination, Nevis.—William Browne; destination, Virginia.—William Milton; destination, Virginia.—William Hosy; destination, Barbadoes.—John ffleming; destination, Virginia.—William More; destination, Virginia.—George Greenway; destination, Virginia.—Anne Hicks; destination, Virginia.

Page 529

John James; destination, Virginia.—Charles Hodges; destination, Virginia.—John Haulbord; destination, Virginia.—Elizabeth Porch; destination, Virginia.—Clemant Applegate; destination, Virginia.—Ann Price; destination, Virginia.—Richard Poole; destination, Virginia.—Elizabeth Daniell; destination, Nevis.—ffrancis Haynes; destination, Barbadoes.—Evan Jones; destination, Nevis.—John Williams; destination, Barbadoes.—John Owen; destination, Barbadoes.

Page 530
Thomas Biford; destination, Barbadoes.—William Biford; destination, Barbadoes.—Walter James; destination, Nevis.—John Serle; destination, Barbadoes.—Jeffery Smale; destination, Barbadoes.—James Williams; destination, Barbadoes.—Evan Edwardes; destination, Barbadoes.—John King; destination, Nevis.—Joan Halloway; destination, Nevis.—Thomas Smith; destination, Barbadoes.—John Roberts; destination, St. Christopher.—Mary Lee; destination, Barbadoes.

Page 531
Henry Seddon; destination, Barbadoes.—Lodwick Gwilliam; destination, Barbadoes.—William Karkeese; destination, Barbadoes.— fflurrance Sinmons; destination, Barbadoes.—Edmund Pritchard; destination, Barbadoes.—Edward Duball; destination, Barbadoes.—John Williams; destination, Nevis.—Roger Strang; destination, Nevis.—Ann Jones; destination, Nevis.—Charles Williams; destination, Antigua.—William Tayler; destination, Nevis.—Walter Hopkins; destination, Nevis.

Page 532
John Haywood; destination, Barbadoes.—John Stone; destination, Barbadoes.—Ellioner Munksly; destination, Nevis.—Sarah Teage; destination, Nevis.—Elizabeth Stand; destination, Nevis.—Elizabeth Owing; destination, Nevis.—Richard Yow; destination, Barbadoes.—George Williams; destination, Barbadoes.—William Lewis; destination, Barbadoes.—Elizabeth Waters; destination, Barbadoes.—Phillip Luen; destination, Barbadoes.—Thomas Trowcock; destination, Nevis.

Page 533
Edward Addis; destination, Nevis.—Lewis Watkins; destination, Nevis.—Risse Thomas; destination, Nevis.—Peter ffontenew; destination, Nevis.—John West; destination, Nevis.—William fflyd; destination, Nevis.—Thomas Garner; destination, Nevis.—Thomas Rees; destination, Nevis.—Robert Banks; destination, Nevis.—George Parker; destination, Nevis.—William Herne; destination, Barbadoes.—Edward James; destination, Nevis.

Page 534
Reynold Galton; destination, Nevis.—Marke Snow; destination, Nevis.—Roger Hunt; destination, Nevis.—William Lluellin; destination, Barbadoes.—Mary Williams; destination, Barbadoes.—Katherine Christopher; destination, Barbadoes.—Margaret Peters; destination, Nevis.—John Johnson; destination, Nevis.—Thomas Gabwell; destination, Nevis.—Thomas Standly; destination, Nevis.—Mary Coulson; destination, Barbadoes.—William Carpenter; destination, Nevis.

Page 535
John Pritchat; destination, Nevis.—John Sheapard; destination, Nevis.—Thomas Webb; destination, Nevis.—Thomas Webb; destination, Nevis.—Mary

Webb ; destination, Nevis.—Thomas Mathews ; destination, Nevis.—Thomas James ; destination, Nevis.—Thomas fflyd ; destination, Nevis.—David James ; destination, Nevis.—Mary Tayler ; destination, Nevis.—Mary Griffis ; destination, Nevis.—John ffreind ; destination, New England.—William Atkinson ; destination, Nevis.

Page 536
Thomas Rollins ; destination, Nevis.—Roger Grizell ; destination, Nevis.—Mary Tayler ; destination, Nevis.—Nathaniell Perks ; destination, Nevis.—Henry Woods ; destination, Nevis.—Mary Atwell ; destination, Nevis.—John Sherwood ; destination, New England.—Elizabeth Creed ; destination, Nevis.—Robert Law ; destination, Nevis.—William Blathern ; destination, Nevis.—Joane Parret ; destination, Nevis.—Alice Hancok ; destination, Nevis.

Page 537
Rebecca James ; destination, Nevis.—Hugh Masters ; destination, Barbadoes.—Robert Crowe ; destination, Barbadoes.—Susan Phillips ; destination, Nevis.—David Beaven ; destination, Nevis.—Mathew Biffard ; destination, Nevis.—Ambbrosse Tayler ; destination, Nevis.—Abraham Royall ; destination, Nevis.—John Everet ; destination, New England.—Thomas Adams ; destination, New England.—Thomas Sturmy ; destination, New England.—Charles Sturmy ; destination, New England.

Page 538
George Norton ; destination, Nevis.—Simple Morees ; destination, Nevis.—Elizabeth Craell ; destination, Nevis.—John Jones ; destination, Nevis.—John Warren ; destination, Nevis.—Robert Yateman ; destination, Nevis.—William Kamson ; destination, Nevis.—John Bricker ; destination, Barbadoes.—John Bennet ; destination, New England.—John Sheapard ; destination, Nevis.—John Briant ; destination, Barbadoes.—William Jones ; destination, New England.

Page 539
ffrancis Olliver ; destination, New England.—Margaret Page ; destination, Nevis.—Ann Page ; destination, Nevis.—John ffreeman ; destination, New England.—Silvanus Davis ; destination, New England.—ffrancis Lightfoot ; destination, Nevis.—John Gorman ; destination, Nevis.—Margaret Morgan ; destination, Barbadoes.—William Gausset ; destination, New England.—William Carraway ; destination, Nevis.—John Carbrash ; destination, Nevis.—Thomas Williams ; destination, Nevis.

Page 540
Sarah Horwood ; destination, Nevis.—ffrancis Richards ; destination, Nevis.—Thomas Jones ; destination, Nevis.—John Barbar ; destination, Nevis.—John Hawker ; destination, Leeward Is.—Ann Reece ; destination, New England.—David Powell ; destination, Nevis.—Richard Tabert ; destination, Nevis.—Edward Leech ; destination, New England.—Richard But ; destination, New England.—Thomas Tayler ; destination, Antigua.—Mary Huffe ; destination, New England.

Page 541
Marrian Nichols ; destination, Nevis.—Allice Dymock ; destination, New England.—John Quarrell ; destination, Nevis.—Thomas Bathum ; destination, Nevis.—Joane Williams ; destination, Antigua.—Hugh Vaughan ; destination,

Nevis.—Henry Young; destination, Barbadoes.—William Brook; destination, Antigua.—Tobias Gregory; destination, Antigua.—Hugh Russy; destination, Montserrat; Dennis Horren; destination, Montserrat.—William Nevis; destination, Nevis.

Page 542
Anne Bates; destination, New England.—Andrew Stepmon; destination, Nevis.—James Baddam; destination, Nevis.—Thomas Baddam; destination, Nevis. —James Bayly; destination, Nevis.—John ffetgard; destination, Nevis.—Ellioner Waite; destination, Antigua.—Allexander Vowles; destination, New England.— Morgan Jones; destination, Nevis.—Jeremiah Clothier; destination, New England. —Richard Cary; destination, New England.—Daniell Chresseham; destination, New England.

Page 543
Jane Grizell; destination, Nevis.—John Williams; destination, Barbadoes.— John Warin; destination, New England.—John Bowen; destination, New England. —John Rudrick; destination, Nevis.—Elizabeth Constable; destination, Nevis.— John Greene; destination, Nevis.—Thomas Jefferis; destination, Nevis.—Henry Evans; destination, Nevis.—John Oburne; destination, Nevis.—John Weeks; destination, Nevis.—John Browne; destination, Nevis.

Page 544
John Hascall; destination, Nevis.—Elizabeth Dibbins; destination, Nevis.— Margery Stone; destination, Nevis.—William Baker; destination, Nevis.—Nicholas Windell; destination, Nevis.—Edward Lowe; destination, Nevis.—Thomas Backster; destination, New England.—Edward Laming; destination, Barbadoes. —Merrian Davis; destination, Barbadoes.—Katherine Juks; destination, Nevis.— George Tirwhitt; destination, Nevis.—William Pew; destination, Nevis.

Page 545
William Andrews; destination, Nevis.—Thomas Chilcott; destination, Nevis. —Michaell Crosly; destination, Nevis.—John Sampson; destination, Nevis.— John Challoner; destination, Nevis.—Katherine Clark; destination, Nevis.— Nicholas ffrost; destination, New England.

END OF BOOK I

Servants to Foreign Plantations

VOL. II, 1663-79

Transcribed by R. Hargreaves-Mawdsley

Page 1
Elizabeth Hoxton ; destination, Nevis.—Edward Parsons ; destination, Nevis. —Walter Higgins ; destination, Nevis.—Edward Butten ; destination, Nevis. —David Powell ; destination, Barbadoes.—Henry Webster ; destination, New England.—Anthony Hulls ; destination, Barbadoes.—Edward Norton ; destination, New England.—William Lees ; destination, Barbadoes.—Thomas Morris ; destination, Barbadoes.—George Crocker ; destination, Barbadoes.

Page 2
Sarah Leveredge ; destination, Barbadoes.—Patrick Taylor ; destination, Barbadoes.—John Cardy ; destination, Barbadoes.—Johannes King ; destination, Barbadoes.—Edward Wallington ; destination, Barbadoes.—Margaret Smith, destination, Barbadoes.—William Haskins ; destination, Barbadoes.—Mary Jefferis ; destination, Nevis.—John Mills ; destination, Barbadoes.—John Murrey ; destination, Nevis.—Thomas Raveing ; destination, Nevis.—William Hodges ; destination, Virginia.

Page 3
John Adlam ; destination, Nevis.—Howell Thomas ; destination, Nevis.— Daniell Puddeford ; destination, Virginia.—Jeremiah Taylor ; destination, Barbadoes.—David Edwards ; destination, Barbadoes.—William Jenkins ; destination, Virginia.—Thomas Edye ; destination, Nevis.—Henry Martin ; destination, Barbadoes.—Humphry Curtis ; destination, Virginia.—Nicholas Evans ; destination, Nevis.—Angell Stephens ; destination, Barbadoes.—Joane Redman ; destination, Barbadoes.

Page 4
Robert ffarmer ; destination, Nevis.—Dorothy ffeild ; destination, Nevis.— Thomas Peate ; destination, Nevis.—Phillip Band ; destination, Virginia.— Robert Pruther ; destination, Nevis.—Richard Davie ; destination, Nevis.—Samuell Harkwood ; destination, Barbadoes.—Elizabeth Davis ; destination, Nevis.—Simon Tiner ; destination, Nevis.—Phillip Johnson ; destination, Nevis.—Joane Lane ; destination, Nevis.—William ffendick ; destination, Nevis.

Page 5
Thomas Taylor ; destination, Virginia.—Robert Davis ; destination, Barbadoes.
—Richard Williams ; destination, Virginia.—John Thomas ; destination, Virginia.
—David Morgan ; destination, Virginia.—William Jinke ; destination, Virginia.—
Arthur Williams ; destination, Barbadoes.—William Harbert ; destination, Virginia.
—Rebeckah Hughes ; destination, Virginia.—Samuell Nowell ; destination, Virginia.
—William Cole ; destination, Virginia.—Robert Lucas ; destination, Virginia.

Page 6
William Pearson ; destination, Virginia.—Andrew Waters ; destination, Virginia.—Mary Wilkins ; destination, Maryland.—Anne Burgesse ; destination, Virginia.—William Sams ; destination, Nevis.—Anne Drew ; destination, Virginia.—John Merreweather ; destination, Nevis.—Walter Williams ; destination, Virginia.—William Briant ; destination, Virginia.—William Merreman ; destination, Virginia.—James Wood ; destination, Virginia.—Jane Clubb ; destination, Virginia.

Page 7
Elizabeth Denton ; destination, Virginia.—Nathaniell ffuller ; destination, Virginia.—Samuell ffuller ; destination, Virginia.—John Price ; destination, Virginia.—William Paniwell ; destination, Virginia.—Richard Davis ; destination, Barbadoes.—Katherine How ; destination, Virginia.—Joseph Tilly ; destination, Virginia.—Robert Howell ; destination, Virginia.—Giles Collins ; destination, Virginia.—Thomas Lord ; destination, Virginia.—John Williams ; destination, Virginia.

Page 8
Mary Cooke ; destination, Nevis.—George Makepeace ; destination, Virginia.—Joane Barksteed ; destination, Virginia.—William Roberts ; destination, Virginia.—James Winniard ; destination, Virginia.—William Osborne ; destination, Virginia.—Sarah Perks ; destination, Virginia.—John Luckman ; destination, Virginia.—Nicholas Terret ; destination, Virginia.—Abraham Rumley ; destination, Virginia.—Henry Thomas ; destination, Virginia.—John Wips ; destination, Virginia.

Page 9
Richard Stevens ; destination, Virginia.—Simon Herring ; destination, Virginia.—William Grimes ; destination, Virginia.—ffrances Gunbry ; destination, Virginia.—Richard Berry ; destination, Virginia.—Margaret Bayly ; destination, Virginia.—George Nicholas ; destination, Virginia.—Samuell Hull ; destination, Virginia.—Katherine ffoster ; destination, Virginia.—Elizabeth hill ; destination, Virginia.—Leonard Southern ; destination, Virginia.—William Henbitch ; destination, Virginia.

Page 10
Hopkin Lewis ; destination, Virginia.—Thomas Lloyd ; destination, Virginia.—William Pinnell ; destination, Virginia.—Mary Ellet ; destination, Virginia.—Walter Watkins ; destination, Virginia.—Christopher Johnson ; destination, Virginia.—Thomas Bryan ; destination, Virginia.—Phillip Mason ; destination, Virginia.—Gabriell Parret ; destination, Virginia.—Thomas Wilson ; destination, Virginia.—John Jones ; destination, Virginia.—Robert Sheapard ; destination, Virginia.

Page 11

Margaret Williams ; destination, Virginia.—Abraham Glasier ; destination, Virginia.—Thomas Simons ; destination, Virginia.—Anne Watkins ; destination, Virginia.—John ffranklin ; destination, Virginia.—Anne Brooks ; destination, Virginia.—James Makall ; destination, Virginia.—Robert Liant ; destination, Virginia. —Anne Wyett ; destination, Virginia.—Thomas ffloyd ; destination, Nevis.— Thomas Trottman ; destination, Maryland.—Joseph Williams ; destination, Maryland.

Page 12

Tobias ffowler ; destination, Maryland.—John Richards ; destination, Virginia. —Samuell Hammon ; destination, Virginia.—Thomas Plannt ; destination, Virginia. —Joseph Salter ; destination, Virginia.—David Davis ; destination, Virginia.— John Cooke ; destination, Virginia.—Ambrose Palmer ; destination, Virginia.—Mary Bicks ; destination, Virginia.—Elizabeth Miles ; destination, Virginia.—Peter Edson ; destination, Virginia.—Richard Rogers ; destination, Virginia.

Page 13

William Waters ; destination, Virginia.—John Skinell ; destination, Virginia. —George Russell ; destination, Virginia.—John Jelloy ; destination, Virginia.— Edward James ; destination, Virginia.—William Knight ; destination, Virginia.— Mary Burk ; destination, Virginia.—John Thomas ; destination, Virginia.—Robert Perreman ; destination, Virginia.—William Wheeler ; destination, Virginia.— Michaell Deloge ; destination, Virginia.—Giles Jenings ; destination, Virginia.

Page 14

George Avis ; destination, Virginia.—James Pricklove ; destination, Virginia.— Jane Williams ; destination, Virginia.—William Maddocks ; destination, Virginia. —Edward Edwards ; destination, Virginia.—William Heed ; destination, Virginia. —Mary Smith ; destination, Virginia.—Sarah Hedges ; destination, Virginia.—John Evans ; destination, Virginia.—Margaret Langdon ; destination, Virginia.—Elizabeth Brinnidge ; destination, Virginia.—Walter Morgan ; destination, Virginia.

Page 15

Lewis Cod ; destination, Virginia.—Thomas Jones ; destination, Virginia.— John Ellis ; destination, Virginia.—Robert Lindsay ; destination, Virginia.—Thomas May ; destination, Virginia.—Peter Oately ; destination, Virginia.—Thompson Carter ; destination, Virginia.—William Rise ; destination, Virginia.—ffrancis Stetchold ; destination, Barbadoes.—Peter Long ; destination, Virginia.—William Sandiford ; destination, Virginia.—Phillip Coop ; destination, Virginia.

Page 16

John Vizard ; destination, Virginia.—John Sheapard ; destination, Virginia.— Elias Edwards ; destination, Virginia.—Edward Harris ; destination, Virginia.— ffilotheus Bowen ; destination, Virginia.—Roger Bowen ; destination, Virginia. —William Dudlett ; destination, Virginia.—William Berry ; destination, Virginia.— John Cooke ; destination, Virginia.—John Price ; destination, Virginia.—William Williams ; destination, Virginia.

Page 17

Anne Brumadge ; destination, Virginia.—John Kendall ; destination, Virginia. —John Jones ; destination, Virginia.—Thomas Elliott ; destination, Virginia.— John Alward ; destination, Virginia.—Thomas Morgan ; destination, Virginia.— Joseph Rich ; destination, Virginia.—Richard Rock ; destination, Virginia.—Thomas Jones ; destination, Virginia.—Thomas Burton ; destination, St. Christopher.— Elizabeth Morgan ; destination, Barbadoes.—Thomas Starte ; destination, Virginia.

Page 18

Jasper Gransome ; destination, Virginia.—Mathew Harrison ; destination, Virginia.—John Cooke ; destination, Barbadoes.—William Miles ; destination, Barbadoes.—Jonathan Tayler ; destination, Barbadoes.—Thomas Roberts ; destination, Virginia.—Lodowick Williams ; destination, St. Christopher.—Thomas James ; destination, St. Christopher.—Thomas George ; destination, St. Christopher.— Nicholas Clement ; destination, St. Christopher.—Thomas Williams ; destination, St. Christopher.—Jane Thomas ; destination, St. Christopher.

Page 19

John Pynon ; destination, St. Christopher.—William Sparkes ; destination, Barbadoes.—Ursula Hall ; destination, St. Christopher.—John ffisher ; destination, Barbadoes.—Marthah Trayden ; destination, Virginia.—ffrith Lyddall ; destination, Virginia.—Thomas Barrow ; destination, Virginia.—Giles Underwood ; destination, Virginia.—Mary Jones ; destination, Virginia.—James Jones ; destination, Virginia.—Hester Bennet ; destination, Virginia.—Jinkin Bowen ; destination, St. Christopher.

Page 20

Katherine Williams ; destination, St. Christopher.—George Poppin ; destination, Barbadoes.—John Powell ; destination, Nevis.—William Rosser ; destination, Nevis.—Edward Wilmot ; destination, Nevis.—Elizabeth Holmes ; destination, Nevis.—George ffryzzan ; destination, Barbadoes.—Mary Jones ; destination, Barbadoes.—Samuel [blank] ; destination, Barbadoes.—Christopher Kirke ; destination, Barbadoes.—Mary Vaughan ; destination, Barbadoes.--Richard Cole ; destination, Barbadoes.

Page 21

Josias Emmett ; destination, Barbadoes.—Evan Thomas ; destination, Barbadoes.—Thomas Cox ; destination, Barbadoes.—Katherine Jones ; destination, Barbadoes.—John Thomas ; destination, Barbadoes.—Thomas Pritchard ; destination, Barbadoes.—Joane Evans ; destination (no place given).—Cicely Pritchard ; destination, Barbadoes.—Mary Lewes ; destination, Barbadoes.—Jennet Lewes ; destination, Barbadoes.—Anne Lewis ; destination, Barbadoes.—Elizabeth Shereman ; destination, Barbadoes.

Page 22

Robert Smith ; destination, Barbadoes.—Jane Tanner ; destination, Barbadoes. —John Cox (of Aimsbury) ; destination, Nevis.—Owen Richards ; destination, Barbadoes.—James Webb ; destination, Barbadoes.—William Knight ; destination, Barbadoes.—William Griffeth ; destination, Barbadoes.—Maudlin Davis ; destination, Barbadoes.—Henery Williams; destination, Nevis.—Thomas Say; destination, New England.—Ann Wattkins; destination, Nevis.—John Higgs; destination (no place given).

Page 23
  Thomas Phillips; destination, Nevis.—Anthoney Holley; destination, Barbadoes.—Blanch Price; destination, Barbadoes.—John Collins; destination, Barbadoes.—William Martin; destination, Barbadoes.—Katherin Symonds; destination, Barbadoes.—Lewis Loyd; destination, Nevis.—ffrancis Hughes; destination, Nevis.—John ffranklin; destination, Barbadoes.—Ann Gould; destination, —Edward Turford; destination, Barbadoes.—Eadogan Jones; destination, Antigua.

Page 24
  Phillip Thomas; destination, Antigua.—Thomas Jones; destination, Antigua. —Christopher Andrewes; destination, Antigua.—Waltar Thomas; destination, Antigua.—James Dicknell; destination, Nevis.—John Provender; destination, New England.—John Wattkins; destination, Barbadoes.—Rowland Davice; destination, Barbadoes.—Martha Waltar; destination, Barbadoes.—Michaell Symkins; destination, New England.—Peter Williams; destination, Antigua.—Roger Apply; destination, Antigua.

Page 25
  Mary Jones; destination, Antigua.—Elianor Lacy; destination, New England. —John Moreton; destination, New England.—Nathaniell Thorneborough; destination, New England.—Mary Caules; destination, Antigua.—Oliver Richards; destination, New England.—Thomas Saunders; destination, Antigua.—Jane Williams; destination, Nevis.—Elizabeth Kedger; destination, Barbadoes.— William Plowman; destination, Barbadoes.—James Lewis; destination, Barbadoes. —William Hill; destination, Nevis.

Page 26
  Thomas Lewis; destination, Barbadoes.—Mathew Phelps; destination, Nevis. —Thomas Vine; destination, Barbadoes.—Robert Miles; destination, Barbadoes.— Thomas Harris; destination, Barbadoes.—William Morgan; destination, Barbadoes.—Marke Giles; destination, New England.—Morris Chamblis; destination, New England.—Elizabeth Hewes; destination, Nevis or Antigua.—Hugh Barnes; destination, New England.—Edmund Davis; destination, Nevis.—John Pitman; destination, New England.

Page 27
  Richard Knight; destination, Barbadoes.—Zacharia Clouter; destination, Barbadoes.—Griffen Morris; destination, Barbadoes.—John Williams; destination, Barbadoes.—Joseph Olford; destination, Barbadoes.—Thomas Trosser; destination, Barbadoes.—ffrancis Bead; destination, Nevis or Caribbees.—John Phillips; destination, Barbadoes or Nevis.—Margaret Brian; destination, Barbadoes.—Edward Jenkins; destination, Barbadoes or Nevis.—Joshua Lamby; destination, Barbadoes or Nevis.—Elizabeth Thomas; destination, Nevis or Leeward.

Page 28
Owen Williams ; destination, Nevis.—Charles Jenkins ; destination, Barbadoes.
—William Burgis ; destination, Barbadoes.—James Guy ; destination, Barbadoes.—
Thomas Riggby ; destination, Nevis.—Joseph Crothwine ; destination, Nevis.
—Thomas Andrewes ; destination, Barbadoes.—Ralph Winn ; destination, Nevis.—
Hugh ffyd ; destination, Nevis.—William Williams ; destination, Barbadoes.—
Eelthian James ; destination, Nevis.—Arthur Bowels ; destination, Barbadoes.
—Anne Lane ; destination, Barbadoes or Caribbees.

Page 29
John Erdeswicke ; destination, Nevis.—Jane Morgan ; destination, Nevis.—
James Parker ; destination, Nevis.—Mary Eves ; destination, Virginia.—Georg
Thomas ; destination, Nevis.—Thomas Radclift ; destination, Barbadoes.—William
ffinnis ; destination, Barbadoes.—Henry Baily ; destination, Barbadoes.—Thomas
Prosly ; destination, Barbadoes.—Edward Clift ; destination, Barbadoes.—Elizabeth
Chune ; destination, Barbadoes.—Edward Williams ; destination, Virginia.

Page 30
John Yeate ; destination, Barbadoes.—Thomas Harper ; destination, Barbadoes.—Joane Stevens ; destination, Barbadoes.—Thomas Browne ; destination,
Barbadoes.—Elizabeth Browne ; destination, Barbadoes.—William Jones ; destination, Virginia.—John Russell ; destination, Virginia.—William Powell ; destination,
Virginia.—Thomas Weston ; destination, Virginia.—William James ; destination, Virginia.—Jonathan Baker ; destination, Virginia.—ffrancis Browne ; destination, Virginia.

Page 31
Julian Leigh ; destination, Virginia.—Welthian Watkins ; destination, Vir-
ginia.—Elinor Phillips ; destination, Virginia.—Margaret Price ; destination, Vir-
ginia.—Anne Clarke ; destination, Virginia.—John Pillsan ; destination, Virginia.
—Grace Wayte ; destination, Virginia.—Christian Davis ; destination, Virginia.—
John Clymer ; destination, Virginia.—Mathew Lewis ; destination, Virginia.—Evan
Lewis ; destination, Virginia.—Henry Baker ; destination, Virginia.

Page 32
Joane Baker ; destination, Virginia.—Jane Cary ; destination, Virginia.—Joane
Cary ; destination, Virginia.—Phillip Sanders ; destination, Virginia.—John
Sanders ; destination, Virginia.—Margaret White ; destination, Virginia.—Joane
Sanders ; destination, Virginia.—Evan Roberts ; destination, Virginia.—Richard
Allen ; destination, Virginia.—James Phillips ; destination, Virginia.—Robert
Evans ; destination, Virginia.—William Davis ; destination, Virginia.

Page 33
Gerrard Warren ; destination, Virginia.—Robert Jones ; destination, Virginia.
—Edward Bastine ; destination, Virginia.—Anne Jenkins ; destination, Barbadoes.—
William Kingsbury ; destination, Virginia.—Humphry Walker ; destination, Vir-
ginia.—Paull Carter ; destination, Virginia.—Robert Blicher ; destination, Nevis.
—Nicholas Raggat ; destination, Nevis.—Teague Lee ; destination, Nevis.—
Thomas Morgan ; destination, Virginia.—Lewis Stephens ; destination, Virginia.

Page 34
Charity Jones ; destination, Virginia.—William Hossam ; destination, Virginia.
—Richard Curtis ; destination, Virginia.—Richard Wildgoose ; destination, Virginia.—John Tayler ; destination, Virginia.—Katherine Semyer ; destination, Virginia.—Mathew Hopwood ; destination, Virginia.—Samuell Jones ; destination, Virginia.—John Darby ; destination, Virginia.—John Johnson ; destination, Virginia.—Mathew Whitfeild ; destination, Virginia.—John Lovell ; destination, Virginia.

Page 35
John Evans ; destination, Virginia.—Thomas Still ; destination, Virginia.—John Cox ; destination, Virginia.—William James ; destination, Virginia.—Edward Sapp ; destination, Virginia.—Henry Price ; destination, Virginia.—Elioner Davis ; destination, Virginia.—Ruth Barrat ; destination, Virginia.—Mary Walker ; destination, Virginia.—John Addams ; destination, Virginia.—John Clarke ; destination, Virginia.

Page 36
William Roberts ; destination, Virginia.—Jane Bowen ; destination, Virginia.—Thomas Preist ; destination, Virginia.—William Wattkins ; destination, Virginia.—William Burdack ; destination, Virginia.—Richard Beate ; destination, Virginia.—Thomas Lewellen ; destination, Virginia.—Jane Dallen ; destination, Virginia.—Edward Harding ; destination, Virginia.—Grace Banner ; destination, Virginia.—Mary Banner ; destination, Virginia.

Page 37
John Williams ; destination, Virginia.—John Carter ; destination, Virginia.—John Whitten ; destination, Virginia.—James Phillips ; destination, Virginia.—Richard Avery ; destination, Virginia.—John Parsons ; destination, Virginia.—Gilbert Lewis ; destination, Virginia.—Edward Hollister ; destination, Virginia.—John Berrow ; destination, Virginia.—Richard Taylor ; destination, Virginia.—Joane Tower ; destination, Virginia.—Mary Lambert ; destination, Virginia.

Page 38
Edmund Tony ; destination, Virginia.—Peter Tony ; destination, Virginia.—Elizabeth Powell ; destination, Virginia.—Margaret Jones ; destination, Virginia.—Ambrose Lloyd ; destination, Virginia.—John Willkins ; destination, Virginia.—John Roberts ; destination, Virginia.—William Perryman ; destination, Nevis.—Mary Phillips ; destination, Virginia.—John Jusale ; destination, Virginia.—Margaret Haines ; destination, Virginia.—Jonathan Phillips ; destination, Nevis.

Page 39
William Harford ; destination, Virginia.—Nathaniell Mathews ; destination, Nevis.—William Smarte ; destination, Virginia.—John Hawkins ; destination, Virginia.—Thomas Hemens ; destination, Virginia.—Elizabeth Merrick ; destination, Virginia.—Elizabeth Protheroe ; destination, Virginia.—John Phillips ; destination, Virginia.—John ffoard ; destination, Virginia.—John Harle ; destination, Virginia.—John Gurlen ; destination, Nevis or Leeward Is.—Symon Warland ; destination, Nevis.

Page 40

William Halliman ; destination, Nevis.—Joane Burt ; destination, Virginia. —Lidiah Silvester ; destination, Virginia.—Bartholomew Romayne ; destination, Nevis.—Mary Latt ; destination, Barbadoes.—John Ames ; destination, Virginia. —Elioner Pearce ; destination, Barbadoes.—James Smith ; destination, Virginia.— John Moore ; destination, Virginia.—John Downe ; destination, Virginia.— Prudence Westbury ; destination, Virginia.—Elizabeth Lewis ; destination, Virginia.

Page 41

Saye Thomas ; destination, Virginia.—Sarah Cheltnam ; destination, Virginia. —Richard Williams ; destination, Virginia.—Robert Chew ; destination, Virginia.— Sarah Dawlas ; destination, Virginia.—James Stampe ; destination, Virginia.— Joane Pitts ; destination, Virginia.—Elizabeth Cullot ; destination, Barbadoes. —George Borse ; destination, Nevis.—William Evans ; destination, Nevis.— William Reece ; destination, Nevis.—David Davis ; destination, Barbadoes.

Page 42

William Harvey ; destination, Nevis.—Samuell Kellsar ; destination, Barbadoes. —John Rae ; destination, Nevis or Caribbees.—Rothero Price ; destination, Barbadoes.—Joseph Paine ; destination, Nevis.—Morgan Williams ; destination, Nevis. —Thomas Speede ; destination, Barbadoes.—Phillip Dawle ; destination, Nevis.— Thomas Morgan ; destination, Nevis.—William Brooke ; destination Nevis.— Thomas Williams ; destination, Nevis.—David Gaines ; destination, Nevis.

Page 43

Edward Pounty ; destination, Barbadoes.—Edmund Thomas ; destination, Barbadoes.—John Parker ; destination, Barbadoes.—John Jones ; destination, Nevis. —William Pullen ; destination, Barbadoes.—Susanna Sawfutt ; destination, Nevis. —Susanna Jones ; destination, Nevis.—Robert Arter ; destination, Nevis.— Mathew Wall ; destination, Nevis.—William Harbett ; destination, Nevis.— Thomas Turner ; destination, Nevis.—Peter Launte ; destination, Nevis.

Page 44

Thomas Dave ; destination, Nevis.—Richard Anderson ; destination, Barbadoes.—David Price ; destination, Nevis.—Evan Rowland ; destination, Nevis.— Mary Russell ; destination, Nevis.—William Tompkins ; destination, Nevis.—Henry Leafe ; destination, Nevis.—John Edwards ; destination, Nevis.—Richard Dauty ; destination, Nevis.—William Sommers ; destination, Nevis.—John Roach ; destination, New England.—Thomas Jones ; destination, Barbadoes.

Page 45

Joane Woollams ; destination, Barbadoes.—Humphry Clifford ; destination, Nevis.—William Davis ; destination, Nevis.—John Inion ; destination, Virginia.— Walter Ciclett ; destination, Virginia.—William Waters ; destination, Virginia.— John Coales ; destination, Virginia.—Walter Harris ; destination, Virginia.—John Creede ; destination, Virginia.—Richard Tracy ; destination, Virginia.—Henry Lewis ; destination, Virginia.—Anne Bassett ; destination, Virginia.

Page 46

Henry Rogers; destination, Virginia.—Robert Brookbanke; destination, Virginia.—John Signett; destination, Virginia.—Richard ffryer; destination, Virginia.—Sarah Smith; destination, Virginia.—Elias Loe; destination, Virginia. —William Russell; destination, Virginia.—Elizabeth Harris; destination, Virginia. —Walter Crow; destination, Virginia.—Thomas Mudd; destination, Virginia.— John Hotter; destination, Virginia.—Hartrude Madler; destination, Virginia.— James Elvard; destination, Virginia.

Page 47

Richard Pew; destination, Virginia.—Robert Holderly; destination, Virginia. —Mary Johnson; destination, Virginia.—John Jenkins; destination, Virginia.— Ursula Palmer; destination, Virginia.—Elizabeth Streete; destination, Virginia. —William Richards; destination, Virginia.—Richard Hatchnutt; destination, Virginia.—Richard Sadler; destination, Virginia.—Nicholas Martin; destination, Virginia.—Christopher Slattford; destination, Virginia.—Margaret Lewis; destination, Virginia.

Page 48

Thomas Pinson; destination, Virginia.—John Hobson; destination, Virginia. —Mary Thomas; destination, Virginia.—Margaret Turner; destination, Virginia. —Joane Jenings; destination, Virginia.—Phillip Clay; destination, Virginia.— Thomas Osburne; destination, Virginia.—Edward Dangerfeild; destination, Maryland.—Morgan Thomas; destination, Virginia.—Thomas Williams; destination, Virginia.—Phillip Thomas; destination, Virginia.—James Monck; destination, Virginia.

Page 49

John Jones; destination, Virginia.—Elizabeth Baily; destination, Virginia.— Richard Smith; destination, Virginia.—Henry Lane; destination, Virginia.— Rebecka Robins; destination, Virginia.—William Willis; destination, Virginia. —Thomas Edwards; destination, Virginia.—Phillip Payton; destination, Virginia. —Richard Smith; destination, Virginia.—Mary Tayler; destination, Virginia.— Anne Smith; destination, Virginia.

Page 50

Phillip Browne; destination, Virginia.—Anne Ernell; destination, Virginia. —Richard Jenkins; destination, Virginia.—Joseph Williams; destination, Virginia. —Rowland Willson; destination, Virginia.—Margaret Morris; destination, Virginia.—Samuell Elliott; destination, Virginia.—Job Upton; destination, Virginia. —Timothy Rogers; destination, Virginia.—Avis Row; destination, Virginia.— Lewis Davis; destination, Virginia.—Jane Powell; destination, Virginia.—John Thomas; destination, Virginia.

Page 51

John Hiley; destination, Virginia.—William ffowle; destination, Virginia.— Benjamin Morratt; destination, Virginia.—Leonard Wray; destination, Virginia. —Rebecka Wray; destination, Virginia.—Elizabeth Beard; destination, Virginia. —Thomas Buttler; destination, Virginia.—John Grafton; destination, Virginia.— John Price; destination, Virginia.—John Viner; destination, Virginia.—Elizabeth Evans; destination, Virginia.—Richard Walling; destination, Virginia.

Page 52

Anne Crasway ; destination, Virginia.—Richard Godfrey ; destination, Virginia.
—Nicholas Houlder ; destination, Virginia.—Elizabeth Jones ; destination, Virginia.
—Mary Kempe ; destination, Virginia.—Aron Powell ; destination, Virginia.—
Edward Bowen ; destination, Virginia.—Henry Knapp ; destination, Virginia.—
Mary Lane ; destination, Virginia.—Robert Curtis ; destination, Virginia.—George
Lewis ; destination, Virginia.—John Alford ; destination, Virginia.

Page 53

Charity Love ; destination ; Virginia.—Thomas Dale ; destination, Virginia.
—John Layns ; destination, Virginia.—John Gill ; destination, Virginia.—Joane
Young ; destination, Virginia.—Sarah Griffen ; destination, Virginia.—Peter
Morgan ; destination, Virginia.—Morgan Thomas ; destination, Virginia.—Thomas
Wadly ; destination, Virginia.—John Player ; destination, Virginia.—William
Lansdowne ; destination, Virginia.—John Lumpe ; destination, Virginia.

Page 54

Richard Davis ; destination, Virginia.—Thomas Williams ; destination, Virginia.
—Elizabeth Hale ; destination, Virginia.—Sarah Horrad ; destination, Virginia.—
John Bullgam ; destination, Virginia.—Benjamin Bramsgrove ; destination, Virginia.
—Anne Pearce ; destination, Virginia.—Susanna Hull ; destination, Virginia.—
David Jones ; destination, Virginia.—Thomas Wales ; destination, Virginia.—
William Jocklin ; destination, Virginia.—John Close ; destination, Virginia.

Page 55

Giles Wilkins ; destination, Virginia.—John Richards ; destination, Virginia.
—Thomas Roach ; destination, Virginia.—William Winbury ; destination, Virginia.
—Mathew Shellam ; destination, Virginia.—Samuell Gardner ; destination, Vir-
ginia.—Christopher Cary ; destination, Virginia.—Gabriell Trusty ; destination,
Virginia.—William Greene ; destination, Virginia.—Phillip Williams ; destination,
Virginia.—John Larcume ; destination, Virginia.—Robert Stone ; destination,
Virginia.

Page 56

John Tether ; destination, Virginia.—Edward Garnesy ; destination, Virginia.
—Sarah Marsfeild ; destination, Virginia.—Nathaniell Tovey ; destination, Virginia.
—Abraham Pullen ; destination, Virginia.—Anne Stork ; destination, Virginia.—
Robert Love ; destination, Virginia.—Richard Travis ; destination, Virginia.—
Margaret Davis ; destination, Virginia.—Samuell Baker ; destination, Virginia.
—James Coles ; destination, Virginia.—Elizabeth Wood ; destination, Virginia.

Page 57

James Edwards ; destination, Virginia.—Elizabeth Young ; destination, Vir-
ginia.—Sarah Parker ; destination, Virginia.—John Mayo ; destination, Virginia.—
Roger Miles ; destination, Virginia.—Thomas Buttler ; destination, Virginia.
—William Marshall ; destination, Virginia.—John Ward ; destination, Virginia.—
Robert Marshall ; destination, Virginia.—Edward Collins ; destination, Virginia.—
John ffrances ; destination, Virginia.—Lettice Powell ; destination, Virginia.

Page 58

Sibbell Higg; destination, Virginia.—Margery Dee; destination, Virginia.—Elizabeth Linard; destination, Virginia.—Anne Steevens; destination, Virginia.—John Chares; destination, Virginia.—Margery Wathen; destination, Virginia.—John Stevens; destination, Virginia.—Richard Steevens; destination, Virginia.—Mary Tayler; destination, Virginia.—Elizabeth Emblin; destination, Virginia.—Susanna Bick; destination, Virginia.—Joane Tower; destination, Virginia.

Page 59

John Gamerell; destination, Virginia.—William Nock; destination, Virginia.—Richard Chambers; destination, Virginia.—William Webb; destination, Virginia.—George White; destination, Virginia.—Elizabeth Tayler; destination, Virginia.—William Raberson; destination, Virginia.—Nicholas Edwards; destination, Barbadoes.—William Cunnaut; destination, Barbadoes.—Robert Toms; destination, Barbadoes.—Elizabeth Nock; destination, Virginia.—Thomas Arrowsmith; destination, Virginia.

Page 60

Thomas Jones; destination, Nevis.—Walter Preece; destination, Virginia.—John Davis; destination, Virginia.—Mary Welch; destination, Virginia.—William Skidmore; destination, Virginia.—William Woodcock; destination, Virginia.—John Bennett; destination, Virginia.—Phillip Pardoe; destination, Virginia.—Thomas Edwards; destination, Virginia.—Alice Norrinuton; destination, Virginia.—John Licky; destination, Barbadoes.—Margaret Griffen; destination, Barbadoes.

Page 61

David Hayce; destination, Barbadoes.—Robert Jones; destination, Virginia.—William Summerhill; destination, Virginia.—John Nicholls; destination, Virginia.—William West; destination, Virginia.—Richard Renn; destination, Virginia.—Joseph Gutheridge; destination, Nevis.—Robert Arthur; destination, Virginia.—Anne Godwin; destination, Virginia.—Thomas Handey; destination, Virginia.—David Jones; destination, Virginia.—Jonah Newman; destination, Virginia.

Page 62

Rowland Vaughan; destination, Virginia.—Edith Window; destination, Virginia.—John Pearce; destination, Virginia.—Katherine Gwillam; destination, Virginia.—John Bullock; destination, Virginia.—ffrancis Rennalls; destination, Virginia.—Robert Kew; destination, Virginia.—Richard Parker; destination, Virginia.—ffrancis Underhill; destination, Virginia.—Constant Underhill; destination, Virginia.—John Ashbey; destination, Barbadoes.

Page 63

Anne Hitchens; destination, Virginia.—John Bick; destination, Maryland.—Walter Gorway; destination, Virginia.—Griffen Morgan; destination, Virginia.—John Hill; destination, Virginia.—Thomas Horton; destination, Virginia.—John Attkins; destination, Virginia.—Samuell England; destination, Virginia.—Richard Baker; destination, Virginia.—ffrancis Creswick; destination, Nevis.—Elizabeth Millsum; destination, Virginia.—John Thomas; destination, Virginia.

I

Page 64

Mary Mare ; destination, Virginia.—Mary Robins ; destination, Virginia.— Walter Griffen ; destination, Virginia.—Joane Babbett ; destination, Virginia.— Robert Hooper ; destination, Virginia.—Margaret Hooper ; destination, Virginia. —Pearce Scrivill ; destination, Virginia.—William Belcher ; destination, Virginia. —Daniell Bishop ; destination, Virginia.—Honnor Rugg ; destination, Virginia.— George Hill ; destination, Virginia.—Margery Davis ; destination, Virginia.

Page 65

George Courtney ; destination, Virginia.—Reece Morgan ; destination, Virginia.—Ratchell Morgan ; destination, Virginia.—William Jefferis ; destination, Nevis.—John ffisher ; destination, Virginia.—John Billat ; destination, Virginia.— Thomas Billat ; destination, Virginia.—Thomas Beard ; destination, Virginia. —Martha Addams ; destination, Virginia.—Thomas Wilkins ; destination, Virginia.—William Ward ; destination, Barbadoes.—Sibbell Arnold ; destination, Virginia.

Page 66

Moses Pearce ; destination, St. Christopher.—Tobias Greene ; destination, St. Christopher.—William Elmes ; destination, St. Christopher.—Thomas Browne ; destination, St. Christopher.—Thomas Huntly ; destination, St. Christopher.— Thomas Pinnall ; destination, St. Christopher.—John Tanner ; destination, St. Christopher.—John Sly ; destination, Barbadoes.—Cornelius Asson ; destination, Barbadoes.—Richard Barly ; destination, Virginia.—Mary Badmington ; destination, Barbadoes.—Daniell Venton ; destination, Virginia.

Page 67

Thomas Venton ; destination, Virginia.—Mary Pindar ; destination, St. Christopher.—Elizabeth Shewell ; destination, St. Christopher.—Susanna Chandler ; destination, St. Christopher.—Richard Thorne ; destination, Barbadoes.—Nicholas Branch ; destination, Jamaica.—Thomas Horsecreste ; destination, Barbadoes.— Jarome Vyerman ; destination, Virginia.—Peter Mager ; destination, Virginia. —John Mallet ; destination, Barbadoes.—Mary Wilson ; destination, Barbadoes.— Thomas Bradburne ; destination, Virginia.

Page 68

John Whusden ; destination, Nevis.—John Woolley ; destination, Nevis.— William Evans ; destination, Nevis.—Phillip Davis ; destination, Barbadoes.— William Norgate ; destination, Barbadoes.—John Angell ; destination, Nevis. —William Sallman ; destination, Nevis.—George Harris ; destination, Nevis.— Edward Clutterbuck ; destination, Barbadoes.—William Grindall ; destination, Barbadoes.—William Baison ; destination, Barbadoes.—John Cecill ; destination, Barbadoes.

Page 69

John Peepe ; destination, Barbadoes.—ffrancis Jelford ; destination, Barbadoes.—Bridget Bowen ; destination, Barbadoes.—William Gay ; destination, Barbadoes.—Mary Clothier ; destination, Barbadoes.—Thomas Chillcutt ; destination, Barbadoes.—Henery Harvey ; destination, Barbadoes.—George Whiteing ;

destination, Barbadoes.—John Cainton; destination, Barbadoes.—William Buck; destination, Barbadoes.—Timothy Paradice; destination, Barbadoes.—William Phelps; destination, Barbadoes.

Page 70
    Thomas Brucy; destination, Barbadoes.—Welthian Dave; destination, Barbadoes.—Edward Jones; destination, Barbadoes.—Richard Banfeild; destination, Barbadoes.—David Peacock; destination, Barbadoes.—Stephen Cornelius; destination, Barbadoes.—John Slade; destination, Barbadoes.—Edward Jones; destination, Barbadoes.—Hugh Mills; destination, Barbadoes.—John Woory; destination, Barbadoes.—John Sheppard; destination, Barbadoes.—Thomas Bull; destination, Barbadoes.

Page 71
    William ffreke; destination, Barbadoes.—John Lamble; destination, Barbadoes.—John Bennett; destination, Barbadoes.—Thomas Evans; destination, Barbadoes.—Mary Hellier; destination, Barbadoes.—William Lawford; destination, Barbadoes.—Margaret Pride; destination, Barbadoes.—Joane Williams; destination, Barbadoes.—Margaret Caffin; destination, Barbadoes.—Richard Brooke; destination, Barbadoes.—Katherine Pow; destination, Barbadoes.— Joane Hopkins; destination, Barbadoes.

Page 72
    ffrancis Swan; destination, Barbadoes.—Henery Bodenar; destination, Barbadoes.—James Lane; destination, Barbadoes.—Thomas Grangely; destination, Barbadoes.—Rebecka Lewis; destination, Barbadoes.—Thomas Jones; destination, New England.—William Jones; destination, Barbadoes.—William Pallmer; destination, Barbadoes.—Thomas Low; destination, Barbadoes.—Jane Cooper; destination, Barbadoes.—George Cooper; destination, Barbadoes.—David Davis; destination, Virginia.

Page 73
    John George; destination, Virginia.—ffrancis Williams; destination, Virginia. —Humphry Thomas; destination, Nevis.—William Littlepage; destination, Virginia.—Henery Sparks; destination, New England.—Henery Swayne; destination, New England.—Christopher Watts; destination, Virginia.—George Lewis; destination, Virginia; William Charleton; destination, Virginia.—Reece ffloyd; destination, Virginia.—William Bale; destination, Virginia.—James Lewis; destination, Virginia.

Page 74
    Mary Manning; destination, Virginia.—William Taylor; destination, Virginia. —John Goldney; destination, Virginia.—Joseph Goldney; destination, Virginia.— Mathew Gubden; destination, Barbadoes or Caribbees.—James Ellis; destination, Virginia.—Katherine Gilbert; destination, Virginia.—John Stone; destination, Virginia.—Sarah Hunt; destination, Virginia.—Richard Cuzens; destination, Virginia.—Christopher Wedge; destination, Virginia.—William Crew; destination, Virginia.

Page 75

Alice Chock; destination, Virginia.—Thomas Wille; destination, Virginia.—William Wille; destination, Virginia.—John Spiller; destination, Maryland.—John Millard; destination, Virginia.—Jacob Gilby; destination, Virginia.—Thomas Ward; destination, Virginia.—Sarah Nethey; destination, Virginia.—William Taylor; destination, Virginia.—William Gandy; destination, Virginia.—John Rawlins; destination, Maryland.—Anthony Rawlins; destination, Maryland.

Page 76

Richard Rawlins; destination, Maryland.—Alice Smith; destination, Barbadoes.—Elizabeth Russle; destination, Virginia.—Ann Churchman; destination, Virginia.—William Bishop, destination, Virginia.—Daniell Dory; destination, Barbadoes.—John Parker; destination, Virginia.—Thomas Baker; destination, Virginia.—Richard Wood; destination, Virginia.—Margaret Williams; destination, Barbadoes.—Thomas Wattkins; destination, Virginia.—Anne Buttler; destination, Virginia.

Page 77

John Barber; destination, Virginia.—Richard Arnsley; destination, Virginia.—Edward Thorneton; destination, Virginia.—Benjamin Caple; destination, Virginia.—John Holwey; destination, Virginia.—Samuell Good; destination, Virginia.—William Bishop; destination, Virginia.—Jonathan Granger; destination, Virginia.—George Granger; destination, Virginia.—John Anthony; destination, Virginia.—Lewis Williams; destination, Virginia.—Elioner Lloyd; destination, Virginia.

Page 78

Charles Phillips; destination, Virginia.—Thomas Glamen; destination, Barbadoes.—Ambrose Lamfere; destination, Virginia.—Mary Perren; destination, Virginia.—Thomas John; destination, Virginia.—Phillip Wornall; destination, Virginia.—Henery Woodland; destination, Virginia.—John King; destination, Virginia.—John Minor; destination, Virginia.—Jane Walker; destination, Virginia.—Joane King; destination, Virginia.—Thomas Barnes; destination, Barbadoes.

Page 79

John Haynes; destination, Barbadoes.—John Ball; destination, Barbadoes.—Rendall Brown; destination, Virginia.—Henery Williams; destination, Virginia.—Welthian Jones; destination, Virginia.—Edward Boylen; destination, Virginia.—Giles Hicks; destination, Virginia.—Thomas Darby; destination, Virginia.—William Betty; destination, Virginia.—James Middleton; destination, Barbadoes.—William Davey; destination, Virginia.—Jacobs (*sic*) Board; destination, Virginia.

Page 80

Thomas Hill; destination, Virginia.—Anne Manning; destination, Virginia.—Samuell Dryer; destination, Virginia.—Charles Rawlins; destination, Virginia.—William Pethicourte; destination, Virginia.—Justian Brankenwell; destination, Virginia.—Elizabeth New; destination, Virginia.—John ffrances; destination, Virginia.—John Burte; destination, Barbadoes.—John Griffen; destination, Virginia.—William Carter; destination, Virginia.—Phillis Chapple; destination, Virginia.

Page 81

Anne ffoard ; destination, Virginia.—Alice Arnold ; destination, Virginia.—John Spracklen ; destination, Virginia.—William ffloyd ; destination, Virginia.—John Greene ; destination, Virginia.—Nicholas Newman ; destination, Virginia.—William Ball ; destination, Barbadoes.—Giles ffoard ; destination, Barbadoes.—John Hicks ; destination, Virginia.—John Collins ; destination, Virginia.—John Vizard ; destination, Virginia.—Martha Vizard ; destination, Virginia.

Page 82

Samuell Abbotts ; destination, Virginia.—Samuell Pearce ; destination, Virginia.—Jonas Rouse ; destination, Virginia.—William Copper ; destination, Virginia.—Robert Thomas ; destination, Virginia.—Thomas Paine ; destination, Virginia.—Joseph Gillrocks ; destination, Virginia.—Andrew ffeltam ; destination, Virginia.—Griffin Morris ; destination, Virginia.—Thomas Arrendon ; destination, Virginia.—Hopkin Williams ; destination, Virginia.—John Williams ; destination, Virginia.

Page 83

Gyles Sydall ; destination, Virginia.—Mary Burrow ; destination, Virginia.—Nicholas Sessum ; destination, Virginia.—Thomas Waller ; destination, Virginia.—Henery Reynolds ; destination, Virginia.—Elizabeth Hicks ; destination, Virginia.—William Ballome ; destination, Virginia.—Gregory Perne ; destination, Virginia.—Thomas Jones ; destination, Virginia.—Arthur Marsh ; destination, Virginia.—John Burris ; destination, Virginia.—John Davis ; destination, Virginia.

Page 84

William Whistons ; destination, Virginia.—John Tomsey ; destination, Barbadoes.—Athanatius Giles ; destination, Virginia.—John Moore ; destination, Virginia.—John Williams ; destination, Virginia.—Elizabeth Conway ; destination, Virginia.—Mary Millsom ; destination, Virginia.—Elizabeth Bushell ; destination, Virginia.—Anne Woodward ; destination, Virginia.—Elizabeth Tucker ; destination, Virginia.—Richard Tucker ; destination, Virginia.—William Tompkins ; destination, Virginia.

Page 85

Thomas Roberts ; destination, Virginia.—Stephen Porter ; destination, Virginia.—Martin Kelly ; destination, Virginia.—Christopher Iles ; destination, Virginia.—John Phillips ; destination, Virginia.—John Habberfeild ; destination, Virginia.—William Martin ; destination, Virginia.—John Tratt ; destination, Virginia.—John Brooks ; destination, Virginia.—Arthur Starte ; destination, Virginia.—Thomas Leage ; destination, Virginia.—Pasco Bellico ; destination, Virginia.

Page 86

Richard Harte ; destination, Virginia.—Anne Jaker ; destination, Virginia.—John Witherly ; destination, Virginia.—Samuell Price ; destination, Virginia.—John Davis ; destination, Virginia.—Richard Gardner ; destination, Virginia.—Edward Gardner ; destination, Virginia.—Thomasin Saull ; destination, Virginia.—Anne ffluice ; destination, Virginia.—James Dave ; destination, Virginia.—John Hargesse ; destination, Virginia.—Bodman Phillips ; destination, Virginia.

Page 87

John Collins ; destination, Virginia.—John Read ; destination, Virginia.—Anne Legge ; destination, Virginia.—Elizabeth Mathen ; destination, Virginia.—James Jones ; destination, Virginia.—James Millford ; destination, Virginia.—Robert Evans ; destination, Virginia.—Ellis Jones ; destination, Virginia.—William Baker ; destination, Virginia.—John Avery ; destination, Virginia.—Rebecka Lovelace ; destination, Virginia.—Grace Darby ; destination, Virginia.

Page 88

Henry Aspray ; destination, Virginia.—John Wetner ; destination, Virginia.—John Winston ; destination, Virginia.—John Stone ; destination, Virginia.—Elizabeth Granger ; destination, Virginia.—Elizabeth Clubb ; destination, Virginia.—Jane Horrard ; destination, Virginia.—Mary Bishop ; destination, Virginia.—Thomasin Harte ; destination, Virginia.—Ambrose Carter ; destination, Virginia.—Pervies Sutten ; destination, Virginia.—Joane Williams ; destination, Virginia.

Page 89

Andrew Attkins ; destination, Virginia.—John Evans ; destination, Virginia.—Elizabeth Evans ; destination, Virginia.—Thomas Rowland ; destination, Virginia.—Robert Willis ; destination, Virginia.—Thomas Chatle ; destination, Virginia.—Jonathan Smadly ; destination, Virginia.—Richard Jelkes ; destination, Virginia.—Richard Bennett ; destination, Virginia.—Margaret Roberts ; destination, Virginia.—William Morgan ; destination, Virginia.—William Daniell ; destination, Virginia.

Page 90

John Strugen ; destination, Virginia.—Mary Turner ; destination, Virginia.—Richard Rodburne ; destination, Virginia.—Abigall Sellwood ; destination, Virginia.—Elizabeth Manly ; destination, Virginia.—Mary Fles ; destination, Virginia.—John Wilcocks ; destination, Virginia.—Robert Boyce ; destination, Virginia.—Phillip Everard ; destination, Virginia.—John Arnell ; destination, Virginia.—Anthony Arnell ; destination, Virginia.—Mary Arnell ; destination, Virginia.

Page 91

Elizabeth Jacquis ; destination, Virginia.—Alice West ; destination, Virginia.—Joane West ; destination, Virginia.—Joane Sloper ; destination, Virginia.—Anne Holwey ; destination, Virginia.—Henry Perry ; destination, Virginia.—William Harbett ; destination, Virginia.—William Williams ; destination, Virginia.—Robert Cocks ; destination, Virginia.—George Hort ; destination, Virginia.—Elizabeth Lee ; destination, Virginia.—Richard Sheard ; destination, Virginia.

Page 92

Jane Merewether ; destination, Virginia.—Gabriell Granwell ; destination, Virginia.—Cornelius Lyons ; destination, Virginia.—Maudlin ffluellen ; destination, Virginia.—Nicholas Lucas ; destination, Virginia.—Richard Gay ; destination, Virginia.—Joyce Warren ; destination, Virginia.—Lidiah Roberts ; destination, Virginia.—William Bacon ; destination, Virginia.—Grace Stone ; destination, Virginia.—Richard Long ; destination, Virginia.—John Richards ; destination, Virginia.

Page 93

Elizabeth Cullimore ; destination, Virginia.—Mary Jones ; destination, Virginia.—William Diddall ; destination, Virginia.—Thomas Adams ; destination, Virginia.—James Hayward ; destination, Barbadoes.—Nathaniell Burtonwood ; destination, Virginia.—Sarah Warner ; destination, Virginia.—Nicholas Sheppard ; destination, Virginia.—Thomasin Rosewell ; destination, Virginia.—John Serjeant ; destination, Barbadoes.—Thomas ffowler ; destination, Barbadoes.—John Mills ; destination, Virginia.

Page 94

ffrancis Kellowhill ; destination, Virginia.—Thomas Rogers ; destination, Virginia.—Judith Jackson ; destination, Virginia.—Elizabeth Jackson ; destination, Virginia.—Elizabeth Stables ; destination, Virginia.—John Massy ; destination, Virginia.—Elizabeth Gellibod (?) ; destination, Virginia.—Sarah Stiff ; destination, Barbadoes.—Thomas Bennett ; destination, Virginia.—Jane Hyatt ; destination, Virginia.—Thomas Jones ; destination, Virginia.—William Gough ; destination, Barbadoes.

Page 95

Richard Barnes ; destination, Virginia.—Joseph Lawrance ; destination, Barbadoes.—Christopher Williams ; destination, Nevis.—Anne Davis ; destination, Virginia.—Charles Bennett ; destination, Virginia.—Anthony Rennals ; destination, Virginia.—William Baldwin ; destination, Virginia.—William Phelps ; destination, Virginia.—Joseph Rowland ; destination, Barbadoes.—Mary Elmes ; destination, Virginia.—Elizabeth Corbill ; destination, Virginia.—Martha Horship ; destination, Virginia.

Page 96

Thomas Attwick ; destination, Virginia.—Howell Morgan ; destination, Virginia.—Thomas Burte ; destination, Virginia.—Morgan Jones ; destination, Virginia.—John Thomas ; destination, Virginia.—Christopher Henton ; destination, Virginia.—Mary Twiste ; destination, Virginia.—Walter Lewis ; destination, Virginia.—James Stowell ; destination, Virginia.—David Williams ; destination, Virginia.—Mary Marvin ; destination, Virginia.—Peter Edson ; destination, Virginia.

Page 97

Lewis Harry ; destination, Virginia.—Edward Price ; destination, Virginia.—Edward Jones ; destination, Virginia.—Elizabeth Morgan ; destination, Virginia.—Jonathan Bateman ; destination, Virginia.—Jennet Jefferis ; destination, Virginia.—Victoria Davis ; destination, Virginia.—Katherine Davis ; destination, Virginia.—Grace Hooke ; destination, Virginia.—Elizabeth Hooke ; destination, Virginia.—James Weaver ; destination, Barbadoes.—Richard Stephens ; destination, Virginia.

Page 98

Phillip Davis ; destination, Virginia.—Arthur Lewis ; destination, Virginia.—Lyson Davis ; destination, Barbadoes.—James Ricketts ; destination, Barbadoes.—Ryer George ; destination, Barbadoes.—Elizabeth Hoyle ; destination, Barbadoes.

—John David; destination, Barbadoes.—Thomas Roberts; destination, Barbadoes.—Elioner Jones; destination, Barbadoes.—Mary Davis; destination, Barbadoes.—ffrancis Hide; destination, Barbadoes.—Thomas Morgan; destination, Barbadoes.

Page 99

Jane Grining; destination, Barbadoes.—Evan Jones; destination, Barbadoes. —David Jones; destination, Barbadoes.—Mary Hicks; destination, Barbadoes.— Evan Lewis; destination, Barbadoes.—Thomas Palmer; destination, Barbadoes.— Elizabeth Collins; destination, Barbadoes.—John Willis; destination, Barbadoes. —Michaell Williams; destination, Barbadoes.—John Willis; destination, Barbadoes.—Evan Davis; destination, Barbadoes.—William Edwards; destination, Barbadoes.

Page 100

Alice Hodgkinson; destination, Barbadoes.—Thomas Smith; destination, Barbadoes.—Elizabeth Goodwen; destination, Barbadoes.—William Jones; destination, Barbadoes.—Robert Durnell; destination, Barbadoes.—Elioner Lewis; destination, Barbadoes.—William Waters; destination, Barbadoes.—Walter Jones; destination, Barbadoes.—Thomas Evans; destination, Barbadoes.—Richard Morgan; destination, Barbadoes.—Thomas Jones; destination, Barbadoes.—Anne James; destination, Barbadoes.

Page 101

Reece Lloyd; destination, Barbadoes.—Thomas Davis; destination, Barbadoes.—Morgan Williams; destination, Barbadoes.—John Wattkins; destination, Barbadoes.—Henry Bartlett; destination, New England.—David Nicholls; destination, Barbadoes.—Joane Blathen; destination, Barbadoes.—John Reevs; destination, Barbadoes.—John Morsley; destination, Barbadoes.—David James; destination, Barbadoes.—William Hampton; destination, Barbadoes.—Elizabeth Bente; destination, Barbadoes.

Page 102

John Hunt; destination, Barbadoes.—Hugh Jones; destination, Virginia.— Elizabeth Jenkins; destination, Barbadoes.—Richard Davis; destination, Barbadoes.—Edward Thomas; destination, Barbadoes.—John Wright; destination, Barbadoes.—John ffrancisco; destination, Barbadoes.—Pedro Pedraldus; destination, Barbadoes.—Griffeth Bowen; destination, Barbadoes.—John Prichard; destination, Barbadoes.—Joane Attwood; destination, Barbadoes.—Joseph Scull; destination, Barbadoes.—William Gilbert; destination, Barbadoes.

Page 103

Arthur Parker; destination, Barbadoes.—John Bird; destination, Barbadoes. —Elinor ffolliott; destination, Barbadoes.—William Game; destination, Barbadoes.—Thomas Middlemore; destination, Barbadoes.—George Haward; destination, Barbadoes.—Elinor Thomas; destination, Barbadoes.—Cicillia Branch; destination, Barbadoes.—William Still; destination, Barbadoes.—Thomas ffarkla; destination, Barbadoes.—George Homittslett; destination, Barbadoes.—John Essington; destination, Barbadoes.—Andrew Hughs; destination, Barbadoes.

Page 104

Penelope Yates ; destination, Barbadoes.—Richard Joanes ; destination, Barbadoes.—Hugh Eades ; destination, Barbadoes.—Anne Sanford ; destination, Barbadoes.—Elizabeth Darby ; destination, Barbadoes.—Addam Perry ; destination, Barbadoes.—Thomas Travell ; destination, Barbadoes.—John Harding ; destination, Virginia.—John Ward ; destination, Barbadoes.—Mary Smith ; destination, Virginia.—Reece Morgan ; destination, Virginia.—John Evans ; destination, Virginia.—Thomas Washington ; destination, Barbadoes.

Page 105

John Steephens ; destination, Barbadoes.—Margery Ames ; destination, Virginia.—Elizabeth Went ; destination, Barbadoes.—Joseph Hemings ; destination, Virginia.—John Standfell ; destination, Barbadoes.—John Morgan ; destination, Virginia.—Blanch Jones ; destination, Virginia.—Elizabeth Grove ; destination, Virginia.—John fflory ; destination, Barbadoes.—Mary Sheapheard ; destination, Virginia.—Mary Atkins ; destination, Virginia.—John Price ; destination, Barbadoes.—Thomas Richardson ; destination, Virginia.

Page 106

John Lotte ; destination, Virginia.—Humphrey Goodwin ; destination, Virginia.—Richard Rawlins ; destination, Barbadoes.—John Popkin ; destination, Barbadoes.—Joane Minson ; destination, Virginia.—Nathaniell Scriven ; destination, Nevis.—Elizabeth Dyer ; destination, Barbadoes.—Joane Lawen ; destination, Virginia.—John Taylor ; destination, Virginia.—Thomas Aylworth ; destination, Barbadoes.—Jane Mathews ; destination, Barbadoes.—Mary Joanes ; destination, Barbadoes.

Page 107

William Whitstone ; destination, Barbadoes.—Anne Davis ; destination, Virginia.—Edward Dagg ; destination, Nevis.—Arthur Norwood ; destination, Virginia.—William Davis ; destination, Virginia.—Hugh Jones ; destination, Virginia.—Lewis Williams ; destination, Virginia.—Thomas Parker ; destination, Barbadoes.—William Bunn ; destination, Nevis.—John Henbury ; destination, Virginia.—Elioner Clarke ; destination, Virginia.—Nathaniell Tucker ; destination, Virginia.—John Hort ; destination, Virginia.

Page 108

John Davis ; destination, Virginia.—George Monke ; destination, Nevis.—William Oadams ; destination, Virginia.—James Hughs ; destination, Virginia.—Precilla Draper ; destination, Virginia.—Elizabeth Morgan ; destination, Virginia.—Anne Perrine ; destination, Barbadoes.—John Rodman ; destination, Barbadoes.—Nicholas Browne ; destination, Virginia.—Elizabeth Ewins ; destination, Virginia.—Edward Wootton ; destination, Virginia.—Thomas Martine ; destination, Virginia.—John Spinner ; destination, Virginia.—Joseph Hedges ; destination, Virginia.

Page 109

Joseph Harding ; destination, Virginia.—Thomas Jones ; destination, Virginia.—Jenkine Jones ; destination, Virginia.—John Reeve ; destination, Virginia.—Davis Dawks ; destination, Virginia.—Mary Pratte ; destination, Virginia.—

Richard Higgens ; destination, Virginia.—Mary Tyle ; destination, Virginia. —Katherine Bastable ; destination, Virginia.—James Mayden ; destination, Virginia.—Charles Corens ; destination, Virginia.

Page 110
Howell Williams ; destination, Virginia.—Jane Leveale ; destination, Barbadoes.—Peter Humphrys ; destination, Virginia.—Thomas Hamms ; destination, Virginia.—James Jones ; destination, Virginia.—Anne Pounsibe ; destination, Virginia.—ffrancis Davis ; destination, Virginia.—John Ames ; destination, Nevis. —Anne Thomas ; destination, Virginia.—John Powell ; destination, Virginia.— Thomas Boyle ; destination, Virginia.—William Russell ; destination, Virginia.

Page 111
John Smith ; destination, Virginia.—William Sparke ; destination, Virginia. —Andrew Mare ; destination, Virginia.—George Browne ; destination, Virginia.— John Dibble ; destination, Virginia.—Robert Smith ; destination, Barbadoes. —Alice Crumpe ; destination, Virginia.—Harbert Williams ; destination, Virginia. —Morrice Williams ; destination, Virginia.—Precilla Drax ; destination, Virginia.— Thomas Ley ; destination, Virginia.—Thomas Waterman ; destination, Virginia.

Page 112
Timothy Howse ; destination, Nevis.—Nicholas Pye ; destination, Virginia.— John Moises ; destination, Virginia.—William Wottner ; destination, Virginia. —Jane Jones ; destination, Virginia.—Mary Cornish ; destination, Barbadoes.— Paull Sladd ; destination, Virginia.—William Mappett ; destination, Virginia. —Phillip Cox ; destination, Virginia.—Julias Thruston ; destination, Virginia.— George Arriall ; destination, Virginia.—John Pope ; destination, Virginia.—John Curtis ; destination, Virginia.

Page 113
Richard Curtis ; destination, Virginia.—John Monke ; destination, Virginia.— Roger Churchill ; destination, Virginia.—Humphry Curtis ; destination, Virginia. —Joane Ayly ; destination, Virginia.—Edith Symmes ; destination, Virginia.— Edith Symmes, jnr. ; destination, Virginia.—Howell Davis ; destination, Nevis. —Susanna Dutton ; destination, Virginia.—Robert Etterick ; destination, Virginia. —Robert ffrancis ; destination, Virginia.—John ffisher ; destination, Virginia.— James Dunning ; destination, Virginia.—Thomas Cradduck ; destination, Virginia.

Page 114
John Balding ; destination, Virginia.—Jane Bagwell ; destination, Virginia.— Joane Toms ; destination, Virginia.—Arthur Ayler ; destination, Virginia.— Edward Ayler ; destination, Virginia.—James Joanesson ; destination, Virginia. —Hosea Cobb ; destination, Virginia.—John Golledge ; destination, Virginia.— Edward Jeffris ; destination, Virginia.—Anne Morrice ; destination, Virginia.— Joseph Godward ; destination, Virginia.

Page 115
William Towers ; destination, Virginia.—Thomas Hunt ; destination, Virginia. —John Hunt ; destination, Virginia.—Sunnell (*sic*) Byron ; destination, Virginia.— John Meads ; destination, Virginia.—Elioner Smith ; destination, Virginia.—John Davis ; destination, Virginia.—Thomas Garnish ; destination, Virginia.

Page 116

Richard Tompson ; destination, Nevis.—John Guppie ; destination, Virginia.
—Samuell Stepney ; destination, Virginia.—Henry Abery ; destination, Virginia.—
Grace Cole ; destination, Virginia.—Mary Brint ; destination, Virginia.—Elizabeth
Bevan ; destination, Nevis.—Elizabeth Manford ; destination, Virginia.—John
Wattkins ; destination, Barbadoes.—Mathias Lewis ; destination, Virginia.—
Thomas Bachellor ; destination, Virginia.—Thomas James ; destination, Virginia.
—Thomas Eden ; destination, Virginia.—Reece Thomas ; destination, Nevis.—
Hester Earney ; destination, Virginia.

Page 117

Thomas Wayte ; destination, Virginia.—Elizabeth Peters ; destination, Virginia.
—Barbara Jones ; destination, Virginia.—William Hart ; destination, Virginia.—
Teage Ishmead ; destination, Virginia.—Thomas Joanes ; destination, Virginia.
—Penelope Pretty ; destination, Virginia.—Pheby Carver ; destination, Virginia.—
Jonas Bennett ; destination, Virginia.—Giles Waters ; destination, Nevis.—Margery
Hughes ; destination, Nevis.—Thomas Bindoco ; destination, Virginia.—John
Trigg, snr. ; destination, Virginia.—John Trigg, jnr. ; destination, Virginia.

Page 118

Walter Graunt ; destination, Virginia.—Thomas Preston ; destination, Virginia.
—Edward Goodman ; destination, Virginia.—John Towers ; destination, Virginia.
—Elizabeth Cox ; destination, Nevis.—Elizabeth Greeneland ; destination, Nevis.—
Elizabeth Richard ; destination, Virginia.—Barbara Towsey ; destination, Virginia.
—Moses Joanes ; destination, Virginia.—William Leachman ; destination, Nevis.—
Samuell James ; destination, Virginia.—William Carpenter ; destination, Virginia.
—John Lawson ; destination, Virginia.

Page 119

Edith Collins ; destination, Virginia.—Thomas Barnes ; destination, Virginia.
—Isaack Caines ; destination, Virginia.—Nathaniell Wiggmore ; destination, Vir-
ginia.—James Caines ; destination, Virginia.—Joane Bayly ; destination, Virginia.
—Joane Hollyer ; destination, Virginia.—Joane Mouly ; destination, Virginia.—
Hugh Barlow ; destination, Virginia.—Walter Hughs ; destination, Virginia.
—John Alloway ; destination, Virginia.—John Ricroft ; destination, Nevis.—Sarah
Bollen ; destination, Virginia.

Page 120

Joane West ; destination, Virginia.—Mary Head ; destination, Virginia.—
John Peach ; destination, Virginia.—John Ellis ; destination, Virginia.—Anne
Yeats ; destination, Virginia.—William Hickman ; destination, Virginia.—Henry
ffollett ; destination, Virginia.—Welthian Thomas ; destination, Virginia.—William
Boysom ; destination, Virginia.—George Davis ; destination, Virginia.—Israll
Prater ; destination, Virginia.—Hopwell Wood ; destination, Virginia.—Mary
Godwin ; destination, Virginia.

Page 121

Thomas Knight ; destination, Nevis.—Elizabeth Mills ; destination, Nevis.—
Thomas George ; destination, Virginia.—Rowland Pitt ; destination, Virginia.—
Richard Millard ; destination, Virginia.—Ecan Thomas ; destination, Virginia.

—William Arnold ; destination, Virginia.—Edward Williams ; destination, Nevis.—
John Straten ; destination, Virginia.—William Essex ; destination, Nevis.—Leonard
Guntur ; destination, Barbadoes.—John Whattly ; destination, Virginia.—John
Williams ; destination, Barbadoes or Leeward Is.—James Williams ; destination,
Barbadoes or Leeward Is.

Page 122

John Hawkins ; destination, Barbadoes or Leeward Is.—James Webb ; destination, Virginia.—William Palmer ; destination, Virginia.—Moses Bunkly ; destination, Virginia.—Roger Corzer ; destination, Barbadoes.—Moses Dunckley ;
destination, Virginia.—Peter Atherton ; destination, Virginia.—John Gibbs ;
destination, Virginia.—John Marrin ; destination, Virginia.—Josias Wilcox ; destination, Nevis.—William Bolcher ; destination, Virginia.—Henry Coopy ; destination, Virginia.—Thomas Hichens ; destination, Virginia.

Page 123

Thomas Hill ; destination, Virginia.—Thomas George ; destination, Virginia.
—Benjamin George ; destination, Virginia.—Anne Borsley ; destination, Virginia.
—Anne Collier ; destination, Virginia.—James Hill ; destination, Virginia.—
Elioner James ; destination, Virginia.—Elizabeth Cary ; destination, Nevis.—John
Shelly ; destination, Virginia.—Richard Poole ; destination, Virginia.—Judith
Coop ; destination, Barbadoes.—Luce Jones ; destination, Barbadoes.—Anne
Perren ; destination, Barbadoes.

Page 124

Richard Roach ; destination, Barbadoes.—Richard Pymm ; destination, Barba-
does.—Griffith Towgood ; destination, Virginia.—John Cuffe ; destination, Virginia.
—ffrancis Street ; destination, Virginia.—Richard Harmer ; destination, Virginia.—
Joane Drew ; destination, Barbadoes.—Joane Golledge ; destination, Virginia.—
Jerimy Hughs ; destination, Barbadoes.—William Browne ; destination, Virginia.
—Richard Hall ; destination, Barbadoes.—William Wayt ; destination, Barbadoes.

Page 125

William Reynald ; destination, Barbadoes.—John George ; destination, Barbadoes.—Elizabeth Lloyd ; destination, Barbadoes.—Jennett Joanes ; destination,
Barbadoes.—Barthollomew Clark ; destination, Barbadoes.—William Allen ; destination, Barbadoes.—Richard Harry ; destination, Barbadoes.—Edward Morgan ;
destination, Barbadoes.—Dorothy Hollway ; destination, Barbadoes.—David Man-
nian ; destination, Barbadoes.—Phillip Jones ; destination, Barbadoes.—Jacob
Perkins ; destination, Barbadoes.—Robert Townsend ; destination, Barbadoes.—
John Barly ; destination, Barbadoes.

Page 126

Margarett Hitchens ; destination, Barbadoes.—Henry Hoper ; destination,
Barbadoes.—Daniell Thomson ; destination, Barbadoes.—Richard Bristoe ; destination, Barbadoes.—Thomas Nutt ; destination, Barbadoes.—Henry Summers ;
destination, Barbadoes.—Evan Davis ; destination, Barbadoes.—William Phelphes ;
destination, Barbadoes.—Mary Elbur ; destination, Barbadoes.—Mathew Phillips ;
destination, Barbadoes.—John Chamberlaine ; destination, Barbadoes.—Henry
Pym ; destination, Barbadoes.

Page 127
Robert Griffis ; destination, Barbadoes.—John Lonnon ; destination, New England.—Thomas Bennett ; destination, Barbadoes.—Thomas Norover ; destination, Barbadoes.—Walter Row ; destination, Barbadoes.—Thomas Davy ; destination, New England.—Darby Brayne ; destination, Barbadoes.—Georg Jinkins ; destination, Barbadoes.—John Ward ; destination, Barbadoes.—Elioner Bott ; destination, Barbadoes.—John Bull ; destination, New England.—Mary Conaway ; destination, New England.

Page 128
John Wright ; destination, Barbadoes.—Jane Evans ; destination, Barbadoes. —Reece Jenkins ; destination, Barbadoes.—Thomas ffry ; destination, New England. —Peter Poyner ; destination, Barbadoes.—Margarett Crompton ; destination, Barbadoes.—Dorothy Tyler ; destination, Barbadoes.—Richard Bayly ; destination, New England.—James Browne ; destination, Barbadoes.—ffrancis Grigory ; destination, Barbadoes.—Anthony Pickett ; destination, Barbadoes.

Page 129
Thomas Wall ; destination, Barbadoes.—John Rose ; destination, Barbadoes or Leeward Is.—Thomas Perrin ; destination, Barbadoes.—Henry Hill ; destination, Barbadoes.—James Pearce ; destination, Barbadoes.—John Chaplin ; destination, Barbadoes.—Anne Munder ; destination, Barbadoes.—William Garland ; destination, Barbadoes.—William Jones ; destination, Barbadoes.—John Davis ; destination, Barbadoes.—Roger Kenny ; destination, Barbadoes.—Georg (*sic*) Spigurnell ; destination, Nevis.

Page 130
Ann Steevens ; destination, Barbadoes.—William Pritchard ; destination, Barbadoes.—John Willis ; destination, Virginia.—John Bethar ; destination, Barbadoes.—John Jones ; destination, Barbadoes.—Elizabeth Jones ; destination, Barbadoes.—William Sherman ; destination, New England.—Margarett Jelfe ; destination, Nevis.—Richard Reece ; destination, New England.—Richard Davis ; destination, Barbadoes and Leeward Is.—Charles Lacon ; destination, Barbadoes or Leeward Is.—Mary Abbutt ; destination, Barbadoes or Leeward Is.

Page 131
Daniell Nicholls ; destination, Virginia.—Job Sims ; destination, Nevis.— Charles Jones ; destination, Nevis.—James Jones ; destination, Nevis.—William Morgan ; destination, Virginia.—John Benson ; destination, Virginia.—Thomas Chamberlin ; destination, Virginia.—John Willmenton ; destination, Nevis.— John Evans ; destination, Barbadoes.—Walter Davis ; destination, Virginia.— Lewis Coner ; destination, Virginia.—Joane Pudding ; destination, Maryland. —Thomas Peirce ; destination, Barbadoes.

Page 132
Mary Davis ; destination, Barbadoes.—John Willson ; destination, Virginia. —Thomas Buttler ; destination, Barbadoes.—Joseph Kettle ; destination, Nevis.— Hester Buck ; destination, Virginia.—Thomas Strowd ; destination, New England. —John Jennings ; destination, Barbadoes or Leeward Is.—Mary Jennings ; destination, Barbadoes or Leeward Is.

Page 133

Thomas Gibbons; destination, Virginia.—Bridgett Wheeler; destination, Virginia.—Thomas Strowd; destination, Virginia.—Sarah Gough; destination, Barbadoes.—Hugh Rowland; destination, Virginia.—George Thorne; destination, Virginia.—Thomas Dabenett; destination, Virginia.—John Bingham; destination, Virginia.—John Price; destination, Virginia.—Mary Wildes; destination, Virginia.—Jane Lewis; destination, Virginia.—Mary Smith; destination, Virginia.

Page 134

James Powell; destination, Barbadoes.—Judith Bowen; destination, Virginia. —Margarett Tyler; destination, Virginia.—Katherine Bray; destination, Virginia. —Elizabeth Stone; destination, Virginia.—William Brockett; destination, Virginia.—William Hartland; destination, Virginia.—Richard Kirke; destination, Virginia.—Rebecca Hill; destination, Virginia.—Thomas Tasker; destination, Virginia.—Robert Wise; destination, Virginia.

Page 135

Peter Kelly; destination, Virginia.—Katherine Eagle; destination, Virginia.— Thomas ffarmer; destination, Virginia.—Edward Morris; destination, Virginia. —George Pustone; destination, Virginia.—William Hawkes; destination, Virginia. —Richard Greene; destination, Virginia.—Anne Cheade; destination, Virginia.— John Haskins; destination, Maryland.—George Wogan; destination, Virginia. —George Thomas; destination, Virginia.—Daniell Hafeild; destination, Virginia.

Page 136

Humphry Symonds; destination, Virginia.—Richard Dubbs; destination, Virginia.—Griffeth Bevan; destination, Virginia.—Martha Wilds; destination, Virginia.—John Meeke; destination, Virginia.—Morgan Jones; destination, Barbadoes.—John Dalby; destination, Virginia.—John Shrubshore; destination, Virginia.—Jeane Chapman; destination, Virginia.—Mary Whiteing; destination, Virginia.—ffrancis South; destination, Virginia.—Richard Edwards; destination, Virginia.

Page 137

Thomas Killpoch; destination, Virginia.—Elizabeth Stoakees; destination, Virginia.—Elizabeth Whitehouse; destination, Virginia.—John Muckfarly (?); destination, Virginia.—David Lloid; destination, Virginia.—William Dixon; destination, Virginia.—Elizabeth Pumfry; destination, Virginia.—Jane Harper; destination, Virginia.—Phillis Edwards; destination, Virginia.—Elizabeth Thomas; destination, Nevis.—Henry Perrisford; destination, Nevis.—Margarett Williams; destination, Nevis.

Page 138

Mary Emannuell; destination, Nevis.—Katherine Williams; destination, Virginia.—Jeremiah Densly; destination, Virginia.—James Martine; destination, Virginia.—Thomas Sheapherd; destination, Virginia.—William Bennoll; destination, Virginia.—William Parry; destination, Virginia.—Edward Russell; destination, Virginia.—Thomas Hillard; destination, Virginia.—William Jones; destination, Virginia.—David Phillips; destination, Virginia.—Mary Jones; destination, Virginia.

Page 139

Elizabeth Jones; destination, Virginia.—Charles Steward; destination, Virginia.—Thomas Horseman; destination, Virginia.—Mary Price; destination, Virginia.—George Pearce; destination, Virginia.—Richard Grindall; destination, Virginia.—David Lewis; destination, Virginia.—Henry Lewis; destination, Virginia.—Miles Darby; destination, Virginia.—Miles Lewis; destination, Virginia.—William Morgan; destination, Virginia.—John Powell; destination, Virginia.

Page 140

George Harper; destination, Virginia.—John Jones; destination, Virginia.—ffabian Arton; destination, Virginia.—Thomas Jay; destination, Virginia.—Mary Jones; destination, Virginia.—Richard Battsly; destination, Virginia.—Phillip Gardner; destination, Virginia.—Jeremy Rod; destination, Virginia.—Henry Bird; destination, Virginia.—Thomas Nicholas; destination, Virginia.—George Oslan; destination, Virginia.—Edward Andrews; destination, Virginia.

Page 141

Davy Parry; destination, Virginia.—Howell Reece; destination, Virginia.—Henry Lewis; destination, Virginia.—Edward Homes; destination, Virginia.—James Evans; destination, Virginia.—Henry Brayne; destination, Virginia.—Thomas Jones; destination, Virginia.—John ffishlock; destination, Virginia.—Ambrose Herriott; destination, Virginia.—Wattkin Thomas; destination, Virginia.—Robert Sopper; destination, Virginia.—Nathan Jones; destination, Virginia.

Page 142

John Smith; destination, Virginia.—John Probert; destination, Virginia.—Jane Wattkin; destination, Virginia.—Thomas Gough; destination, Virginia.—John Kayes; destination, Virginia.—Richard Bowen; destination, Virginia.—John Colstemy; destination, Virginia.—James Pearce; destination, Virginia.—Richard Nicholas; destination, Virginia.—Ann Baker; destination, Virginia.—James Winard; destination, Virginia.—John Dickfeild; destination, Virginia.

Page 143

John Macholl; destination, Virginia.—Evan Price; destination, Virginia.—John Willis; destination, Virginia.—John Street; destination, Virginia.—Daniell Thomas; destination, Virginia.—Edward Yearsly; destination, Virginia.—John Probaut; destination, Virginia.—Robert Wash; destination, Virginia.—Robert White; destination, Virginia.—George Truelove; destination, Virginia.—William Croucher; destination, Virginia.—Richard Hubbard; destination, Virginia.

Page 144

John Powell; destination, Virginia.—Ezekill Jack; destination, Virginia.—John Andrews; destination, Virginia.—Sarah Garvard; destination, Virginia.—Elizabeth Parry; destination, Virginia.—James Rodgers; destination, Virginia.—Charles Harrington; destination, Virginia.—Anne Steane; destination, Virginia.—Griffith Jones; destination, Virginia.—Evan Richard; destination, Virginia.—John Davis; destination, Virginia.—John Webster; destination, Virginia.

Page 145

Mark Saltehouse; destination, Virginia.—William ffletcher; destination, Virginia.—James Scofeild; destination, Virginia.—Samuell Hill; destination, Virginia. —George Whaley; destination, Virginia.—William Evan; destination, Virginia.— Mary Bason; destination, Virginia.—Margaret Cheadle; destination, Virginia.— William Cheadle; destination, Virginia.—Thomas Stott; destination, Virginia. —Richard Evans; destination, Virginia.—John Ayres; destination, Virginia.

Page 146

Alice Stevens; destination, Virginia.—James Cleyton; destination, Virginia. —Joane Wall; destination, Virginia.—Edward Allen; destination, Virginia.— Enock Ellor; destination, Virginia.—Winifred Mosse; destination, Virginia. —Thomas Davy; destination, Virginia.—Lewis Williams; destination, Virginia.— Thomas Collins; destination, Virginia.—Thomas Phillips; destination, Nevis. —Abraham Dawson; destination, Virginia.—Anthony Underwood; destination, Nevis.

Page 147

William Carter; destination, Virginia.—Walter Lane; destination, Barbadoes. —Jeremy Parry; destination, Virginia.—John Willson; destination, Virginia.— Richard Shippy; destination, Virginia.—Christopher Tomlin; destination, Virginia.—William Bane; destination, Virginia.—John Hughs; destination, Virginia. —Evan Thomas; destination, Virginia.—Charles Cox; destination, Virginia.— Mary Coleman; destination, Virginia.—Stephen Shank; destination, Barbadoes.

Page 148

Benjamin Thomas; destination, Virginia.—William Jones; destination, Virginia.—Thomas Roberts; destination, Virginia.—John Hobson; destination, Virginia.—Margarett Mettham; destination, Virginia.—Henry Allen; destination, Virginia.—Daniell Gallant; destination, Virginia.—Margarett Paine; destination, Virginia.—William Greene; destination, Barbadoes.—John Morgan; destination, Virginia.—Moses Dale; destination, Virginia.—William Wood; destination, Virginia.

Page 149

Reynold ffuloflove; destination, Virginia.—Richard Sutton; destination, Virginia.—Walter Sutton; destination, Virginia.—Robert Tayler; destination, Virginia.—Thomas Curtis; destination, Virginia.—Elizabeth Griffis; destination, Virginia.—John Cunney; destination, Virginia.—Hugh Jones; destination, Virginia.—John Wilks; destination, Virginia.—Henry Knight; destination, Virginia. —Morgan Wattkins; destination, Virginia.—William Kettle; destination, Virginia.

Page 150

John Tayler; destination, Virginia.—George Parker; destination, Virginia.— Morgan Pranch; destination, Virginia.—Sarah Tippett; destination, Virginia. —James Lewis; destination, Virginia.—Thomas Davis; destination, Virginia.— James Jones; destination, Virginia.—Charles Barnes; destination, Virginia.—Joseph Smith; destination, Virginia.—David Williams; destination, Virginia.—John Marrile; destination, Virginia.—John Daine; destination, Virginia.

Page 151

Thomas Holland ; destination, Virginia.—Jeremy Densly ; destination, Virginia.—George Wattkin ; destination, Virginia.—Phillip Thomas ; destination, Virginia.—John Thomas ; destination, Virginia.—Richard Winter ; destination, Virginia.—John Tayler ; destination, Virginia.—Thomas Williams ; destination, Virginia.—David Williams ; destination, Virginia.—William Jinkin ; destination, Virginia.—Richard John ; destination, Virginia.—Isaack Newton ; destination, Barbadoes.

Page 152

John Organ ; destination, Virginia.—Jarvis Riseton ; destination, Virginia.—Richard West ; destination, Virginia.—Richard ffletcher ; destination, Virginia.—Elizabeth Hopkins ; destination, Virginia.—Thomas Harrison ; destination, Virginia.—John Husband ; destination, Virginia.—Jinkin Price ; destination, Virginia.—Anthony Hathur ; destination, Virginia.—Warren Hathur ; destination, Virginia.—Joseph Curd ; destination, Virginia.—Mary Morgan ; destination, Virginia.

Page 153

William Bourne ; destination, Virginia.—Christopher Miles ; destination, Barbadoes.—Henry Jinkins ; destination, Virginia.—David Williams ; destination, Virginia.—Robert Blaketon ; destination, Barbadoes.—James Sloe ; destination, Virginia.—Nathaniell Lewis ; destination, Virginia.—Thomas Hill ; destination, Virginia.—Thomas Appleyard ; destination, Virginia.—Olliver Davis ; destination, Virginia.—John Hooper ; destination, Barbadoes.—James Coder ; destination, Virginia.

Page 154

Richard Butterfeild ; destination, Virginia.—Thomas Brothest ; destination, Virginia.—John Richards ; destination, Virginia.—George Jones ; destination, Virginia.—Richard Linton ; destination, Virginia.—Edward Jones ; destination, Virginia.—Anthony Markeman ; destination, Virginia.—Richard Parry ; destination, Virginia.—Richard Brooke ; destination, Virginia.—John Dembry ; destination, Virginia.—Archball (?) Millard ; destination, Virginia.—Richard Mathews ; destination, Virginia.

Page 155

Lawrence White ; destination, Virginia.—Richard Maykins ; destination, Virginia.—Jane Williams ; destination, Virginia.—William Sympson ; destination, Virginia.—Edith Sturgis ; destination, Virginia.—Ambrose Chappell ; destination, Virginia.—Richard Owen ; destination, Virginia.—Rebecca Gibbs ; destination, Virginia.—Wilban Pearce ; destination, Virginia.—Edward Emmont ; destination, Virginia.—Robert Saunders ; destination, Virginia.—Sarah Paine ; destination, Virginia.—Elizabeth Peeke ; destination, Virginia.

Page 156

Susanna Edmonds ; destination, Virginia.—John Cottle ; destination, Barbadoes.—Margaret Nott ; destination, Barbadoes.—John Jones ; destination, Virginia.—James Morse ; destination, Nevis.—Margaret Carter ; destination, Virginia.—William Dellahay ; destination, Virginia.—Joseph Ward ; destination, Nevis.—

K

Margarett Lewis ; destination, Virginia.—Anne Birch ; destination, Virginia.
—Humphrey Mire ; destination, Virginia.—Elizabeth Buttler ; destination, Virginia.—Lishom Howell ; destination, Virginia.—Mary Woods ; destination, Virginia.

Page 157

Thomas Richards ; destination, Virginia.—Thomas Stone ; destination, Virginia.—Thomas Belcher ; destination, Virginia.—Gabriel Tayler ; destination, Virginia.—William Gay ; destination, Virginia.—Ann Pitter ; destination, Virginia.—John Kelly ; destination, Virginia.—ffrancis Powle ; destination, Nevis.—John Bannam ; destination, Virginia.—John Roach ; destination, Virginia.—Christian Pew ; destination, Nevis.—George Lewis ; destination, Nevis.—Andrew Roger ; destination, Nevis.—Thomas Langford ; destination, Virginia.—Mary Evans, destination, Virginia.

Page 158

Edward Booth ; destination, Virginia.—William Horton ; destination, Nevis.—George Hall ; destination, Nevis.—Philip David ; destination, Nevis.—Richard Chedbun ; destination, Virginia.—Rebecca Webb ; destination, Virginia.—Joane Davis ; destination, Virginia.—Griffeth Phillips ; destination, Virginia.—Richard Davis ; destination, Barbadoes.—John Charles ; destination, Nevis.—Richard Bennett ; destination, Nevis.—Thomas Kellway ; destination, Nevis.—Robert Upward ; destination, Nevis.—Edith Kettle ; destination, Nevis.—Thomas Williams ; destination, Nevis.

Page 159

John Sharp ; destination, Virginia.—Henry Willoughby ; destination, Virginia.—Joseph Pinson ; destination, Virginia.—John ffarclue ; destination, Virginia.—Griffeth Daniell ; destination, Virginia.—Henry Comes ; destination, New England.—George Daw ; destination, Virginia.—Marke Snow ; destination, Barbadoes.—James Wood ; destination, Nevis.—Mary Rogers ; destination, Nevis.—Thomas James ; destination, Barbadoes.—Thomas Currier ; destination, Virginia.—Thomas Jones ; destination, Nevis.—John Mallett ; destination, Virginia.—Thomas ffilkins ; destination, Virginia.—Mathew Roberts ; destination, Virginia.

Page 160

Walter Drawey (?) ; destination, Virginia.—Jerman Beaton ; destination, Virginia.—Peter Buttler ; destination, Virginia.—Thomas Buttler ; destination, Virginia.—Thomas Frome ; destination, Barbadoes.—John Paviott ; destination, New England.—Thomas Williams ; destination, Barbadoes.—Robert Brayne, destination, New England.—Thomas Phillips ; destination, Barbadoes.—Susanna Parsons ; destination, Nevis.—Samuell Pew ; destination, Nevis.—Henry Webb ; destination, Nevis.—Susanna Parsons ; destination, Virginia.

Page 161

John Humphry ; destination, Barbadoes.—Moses Hughs ; destination, Virginia.—Alexander Romsy ; destination, Nevis.—Hugh Sheaperd ; destination, Nevis.—Joane Davis ; destination, Nevis.—Edward Morrice ; destination, Nevis.—Walter Howell ; destination, Nevis.—John Somers ; destination, Nevis.—William Roberts ;

destination, Virginia.—Phillip Lewis; destination, Nevis.—Robert Lattimore; destination, Nevis.—John Symonds; destination, Nevis.—John Thomas; destination, Nevis.

Page 162

William Daves; destination, New England.—Joane Pearcy; destination, Virginia.—Tarloughe Brian; destination, Barbadoes.—Jehadah Jones; destination, Nevis.—Susan Prest; destination, Nevis.—Thomas Hughes; destination, New England.—John ffryer; destination, New England.—John Trowbridg; destination, New England.—Thomas Lloid; destination, Virginia.—John Wood; destination, New England.—William Hayes; destination, Barbadoes.—Edward Tucker; destination, New England.—Andrew Bevans; destination, Virginia.—Dorothy Vaughan; destination, Barbadoes.—John Peckman; destination, Virginia.

Page 163

ffrances Betts; destination, Barbadoes.—Robert Jones; destination, Virginia. —John Leaff; destination, Virginia.—John Hood; destination, Virginia.—John Edwards; destination, Virginia.—John Clhoone; destination, New England.— Joseph Allen; destination, Virginia.—John Dickeson; destination, New England. —Ann Parr; destination, Virginia.—William Price; destination, Virginia.—John Smith; destination, Barbadoes.—James Alexander; destination, Virginia.—William Jones; destination, Barbadoes.—Adam Arton; destination, Virginia.—James Barnard; destination, Virginia.—William Seymor; destination, Virginia.

Page 164

Arthur Spenser; destination, Virginia.—Thomas Webb; destination, Virginia. —ffrancis Hobson; destination, Nevis.—Georg ffrapwell; destination, Virginia.— Thomas Harris; destination, Virginia.—John Merriwether; destination, Virginia. —James Dicks; destination, Virginia.—Richard Browne; destination, Barbadoes. —Mary Barnutt; destination, Virginia.—ffrancis Hancock; destination, Virginia.— Thomas Young; destination, Virginia.—Henry Hughs; destination, Virginia. —Daniell Rowland; destination, Virginia.—Howell Davis; destination, Virginia. —John James; destination, Virginia.

Page 165

William Morgan; destination, Nevis.—Richard Davy; destination, Nevis.— Susanna Barber; destination, Virginia.—Charles Grindley; destination, Virginia. —Rowland Davis; destination, Virginia.—Edward Way; destination, Virginia.— Eliza Stone; destination, Virginia.—Mary Short; destination, Virginia.—William Marratt; destination, Virginia.—Thomas Davis; destination, Virginia.—Phillip Morrice; destination, Virginia.—John Williams; destination, Virginia.—Peter Williams; destination, Nevis.—James Pritchard; destination, Virginia.—David Jones; destination, Virginia.—Humphry Chayton; destination, Nevis.—Margarett Hitchins; destination, Virginia.

Page 166

Ann Mallpus; destination, Nevis.—John Brand; destination, Virginia.— John Lidden; destination, Virginia.—Rebeckah Radford; destination, Virginia. —William Mathews; destination, Virginia.—Thomas Williams; destination, Virginia.—William Jinkins; destination, Virginia.—John Lloid; destination,

Virginia.—James Brimble ; destination, Virginia.—Mary Mathews ; destination, Virginia.—John Moore ; destination, Virginia.—Olliver Morgan ; destination, Virginia.—John Evans ; destination, Virginia.—Christopher Roberts ; destination, Virginia.—John Allen ; destination, Nevis.—Sarah Crew ; destination, Virginia.

Page 167
Joseph Sheappard ; destination, Virginia.—John Lewis ; destination, Virginia.—Phillip Pie ; destination, Virginia.—William Jeapson ; destination, Virginia.—Joseph Apharry ; destination, Virginia.—Elizabeth Mathews ; destination, Virginia.—Dorothy ffox ; destination, Virginia.—Thomas Lewis ; destination, Virginia.—Ann Clark ; destination, Virginia.—William Powell ; destination, Virginia.—Ann Newan ; destination, Virginia.—Margarett Burford ; destination, Virginia.—William Bagg ; destination, Virginia.—Mary ffletcher ; destination, Virginia.—Honour Hall ; destination, Nevis.—Jane Taman ; destination, Nevis.

Page 168
Joane Smith ; destination, Nevis.—William Man ; destination, Nevis.—Charles Pritchard ; destination, Virginia.—Mary Weight ; destination, Nevis.—John Browne ; destination, Virginia.—John Dowling ; destination, Virginia.—Bartholomew Morsell ; destination, Virginia.—Anthony Dollery ; destination, Virginia.—Mary Bourton ; destination, Virginia.—Mary Pickford ; destination, Virginia.—Grace Good ; destination, Virginia.—Jane Bayly ; destination, Virginia.—Dorothy Davis ; destination, Nevis.—Ann Pickerin ; destination, Virginia.—Alice Bayly ; destination, Virginia.—Mary Haines ; destination, Virginia.

Page 169
Mary Howell ; destination, Virginia.—William Johnston ; destination, Virginia.—John Avery ; destination, Virginia.—Gartry Avery ; destination, Virginia.—Sarah Chamberlaine ; destination, Virginia.—Elioner Richman ; destination, Virginia.—William Morgan ; destination, Virginia.—Reece Jones ; destination, Virginia.—Reynold Davis ; destination, Virginia.—Elizabeth Blessly ; destination, Virginia.—Ann Jones ; destination, Virginia.—Mary Percivall ; destination, Virginia.—Jane Reece ; destination, Virginia.—ffrances Tuffen ; destination, Virginia.—Margaret Roberts ; destination, Barbadoes.—Grace Davis ; destination, Barbadoes.

Page 170
Mary Holbrooke ; destination, Virginia.—Margaret Holbrooke ; destination, Virginia.—Sybell Peters ; destination, Virginia.—Mary Budding ; destination, Virginia.—Susanna Budden ; destination, Virginia.—Katherine Mann ; destination, Virginia.—Dorcus Willmet ; destination, Virginia or Barbadoes.—Joane Joyce ; destination, Virginia.—John Jacob ; destination, Virginia.—Ann Richardson ; destination, Virginia.—Margery Rawley ; destination, Virginia.—Barbara Hill ; destination, Virginia.—Richard Briant ; destination, Virginia.—Dorothy Clarke ; destination, Virginia.—Richard Williams ; destination, Virginia.—Thomas Strashing ; destination, Virginia.

Page 171
Arthur Hay ; destination, Virginia.—Elizabeth Jame ; destination, Barbadoes.—Joan Clarke ; destination, Virginia.—John Samm ; destination, Virginia.—

Samuell Sunderland ; destination, Virginia.—John King ; destination, Virginia. —Evan Thomas ; destination, Virginia.—Jane Tuich ; destination, Virginia.— Winifred James ; destination, Virginia.—Thomas Jenkins ; destination, Virginia. —Richard Lewis ; destination, Virginia.—Richard Jones ; destination, Virginia.— Edward William ; destination, Virginia.—Daniell Lewis ; destination, Virginia.— Edward Hart ; destination, Virginia.—Thomas Hart ; destination, Virginia.

Page 171 (*sic*)
George Mackalla ; destination, Virginia.—George Morgan ; destination, Virginia.—Auffris Gueff ; destination, Nevis.—George Garmant ; destination, Virginia.—John ffeare ; destination, Virginia.—Robert Peacock ; destination, Virginia.—George Hambleton ; destination, Virginia.—John Rosser ; destination, Virginia.—James Mitchell ; destination, Virginia.—John Allery ; destination, Virginia.—Morgan Hammons ; destination, Virginia.—John Harris ; destination, Virginia.—John Brookes ; destination, Virginia.—Christopher Hore ; destination, Virginia.—James Silvester ; destination, Virginia.—Harman Jonson ; destination, Virginia.

Page 172
Robert Hallwell ; destination, Virginia.—Grace Gray ; destination, Virginia. —Jane Gardner ; destination, Virginia.—Richard Turner ; destination Virginia.— Ann Yate ; destination, Virginia.—Robert Lord ; destination, Virginia.—Edward Barne ; destination, Virginia.—Rachell Williams ; destination, Virginia.—William Hughs ; destination, Virginia.—Onor Macarty ; destination, Virginia.—fflorence Driscoll ; destination, Virginia.—David James ; destination, Virginia.—Edward ffelton ; destination, Virginia.—Samuell Munday ; destination, Virginia.—Michaell Grayer ; destination, Virginia.

Page 173
George Lockyear ; destination, Virginia.—Joane Harris ; destination, Virginia. —William Johnson ; destination, Virginia.—William Rise ; destination, Virginia.— John Hogg ; destination, Nevis.—Joseph ffick ; destination, Virginia.—Elizabeth ffick ; destination, Virginia.—Samuell Minard ; destination, Virginia.—Georg Hollard ; destination, Virginia.—John Dowell ; destination, Virginia.—Thomas Hodge ; destination, Virginia.—William Dicker ; destination, Virginia.—Thomas Collins ; destination, Virginia.—Jenkine Thomas ; destination, Nevis or Antigua.— Mary Dyer ; destination, Nevis.—Jane Robison ; destination, Nevis.

Page 174
John Caley ; destination, Montserrat.—John Winslory ; destination, Nevis.— Evan Rice ; destination, Barbadoes.—John Bryan ; destination, Barbadoes.—John Dorreman ; destination, Barbadoes.—Edward Dyer ; destination, Barbadoes or Leeward Is.—Joseph Shorney ; destination, Barbadoes.—William Jay ; destination, Barbadoes.—John Potter ; destination, Barbadoes.—John Williams ; destination, Barbadoes.—James Powell ; destination, Virginia.—Richard Gribble ; destination, Barbadoes.—William Clarke ; destination, Barbadoes.—John Madden ; destination, Barbadoes.—John Lewis ; destination, Barbadoes.—Elizabeth Andersey ; destination, Barbadoes.

Page 175

Mary Lane ; destination, Virginia.—Thomas Parker ; destination, Virginia.— William Tayler ; destination, Virginia.—Thomas Williams ; destination, Barbadoes.—Morgan Williams ; destination, Virginia.—John Irish ; destination, Barbadoes.—Phillip Edmund ; destination, Barbadoes.—Mary Evan ; destination, Virginia.—Sidrach Hardick ; destination, Barbadoes.—Adam Clarke ; destination, Barbadoes.—Archiman Dodds ; destination, Jamaica.—William Kingscutt ; destination, Barbadoes.—Richard Whately ; destination, Barbadoes.—Ann Mason ; destination, Nevis.—John Peeney ; destination, Nevis.—Jane Williams ; destination, Barbadoes.

Page 176

William Pouley ; destination, Barbadoes.—Thomas ffoster ; destination, Barbadoes.—George Jones ; destination, Barbadoes.—Cicely ffeare ; destination, Nevis.—Regee (?) Browne ; destination, Nevis.—John Jones ; destination, Jamaica. —Richard Jones ; destination, Jamaica.—Richard Jones ; destination, Jamaica.— William Neale ; destination, Nevis.—Phillip Webb ; destination, Virginia.—John Vaughan ; destination, Virginia.—Elizabeth ffisher ; destination, Nevis.—Martha Peeterson ; destination, Virginia.—Richard Carter ; destination, Nevis.—William Mulgrove ; destination, Nevis.

Page 177

William Browne ; destination, Nevis.—John Morgan ; destination, Nevis.— Ephraim Browne ; destination, Barbadoes.—Humphrey Cockshut ; destination, Barbadoes.—Edmund Waymor ; destination, Jamaica.—Jane Olton ; destination, Nevis.—William Dyer ; destination, Nevis.—Elizabeth Price ; destination, Jamaica. —David Jones ; destination, Virginia.—Elizabeth Pye ; destination, Barbadoes.— Elizabeth Williams ; destination, Nevis.—William Perrin ; destination, Jamaica.— Reece Jones ; destination, Nevis.—John Lewis ; destination, Barbadoes.—David Binons ; destination, Barbadoes.—Edith Watkins ; destination, Nevis.

Page 178

John Williams ; destination, Nevis.—John Women ; destination, Nevis.— Joane Blunt ; destination, Nevis.—Thomas Rogers ; destination, Jamaica.—John Qunee (*sic*) ; destination, Nevis.—Thomas Slade ; destination, Nevis.—Thomas Slade ; destination, Nevis.—Edward ffuse ; destination, Nevis.—Katherine Williams ; destination, Nevis.—George Greene ; destination, Nevis.—David Williams ; destination, Nevis.—George Johnson ; destination, Nevis.—John Combs ; destination, Nevis.—William Harris ; destination, Barbadoes.—Thomas Tucker ; destination, Nevis.—Elizabeth Randall ; destination, Nevis.

Page 179

John Williams ; destination, Nevis.—James Hulland ; destination, Barbadoes. —Thomas Sheappard ; destination, Nevis.—John Davis ; destination, Nevis.— Evan Jones ; destination, Barbadoes or Nevis.—Thomas Williams ; destination, Barbadoes.—John Tripplett ; destination, Nevis.—John Symkins ; destination, Barbadoes or Nevis.—William Willmett ; destination, Barbadoes.—Daniell Munday ; destination, Barbadoes.—ffrancis Harris ; destination, Barbadoes or Nevis.

—Mary Steevens ; destination, Barbadoes or Nevis.—Perrin Tayler ; destination, Nevis.—ffaulke Edwards ; destination, Barbadoes.—William Downton ; destination, Nevis.—Stephen Howard ; destination, Montserrat.

Page 180
John Jones ; destination, Montserrat.—John Deane ; destination, Barbadoes. —James Rawlins ; destination, Barbadoes.—John Williams ; destination, Montserrat.—Thomas Hall ; destination, Nevis.—George Williams ; destination, Nevis. —Elizabeth James ; destination, Barbadoes.—Mary Nash ; destination, Barbadoes. —William Millard ; destination, Montserrat.—Elias Coles ; destination, Nevis.— Thomas Moody ; destination, Nevis.—Thomas ffroame ; destination, New England. —Giles Wattkins ; destination, Nevis.—Robert Symms ; destination, Nevis.— Thomas Windall ; destination, Montserrat.—Henry Richard ; destination, Montserrat.—Hugh Jones ; destination, New England.

Page 181
Abraham Jones ; destination, Barbadoes.—William Jones ; destination, Barbadoes.—William Andrews ; destination, Nevis.—John Dodd ; destination, Nevis. —Sarah Thomas ; destination, New England.—Ann Bayly ; destination, Nevis.— William Cosens ; destination, Barbadoes.—Thomas Holborne ; destination, New England.—William Jones ; destination, Barbadoes.—Mary Thorne ; destination, Barbadoes.—Robert Jinkins ; destination, Nevis.—William Spickett ; destination, Nevis.—John Long ; destination, Nevis.—William Lane ; destination, Barbadoes. —John Smart ; destination, Nevis.—John Smart ; destination, Nevis.—Thomas Davis ; destination, Nevis.

Page 182
William Lewis ; destination, Montserrat.—Peter ffysher ; destination, Nevis.— John Davis ; destination, Nevis.—William James ; destination, Nevis.—Samuell Souther ; destination, Nevis.—William Everell ; destination, Nevis or Montserrat. —William Smith ; destination, Nevis.—William Smith ; destination, Nevis.— Samson Burch ; destination, Montserrat.—Roger Winslow ; destination, Virginia. —Katherine Williams ; destination, Nevis.—Rowland Lentall ; destination, Nevis. —Christopher Carr ; destination, Nevis.—Samuell Beale ; destination, New England.—John Williams ; destination, New England.

Page 183
Joseph Colston ; destination, New England.—Samuell Hopkins ; destination, Nevis.—Roger Price ; destination, Barbadoes.—Joan James ; destination, Nevis.— Johannes Heale ; destination, Virginia.—Samuell Davis ; destination, Nevis.— George Heunnan (?) ; destination, Virginia.—Richard William Roberts ; destination, Virginia.—Jonathan Madgwick ; destination, Virginia.—Joseph ffranckum ; destination, Virginia.—Maurice Williams ; destination, Barbadoes.—William Edward ; destination, New England.—Adam Wallis ; destination, Virginia.— Nathaniel Parker ; destination, Barbadoes.—John Jacob ; destination, Barbadoes.— Joane Kent ; destination, Barbadoes.—ffrancis William ; destination, Virginia.

Page 184
Thomas Jones ; destination, Barbadoes.—Samuell Jones ; destination, Virginia. —John Brookes ; destination, Virginia.—Joane Morgan ; destination, Virginia.—

Elizabeth Griffen ; destination, Nevis.—Edith ffrankes ; destination, Barbadoes.
—Thomas Homes ; destination, Barbadoes.—John Bacon ; destination, Virginia.—
John Townsend ; destination, Virginia.—Sare ffee (*sic*) James ; destination,
Nevis.—Thomas James ; destination, Nevis.—Thomas Mountford ; destination,
Virginia.—Richard Bush ; destination, Virginia.—Bartholomew Penn ; destina-
tion, Virginia.—Richard Kerswell ; destination, Nevis.—Robert Thare ; destination,
Nevis.—John Morgan ; destination, Virginia.

Page 185
      Jenkin Williams ; destination, Virginia.—Mary Doore ; destination, Nevis.—
Sara Street ; destination, Virginia.—Emanuell Evans ; destination, Virginia.
—Richard Day ; destination, Nevis.—John Bowler ; destination, Nevis.—Deborah
Bowler ; destination, Nevis.—Elizabeth Jones ; destination, Nevis.—Margarett
Jones ; destination, Virginia.—Thomas Higgs ; destination, Nevis.—Mary Davis ;
destination, Nevis.—William Lingham ; destination, Nevis.—Richard Maylerd ;
destination, Nevis.—Timothy Clare ; destination, Nevis.—ffrances Belcher ; destination, Nevis.—Margarett Clarke ; destination, Virginia.—Edward Clarke ; destination, Virginia.—John Rennolls ; destination, Virginia.

Page 186
      Mathew Walter ; destination, Virginia.—William Rudman ; destination,
Maryland.—Thomas Lewellin ; destination, Nevis.—Richard Howard ; destina-
tion, Nevis.—William Jenkins ; destination, Nevis.—Thomas Davis ; destination,
Virginia.—Margarett Griffin ; destination, Virginia.—Joice Griffeth ; destination,
Virginia.—Judith Davis ; destination, Nevis.—Stephen Hartly ; destination, Vir-
ginia.—John Tripp ; destination, Virginia.—William Jones ; destination, Barbadoes.
—John fflowers ; destination, Virginia.—William Williams ; destination, Virginia.—
Walter Williams ; destination, Barbadoes.—Rebecca Hellier ; destination, Nevis.
—Mary Vinson ; destination, Virginia.—Joane Chechy ; destination, Maryland.

Page 187
      Anthony Ewen ; destination, Virginia.—John Ansin ; destination, Virginia.
—Mary Williams ; destination, Virginia.—John Walby (*Katherine*) ; destination,
Virginia.—William Hort ; destination, Virginia.—William Beard ; destination,
Virginia.—Thomas Morgan ; destination, Maryland.—John Arden ; destination,
Virginia.—John Thomas ; destination, Virginia.—Prudence Punny ; destination,
Virginia.—John Thomas ; destination, Virginia.—Isabell Clarke ; destination, Vir-
ginia.—Phillip Teverton (*Society*) ; destination, Maryland.—John ffreeman (*Sub-
mission*) ; destination, Virginia.—Georg Martin (*Submission*) ; destination, Virginia.
—Timothy Channter (*True Love*) ; destination, Virginia.—Elioner Kirby ; destina-
tion, Virginia.—Ann Rowly ; destination, Virginia.

Page 188
      Richard Mason ; destination, Virginia.—William Durbin (*Nevis Adventure*) ;
destination, Nevis.—Margarett Reece ; destination, Virginia.—Phillip Tyler ;
destination, Virginia.—Richard ffoskew (*Content*) ; destination, New England.—
Mary Nilston ; destination, Virginia.—Thomas Lloyd ; destination, Virginia.
—Robert Johnson ; destination, Virginia.—Nevill Draint ; destination, Virginia.—
Walter Welsh ; destination, Virginia.—Robert Wattkins ; destination, Virginia.—

Edward Curtis; destination, Virginia.—John Hawkes (*Samuel and Mary*); destination, Virginia.—Edward Phillip; destination, Virginia.—Robert Hort; destination, Virginia.—Christopher Parsons; destination, Virginia.—John ffisher (*Katherine*); destination, Virginia.

Page 189
    William Phillips; destination, Virginia.—Robert Lewis; destination, Virginia. —Reece Evans; destination, Nevis.—George Dodderidge; destination, Virginia. —William Wintor; destination, Maryland.—John ffloyd; destination, Virginia.— George Soley; destination, Virginia.—Alice Soley; destination, Virginia.—John ffaddery; destination, Virginia.—Richard Jones; destination, Virginia.—John Drewett; destination, Virginia.—William Payne; destination, Virginia.—Ann Morgan; destination, Virginia.—Jane Bottle; destination, Virginia.—John Mathyson; destination (no place given).—Andrew Lloyd (*Katherine*); destination, Virginia.—Barnaby Samborne; destination, Barbadoes.—John Burges (*Unichorne*); destination, Virginia.

Page 190
    Jane Stevenson (*William and Ann*); destination, Virginia.—Jane Spurry (*Society*); destination, Virginia.—Katherine Jones (*Society*); destination, Virginia. —John Dodderidge (*Society*); destination, Virginia.—John Adely (*Society*); destination, Virginia.—John ffidoe (*Samuell and Mary*); destination, Virginia.—Robert ffidoe (*Samuell and Mary*); destination, Virginia.—Joell Perry (*Society*); destination, Virginia.—Richard Ricketts; destination, Virginia.—Mante (?) Bisgood (*Katherine*); destination, Virginia.—John Clarke (*William and Ann*); destination, Virginia.—Mary Howell; destination, Virginia.—Israell Batt (*Submission*); destination, Virginia.—John Turner (*Katherine*); destination, Virginia.—John Craze (*Samuell and Mary*); destination, Virginia.—Benjamin Stringer (*Richard James* [*sic*]); destination, Virginia.—Edward Gilson (*William and Ann*); destination, Virginia.

Page 191
    Mary Benson (*Nevis Adventure*); destination, Nevis.—Katherine Oakeford (*Richard*); destination, Barbadoes.—Elizabeth Oakeford (*Richard*); destination, Barbadoes.—James Wright (*Joseph*); destination, Virginia.—John Wathen (*ffrancis and Mary*); destination, Maryland.—Thomas Jones (*ffrancis and Mary*); destination, Virginia.—John Roberts (*Katherine*); destination, Virginia.—Roger Williams (*Nevis Adventure*); destination, Nevis.—Walter Griffis (*Society*); destination, Virginia.—John Bateman (*Joseph*); destination, Virginia.—Richard Hally (*Unichorne*); destination, Virginia.—Thomas Wootten (*Unichorne*); destination, Virginia. —John Wootten (*Unichorne*); destination, Virginia.—Robert Sparkes (*Society*); destination, Maryland.—Thomas Lewis (*True Love*); destination, Virginia.— Thomas Clement (*Richard*); destination, Barbadoes.—John Batchelle (*ffrancis and Mary*); destination, Virginia.

Page 192
    John Bowen (*ffrancis and Mary*); destination, Virginia.—John Owen (*ffrancis and Mary*); destination, Virginia.—Robert Champion (*Agreement*); destination, Virginia.—John Clarke; destination, Nevis.—Richard Martin (*William and Ann*);

destination, Virginia.—John Browneing (*Richard*) ; destination, Barbadoes.—
Ann Browneing (*Richard*) ; destination, Barbadoes.—William Benham ; destina-
tion, Nevis.—George Williams (*Agreement*) ; destination, Virginia.—Robert Aler ;
destination, Virginia.—Abraham Richards (*True Love*) ; destination, Virginia.—
Richard Lightwood (*Richard and James*) ; destination, Maryland.—Mary Tanner
(*Richard and James*) ; destination (no place given).—Benjamin Thorneton (*Society*) ;
destination, Virginia.—John Snow (*Samuell and Mary*) ; destination, Virginia.
—William Jenkins (*Richard and James*) ; destination, Maryland.

Page 193
    Edward Gelson (*William and Ann*) ; destination, Virginia.—Anthony Norton ;
destination, Virginia.—Thomas Harris ; destination, Maryland.—Elizabeth Ship-
boy ; destination, Maryland.—Grace Upton (*Richard and James*) ; destination,
Maryland.—Elizabeth Horwood (*Agreement*) ; destination, Virginia.—Benjamin
Littlehales (*John*) ; destination, Barbadoes.—Thomas Gild (*Richard and James*) ;
destination, Virginia.—Edward Serman (*True Love*) ; destination, Virginia.—
Thomas Harris (*William and Ann*) ; destination, Virginia.—Nicholas Jones (*Unichorne*) ; destination, Virginia.—Zachery Cadle (*Society*) ; destination, Virginia.—
Richard Andrew (*John*) ; destination (no place given).—Samuell Deareing (*Uni-
chorne*) ; destination (no place given).—Thomas Nicholas (*Society*) ; destination,
Virginia.—Robert Skelton (*True Love*) ; destination, Virginia.

Page 194
    Christopher Jones (*Jacob*) ; destination, Montserrat.—John Edwards ; destina-
tion, Virginia.—John Spencer ; destination, Virginia.—Mary Bouton ; destination,
Virginia.—Lewis Griffeth ; destination, Virginia.—Griffey Lloyd ; destination,
Virginia.—William Nicholas (*Agreement*) ; destination, Virginia.—Edmund Punford
(*Unichorne*) ; destination, Virginia.—Christian Jones (*Armes of Bristoll*) ; destination,
Barbadoes.—John Rawlins (*Agreement*) ; destination, Virginia.—Charles Williams
(*Unichorne*) ; destination, Virginia.—Thomas Powell (*Agreement*) ; destination,
Virginia.—John Stallard (*Agreement*) ; destination, Virginia.—James Sarsaine ;
destination, Virginia.—Elizabeth Curtis (*Unichorne*) ; destination, Maryland.—
Robert Smith (*Unichorne*) ; destination, Maryland.

Page 195
    James Browne (*Gabriell*) ; destination, Nevis.—Thomas Harry ; destination,
Montserrat.—William Harris (*Unichorne*) ; destination, Virginia.—Christopher
Rowning (*Unichorne*) ; destination, Maryland.—William George ; destination,
Virginia.—Thomas Olliver (*Agreement*) ; destination, Virginia.—Thomas Spencer
(*Agreement*) ; destination, Virginia.—Jane Godson (*Seaflower*) ; destination, Barba-
does.—Edward Ledden ; destination, Virginia.—Launcelett Webb (*Unichorne*) ;
destination, Virginia.—Elizabeth Kingson (*Unichorne*) ; destination, Virginia.—
Judith Reeve (*Seaflower*) ; destination, Barbadoes.—Henry Windard (*Seaflower*) ;
destination, Barbadoes.—Grace Long (*Unichorne*) ; destination, Virginia.—Patience
Moore (*Unichorne*) ; destination, Virginia.—Thomas Rendall (*Unichorne*) ; destination, Virginia.

Page 196
    Samuell Holliday (*Unichorne*) ; destination, Virginia.—Morgan Thomas
(*Jacob*) ; destination, Jamaica.—Isaac Jones ; destination, Montserrat.—Thomas

Nicholls ; destination, Barbadoes.—William Lewis (*Unichorne*) ; destination, Virginia.—Robert Sharpe (*Agreement*) ; destination, Virginia.—David Penery (*Jacob*) ; destination, Montserrat.—Jane Chegley ; destination, Barbadoes.—Henry Phillips (*Jacob*) ; destination, Nevis.—Richard Smith (*Jacob*) ; destination, Montserrat.—John Willis ; destination, Barbadoes.—Andrew Phillips ; destination, Virginia.—Lewis Jones (*Gabriell*) ; destination, Nevis.—John Welch ; destination, Jamaica.—Charles Slaughter (*Agreement*) ; destination, Virginia.—John Bayly (*Gabriell*) ; destination, Nevis.

Page 197

Mary Jefferys (*Agreement*) ; destination, Virginia.—Samuell Jones ; destination, Virginia.—Robert Gilling (*Love's Increase*) ; destination, Nevis.—Margarett Seaward (*Jacob*) ; destination, Nevis.—Thomas Webb ; destination, Barbadoes.—William Battle ; destination, Nevis.—Dorothy Katherine (*Love's Increase*) ; destination, Nevis. —Phillip Davy (*Elizabeth of Gloucester*) ; destination, Jamaica.—Edward Liddiard (*Elizabeth of Gloucester*) ; destination, Jamaica.—Hugh Pew ; destination, Nevis. —George Quarrells (*Elizabeth of Gloucester*) ; destination, Jamaica.—Henry Triptoe (*Elizabeth*) ; destination, Jamaica.—Thomas Mitchell ; destination, Jamaica.— Edward Robert (*Golden Lyon*) ; destination, Barbadoes.—Margarett Hutchins (*Elizabeth of Gloucester*) ; destination, Jamaica.—David Collins (*Jacob*) ; destination, Montserrat.

Page 198

David Price (*Reformation*) ; destination, Barbadoes.—Thomas Newman (*Elizabeth of Gloucester*) ; destination, Jamaica.—Peter Legg (*Reformation*) ; destination, Barbadoes.—James Daulton (*Gabriell*) ; destination, Nevis.—Richard Trew (*Elizabeth*) ; destination, Jamaica.—Howell Winny (*Gabriell*) ; destination, Montserrat.—John Ives (*Elizabeth*) ; destination, Nevis or Jamaica.—Robert Richardson (*Bristoll Armes*) ; destination, Barbadoes.—William Blewett (*Reformation*) ; destination, Barbadoes.—Roger ffloyd (*Gabriell*) ; destination, Nevis.—Abraham Williams (*Robert*) ; destination, Barbadoes.—Peter ffuller (*Love's Increase*) ; destination, Nevis.—Richard Martin (*Reformation*) ; destination, Barbadoes.—Andrew Baker (*Robert*) ; destination, Barbadoes.—Joane Wike (*Robert*) ; destination, Barbadoes. —John Lucas ; destination, Jamaica.

Page 199

John Ebden (*Reformation*) ; destination, Barbadoes.—Edward Hooper (*Gabriell*) ; destination (no place given).—Walter Howell ; destination, Nevis.— William Hide ; destination, Barbadoes.—William Knight ; destination, Barbadoes. —Richard Smith (*Reformation*) ; destination, Barbadoes.—Henry Leafe (*Robert*) ; destination, Barbadoes.—Charles Iles (*Hope*) ; destination, Barbadoes.—Daniell Curry (*Golden Lion*) ; destination, Barbadoes.—Thomasin Curry (*Golden Lion*) ; destination, Barbadoes.—Ann Smith (*Robert*) ; destination, Barbadoes.—Turberville [blank] (*Gabriell*) ; destination (no place given).—Hector Lewis (*Elizabeth of Gloucester*) ; destination, Jamaica.—Morgan Reece (*Love's Increase*) ; destination, Nevis.—John Low (*Robert*) ; destination, Barbadoes.—William Thomas (*Gabriell*) ; destination, Nevis.

Page 200

Jane Peale (*Gabriell*) ; destination, Nevis.—Robert Chivers (*Reformation*) ; destination, Barbadoes.—Thomas Munbedd ; destination, Jamaica.—Grispian

Downeing (*Gabriell*) ; destination, Barbadoes and Leeward Is.—John Skinner (*Gabriell*) ; destination, Barbadoes and Leeward Is.—Simon Wall ; destination, Jamaica.—Zacharia Hancock (*Robert*) ; destination, Barbadoes.—John Parry ; destination, Nevis.—William Jones (*Love's Increase*) ; destination, Nevis.—Walter Tacy (*Love's Increase*) ; destination, Nevis.—Reece Williams (*Love's Increase*) ; destination, Nevis.—David Knowles (*Love's Increase*) ; destination, Nevis.— Elizabeth Hawkins (*Love's Increase*) ; destination, Nevis.—ffrancis Bourne (*Love's Increase*) ; destination, Nevis.—Richard Jackson (*Love's Increase*) ; destination, Nevis.—John Davis (*Love's Increase*) ; destination, Antigua.

Page 201
    John Bacon (*Love's Increase*) ; destination, Nevis.—Thomas Davis (*Blackamore*) ; destination, Nevis.—Jeremy Clarke (*The ffrench ship of Boston*) ; destination, New England.—George Harris (*Robert and Hester*) ; destination, New England.— Thomas Mash (*Jeremy*) ; destination, Nevis.—David Teague (*Jeremy*) ; destination, Nevis.—James Brewer (*Jeremy*) ; destination, Nevis.—Elizabeth Cox (*Jeremy*) ; destination, Nevis.—David Seard (*Jeremy*) ; destination, Nevis.—David Phillips ; destination, Nevis.—Miles Pinil ; destination, Nevis.—Hannah Bicker (*Jeremy*) ; destination, Nevis.—Thomas James ; destination, Nevis.—Anthony Sloper (*The ffrench ship of Boston*) ; destination, New England.—John Harris ; destination, New England.—Michael Morgan ; destination, Nevis.—Thomas Corsey (*Jeremy*) ; destination, Nevis.

Page 202
    Robert James (*Unity*) ; destination, Nevis.—Nicholas Wattkin (*Jeremy*) ; destination, Antigua.—John Paine (*Jeremy*) ; destination, Nevis.—John Burle (*Jeremy*) ; destination, Nevis.—Mary Davis ; destination, Nevis.—James Ash (*Jeremy*) ; destination, Antigua.—Robert Churchill (*Society*) ; destination, New England.—Lewis Thomas (*Jeremy*) ; destination, Nevis.—Jenkin Rice (*Jeremy*) ; destination, Nevis.—George Bartley (*Jeremy*) ; destination, Nevis.—Anne May ; destination, Antigua or Caribbee Is.—Mathew Shepherd (*Neptune*) ; destination, Barbadoes.—John Short ; destination, Antigua or Caribbee Is.—Robert Millard ; destination, New England.

Page 203
    John Hort (*Neptune*) ; destination, Barbadoes.—Joane Martin ; destination, New England.—Thomas Minny (*New found Land Merchant*) ; destination, New England.—Isaac Wiley (*Laurell*) ; destination, Barbadoes.—Robert Richard ; destination, Barbadoes.—John Evans (*Neptune*) ; destination, Barbadoes.—James Williams ; destination (no place given).—Daniell Jones ; destination, Nevis.—Timothy Burton (*Neptune*) ; destination, Barbadoes.—John Hopkins (*Laurell*) ; destination, Nevis or Jamaica.—George Slayler (*Hopefull Katharine*) ; destination, Jamaica.—Thomas Davy (*Hopefull Katharine*) ; destination, Jamaica.—John Price ; destination, Jamaica or Barbadoes.—Edmund Howell (*Laurell*) ; destination, Nevis.—Nathaniell Benson (*Laurell*) ; destination, Nevis or Jamaica.

Page 204
    Thomas Davis (*Laurell*) ; destination, Nevis, Jamaica or New England.— William Badger (*Laurell*) ; destination, Nevis.—William Harding (*Laurell*) ; destination, Jamaica.—Walter Berry (*Laurell*) ; destination, Jamaica.—Henery Masy ;

destination, Virginia.—William Davis (*Katherine*) ; destination, Virginia.—Thomas Watkins (*Lion*) ; destination, Jamaica.—Edward Davis (*Planter*) ; destination, Barbadoes.—Phillip Tiler (*Planter*) ; destination, Barbadoes.—Theophilus Harkett (*Lyon*) ; destination, Jamaica.—Thomas Deare (*Patience*) ; destination, Virginia.— Ellis Jones (*Planter*) ; destination, Barbadoes.—Anne Shay (*Planter*) ; destination, Barbadoes.

Page 205
Jane Caple (*Society*) ; destination, Virginia.—ffrancis Reese (*Society*) ; destination, Virginia.—Elizabeth Iles (*Patience*) ; destination, Virginia.—Edward Whittman (*Society*) ; destination, Virginia.—George Hughs (*Society*) ; destination, Virginia.—Mary Jones (*Triall*) ; destination, Virginia.—Jane Gray (*Triall*) ; destination, Virginia.—Edward Andreges (*Society*) ; destination, Virginia.—Isaac Gingell (*Society*) ; destination, Virginia.—Hugh Cartwright (*Katharine*) ; destination, Virginia.—Charles ffeakley (*Katharine*) ; destination, Virginia.—Margeret Richard (*Katharine*) ; destination, Virginia.

Page 206
Thomas Murphe (*Richard and James*) ; destination, Virginia.—Anne Stradling (*Richard and James*) ; destination, Virginia.—Anne Baker (*Society*) ; destination, Virginia.—Mary Sharrett (*Society*) ; destination, Virginia.—William Cole (*Society*) ; destination, Virginia.—Susan Peters (*Society*) ; destination, Virginia.—Richard Scarrutt (*Thomas and Mary*) ; destination, Nevis.—William Davis (*Triall*) ; destination, Virginia.—Peter Hellier (*Katharine*) ; destination, Virginia.—William Townsend (*Triall*) ; destination, Virginia.—Hugh Rice ; destination, Jamaica.—Shadrick George (*Katharine*) ; destination, Virginia.

Page 207
Thomas Moggs (*Triall*) ; destination, Virginia.—David Lloyd (*Thomas and Mary*) ; destination, Nevis.—Hugh Lloyd (*Thomas and Mary*) ; destination, Nevis. —David Richard (*Triall*) ; destination, Virginia.—Martha Peterson (*Triall*) ; destination, Virginia.—Richard Weaver (*Restauration*) ; destination, Virginia.— Johannes Chambers (*Restauration*) ; destination, Virginia.—Mary Medems (*Lyon*) ; destination, Jamaica.—Daniell Dune (*Lyon*) ; destination, Jamaica.—Mathias Dring (*Society*) ; destination, Virginia.—James Harris (*Society*) ; destination, Virginia.— Thomas Browne (*Society*) ; destination, Virginia.

Page 208
Richard Evans (*Triall*) ; destination, Virginia.—Abraham Joslin (*Restauration*) ; destination, Virginia.—Robert Pumphret (*Katharine*) ; destination, Virginia.— Thomas Marshall (*Katharine*) ; destination, Virginia.—John Ingrum ; destination, Virginia.—Bryan Doubty (*Triall*) ; destination, Virginia.—John White (*Triall*) ; destination, Virginia.—John Bennett (*Katharine*) ; destination, Virginia.—Thomas Ellmore (*Society*) ; destination, Virginia.—Walter Benford (*Katharine*) ; destination, Virginia.—Thomas Turton (*William*) ; destination, Nevis or Virginia.—John Andrews (*Society*) ; destination, Virginia.

Page 209
John Norrish (*Triall*) ; destination, Virginia.—Morgan Thomas (*Triall*) ; destination, Virginia.—William Williams (*Stephen*) ; destination, Virginia.—Rebecca

Knight (*Hercules*) ; destination, Virginia.—James Pendergras (*Triall*) ; destination, Virginia.—Richard Lase (*Triall*) ; destination, Virginia.—William Whittfeild (*Triall*) ; destination, Virginia.—Sara Williams (*Triall*) ; destination, Virginia.— Abraham Ames ; destination, Virginia.—Roger Reece ; destination, Virginia.— Thomas Sheard (*Triall*) ; destination, Virginia.—Thomas Wright ; destination, Virginia.

Page 210
John Clarke (*Katherine*) ; destination, Virginia.—Joane Bleathen ; destination, Virginia.—Anne Attkins ; destination, Virginia.—Thomas House ; destination, Virginia.—Thomas King ; destination, Virginia.—Richard Whitturd ; destination, Nevis.—Thomas Lewis (*Triall*) ; destination, Virginia.—Joseph Powell ; destination, Virginia.—George Harbert ; destination, Virginia.—John Hayden (*Triall*) ; destination, Virginia.—Anne Davis ; destination, Virginia.—Reece Price ; destination, Virginia.

Page 211
Thomas Newman ; destination, Virginia.—John Hand ; destination, Virginia. —Thomas Harris ; destination, Virginia.—Jonathan St. Alban ; destination, Barbadoes.—Hester Garberry (*Steven*) ; destination, Virginia.—Leonard Coate ; destination, Virginia.—James Morgan ; destination, Virginia.—John Prance (*ffenix*) ; destination, Virginia.—Susannah Davis ; destination, Maryland.—Thomas Gollidge (*Steven*) ; destination, Virginia.—Elizabeth Gollidge (*Steven*) ; destination, Virginia. —Daniell Edwards ; destination, Virginia.

Page 212
Robert Thomas ; destination, Virginia.—Goodlove Bright (*ffrancis and Mary*) ; destination, Virginia.—William Brooke ; destination, Barbadoes.—Daniell Howell (*Katharine*) ; destination, Virginia.—Walter Lewis (*ffrancis and Mary*) ; destination, Virginia.—William Bowen (*ffrancis and Mary*) ; destination, Virginia.—John Richards (*ffrancis and Mary*) ; destination, Virginia.—Thomas Wates (*ffenix*) ; destination, Virginia.—Edward Provin (*Richard and James*) ; destination, Virginia. —Mary Boyd (*ffrancis and Mary*) ; destination, Virginia.—Thomas Pitchard (*ffrancis and Mary*) ; destination, Virginia.—Hugh Evans (*ffrancis and Mary*) ; destination, Virginia.

Page 213
James Garolls (*ffrancis and Mary*) ; destination, Virginia.—Thomas James (*ffrancis and Mary*) ; destination, Virginia.—Thomas Hooke (*ffrancis and Mary*) ; destination, Virginia.—John Wines ; destination, Virginia.—ffrancis Baker (*Samuell and Mary*) ; destination, Virginia.—Richard Dummutt (*Nevis Adventure*) ; destination, Nevis.—Lewis Howell ; destination, Virginia.—Mary Hull ; destination, Barbadoes.—John Gouldby ; destination, Virginia.—Thomas Webb ; destination, Virginia.—William Wills (*ffrancis and Mary*) ; destination, Virginia.—Sarah Jennyns ; destination, Virginia.

Page 214
Jane Jones (*Richard and James*) ; destination, Virginia.—Mary Browne ; destination, Virginia.—William Jones (*Lion*) ; destination, Barbadoes.—Katharine Harris (*Samuell and Mary*) ; destination, Virginia.—Margaret Whitehead (*Nevis*

Adventure) ; destination, Nevis.—Edward Phillips (*Richard*) ; destination, Nevis.—
Robert Dennis (*Richard and James*) ; destination, Virginia.—Anne Lercock (*Pearle*) ;
destination, Virginia.—John Johns ; destination, Virginia.—Edward Avery (*Richard
and James*) ; destination, Virginia.—Henery Tatlock (*William and Anne*) ; destination, Virginia.—Henery Brombill (*William and Anne*) ; destination, Virginia.

Page 215
Thomas Bridg (*William and Anne*) ; destination, Virginia.—ffaithfull Gording
(*Nevis Adventure*) ; destination, Nevis.—Edward Phillips (*Merryland Merchant*) ;
destination, Virginia.—Thomas Attwood (*Pearle*) ; destination, Virginia.—William
Goose (*ffrancis and Mary*) ; destination, Virginia.—Judith Martin (*Richard and
James*) ; destination, Virginia.—Barbary More (*Agreement*) ; destination, Virginia.
—Sarah ffowler ; destination, Maryland.—William Hathaway (*Richard*) ; destina-
tion, Barbadoes.—Mary Weakley (*John ffrigatt*) ; destination, Barbadoes.—Mary
Jones (*John ffrigatt*) ; destination, Barbadoes.—Lewis William ; destination,
Virginia.

Page 216
Zacharias Thomas ; destination, Virginia.—Rowland Minton (*Maryland
Merchant*) ; destination, Virginia.—Thomas Whiting (*ffrancis and Mary*) ; destina-
tion, Maryland.—Henery Mores ; destination, Virginia.—John Bruiny ; destination,
Virginia.—William Sage (*Seafflower*) ; destination, Barbadoes.—Giles Rendall ;
destination, Maryland.—Thomas Hughs (*Unicorne*) ; destination, Virginia.—John
Obonny (*Baltimore*) ; destination, Virginia.—Walter Garratt ; destination, Barba-
does.—William John Jenkins (*Unicorne*) ; destination, Virginia.—Reece Thomas
(*Unicorne*) ; destination, Virginia.

Page 217
William Williams (*Unicorne*) ; destination, Virginia.—Henery Butler (*Balti-
more*) ; destination, Virginia.—Grace Jones (*Samuell and Mary*) ; destination,
Virginia.—Mary Lambert (*Samuell and Mary*) ; destination, Virginia.—Thomas
Eliott (*Samuell and Mary*) ; destination, Virginia.—Thomas Williams (*Samuell and
Mary*) ; destination, Virginia.—Moses Kingman (*Richard*) ; destination, Barbadoes.
—Sarah Owen ; destination, Virginia.—Elizabeth Williams ; destination, Virginia.
—George Butler (*Agreement*) ; destination, Virginia.—John Matthews (*Agreement*) ;
destination, Virginia.—Christopher Baldwin (*Richard*) ; destination, Virginia.

Page 218
Matthew Pope (*Unicorne*) ; destination, Virginia.—Jennett Phillips (*Gabriel*) ;
destination, Nevis.—David Bowen (*Richard*) ; destination, Barbadoes or Nevis.—
Benjamine Tovey (*Richard*) ; destination, Barbadoes.—Richard Lamforth (*Agree-
ment*) ; destination, Virginia.—Anne fuller ; destination, Virginia.—Aron Elsden ;
destination, Virginia.—Elizabeth Williams (*Agreement*) ; destination, Virginia.—
Richard Cole (*Richard*) ; destination, Barbadoes.—Peter Edwards (*Barbadoes
Merchant*) ; destination, Virginia.—William Thomas ; destination, Barbadoes.—
Edward Wallis (*Gabriell*) ; destination, Nevis.

Page 219
Joseph Hunt ; destination, Nevis.—Richard Scammell (*Barbadoes Merchant*) ;
destination, Virginia.—Charles Lewis (*Agreement*) ; destination, Virginia.—Joseph

David (*Agreement*); destination, Virginia.—James Moody; destination, Virginia.
—Thomas Lepper (*Agreement*); destination, Virginia.—Robert Jarvis (*Gabriell*);
destination, Nevis.—William Brewerton (*Agreement*); destination, Virginia.—
Samuell Willett (*Barbadoes Merchant*); destination, Virginia.—Mary Acres (*Agreement*); destination, Virginia.—Jone Good (*Gabriell*); destination, Nevis.—Mary
Dennum (*Gabriell*); destination, Nevis.

Page 220
Phillip Olliver (*Nevis Merchant*); destination, Nevis.—John Browne (*Nevis
Merchant*); destination, Nevis.—William Biles (*Nevis Merchant*); destination,
Nevis.—Roger Monke (*Gabriell*); destination, Nevis.—James Bridduck; destination, Nevis.—John Anderson (*Gabriell*); destination, Nevis.—Christopher Blunt;
destination, Nevis.—John West; destination, Nevis.—George Hopkins (*Nevis
Merchant*); destination, Nevis.—Robert Player; destination, Nevis.—Joane Burgey
(*Jeremy*); destination, Nevis.—Thomas Sam (*Jeremy*); destination, Nevis.

Page 221
Richard Hill (*Nevis Merchant*); destination, Nevis.—Richard Wells (*Nevis
Merchant*); destination, Montserrat.—George Thomas (*Nevis Merchant*), destination, Montserrat.—Morgan Thomas; destination, Jamaica.—Laurence ffrier
(*Nevis Merchant*); destination, Montserrat.—francis Pester; destination, Barbadoes
or Leeward Is.—James Lewis; destination, Nevis.—Mary Goulding; destination,
Nevis.—William Jones; destination, Nevis.—Charles Rosser (*Nevis Merchant*);
destination, Montserrat.—Elizabeth Barber; destination, Nevis.—francis Norcomb;
destination, Nevis or Barbadoes.—Anthony Bayly; destination, Nevis.—Anne
Glover; destination, Nevis.—William Boudley, snr.; destination, Montserrat.

Page 222
William Boudley, jnr.; destination, Montserrat.—John Boudley; destination,
Montserrat.—Elizabeth Jones (*Nevis Merchant*); destination, Nevis.—Thomas
Barnes (*Nevis Merchant*); destination, Nevis.—John Merrill (*Exchange*); destination, Barbadoes.—John Gwilliam (*Nevis Merchant*); destination, Nevis.—Maudlin
Shaw; destination, Barbadoes.—Hanna Bayly; destination, Barbadoes.—Giles
Jones; destination, Montserrat.—John White; destination, Jamaica.—David
Spurle; destination, Jamaica.—George Jefferis; destination, .Jamaica.—John
Jones; destination, Barbadoes.—Hugh Parry; destination, Virginia.

Page 223
Robert Hughs; destination, Virginia.—John Hibbs (*Society*); destination,
Virginia.—Matthias Williams; destination, Virginia.—Thomas Harris (*Triall*);
destination, Virginia.—Elizabeth Tayler; destination, Virginia.—William Evans;
destination, Virginia.—Peter Major (*Triall*); destination, Virginia.—John Lovering;
destination, Virginia.—John ffoord (*Joseph*); destination, Virginia.—Phillip Cox
(*Joseph*); destination, Virginia.—William Bullock; destination, Virginia.—John
Lewis (*Society*); destination, Virginia.—Martha Price; destination, Virginia.—
Margaret Miskell; destination, Virginia.

Page 224
Sarah Price; destination, Virginia.—John Russell; destination, Virginia.—
John Ditcher; destination, Virginia.—Thomas Olliver; destination, Virginia.

—John Pope; destination, Virginia.—William Lewis; destination, Jamaica or Caribbee Is.—John Bruton; destination, Virginia.—John Pye; destination, Virginia.—John Bridgeman; destination, Virginia.—Anthony Gerrard; destination, Virginia.—William Horwood; destination, Virginia.—Charles Barneshaw (*Triall*); destination, Virginia.—George Pearce (*Society*); destination, Virginia.—William Penderton; destination, Virginia.

Page 225
Joshua Nason; destination, Virginia.—John Phillips; destination, Virginia.—William Evans; destination, Virginia.—John Reede (*Sarah and Elizabeth*); destination, Virginia.—Robert Poore; destination, Virginia.—Grace Silcockes (*Triall*); destination, Virginia.—Elioner Luffe; destination, Virginia.—Morgan Jones; destination, Virginia.—James Symons; destination, Jamaica.—Edward Love; destination, Virginia.—William Mishew; destination, Maryland.—William Plovey; destination, Maryland.—William Hall; destination, Maryland.—Thomas Ward; destination, Maryland.

Page 226
George Horne; destination, Maryland.—Walter Kerswell; destination, Virginia.—George King (*Richard and James*); destination, Virginia.—Thomas Tyler; destination, Virginia.—John Walner; destination, Barbadoes.—Stephen Marshall (*Tryall*); destination, Virginia.—John Marshall (*Tryall*); destination, Virginia.—William Smith; destination, Virginia.—John Veltum; destination, Virginia.—John Perry (*Joseph*); destination, Virginia.—Abraham Matthews; destination, Virginia.—William Mills (*Triall*); destination, Virginia.—Mary Haines (*Society*); destination, Virginia.—Thomas Wells; destination, Virginia.

Page 227
James Temple (*Katharine*); destination, Virginia.—James Willkins (*Katharine*); destination, Virginia.—Thomas Willkins (*Katharine*); destination, Virginia.—Elizabeth Gowing (*Katharine*); destination, Virginia.—Agnis Temple (*Katharine*); destination, Virginia.—Mary Loder (*Katharine*); destination, Virginia.—Matthew Warren; destination, Virginia.—William Tiley (*Concord*); destination, Virginia.—Robert Phipps (*Samuell and Mary*); destination, Virginia.—William Sheppard (*Samuell and Mary*); destination, Virginia.—Richard Mannington; destination, Virginia.—William Talley (*Triall*); destination, Virginia.—William Roberts (*Society*); destination, Virginia.—James Younge (*Society*); destination, Virginia.

Page 228
Richard Willcox (*Triall*); destination, Virginia.—John Williams (*Stephen*); destination, Virginia.—William Price; destination, Virginia.—Ann Lewis; destination, Virginia.—Able Norrice (*Society*); destination, Virginia.—Mary George (*Adventure*); destination, Nevis.—Margarett Margan (*sic*); destination, Nevis.—Thomas Jenkins; destination, Virginia.—Howell Jones; destination, Virginia.—John Suger (*Stephen*); destination, Virginia.—Richard Porcher (*Stephen*); destination, Virginia.—John Lewis (*Thomas and Mary*); destination, Virginia.—Jane Badge (*Triall*); destination, Virginia.—Thomas Evans (*William and Ann*); destination, Virginia.

L

Page 229

Elizabeth Probbin (*Society*) ; destination, Virginia.—Bartholomew Wolfe ; destination, Virginia.—Richard Andrews ; destination, Virginia.—Rachaell Robins (*Samuell and Mary*) ; destination, Virginia.—David Griffin ; destination, Nevis.— Thomas Baker ; destination, Virginia.—John Baker ; destination, Virginia.—George Howell (*Stephen*) ; destination, Virginia.—William Smith (*Stephen*) ; destination, Virginia.—John Heath ; destination, Virginia.—John Tucker ; destination, Virginia. —John Cluck ; destination, Virginia.—William Haukes ; destination, Virginia.— Deborah Watts ; destination, Virginia.—William ffoord ; destination, Barbadoes. —James Thomas ; destination, Virginia.

Page 230

Joseph Rogers (*Elizabeth and Sarah*) ; destination, Virginia.—John Buxton ; destination, Virginia.—Benjamin Blacklock ; destination, Virginia.—William Reade ; destination, Virginia.—Charles Jones ; destination, Maryland.—Robert Phillips ; destination, Virginia.—John Knight ; destination, Virginia.—William Poun ; destination, Virginia.—Henery Davis ; destination, Virginia.—William Wheler ; destination, Virginia.—Thomas Mitchell ; destination, Virginia.—Thomas Skudamore ; destination, Virginia.—Susannah Wray ; destination, Virginia.—James Johnson ; destination, Jamaica.

Page 231

John Hartily (*Richard and James*) ; destination, Maryland.—William Holland ; destination, Maryland.—Thomas Camme ; destination, Maryland.—Edward Smith ; destination, Maryland.—Stephen Pegg ; destination, Maryland.—Thomas Roe ; destination, Maryland.—John Dammes ; destination, Maryland.—Grace Turner ; destination, Maryland.—Richard Attkison ; destination, Maryland.—Jane Windsor ; destination, Virginia.—Thomas Griffith ; destination, Virginia.—Abraham Morgan ; destination, Virginia.—Thomas Petley (*Endeavour*) ; destination, Virginia.—Symon Purdue ; destination, Virginia.

Page 232

Thomas Crumpton ; destination, Virginia.—Elizabeth Davis ; destination, Virginia.—George Davis ; destination, Virginia.—Thomas Cooke ; destination, Virginia.—Nicholas Holloway ; destination, Virginia.—Thomas Nervill ; destination, Virginia.—John Crumpe ; destination, Virginia.—Ann Salisbury ; destination, Virginia.—Dorothy Bayly ; destination, Maryland.—Josias Hussey ; destination, Virginia.—Anne Juce ; destination, Virginia.—Anne Rider ; destination, Virginia. —Daniell Haines ; destination, Virginia.—Griffith Griffiths ; destination, Virginia.

Page 233

John Stronge ; destination, Virginia.—James Chalcraft ; destination, Virginia.—Richard Cobner ; destination, Virginia.—William Lodum ; destination, Virginia.—John Baldwin ; destination, Virginia.—David Stradling ; destination, Virginia.— fflorence Stradling ; destination, Virginia.—Joane Crocker ; destination, Virginia.—Thomas Wrentmore ; destination, Virginia.—John Membry ; destination, Virginia.—Benjamine Vickrey ; destination, Virginia.—John Gefford ; destination, Virginia.—Morgan Davis ; destination, Virginia.—John Bowell ; destination, Virginia.

Page 234

Alice Games ; destination, Virginia.—Joseph Almond ; destination, Virginia.
—Mary Jones ; destination, Virginia.—Martha Short ; destination, Barbadoes.—
William Hickes ; destination, Virginia.—George Webber ; destination, Barbadoes.
—Thomas New ; destination, Virginia.—Alice Onion ; destination, Virginia.—
Lachariah Deane ; destination, Virginia.—John Phillips ; destination, Barbadoes.
—Richard Lane ; destination (no place given).—Matthew Hoppells ; destination,
Virginia.—William Christopher ; destination, Virginia.—ffrancis David ; destina-
tion, Virginia.

Page 235

Dorothy England ; destination, Nevis.—John Paine ; destination, Virginia.
—Roger Groves ; destination, Virginia.—John Jones ; destination, Virginia.—John
Sansbury ; destination, Virginia.—Thomas Harding ; destination, Virginia.—
Henery Ayles ; destination, Virginia.—Richard Williams ; destination, Virginia.
—Alice Williams ; destination, Virginia.—Elizabeth Penduck ; destination, Vir-
ginia.—Robert Lock ; destination, Virginia.—Sarah ffowler ; destination, Virginia.
—Thomas Harris ; destination, Virginia.—Thomas Bassant ; destination, Virginia.—
John Guyett ; destination, Virginia.

Page 236

Robert Briant ; destination, Virginia.—Joseph Jenkins ; destination, Nevis.—
Reice Thomas ; destination, Virginia.—John Davis ; destination, Virginia.—John
Wely ; destination, Virginia.—Thomas Richards ; destination, Virginia.—Thomas
Cuffe ; destination, Virginia.—Richard Rake ; destination, Virginia.—Phillip
Lawrance ; destination, Virginia.—Anne Jones ; destination, Virginia.—Richard
Denham ; destination, Virginia.—John Owen ; destination, Virginia.—Anne
Peddement ; destination, Virginia.—Dennis Clarke ; destination, Virginia.—Robert
Hughs ; destination, Virginia.—Anne ffoord ; destination, Virginia.

Page 237

John Thornehull ; destination, Virginia.—William Widows ; destination,
Virginia.—William Border ; destination, Virginia.—William Lester ; destination,
Virginia.—Edward Rann ; destination, Virginia.—William Lightley ; destina-
tion, Virginia.—Giles Rockett ; destination, Virginia.—Joane Hill ; destination,
Virginia.—Mary Grigg ; destination, Virginia.—John Whafer ; destination, Vir-
ginia.—Phillip Streete ; destination, Virginia.—Robert Mens (?) ; destination,
Virginia.—John Bushell ; destination, Virginia.—Roger Cooke ; destination, Vir-
ginia.—Elizabeth Villers ; destination, Virginia.—Robert Trevent ; destination,
Virginia.

Page 238

John Cooper ; destination, Virginia.—George Tomson ; destination, Virginia.
—Mary Evans ; destination, Virginia.—Cicly (*sic*) Evans ; destination, Virginia.—
William Hodge ; destination, Nevis.—Henry Whitehead ; destination, Nevis.
—Evan Barrett ; destination, Barbadoes.—Anthony Quarrell ; destination, Vir-
ginia.—John Weaver ; destination, Barbadoes.—David Edwards ; destination,
Virginia.—Michaell Rous ; destination, Barbadoes.—George ffoorde ; destination,
Virginia.—Richard Hopkins ; destination, Virginia.—Elizabeth Jones ; destina-

tion, Virginia.—Katherine Jones ; destination, Virginia.—Richard Climer ; destination, Virginia.—William ffelton ; destination, Barbadoes.—Prudence Davis ; destination, Virginia.

Page 239

John Auter ; destination, Virginia.—Mary Probert ; destination, Nevis.—Austin Jenkins ; destination, Virginia.—Richard Pope ; destination, Nevis.—George Loshley ; destination, Barbadoes.—Elizabeth Norman ; destination, Barbadoes.—Thomas Jones ; destination, Nevis.—John Jones ; destination (no place given). —George Dobbins ; destination, Nevis.—John Boore ; destination, Barbadoes.—Cornelius Larden ; destination, Virginia.—John Tayler ; destination, Nevis.—Joseph Muspott ; destination, Virginia.—Alice Read ; destination, Barbadoes.—Mary Williams ; destination, Virginia.—Elizabeth Jones ; destination, Nevis.

Page 240

Gartres Cottle ; destination, Virginia.—Charles Harris ; destination, Barbadoes.—William Low ; destination, Maryland.—Elizabeth Barnelines ; destination, Barbadoes.—Hannah Brideley ; destination, Barbadoes.—Joane Page ; destination, Virginia.—John Parker ; destination, Virginia.—Katherine Reynolds ; destination, Barbadoes.—Gregory Reyland ; destination, Virginia.—Maurice Benfcold (?) ; destination, Virginia.—Thomasin Webb ; destination, Nevis.—Sarah Northorne ; destination, Nevis.—Thomas Window ; destination, Nevis.—Daniel Price ; destination, Virginia.—Mary Sheppley ; destination, Virginia.—Richard Lewis ; destination, Virginia.

Page 241

William Hopkins ; destination, Virginia.—William Pridley ; destination, Maryland.—Edward Smith ; destination, Virginia.—Thomas Hagget ; destination, Virginia.—Thomas Reece ; destination, Virginia.—Henry Gupway ; destination, Virginia.—Jane Pritchard ; destination, Virginia.—Robert ffoorte ; destination, Virginia.—ffrancis Thomas ; destination, Virginia.—Robert Evans ; destination, Virginia.—Dorothy Kezle ; destination, Virginia.—John Wade ; destination, Virginia.—John Minthen ; destination, Virginia.—Thomas Shine ; destination, Virginia.—Timothy Shine ; destination, Virginia.—Henry Strickland ; destination, Virginia.

Page 242

William Nauty ; destination, Virginia.—Edward Wise ; destination, Virginia. —Elizabeth Carr ; destination, Virginia.—Thomas Hopkins ; destination, Virginia. —John Scripture ; destination, Virginia.—Richard Wigg ; destination, Virginia.—Thomas Tayler ; destination, Virginia.—Mary Nash ; destination, Virginia.—Elioner Smart ; destination, Virginia.—John Nicholl ; destination, Virginia.—John Lullet ; destination, Virginia.—Anne Masters ; destination, Virginia.—Anne Hewell ; destination, Virginia.—Thomas Williams ; destination, Virginia.—James Leeke, destination, Virginia.

Page 243

John Mills ; destination, Maryland.—Hopkin Williams ; destination, Virginia.—Thomas Barrow ; destination, Virginia.—William Thomas ; destination, Virginia. —Anne Waters ; destination, Maryland.—David Vaughan ; destination, Virginia.

—John Wills; destination, Virginia.—Thomas Merrifield; destination, Virginia.—
John Orchard; destination, Virginia.—Anne Thomas; destination, Jamaica.—John
Lowrin; destination, Virginia.—John Griffeth; destination, Virginia.—Lettice
ffoord; destination, Maryland.—Mary Huskins; destination, Virginia.—Mary
Hobson; destination, Jamaica.—Evan Jones; destination, Virginia.

Page 244
John Jones; destination, Virginia.—Anne Markes; destination, Virginia.—
Avis Howman; destination, Virginia.—John Lullet; destination, Virginia.—Henry
Howard; destination, Virginia.—Theophilus Wattkins; destination, Virginia.—
John Sheppard; destination, Virginia.—John Williams; destination, Virginia.—
Thomas Manson; destination, Virginia.—John Plummer; destination, Virginia.
—John Bridges; destination, Virginia.—John Mottershitt; destination, Virginia.
—William Penkston; destination, Virginia.—John Bate; destination, Virginia.—
Stephen Beutler; destination, Virginia.—Phillip Mattson; destination, Virginia.

Page 245
Thomas Safford; destination, Virginia.—Andrew Brady; destination, Virginia.
—John Searle; destination, Virginia.—Cicely Hall; destination, Virginia.—Samuell
Britten; destination, Virginia.—Richard Wood; destination, Virginia.—Dorothy
Swettman; destination, Virginia.—Anne Hurdidge; destination, Virginia.—
Richard Drake; destination, Virginia.—Cicely Peasely; destination, Virginia.
—John Thomas; destination, Virginia.—Thomas Oliver; destination, Virginia.—
James Blunt; destination, Virginia.—Thomas Dax (?); destination, Virginia.

Page 246
William Pilchert; destination, Virginia.—Henry Benfield; destination, Vir-
ginia.—William Morgan; destination, Virginia.—John Mortimore; destination,
Virginia.—Richard Burgis; destination, Virginia.—John Guilliam; destination,
Virginia.—James Alwood; destination, Virginia.—Mary Williams; destination,
Virginia.—Susanna Grandier; destination, Virginia.—Mary ffowler; destina-
tion, Virginia.—Robert Williams; destination, Virginia.—John Harker; destina-
tion, Virginia.—Robert Ellis; destination, Barbadoes.—Mary Evans; destination,
Virginia.—Thomas Lloyds; destination, Virginia.—Richard Hopkins; destination,
Virginia.

Page 246 (sic)
William Mundey; destination, Virginia.—Thomas Chick; destination, Virginia.
—Katherine Macy; destination, Virginia.—Nicholas Huskstone; destination,
Virginia.—George Lloyd; destination, Virginia.—Anthony Guest; destination,
Stanton Drue.—Samuell Ellis; destination, Nevis.—Ursula Hammell; destination, Virginia.—Sarah Edwards; destination, Virginia.—William Greatehead;
destination, Virginia.—Robert Andrewes; destination, Virginia.—Robert Burnoll;
destination, Virginia.—Thomas Andrewes; destination, Virginia.—John Hill;
destination, Maryland.—Thomas Percivall; destination, Virginia.—Joane Wood;
destination, Nevis.

Page 247
Anne Thoms; destination, Virginia.—Charles Baker; destination, Virginia.
—Thomas Wakefield; destination, Virginia.—Henry Evans; destination, Virginia.

—William Lucas ; destination, Nevis.—Thomas Haswell ; destination, Nevis.—Richard Parkar ; destination, Nevis.—Richard Downton ; destination, Nevis.—John Sharrow ; destination, Nevis.—William Jones ; destination, Nevis.—John Jones ; destination, Nevis.—William Poole ; destination, Nevis.—Baldwine Thomas ; destination, Nevis.—Peter Tithing ; destination, Nevis.—William Eyres ; destination, Nevis.—Charles Digby ; destination, Montserrat.

Page 248

William Bick ; destination, Nevis.—William Jones ; destination, Nevis.—William Hughes ; destination, Nevis.—Richard Eastbury ; destination, Barbadoes.—Thomas Dale ; destination, Barbadoes.—Annah Coleman ; destination, Barbadoes.—John Shipsea ; destination, Barbadoes.—John Aylesworth ; destination, New England.—Richard Stophill ; destination, Nevis.—Thomas Millson ; destination, Barbadoes.—Sylvester Washing ; destination, Barbadoes.—John Williams ; destination, Barbadoes.—Thomas Jones ; destination, New England.—Matthew Tayler ; destination, New England.—Jeremiah Bridges ; destination, Nevis.—Morgan Jones ; destination, Nevis.—Joane Jarvis ; destination, New England.

Page 249

Arthur Challoner ; destination, New England.—Lenox Beverlin ; destination, New England.—William Drew ; destination, Barbadoes.—William Davis ; destination, Nevis.—Thomas Bick ; destination, Nevis.—Thomas Turner ; destination, Nevis.—John Hunt ; destination, Nevis.—Benjamin Rolfe ; destination, Nevis.—Jeremiah Longden ; destination, Nevis.—William Bowen ; destination, Nevis.—Thomas Rigges ; destination, Nevis.—Elizabeth Turner ; destination, Nevis.—John Roberts ; destination, New England.—John Baugh ; destination, Barbadoes.—Christian Pendelin ; destination, Barbadoes.—John Long ; destination, Nevis.—William Plomer ; destination, Nevis.—Thomas Smith ; destination, Nevis.

Page 250

Lidia Carter ; destination, Virginia.—Elizabeth White ; destination, Barbadoes.—John Oldburge ; destination, Barbadoes.—Edward Chichester ; destination, Nevis.—Walter Jackson ; destination, Nevis.—Thomas Griffen ; destination, Barbadoes and Nevis.—Henry Webb ; destination, Virginia.—Lucy Byes ; destination, Nevis.—Thomas Baker ; destination, New England.—Humphry Wall ; destination, New England.—John Sclanders ; destination, New England.—Martha Round ; destination, New England.—Elizabeth Morgan ; destination, Barbadoes.—Elizabeth Polden ; destination, Barbadoes.—John Harrington ; destination, Nevis.—Mary Veere ; destination, Nevis.—John Geare ; destination, New England.—John Dodge ; destination, New England.—Daniell Langley ; destination, Virginia.

Page 251

Henry Thomas ; destination, Barbadoes or Virginia.—Giles Brace ; destination, Barbadoes or Virginia.—Richard Turk ; destination, Barbadoes or Virginia.—William Hawkins ; destination, Barbadoes or Virginia.—William Ashbey ; destination, Virginia.—Joseph Hill ; destination, Barbadoes.—Jacob Wall ; destination, Nevis.—David Jenkins ; destination, Maryland.—John Williams ; destination, Virginia.—Ellis Northerne ; destination, Nevis.—John Reade ; destination, Nevis.—Mary Slade ; destination, Barbadoes.—Elizabeth ffarley ; destination, Virginia.—

John Rigges ; destination, Virginia.—John Combes ; destination, Virginia.—Joane fford ; destination, Virginia.—Rebecca Cuffe ; destination, Virginia.—Walter Parrey ; destination, Virginia.—William Gadd ; destination, Virginia.—Rendall David ; destination, Virginia.—John Wood ; destination, Virginia.—James Williams ; destination, Nevis.

Page 252

James Publin ; destination, Virginia.—Henry Parry ; destination, Virginia.— Sarah Smith ; destination, Virginia.—Anne Husdey ; destination, Virginia.—Anne Chelcutt ; destination, Nevis.—Maudlin Jones ; destination, Virginia.—Griffeth Jones ; destination, Virginia.—William Lowrey ; destination, Virginia.—William Jenkins ; destination, Virginia.—Jane Ketty ; destination, Virginia.—Edward Jenkins ; destination, Virginia.—William Reece ; destination, Virginia.—George Walter ; destination, Virginia.—Thomas Pritchard ; destination, Virginia.—Reice Evan ; destination, Virginia.—John Morgan ; destination, Virginia.—William Robinson ; destination, Virginia.—John Allen ; destination, Virginia.—Welthian Williams ; destination, Maryland.—Sarah Rennolls ; destination, Virginia.—John Sherry ; destination, Virginia.

Page 253

George Matthewes ; destination, Virginia.—Richard Thompson ; destination, Barbadoes.—Anne Gardener ; destination, Nevis.—Evan Jones ; destination, Maryland.—Luke Yerden ; destination, Barbadoes.—Sarah Bifield ; destination, Barbadoes.—Charles Harris ; destination, Virginia.—Cicely Williams ; destination, Maryland.—Mary Randell ; destination, Virginia.—Katherine Reade ; destination, Virginia.—William Reade ; destination, Virginia.—John Gale ; destination, Virginia.—William Ricketts ; destination, Virginia.—John Hillton ; destination, Virginia.—Matthew Perry ; destination, Virginia.—ffrancis Roode ; destination, Virginia.—Richard Price ; destination, Virginia.—Margaret Phillips ; destination, Virginia.—Hannah Ware ; destination, Virginia.—Elizabeth Clarke ; destination, Virginia.—Edward Evans ; destination, Virginia.—Mary Browne ; destination, Virginia.

Page 254

Maudlin Lewis ; destination, Barbadoes.—Rowland Williams ; destination, Virginia.—Matthew Willes ; destination, Barbadoes.—Margaret Sallett ; destination, Virginia.—Anne Muttlebury ; destination, Virginia.—John Price ; destination, Virginia.—Elizabeth Prudrow ; destination, Virginia.—Nicholas Jones ; destination, Virginia.—Joseph Browne ; destination, Virginia.—Simon Smith ; destination, Virginia.—Martha Upton ; destination, Virginia.—Elizabeth Collins ; destination, Virginia.—William Ithill ; destination, Virginia.—William Wassard ; destination, Nevis.—John Hughes ; destination, Virginia.—John Hollis ; destination, Virginia.—Richard Baron ; destination, Virginia.—Roger Bishop ; destination, Virginia.—David Evans ; destination, Virginia.—Reece Jones ; destination, Virginia.—Mary Gay ; destination, Virginia.

Page 255

Edward Washer ; destination, Virginia.—Richard Wattkins ; destination, Nevis.—Henry Perry ; destination, Nevis.—George Morgan ; destination, Virginia.

—Robert ffletcher ; destination, Virginia.—William Court ; destination, Virginia.
—John Court ; destination, Virginia.—Henry Grazier ; destination, Virginia.—
Joseph Strickland ; destination, Virginia.—Richard Hogchitch ; destination, Vir-
ginia.—Richard Jarvis ; destination, Virginia.—James Hogchitch ; destination,
Virginia.—Richard Priestly ; destination, Virginia.—Arthur Scriven ; destination,
Virginia.—Thomas Bayly ; destination, Virginia.—James Griffen ; destination, Vir-
ginia.—Robertus Phillips ; destination, Virginia.—William Sydenham ; destination,
Virginia.—Israell Watham ; destination, Virginia.—John Light ; destination, Virginia.—Margaret Trippick ; destination, Virginia.—Elizabeth Blackwell ; destination, Nevis.

Page 256
    Giles Barrett ; destination, Virginia.—Bartholomew Avenell ; destination,
Nevis.—Richard Avenell ; destination, Nevis.—Anne Roberts ; destination, Vir-
ginia.—Grace Jones ; destination, Virginia.—Walter Evans ; destination, Virginia.
—Thomas Knight ; destination, Nevis.—Henry Reece ; destination, Nevis.—
Samuell Ostler ; destination, Virginia.—George Young ; destination, Virginia.—
Robert Davis ; destination, Virginia.—John Jacob ; destination, Virginia.—Edward
Mills ; destination, Virginia.—William Hill ; destination, Virginia.—Thomas
Bowden ; destination, Nevis.—Margarett ffarmer ; destination, Virginia.—Richard
Gill ; destination, Virginia.—William Carter ; destination, Barbadoes.—William
Meeke ; destination, Virginia.—Thomas Willson ; destination, Virginia.—Richard
Williams ; destination, Barbadoes.—John Vincent ; destination, Nevis.—Robert
Carver ; destination, Nevis.

Page 257
    Theodorus Lewis ; destination, Virginia.—John Beare ; destination, Virginia.
—John Wallway ; destination, Virginia.—John Williams ; destination, Maryland.—
John Merrick ; destination, Virginia.—William Wilkins ; destination, Virginia.—
Joane Watts ; destination, Virginia.—Samuell Warner ; destination, Virginia.
—Susannah Abbott ; destination, Virginia.—William Norcutt ; destination,
Virginia.—Henricus Rogers ; destination, Virginia.—Henry Williams ; destina-
tion, Virginia.—Elizabeth Arnold ; destination, Virginia.—Moses Jones ; destina-
tion, Virginia.—Nicholas Stafford ; destination, Nevis.—Edward Short ; desti-
nation, Virginia.—Richard Thomkins ; destination, Virginia.—Howell ffrancis ;
destination, Virginia.—William Wilkes ; destination, Virginia.

Page 258
    Mabell Uxley ; destination, Virginia.—Thomas Boules ; destination, Vir-
ginia.—Joseph Gouldsney ; destination, Virginia.—Anne Johnson ; destination,
Virginia.—Elizabeth Williams ; destination, Virginia.—Rowland Williams ; destination, Virginia.—Mary Bull ; destination, Virginia.—George Turley ; destination,
Virginia.—William fferryman ; destination, Barbadoes.—William Howard ; destination, Virginia.—Wattkin Andrewes ; destination, Barbadoes.—Richard Andrewes ;
destination, Barbadoes.—George Jones ; destination, Nevis.—Jane Reece ; destina-
tion, Nevis.—James Richards ; destination, Barbadoes.—Thomas Wickham ; desti-
nation, Barbadoes.—John Lambert ; destination, Nevis.—John Lung ; destination,
Nevis.

Page 259

Owen Jones ; destination, Barbadoes.—Elizabeth Bolton ; destination, Nevis.—
Thomas Hughes ; destination, Nevis.—Morgan Williams ; destination, Nevis.—
Thomas Nilie ; destination, Nevis.—Edward Jones ; destination, Nevis.—Edmund
Rogers ; destination (no place given).—Edward Lewis ; destination, Nevis.—Richard
Sandell ; destination, Barbadoes.—James Kendall ; destination, Barbadoes or
Nevis.—William Morgan ; destination, Nevis.—Anthony Coles ; destination,
Nevis.—John Clarke ; destination, Nevis.—Johannes Jones ; destination, Barbadoes.
—John Roswell ; destination, Barbadoes.—Robert Browne ; destination, Barbadoes.
—William Stuckey ; destination, Barbadoes.

Page 260

Joane Jones ; destination, Barbadoes.—William Avent ; destination, Nevis.—
Elizabeth Gardener ; destination, Barbadoes.—Thomas Bull ; destination, Nevis.
—Richard Jones ; destination, Nevis.—Matthew Bland ; destination, Nevis.—
Saunder Judicott ; destination, Nevis.—Joseph Horton ; destination, Nevis.—
George Sterte ; destination, Barbadoes.—James Sprake ; destination, Nevis.—
William Lawrence ; destination, Nevis.—Edward Ansell ; destination, Nevis.—
William Chedsey ; destination, Nevis.—Edward Thomas ; destination, Nevis.
—Nathan Bayly ; destination, Nevis.—Henry Reekes ; destination, Nevis.

Page 261

Thomas Ellison ; destination, Nevis.—Richard Browne ; destination, Nevis.—
Richard Richardson ; destination, Nevis.—Thomas ffitz-Gerard ; destination,
Nevis.—Thomas Preece ; destination, Nevis.—Thomas Haines ; destination, Nevis.
—Jeremiah Rose ; destination, Nevis.—John Richardson ; destination, Nevis.—
Alexander Killman ; destination, Nevis.—Edward Puberly ; destination, Nevis.—
George Jenkins ; destination, Nevis.—John Parry ; destination, Nevis.—Joane
Edwards ; destination, Nevis.—Thomas Woodley ; destination, Barbadoes.—Howell
Thomas ; destination, Nevis.

Page 262

William Edwards ; destination, Nevis.—Jane Parry ; destination, Nevis.—Anne
Hunt ; destination, Nevis.—Lewis Sherive ; destination, Nevis.—Peter Sherive ;
destination, Nevis.—Nicholas Aust ; destination, Nevis.—Llewellin Morgan ; destination (no place given).—George Morris ; destination, Nevis.—Thomas Gengill ;
destination, Nevis.—John Pester ; destination, Barbadoes.—Reece Morgan ; destination, Nevis.—Sarah Treverd ; destination, Nevis.—William Gramford ; destination, Nevis.—Richard ffisher ; destination, Montserrat.—Sarah Cullymore ;
destination, Nevis.—John ffroud ; destination, Nevis.

Page 263

John Woods ; destination, Nevis.—Evan Davis ; destination, Nevis.—
William Greenall ; destination, Nevis.—Anthony Davoly ; destination, Nevis.—
John Ballard ; destination, Montserrat.—Thomas Casum ; destination, Montserrat.
—Edward Minord ; destination, Nevis.—Edward Lewis ; destination, Nevis.—
Penelope Grubb ; destination, Nevis.—Elizabeth fforley ; destination, Nevis.
—Robert Roger ; destination, Nevis or Antigua.—Charles Roe ; destination, Nevis.
—Susannah Clarke ; destination, Nevis.—Katherine Jones ; destination, Nevis.—
Thomas Woodward ; destination, Nevis.

Page 264

Edmond Day ; destination, Nevis or Antigua.—Samuel Hurlestone ; destination, Nevis.—John Anderton ; destination, Nevis.—Ann Buggin ; destination, Nevis.—Roger Collins ; destination, Nevis.—Gabriell Allen ; destination, Nevis. —John Haines ; destination, Nevis.—William Reed ; destination, Antigua.— George Burford ; destination, Montserrat ; destination, Leversedge Huxley ; destination, Nevis.—Edward Wolfe ; destination, Nevis.—William Thomas ; destination, Nevis.—Thomas Steliard ; destination, Nevis.—Jacob Johnsons ; destination, Nevis.

Page 265

John Parmiter ; destination, Nevis.—James Herring ; destination, Nevis.— Jane Martin ; destination, Nevis.—Anne Powell ; destination, Nevis.—John Hullett ; destination, Nevis.—John West ; destination, Nevis.—Thomas Martin ; destination, Nevis.—Thomas Wells ; destination, Nevis.—Thomas Rossome ; destination, Nevis.—William ffisher ; destination, New England.—Jane Taylor ; destination, Nevis.—Katherine Purvice ; destination, Nevis.—Rice Griffen ; destination, New England.—Robert Legg ; destination, Barbadoes.—Nathaniell Boyer ; destination, Barbadoes.—ffrancis Baker ; destination, Nevis.

Page 266

Deborah Jefferies ; destination, Nevis.—William Robins ; destination, New England.—Richard Stone ; destination, New England.—Charles Powell ; destination, Nevis.—John Stout ; destination, Nevis.—Llewis Price ; destination, Barbadoes.—Joane Harris ; destination, Barbadoes.—Mellisant Fry ; destination, Barbadoes.—Elizabeth Phillips ; destination, Barbadoes.—Emanuell Stringer ; destination, Barbadoes.—Richard Phelps ; destination, Barbadoes.—Margaret Mills ; destination, Barbadoes.—Martin Yeamanson ; destination, Barbadoes.—Thomas Edwards ; destination, Montserrat.—David Griffeth ; destination, Antigua, Montserrat or Nevis.—Reece Gwinne ; destination, Antigua, Montserrat or Nevis.—Gabriell Joice ; destination, Nevis.—Joseph Gooding ; destination, Nevis.—John Stoute ; destination, Nevis.—Esekiell Langley ; destination, Nevis.—William Cotton ; destination, Jamaica.

Page 267

William Jones ; destination, Nevis.—William Harris ; destination, Jamaica.— Howell Thomas ; destination, Nevis.—Daniell Lawson ; destination, Nevis.— Alexander Morgan ; destination, Barbadoes.—Elizabeth Harrison ; destination, Jamaica.—Mary Hawkins ; destination, Jamaica.—Charles Prattin ; destination, Nevis.—Thomas Jones ; destination, Nevis.—William Powell ; destination, New England.—William Morris ; destination, New England.—John Robert ; destination, New England.—Thomas Waynehouse ; destination, New England.—Evan Davis ; destination, New England.—Andrew Lugg ; destination, New England.—Anthony Wood ; destination, Virginia.—Joan Buddin ; destination, Jamaica.—William Cosser ; destination, Jamaica.—John Woodman ; destination, Jamaica.—John Window ; destination, Barbadoes.—Thomas Cooke ; destination, Barbadoes.— William Pen ; destination, New England.—Howell Thomas ; destination, Virginia.

Page 268

Richard Lambert ; destination, Barbadoes.—William Thomas ; destination, Barbadoes.—Charles Waters ; destination, Barbadoes.—Richard Thous ; destination, Virginia.—William Salmun; destination, Virginia.—John ffokes; destination, Virginia.—George Roberts; destination, Virginia.—Howell Jones; destination, Virginia.—Kingsmill Maynard; destination, Virginia.—William Moore; destination, Virginia.—John Jones; destination, Virginia.—Margaret May; destination, Virginia.—William Winter; destination, Virginia.—Thomas Warmer; destination, Virginia.—John Mathias; destination, Virginia.—George Wadham; destination, Virginia.—John Bartlett; destination, Virginia.—John Nickolls; destination, Jamaica.

Page 269
Thomas Lees; destination, Virginia.—John Higgins; destination, York River. —John Hughes; destination, Virginia.—Barbara Andrews; destination, Virginia.— Thomas Higgins; destination, Virginia.—Ellioner Langford; destination, Virginia.—Henry Williams; destination, Virginia.—Charles Lewis; destination, Virginia.—John Trapni; destination, Virginia.—William Conner; destination, Virginia.—John Price; destination, Virginia.—Anne Jones; destination, Virginia. —Ruth West; destination, Virginia.—Ellioner Cullis; destination, Virginia.— Blanch Jones; destination, Maryland.—Joane Jones; destination, Virginia.— William Winthrip; destination, Virginia.—James Edwards; destination, Virginia. —Giles Olpin; destination, Virginia.—John Holliday; destination, Virginia.— James Bendall; destination, Virginia.—John Bath; destination, Virginia.—Daniell Auston; destination, Virginia.—Nicholas Haskins; destination, Virginia.

Page 270
Mary Harford; destination, Virginia.—Thomas Marshall; destination, Virginia.—Blewett Beamont; destination, Virginia.—Jane Case; destination, Virginia. —Rebecca Jee; destination, Virginia.—Watkin Llewis; destination, Maryland.— Daniell Peirce; destination, Virginia.—James Benning; destination, Virginia.— James Richards; destination, Virginia.—Thomas Richards; destination, Virginia. —David Roberts; destination, Virginia.—James Hardy; destination, Maryland. —Mary James; destination, Virginia.—Thomas Mathews; destination, Virginia.— Walter White; destination, Virginia.—Elizabeth Solomon; destination, Virginia. —Mathew Gaudrum; destination, Virginia.—William Woodly; destination, Virginia.—Thomas Goodwin; destination, Virginia.—Robert Smith; destination, Virginia.—John Heale; destination, Virginia.—Abraham Butcher; destination, Virginia.

Page 271
Robert Brock; destination, Virginia.—Samuell Wheeler; destination, Virginia. —Evans Thomas; destination, Virginia.—Mary Martin; destination, Virginia.— John Strude; destination, Virginia.—George Nest; destination, Virginia.— William Hardin; destination, Virginia.—Mary Nest; destination, Virginia.—Mark Kelly; destination, Virginia.—George Childs; destination, Virginia.—Katharine Clarke; destination, Virginia.—Walter Lewis; destination, Virginia.—John Percell; destination, Virginia.—Jane Willson (*Nevis Merchant*); destination, Virginia.— Roger Evans; destination, Virginia.—Mart Wall; destination, Virginia.—Michaell Conway; destination, Virginia.—Jane Price; destination, Virginia or Barbadoes.— Thomas Lewis; destination, Virginia.—Morgab Phillips; destination, Virginia.— Evan Thomas; destination, Virginia.—Elizabeth Crindall; destination, Richard Band; destination, Virginia.

Page 272
Richard Winn ; destination, Virginia.—James Hurne ; destination, Virginia. —John Smith ; destination, Virginia.—Elizabeth Wooly ; destination, Virginia.— William Woodly ; destination, Virginia.—John Lafwell ; destination, Virginia. —James Upadine ; destination, Virginia.—John Jones ; destination, Virginia.— James Jobbins ; destination, Virginia.—Elizabeth Grindall ; destination, Virginia.— Thomas Gilbert ; destination, Barbadoes.—Edward Jenkin ; destination, Virginia. —Maria West ; destination, Virginia.—Mary West ; destination, Virginia.—Sarah West ; destination, Virginia.—Elizabeth Mantell ; destination, Virginia.—John Blanch ; destination, Virginia.—Elizabeth Bush ; destination, Barbadoes.—Abraham ffoord ; destination, Virginia.—Carnan Hutton ; destination, Virginia.—Humphry Jones ; destination, Virginia.—Joseph Merryweather ; destination, Virginia.—Mary Miller ; destination, Virginia.—Richard Rugg ; destination, Virginia.

Page 273
John Rugg ; destination, Virginia.—Michaell Godwin ; destination, Virginia. —James Cousins ; destination, Virginia.—Richard Sutton ; destination, Barbadoes. —James Bridgeford ; destination, Virginia.—Daniell Cooksey ; destination, Virginia.—George Elze ; destination, Virginia.—Edward Richards ; destination, Virginia.—Joan Elze ; destination, Virginia.—Michaell Harpfeild ; destination, Virginia.—Edward Jones ; destination, Virginia.—Thomas Newsham ; destination, Virginia.—Leonard Newsham ; destination, Virginia.—Elizabeth Jones ; destination, Virginia.—Susanna Stone ; destination, Virginia.—Henry Warnfoord ; destination, Virginia.—Paule Williams ; destination, Virginia.—Bridgett Lowe ; destination, Nevis.—John Berryman ; destination, Virginia.—John Leake ; destination, Virginia.—Edward Morgan ; destination, Virginia.—John Roberts ; destination, Virginia.—Margaret Gregory ; destination, Virginia.

Page 274
John Rogers ; destination, Virginia.—Benjamin Bevis ; destination, Maryland.—William Brittin ; destination, Virginia.—William Easton ; destination, Virginia.—Thomas Richards ; destination, Virginia.—Thomas Cooke ; destination, Virginia.—John Knowling ; destination, Virginia.—Moses Horton ; destination, Virginia.—Thomas Turner ; destination, Virginia.—Mary Limore ; destination, Virginia.—Elizabeth Gaine ; destination, Virginia.—Richard Glover ; destination, Virginia.—Sarah Nash ; destination, Virginia.—John Browne ; destination, Virginia.—Henry Harris ; destination, Virginia.—Andrew Wright ; destination, Virginia.—Jane Payne ; destination, Virginia.—Charles Young ; destination, Virginia.—William Phillips ; destination, Virginia.—John Staty ; destination, Virginia.—Elizabeth Rawbone ; destination, Virginia.—Elizabeth Bartlam ; destination, Virginia.

Page 275
Richard Wells ; destination, Nevis.—Daniell Taylor ; destination, Virginia.— Richard Newman ; destination, Virginia.—Thomas Heath ; destination, Virginia. —Daniell Galland ; destination, Jamaica.—William Luton ; destination, Virginia.— Robert Brocklesby ; destination, Virginia.—William Braine ; destination, Virginia. —Deborah Cozens ; destination, Virginia.—Mary Holder ; destination, Virginia.— Onner Blake ; destination, Virginia.—Thomas Bissell ; destination, Vir-

ginia.—William Moody ; destination, Virginia.—John White ; destination, Virginia.
—William Thomas ; destination, Virginia.—Thomas Maddox ; destination, Virginia.—Richard Carter ; destination, Virginia.—Mary Gwillim ; destination, Virginia.—Hester Handy ; destination, Virginia.—Samuell ffranklyn ; destination, Virginia.—Thomas West ; destination, Virginia.—Sarah Dawson ; destination, Virginia.—Elizabeth Lowe ; destination, Virginia.

Page 276
John ffarmer ; destination, Barbadoes.—Dorothy Jones ; destination, Virginia.—Peter Steward ; destination, Virginia.—Mary Burges ; destination, Virginia.—James Shute ; destination, Virginia.—Mary Thomas ; destination, Virginia.—Elizabeth Thomas ; destination, Virginia.—John Thomas ; destination, Virginia.—Thomas Williams ; destination, Virginia.—William End ; destination, Virginia.—Griffin Evans ; destination, Virginia.—Ursula Thomas ; destination, Virginia.—Phillip Watts ; destination, Virginia.—William Powell ; destination, Virginia.—James Wall ; destination, Virginia.—John Stutchberry ; destination, Virginia.—John Tucker ; destination, Virginia.—Stephen Peterson ; destination, Virginia.—William Baker ; destination, Virginia.—William Thomas ; destination, Virginia.—John Harris ; destination, Virginia.—William Popley ; destination, Virginia.

Page 277
Susan Dempston ; destination, Virginia.—Anne Kenner ; destination, Virginia.—Thomas Mountslow ; destination, Virginia.—Samuell Painter ; destination, Virginia.—John Allen ; destination, Virginia.—Joseph Moxham ; destination, New England.—Joseph ffry ; destination, Maryland.—James Bayliffe ; destination, Maryland.—David Jones ; destination, Maryland or Virginia.—Thomas Palmer ; destination, Virginia.—Henry ffish ; destination, Barbadoes.—John Burroughs ; destination, Virginia.—Blanch Pritchett ; destination, Virginia.—Thomas Perry ; destination, Virginia.—Edward Slade ; destination, Virginia.—Thomas Hidde ; destination, Virginia.—Edward Hidde ; destination, Virginia.—Joshua Lee ; destination, Virginia.—Thomas Jones ; destination, Virginia.

Page 278
Mary ffishpell ; destination, Virginia.—John Hoskins ; destination, Virginia.—Bridgett Morgan ; destination, Virginia.—William Davis ; destination, Virginia.—Robert Leather ; destination, Virginia.—Thomas Clarke ; destination, Virginia.—Thomas Larrimur ; destination, Virginia.—Edward Ellis ; destination, Virginia.—Mary Eastmett (*Lilly of Bristol*) ; destination, Virginia.—Jonathan Smith (*Althea*) ; destination, Virginia.—William Hipsly (*Stephen*) ; destination, Virginia.—Edward Jones (*Althea*) ; destination, Virginia.—David Bevan (*Stephen*) ; destination, Virginia.—Arthur Davis (*Stephen*) ; destination, Virginia.—Morgan Lysons (*Providence*) ; destination, Virginia.—Alexander Richard (*William and Anne*) ; destination, Virginia.—Henry Piper (*Lyon*) ; destination, Barbadoes.—Rebecca Langton (*Lilly of London*) ; destination, Virginia.—John Price (*Starr*) ; destination, Virginia.

Page 279
Thomas Napper (*Exchange*) ; destination, Virginia.—Anne Ireland (*William and Anne*) ; destination, Virginia.—William Spuraway (*Althea*) ; destination, Virginia.—Charles Low (*Althea*) ; destination, Virginia.—Robert Tayler (*Loves Increase*) ; destination, Virginia.—Charles Berrow (*Loves Increase*) ; destination, Virginia.—John Bowles (*Loves Increase*) ; destination, Virginia.—Michaell Webb

(*Loves Increase*) ; destination, Virginia.—Joseph Thomas (*Loves Increase*) ; destination, Virginia.—John Smith (*Prosperous Catch*) ; destination, Montserrat.—Lawrence Pratt (*Constant Martha*) ; destination, Virginia.—Michaell Whitewood (*Prosperous Catch*) ; destination, Montserrat.—Griffin Evans (*William and Anne*) ; destination, Virginia.—Joseph Poynt (*William and Anne*) ; destination, Virginia.—John Wynn (*Lilly Dogger*) ; destination, Virginia.—William Marrow (*William and Anne*) ; destination, Virginia.

Page 280

Richard Prece (*William and Anne*) ; destination, Virginia.—Thomas Boulton (*Dogger of Yarmouth*) ; destination, Virginia.—Christopher Veale (*Dogger of Yarmouth*) ; destination, Virginia.—John Boulton (*Dogger of Yarmouth*) ; destination, Virginia.—William Abbis (*Exchange of Bristoll*) ; destination, Nevis, Antigua or Virginia.—John Downe (*Stephen*) ; destination, Virginia.—Simon Rice (*Althea*) ; destination, Virginia.—Joan ffry (*Starr*) ; destination, Virginia.—Thomas Marlique (*Love's Increase*) ; destination, Virginia.—Robert Price (*Love's Increase*) ; destination, Virginia.—John Woodheard (*Love's Increase*) ; destination, Maryland.—Mary Evans (*Love's Increase*) ; destination, Virginia.—William Beedle (*John of Bristoll*) ; destination, Virginia.—Andrew Lake (*John of Bristoll*) ; destination, Virginia.— Mary Sprake (*Constant Martha*) ; destination, Virginia.—James Peale (*John of Bristoll*) ; destination, Virginia.—William Stand (*Neptune of Bristoll*) ; destination, Jamaica.

Page 281

George Beaker (*John of Bristoll*) ; destination, Virginia.—William Powell (*Starr*) ; destination, Virginia.—William Richardson (*John of Bristoll*) ; destination, Virginia.—James Parry (*Loves Increase*) ; destination, Virginia.—William Glue (*Loves Increase*) ; destination, Virginia.—John Alderton (*Constant Martha*) ; destination, Virginia.—William Johns (*Starr*) ; destination, Virginia.—Richard John Morsly (*Starr*) ; destination, Virginia.—John Jenkin Davy (*Starr*) ; destination, Virginia.—Sylvester Saunders ; destination, Virginia.—Thomas James (*Constant Martha*) ; destination, Virginia.—Richard Lloyd (*Constant Martha*) ; destination, Virginia.—Thomas Perry (*Reformation*) ; destination, Virginia.—Richard Stone (*Reformation*) ; destination, Virginia.—Anne Tayler (*Constant Martha*) ; destination, Virginia.—Mary Davis (*Constant Martha*) ; destination, Virginia.—Lewis Davis (*Constant Martha*) ; destination, Virginia.—John Smith ; destination, Virginia.— Daniell Bugle ; destination, Virginia.

Page 282

More Morgan (*Starr*) ; destination, Virginia.—Henry Jenkins (*Starr*) ; destination, Virginia.—Thomas Hughes (*Starr*) ; destination, Virginia.—Joseph Hunt (*Constant Martha*) ; destination, Virginia.—Ellioner ffrank (*Constant Martha*) ; destination, Virginia.—James ffrank (*Constant Martha*) ; destination, Virginia.— Jonas Lewis ; destination, Virginia.—Joseph Crumpe (*Starr*) ; destination, Maryland. —William Jones ; destination, Virginia.—Valentine Stephenson (*Constant Martha*) ; destination, Virginia.—ffrancis Weekfull (*Constant Martha*) ; destination, Virginia.— Mabella Tent (*Constant Martha*) ; destination, Virginia.—Arthur Whiteby (*Constant Martha*) ; destination, Maryland.—Guilliam Thomas (*Reformation*) ; destination, Virginia.—Thomas Hanman (*Starr*) ; destination, Virginia.—Robert Wayte (*Constant Martha*) ; destination, Virginia.

Page 283
     William Stretch (*Constant Martha*) ; destination, Virginia.—William Lambert (*Reformation*) ; destination, Virginia.—Samuell Churchhouse (*Constant Martha*) ; destination, Virginia.—Walter Dodimet (*Katharine*) ; destination, Barbadoes.— Elizabeth Osborne ; destination, Barbadoes.—John ffryer ; destination, Virginia. —John Williams ; destination, Barbadoes.—John Tally (*Katharine*) ; destination, Barbadoes.—Grace Phellps (*Nathaniel of London*) ; destination, Barbadoes.—Henry Belshire (*Gabriell*) ; destination, Barbadoes.—Elizabeth Osborne (*Gabriell*) ; destination, Barbadoes.—Reece Williams (*Baltemore*) ; destination, Virginia.—Joseph Hall ; destination, Barbadoes.—John Wakecombe (*Katharine*) ; destination, Barbadoes.—John Haggason ; destination, Barbadoes.

Page 284
     William Tiley ; destination, Virginia.—Charles Mines (*Baltemore*) ; destination, Virginia.—John Gardner (*Baltemore*) ; destination, Virginia.—Thomas Deane (*Baltemore*) ; destination, Virginia.—Robert Shuring (*Katharine of Bristoll*) ; destination, Barbadoes.—John Price (*Gabriell*) ; destination, Caribbee Is.—Robert Browne (*Gabriell*) ; destination, Caribbee Is.—Robert Webb (*Baltemore*) ; destination, Virginia.—Reece Williams (*Baltemore*) ; destination, Virginia.—Theophilus Watkins (*Baltemore*) ; destination, Virginia.—John Jones (*Baltemore*) ; destination (no place given).—John Evans (*Rotchell Merchant*) ; destination, Virginia.—Thomas Harris (*Baltemore*) ; destination, Virginia.—John Russell (*Katharine*) ; destination, Barbadoes.—ffrancis Knowles (*Nathaniell of London*) ; destination, Barbadoes.

Page 285
     Thomas Marder (of Tanton, *Baltmore* [*sic*]) ; destination, Virginia.—Richard Reeves (*Rotchell Merchant*) ; destination, Virginia.—Richard Griffin (*Rotchell Merchant*) ; destination, Virginia.—Evan Jones (of Carmarthen, *Baltmore* [*sic*]) ; destination, Virginia.—Herbert Morgan (of Panteage, *John*) ; destination, Virginia.—Thomas Ree (of Aus [?], *Katharin*) ; destination, Barbadoes.—Jane Hodges (*Rotchell Merchant*) ; destination, Virginia.—Michaell Smith (of Bristoll, *America Merchant*) ; destination, Jamaica.—Mary Manning ; destination, Barbadoes.— Thomas Phillips ; destination, Jamaica.—Elinor Jones (of Aresmon, *America Merchant*) ; destination, Jamaica.—Richard Constanc (*sic*) ; destination, Jamaica.— Thomas Allen (*Primrose*) ; destination, Jamaica.—Maurice Phillips ; destination, Jamaica.—Robert Pollman ; destination (no place given).—John Williams ; destination, Barbadoes.—David Nicholas (*Primrose*) ; destination, Barbadoes.—Simon Griffin (*Primrose*) ; destination, Barbadoes.—Daniell Close (of Shudwater, *Primrose*) ; destination, Jamaica.

Page 286
     Ann Tuston (of Whithington, *America Merchant*) ; destination (no place given). —Isaack Lane (of Petworth, *America Merchant*) ; destination (no place given).— Thomas Bradshaw (of Winsell, *Success*) ; destination, Barbadoes.—Samuell Tayler (*Success*) ; destination, Barbadoes.—Nicholas Greene ; destination, Newfoundland. —Richard Strange ; destination, Nevis.—Hugh Tayler ; destination, Nevis.—David Williams ; destination, Nevis.—John Harburt (*Blackmore*) ; destination, Barbadoes or Virginia.—Charles Davis (*Blackmore*) ; destination, Barbadoes or Virginia. —George Edwards (overwritten) (*Blackmore*) ; destination, Barbadoes or Virginia.—Henry Jones (*Phenix*) ; destination, Virginia.—William Jones (*Nevis Mer-*

chant) ; destination, Virginia.—ffrances Strattford (*Alexander*) ; destination, Virginia.
—James Ash (*Bristoll Merchant*) ; destination, Virginia.—Alice Edwards (*Nevis Merchant*) ; destination, Virginia.—Elizabeth Offer (*Nevis Merchant*) ; destination, Virginia.—Ellinor ffell ; destination, Virginia.—Mary James ; destination, Virginia.—Humphry Scott (*Nevis Merchant*) ; destination, Virginia.—Richard ffloyd ; destination, Virginia.—Robert Evans ; destination, Virginia.—Richard Jones ; destination, Virginia.—John Dowty ; destination, Virginia.

Page 287

Henry Raily (*Alexander*) ; destination, Virginia.—John Salter (*Alexander*) ; destination, Virginia.—Edward Rawlins (*Richard and James*) ; destination, Virginia. —Edward Weston (*Nevis Merchant*) ; destination, Virginia.—Benjamin Addington (*Richard and James*) ; destination, Virginia.—William Blackgrove (*Batchellor*) ; destination, Virginia.—Richard ffarmer (*Richard and James*) ; destination, Virginia.—John ffransum (*Stephen*) ; destination, Virginia.—Hester Marchfeild (*Phenix*) ; destination, Virginia.—Thomas Baker (*Richard and James*) ; destination, Virginia. —Roger Squire (*Stephen*) ; destination, Virginia.—Edward Lawrence (*Unicorn*) ; destination, Virginia.—Samuell Gerrard (*Nevis Merchant*) ; destination, Virginia.—John Bevill (*Richard and James*) ; destination, Virginia.—William Parker (*Maryland Merchant*) ; destination, Virginia.—John Phillips (*Maryland Merchant*) ; destination, Virginia.—Richard Sidenham (*Blackmore*) ; destination, Barbadoes.

Page 288

Mary Horseman (*Phenix*) ; destination, Virginia.—Richard Knight (*Bristoll Merchant*) ; destination, Virginia.—Richard Glosty (*Batchellor*) ; destination, Virginia.—John Bradshaw (*Endeavor Ketch*) ; destination, Nevis.—Jane Woods (*Phenix*) ; destination, Virginia.—George Mathews (*Bristoll Merchant*) ; destination, Virginia.—William Harris (*Phenix*) ; destination, Virginia.—Thomas Compton (*Unicorn*) ; destination, Virginia.—Samuell Gayner ; destination, Virginia.—Thomas Ward ; destination, Virginia.—Susana Brayne (*Susan*) ; destination, Maryland.— Hanna fford (*Bristoll Merchant*) ; destination, Virginia.—Edward Wallis (*Bristoll Merchant*) ; destination, Virginia.—John Thomas (*Nevis Merchant*) ; destination, Virginia.—Lewis ffrancis (*Richard and James*) ; destination, Virginia.—James Russe (*John*) ; destination, Virginia.—Joseph ffarworth ; destination, Virginia.

Page 289

John Taylor (*George*) ; destination, Virginia.—Henry Kent (*Unicorn*) ; destination, Virginia.—Nicholas Westcott (*Agreement*) ; destination, Virginia.—James Prince (*Agreement*) ; destination, Virginia.—Mary Coles (*Susanna*) ; destination, Virginia.—Joseph Edmund (*Edward and James*) ; destination, Virginia.—Elizabeth Chamberlin (*Batchellor*) ; destination, Virginia.—James Penn (*St. John*) ; destination, Virginia.—Robert Bickam (*Susanna*) ; destination, Virginia.—Brydgett Shippman (*Maryland Merchant*) ; destination, Virginia.—William Seye (*Susanna*) ; destination, Maryland.—Richard Powell ; destination, Maryland.—Thomas Price ; destination, Maryland.—Mary Jenkins ; destination, Maryland.—Jane Boole ; destination, Maryland.—Edward Boole ; destination, Maryland.

Page 290

John Jones (*Nevis Merchant*) ; destination, Virginia.—William Harrwarr (*Susanna*) ; destination, Virginia.—Edward Phillips (*William and John*) ; destination, Virginia.—Robert White (*Batchellor*); destination, Virginia.—Sarah Bay (*William and Ann*); destination, Virginia.—Rebecca Stephens (*Bristoll Merchant*); destination, Virginia.—Anthony Blanchard (*Unicorn*); destination, Virginia.— Jenkin Thomas (*Unicorn*); destination, Virginia.—Alice James (*Susanna*); destination, Pottuxon.—Christopher Norton (*Unicorn*); destination, Virginia.—Walter Wheath (*Richard and James*); destination, Virginia.—Thomas Jenkin (*Unicorn*); destination, Virginia.—Charles Greene (*Bristoll Merchant*); destination, Virginia.— Thomas Goodwin (*Unicorne*); destination, Virginia.—William Sely; destination, Maryland.—Margery Lewis; destination, Maryland.

Page 291

Herbert Power (*Agreement*); destination, Virginia.—Richard Bayneham (*Susanna*); destination, Virginia.—Henry ffreke (*Maryland Merchant*); destination, Virginia.—Phillip Dennis (*Richard and James*); destination, Virginia.— Edith Collins (*Agreement*); destination, Virginia.—Mary Price (*Maryland Merchant*); destination, Virginia.—Roger Davis (*Maryland Merchant*); destination, Virginia.—Richard Howell; destination, Jamaica.—Daniell Hurly (*Maryland Merchant*); destination, Virginia.—Robert Seword; destination, Nevis.—Mary White (*Maryland Merchant*); destination, Virginia.—George Millard (*Sarah*); destination, Nevis.—Thomas Crippin (*William and Anne*); destination, Virginia. —Richard Tomlinson (*Maryland Merchant*); destination, Virginia.—Hester Price (*Maryland Merchant*); destination, Virginia.—David Evans (*Maryland. Merchant*); destination, Virginia.—John Davis (*Maryland Merchant*); destination, Virginia.— John Price (*Maryland Merchant*); destination, Virginia.

Page 292

Thomas Bevan (*Maryland Merchant*); destination, Maryland.—Richard Winson (*Maryland Merchant*); destination, Maryland.—Mary Ano (*Maryland Merchant*); destination, Maryland.—Elizabeth Wedmore (*Maryland Merchant*); destination, Virginia.—Elizabeth Austin (*William and Anne*); destination, Virginia. —James Sutton (*ffrancis and Mary*); destination, Virginia.—John Smith (*William and Anne*); destination, Virginia.—Martha Steven (*William and Anne*); destination, Virginia.—Nathaniell Mason (*William and Anne*); destination, Virginia.— Hannah Pate (*ffrancis and Mary*); destination, Virginia.—John Thompson (*ffrancis and Mary*); destination, Virginia.—Mordecay Jones (*ffrancis and Mary*); destination, Virginia.—Thomas Price; destination, Virginia.—Joseph Parry; destination, Virginia.—Jane Harvy; destination, Virginia.—Benjamin Gildar (*George*); destination, Virginia.—Dorothy Adams (*ffrancis and Mary*); destination, Virginia.—Mary Gardner (*George*); destination, Virginia.

Page 293

Rachell Shelton (*William and Ann*); destination, Virginia.—John Downing (*William and Ann*); destination, Virginia.—Jane Powter (*ffrancis and Mary*); destination, Virginia.—Nicholas Savory; destination, Nevis.—John Wattkins (*ffrancis and Mary*); destination, Virginia.—Elinor ffoord (*ffrancis and Mary*); destination, Virginia.—Elizabeth Constant (*ffrancis and Mary*); destination, Virginia.—George Hanks (*ffrancis and Mary*); destination, Virginia.—Thomas Rake; destination, Virginia.—John Collins (*William and Ann*); destination, Virginia.—Reece Jenkins (*ffrancis and Mary*); destination, Virginia.—Stephen

M

Morgan (*ffrancis and Mary*); destination, Virginia.—Thomas Jenkins (*ffrancis and Mary*); destination, Virginia.—William Morgan (*ffrancis and Mary*); destination, Virginia.—Ann Davis (*ffrancis and Mary*); destination, Virginia.—John How (*William and Ann*); destination, Virginia.—Jeremiah Perry (*William and Ann*); destination, Virginia.

Page 294

Hannah ffoord (*George*); destination, Virginia.—Richard Sherman (*ffrancis and Mary*); destination, Virginia.—Elizabeth Sampson (*George*); destination, Virginia.—John Warrell (*William and Ann*); destination, Virginia.—Daniell Underwood (*George*); destination, Virginia.—Richard Tarbutt (*ffrancis and Mary*); destination, Virginia.—Joseph Roberts (*ffrancis and Mary*); destination, Virginia.—Diana Nokes (*Mary*); destination, Antigua.—John Reeves (*George*); destination, Virginia.—Robert Davis (*George*); destination, Virginia.—Elienor Evans (*Mary*); destination, Antigua.—Rowland Gwin (*Planter*); destination, Nevis.—David Philipps (*ffrancis and Mary*); destination, Virginia.—Isaac Bishopp (*George*); destination, Virginia.—Ann Crow (*ffrancis and Mary*); destination, Virginia.—Daniell Simon (*ffrancis and Mary*); destination, Virginia.—Thomas Richards (*George*); destination, Virginia.—Elizabeth Cooper (*Sarah and Elizabeth*); destination, Virginia.

Page 295

Joane Leeke (*Sarah and Elizabeth*); destination, Virginia.—Elizabeth Edmonds (*George*); destination, Virginia.—David Rosser (*ffrancis and Mary*); destination, Virginia.—Robert Berkly (*ffrancis and Mary*); destination, Virginia.—Henry Powter (*George*); destination, Virginia.—Lewis Williams (*Alithea*); destination, Maryland.—Hugh Addison (*ffrancis and Mary*); destination, Virginia.—Thomas Whittchelly (*ffrancis and Mary*); destination, Virginia.—Margarett Harris (*William and Ann*); destination, Virginia.—Michaell Davis (*Batchelor*); destination, Barbadoes.—Philipp Evans (*America Merchant*); destination, Jamaica.—Richard Widdus (*George*); destination, Virginia.—John Radford (*William and Anne*); destination, Virginia.—Reece Davis (*George*); destination, Virginia.—William Davis (*Charles*); destination, Virginia.—John Adis (*Loves Increase*); destination, Nevis.

Page 296

Cornelius Giles (*America Merchant*); destination, Jamaica.—Benjamin Thomas (*Golden Lyon*); destination, Barbadoes.—Robert Vibian (*sic*) (*America Merchant*); destination, Jamaica.—Robert Window (*America Merchant*); destination, Jamaica.—Alice Dickes (*America Merchant*); destination, Jamaica.—Elizabeth Collins (*America Merchant*); destination, Jamaica.—John Curtis (*America Merchant*); destination, Jamaica.—Abraham Nicholas (*America Merchant*); destination, Jamaica.—John Newman (*America Merchant*); destination, Jamaica.—Welthian Savage (*America Merchant*); destination, Jamaica.—John Brebery (?) (*Batchelor*); destination, Barbadoes.—Charles Buttler (*Batchelor*); destination, Barbadoes.—Robert Nickins (*Golden Lyon*); destination, Barbadoes.—Samuel Curtis (*Mary and Joane*); destination, Newfoundland.—John Bushell (*Exchange*); destination, Nevis.—Ansell Williams (*Exchange*); destination, Nevis.—Stephen Goun (*Batchelor*); destination, Barbadoes.—Daniell Millard (*Society*); destination, Barbadoes.—Rose Brindall (*Batchelor*); destination, Barbadoes.

Page 297

Katharine Howell (*Batchelor*); destination, Barbadoes.—Robert Sprewell (*Exchange*); destination, Nevis.—William Denham (*Exchange*); destination, Nevis. —John Hewins (*Exchange*); destination, Nevis.—William Baylis (*Loves Increase*); destination, Barbadoes.—Lawrence ffoweracres (*Golden Lyon*); destination, Barbadoes.—Philipp Saunders (*Jacob*); destination, Newfoundland.—Owen Hughs (*Exchange*); destination (no place given).—Richard Cullin (*Batchelor*); destination, Barbadoes.—Thomas Newcome (*Exchange*); destination, Nevis.—Henry Williams (*Exchange*); destination, Nevis or Antigua.—William Whiteacre (*Gabriell*); destination, Barbadoes.—Giles English (*Gabriell*); destination, Barbadoes.—William English (*Gabriell*); destination, Barbadoes.—Thomas Lawrence (*Isabella*); destination, Jamaica.—Robert Cripps (*Jacob*); destination, Newfoundland.—George Capp (*Batchelor*); destination, Barbadoes.—Elienor Peirce (*Batchelor*); destination, Barbadoes.

Page 298

Rebeccah Browne (*Batchelor*); destination, Barbadoes.—Edmund ffarre (*Gabriell*); destination, Nevis.—Sarah Pope (*Dolphin*); destination, Barbadoes.— Robert Anderson; destination, Jamaica.—Hannah Legg (*Isabella*); destination, Jamaica.—William Harris (*Isabella*); destination, Jamaica.—Thomas Whittle (*Speedwell*); destination, New England.—Charles Lane (*Daniell*); destination, New England.—John Webb (*Isabella*); destination, Jamaica.—Margarett Howell (*Isabella*); destination, Jamaica.—Edward Knight (*Primrose*); destination, Jamaica.—John Parke (*Primrose*); destination, Jamaica.—James Pew (*Isabella*); destination, Jamaica.—Richard Cuffe (*Isabella*); destination, Jamaica.—Bartholomew Gornby (*Primrose*); destination, Jamaica.—Darby Hanning (*Primrose*); destination, Jamaica.

Page 299

Thomas Archer (*Primrose*); destination, Jamaica.—Samuell Berry (*Primrose*); destination, Jamaica.—ffrancis Beard (*Hopewell*); destination, Newfoundland.— Robert Gillum (*Primrose*); destination, Jamaica.—Richard Davis (*Hopewell*); destination, Newfoundland.—William Hopkins (*Mary*); destination, Jamaica.— Evan Phillipps (*Hopewell*); destination, Newfoundland.—Thomas Price (*Susanna*); destination, Virginia.—David Dennis (*Bristoll Merchant*); destination, Virginia.— Thomas Hillman (*Susanna*); destination, Virginia.—William Southern (*Susanna*); destination, Virginia.—Thomas Gilbert (*Susanna*); destination, Virginia.—James Gilbert (*Susanna*); destination, Virginia.—Nathaniel Williams (*Saphire Ketch*); destination, Virginia.—Morgan Howell (*Susanna*); destination, Virginia.—Ann Bone (*Susanna*); destination, Virginia.—Elias Edins (*Blackmore*); destination, Virginia.

Page 300

ffrancis Ward (*Susanna*); destination, Virginia.—Daniell Holmes (*Saphire Ketch*); destination, Virginia.—Thomas Harly (*Susanna*); destination, Virginia.— John Hicks (*Susanna*); destination, Virginia.—Edward Ellis (*Susanna*); destination, Virginia.—Thomas Hill (*Blackmore*); destination, Virginia.—Abigall Mayfeild (*Susanna*); destination, Virginia.—Jerves Williams (*Bristoll Merchant*); destination, Virginia.—Katharine Williams (*Susanna*); destination, Virginia.—Jeremy Warner (*Susannah*); destination, Virginia.—Thomas Seabrett (*Saphire Ketch*); destination, Virginia.—Joseph Holt (*Susanna*); destination, Virginia.—Mary Wyatt (*Saphire Ketch*); destination, Maryland.—Alice Bird (*Susanna*); destination, Maryland.—Thomas James (*Susanna*); destination, Maryland.—Jeremy Harris (*Susanna*); destination, Maryland.—John ffoord (*Susanna*); destination, Virginia. —George Radford (*Susanna*); destination, Virginia.—William Bunchcombe (*Susanna*); destination, Virginia.—George Martyn (*Susanna*); destination, Virginia.—John Reece (*Bristoll Merchant*); destination, Virginia.

Page 301

Mary Searle (*Bristoll Merchant*); destination, Virginia.—Daniell Banks (*Bristoll Merchant*); destination, Virginia.—Thomas Hinson (*New England Merchant*); destination, Virginia.—Sarah Rawleigh; destination, Virginia.—Ann Peck (*Bristoll Merchant*); destination, Virginia.—Jenkin Rogers (*Bristoll Merchant*); destination, Virginia.—Robert Meredith (*Blackmore*); destination, Virginia.—Sarah Muskett (*Bristoll Merchant*); destination, Virginia.—John Hughs (*Maryland Merchant*); destination, Maryland.—Elizabeth Soloman (*Nevis Merchant*); destination, Virginia.—Nicholas Windover (*Nevis Merchant*); destination, Virginia.—Anthony Drew (*Nevis Merchant*); destination, Virginia.—John Allen (*Lambe*); destination, Jamaica.—John Giles (*Richard and James*); destination, Virginia.—Mary Morgan (*New England Merchant*); destination, Virginia.—Edward Creed (*John*); destination, Virginia.—Susannah Norcutt (*New England Merchant*); destination, Virginia. —Elienor Price (*Maryland Merchant*); destination, Maryland.

Page 302

Alice Trow (*Maryland Merchant*); destination, Maryland.—Edward Williams (*Unicorne*); destination, Virginia.—Margarett Smith (*John*); destination, Virginia. —Thomas Baily (*Unicorne*); destination, Virginia.—Thomas Jeanes (Susanna); destination, Virginia.—George Stanly (*Maryland Merchant*); destination, Virginia. —William Jones; destination, Virginia.—Mary Major (*Unicorne*); destination, Virginia.—William Lawrence (*Nevis Merchant*); destination, Virginia.—Nathaniell Davis (*Maryland Merchant*); destination, Virginia.—Thomas Carline (Stephen); destination, Virginia.—John Tackley (*Maryland Merchant*); destination, Virginia. —William Tackley (*Maryland Merchant*); destination, Virginia.—John Williams; destination, Virginia.—Elizabeth Pope (*Lamb*); destination, Virginia.—Benjamin Ricketts (*Lamb*); destination, Virginia.—Joyce Holder (*Lamb*); destination, Virginia.—Henry Gosmoore (*Expectation*); destination, Virginia.—Ann Nagis (*Comfort*); destination, Virginia.—William Jones (*Nevis Merchant*); destination, Virginia.

Page 303

Mary Hancock (*Lamb*); destination, Jamaica.—James Briant (*Unicorne*); destination, Virginia.—William Bassett (*Expectation*); destination, Virginia.— James Clubb (*John*); destination, Virginia.—Richard Symonds (*Expectation*); destination, Virginia.—Ann Okey (*Stephen*); destination, Virginia.—Henry Williams (*Stephen*); destination, Virginia.—Ephraim Axford (*Bristoll Merchant*); destination, Virginia.—Barbara Collins (*Abraham and Isaac*); destination, Virginia.—William Wadly; destination, Virginia.—Richard Hawkins (*Alathea*); destination, Virginia. —Charles Charles (*sic*) Jones; destination, Virginia.—Robert Watts; destination, Virginia.—Hesekiah Blank (*Comfort*); destination, Virginia.—Hannah Siley (*Bristoll Merchant*); destination, Virginia.—John Harding (*ffrancis and Mary*); destination,

Virginia.—John Storks (*Maryland Merchant*); destination, Virginia.—William Legg (*ffrancis and Mary*); destination, Virginia.—ffrances ffolkner (*ffrancis and Mary*); destination, Virginia.—Elizabeth Griffiths (*ffrancis and Mary*); destination, Virginia.—Thomas Lockyer (*Comfort*); destination, Virginia.—Samuell Jones (*Sarah and Elizabeth*); destination, Virginia.—Nathaniel Dayes (*Bristoll Merchant*); destination, Virginia.—Griffith Griffiths (*Bristoll Merchant*); destination, Virginia.

Page 304

Richard Reed (*Bristoll Merchant*); destination, Virginia.—John Haskins (*Sarah and Elizabeth*); destination, Virginia.—John Stone (*Maryland Merchant*); destination, Virginia.—Christopher Earle (*Maryland Merchant*); destination, Virginia.—Jonathan Budge (*George*); destination, Virginia.—Josias Budge (*George*); destination, Virginia.—Thomas Gough (*George*); destination, Virginia.—Isaac Hopkins (*George*); destination, Virginia.—Thomas Collins (*George*); destination, Virginia.—Mary Thomas (*ffrancis and Mary*); destination, Virginia.—William Cox; destination, Nevis.—Henry Wall (*Bristoll Merchant*); destination, Virginia.—Joane Twist; destination, Virginia.—Bridgett Griffith (*Maryland Merchant*); destination, Virginia.—Henry Symons (*Maryland Merchant*); destination, Virginia.—Robert Kellway (*America Merchant*); destination, Jamaica.—Christopher Legg (*America Merchant*); destination, Jamaica.—Richard Attwood (*ffrancis and Mary*); destination, Virginia.—Richard Pritchatt (*Sarah and Elizabeth*); destination, Virginia.—Thomas Greenfeild (*Maryland Merchant*); destination, Virginia.—Andrew Bomer (*Sarah and Elizabeth*); destination, Virginia.

Page 305

Richard Somersett (*America Merchant*); destination, Jamaica.—William Burgis (*George*); destination, Virginia.—ffrancis Thomas (*George*); destination, Virginia.—Humfry Mills (*ffrancis and Mary*); destination, Maryland.—Edward Millard (*ffrancis and Mary*); destination, Virginia.—William Johnson (*ffrancis and Mary*); destination, Virginia.—William Morris (*Agreement*); destination, Virginia.—ffrancis Meeke (*ffrancis and Mary*); destination, Virginia.—William Games (*George*); destination, Virginia.—William Window (*ffrancis and Mary*); destination, Maryland.—Phyllis Goulding (*ffrancis and Mary*); destination, Virginia.—Edward Watts (*Agreement*); destination, Virginia.—William Harris (*Agreement*); destination, Virginia.—William Shaw (*Agreement*); destination, Virginia.—Henry Isdill (*George*); destination, Virginia.—David Jones (*George*); destination, Virginia.—Edward Rokly; destination, Virginia.—John Richards (*Reformation*); destination, Virginia.—Thomas Tucker (*Olive Tree*); destination, Barbadoes.—James Brookes (*Reformation*); destination, Virginia.—Richard Leech (*Humility*); destination, Barbadoes.—William Mason (*Agreement*); destination, Virginia.

Page 306

Mary Powell (*Agreement*); destination, Virginia.—James Curnock (*Primrose*); destination, Jamaica.—John Baker (*Batchelor*); destination, Barbadoes.—Sarah Perrin (*Agreement*); destination, Virginia.—Howell Price (*Primrose*); destination, Jamaica.—Stephen Jones (*Angell Gabriell*); destination, Barbadoes.—David Clarke (*Exchange*); destination, Nevis.—Joane Curtis (*Angell Gabriell*); destination, Virginia (in Wickacomico).—Hugh Jones (*Angell Gabriell*); destination, Virginia.—Ann Madocks (*Society*); destination, Barbadoes.—John Ittry (*Angell Gabriell*); destination, Virginia.—Simon Hughes (*Angell Gabriell*); destination, Virginia.—Jane

Wilkins (*Batchelor*); destination, Barbadoes.—John ffoord; destination, Virginia.—Thomas Humphreys (*Exchange*); destination, Nevis.—Arthur Springnesh (*Angell Gabriell*); destination, Virginia.—Richard Worgan (*William and Ann*); destination, Barbadoes.—John Durban; destination, Barbadoes.—Benjamin Charme (*Angell Gabriell*); destination, Virginia.—William Mitchell (*William and Ann*); destination, Barbadoes.

Page 307

William Banfeild (*Exchange*); destination, Nevis.—Mary Webb (*Exchange*); destination, Nevis.—Thomas Hitchman (*Charity Ketch*); destination, Virginia.—Thomas Davis (*ffellowshipp*); destination, Antigua.—John Kirtland (*Gabriell*); destination, Virginia.—James Hallings (*Arthur and Mary*); destination, Barbadoes.—[Blank] Cannum (*Arthur and Mary*); destination, Barbadoes.—Mathew Payne (*Gabriell*); destination, Nevis.—Thomas Sheppard (*Gabriell*); destination, Nevis.—John Morris (*Gabriell*); destination, Nevis.—Mary Syms (*Gabriell*); destination, Nevis.—Thomas White (*Mary*); destination, Barbadoes.—Ann Payne (*Two Brothers*); destination, Barbadoes.—Samuel fferris (*Bristoll Merchant*); destination, Virginia.—Moses ffound (*Retorne of Boston*); destination, New England.—Katharine Griffin (*Unicorne*); destination, Virginia.—Richard Land (?) (*Bristoll ffactor*); destination, Virginia.—Sarah Clarke (*Bristoll ffactor*); destination, Virginia.—Ann Tidcombe (*Retorne of Boston*); destination, New England.—Mary Ball (*Retorne of Boston*); destination, New England.—Ann Wharton (*Retorne of Boston*); destination, New England.

Page 308

William Bastin (*Bristoll ffactor*); destination, Virginia.—Elizabeth Poticary (*Bristoll ffactor*); destination, Virginia.—Ann Matthewes (*Bristoll ffactor*); destination, Virginia.—Christopher Meade (*Martha and Sarah*); destination, Virginia.—Andrew Dyer (*Bristoll ffactor*); destination, Virginia.—Thomas Lewes (*Bristoll ffactor*); destination, Virginia.—Milsy Williams (*Martha and Sarah*); destination, Virginia.—John Thomas; destination, Virginia.—David Jones (*Nevis Merchant*); destination, Virginia.—Mary Dorman (*Bristoll ffactor*); destination, Virginia.—Hanna Elvins (*Nevis Merchant*); destination, Virginia.—Joshua Jackson; destination, Virginia.—Katharine Jones (*Retorne*); destination, New England.—Priscilla Wattkins (*Retorne*); destination, New England.—Philipp May (*Bristoll ffactor*); destination, Virginia.—Thomas Jenkins (*Victory*); destination, Virginia.—Humfry Axall (*Releife of Boston*); destination, New England.—Elizabeth Pittman (*Bristoll Merchant*); destination, Virginia.—William Lucus (*Mary and Joane*); destination, Virginia.—Elizabeth Harding (*Bristoll ffactor*); destination, Virginia.

Page 309

Mary Dorney (*Victory*); destination, Virginia.—Jonathan Hurd (*Unicorne*); destination, Virginia.—Elizabeth Howell (*Victory*); destination, Virginia.—Joane Morris (*Nevis Merchant*); destination, Virginia.—Richard Martyn (*Bristoll Merchant*); destination, Virginia.—Katharine Griffin (*Victory*); destination, Virginia.—James Williams (*Victory*); destination, Virginia.—Robert Lindsay (*Concord*); destination, Virginia.—Mary Dollman (*Blackmore*); destination, Virginia.—Jennet Edwards (*Expectation*); destination, Virginia.—Mary Haverd (*Nevis Merchant*); destination, Virginia.—Michaell Dare (*Bristoll Merchant*); destination, Virginia.—Henry Brice (*Bristoll Merchant*); destination, Virginia.—John Hughes (*Bristoll*

Merchant); destination, Virginia.—John Anderson (*Sarah and Elizabeth*); destination, Virginia.—ffrancis Sutton (*Victory*); destination, Virginia.—William Jones (*Victory*); destination, Virginia.—Thomas Blake (*Blackmore*); destination, Virginia.—George Browne (*Sarah and Elizabeth*); destination, Virginia.

Page 310

Richard Shepherd (*Victory*); destination, Virginia.—Sarah Killuck (*Victory*); destination, Virginia.—Ann Otridge (*Victory*); destination, Virginia.—Dorothy Haverd (*Reformation*); destination, Virginia.—Robert Smith (*Victory*); destination, Virginia.—John Collins (*Bristoll Merchant*); destination, Virginia.—Welthian Jones (*George*); destination, Virginia.—John Chapman (*Richard of Bristoll*); destination, Virginia.—Thomas Turner (*Bristoll Merchant*); destination, Virginia.—William Edwards (*Bristoll Merchant*); destination, Virginia.—Elizabeth Abbott (*Victory*); destination, Virginia.—John Carroll (*Sarah and Elizabeth*); destination, Virginia.—John Poole (*Sarah and Elizabeth*); destination, Virginia.—Edward Clement (*Victory*); destination, Virginia.—Charles Glover (*Maryland Merchant*); destination, Virginia.—John Bowers (*Victory*); destination, Virginia.—John Spencer (*Bristoll Merchant*); destination, Virginia.—Elizabeth Bache (*Blackmore*); destination, Virginia.—Elizabeth Daybrinke (*Blackmore*); destination, Virginia.—Grace Tammas (?) (*John and Joane*); destination, Virginia.

Page 311

John Coward (*Blackmore*); destination, Virginia.—John Singer (*Blackmore*); destination, Virginia.—John Rogers (*Expectation*); destination, Virginia.—Alice Wattkins; destination, Virginia.—William Morgan (*Sarah and Elizabeth*); destination, Virginia.—Priscilla Kingman (*Maryland Merchant*); destination, Virginia.—John Thedam (*Victory*); destination, Virginia.—Joseph Merchant (*Victory*); destination, Virginia.—Mary Powell (*Victory*); destination, Virginia.—Christopher Harrell (*Victory*); destination, Virginia.—Henry Harrell (*Victory*); destination, Virginia.—George Semine (*Alithea*); destination, Virginia.—George Wattkis (*sic*) (*Alithea*); destination, Virginia.—Margaret Jones (*Sarah and Elizabeth*); destination, Virginia.—ffrancis Cotton (*Sarah and Elizabeth*); destination, Virginia.—William Stidman (*Expectation*); destination, Virginia.—Arthur Williams (*Katharine*); destination, New York.—Edward Williams; destination, New York.—Samuell Minor; destination, New York.—John Lokyer (*John*); destination, Virginia.—Rebecca Walter (*Maryland Merchant*); destination, Virginia.

Page 312

Edward Badman (*Mary and Joane*); destination, Virginia.—Martha Barnett (*Mary and Joane*); destination, Virginia.—David Llewellin (*Victory*); destination, Virginia.—Jane Shakefoote (*New England Merchant*); destination, Nevis.—Roger Meredith (*ffrancis and Mary*); destination, Virginia.—Thomas Ward (*Agreement*); destination, Virginia.—Patience Walker (*Richard*); destination, Virginia.—Constant Cotton (*Richard*); destination, Virginia.—John David (*Victory*); destination, Virginia.—Thomas Tanner (*Richard*); destination, Virginia.—William Watts (*Richard*); destination, Virginia.—James Eton (*Victory*); destination, Virginia.—William Edwards (*George*); destination, Virginia.—Sarah Bennett (*George*); destination, Virginia.—Timothy Haines (*John*); destination, Virginia.—Richard Daggett (*Agreement*); destination, Maryland.—Mary Couzens (*Agreement*); destination,

Virginia or Maryland.—John Rice (*Richard and James*); destination, Virginia.—Thomas ffreeman (*Agreement*); destination, Virginia.—John Jones (*ffrancis and Mary*); destination, Virginia.—William Penbrooke (*Agreement*); destination, Maryland.—George Beard (*Antego Merchant*); destination, Nevis.

Page 313
John Roberts (*Maryland Merchant*); destination, Virginia.—Richard Williams (*George*); destination, Virginia.—Thomas Kirby (*Exchange*); destination, Barbadoes.—George Curryer (*Maryland Merchant*); destination, Virginia.—George Hartupp (*George*); destination, Virginia.—John Johnson (*Maryland Merchant*); destination, Virginia.—Margaret Dugden (*George*); destination, Virginia.—Anthony Poole (*George*); destination, Virginia.—Thomas Sweete (*Maryland Merchant*); destination, Virginia.—John Turner (*Maryland Merchant*); destination, Maryland. —Thomas Barker (*Maryland Merchant*); destination, Maryland.—Thomas ffowler (*Maryland Merchant*); destination, Maryland.—William Williams (*ffrancis and Mary*); destination, Virginia.—Ann Deverell (*Maryland Merchant*); destination, Virginia.—Mary Young (*Rainbowe*); destination, Virginia.—Thomas Griffith (*George*); destination, Virginia.—John Burnett (*William and Joseph*); destination, Virginia.—George Wilkenson (*George*); destination, Virginia.—Thomas Powell (*Maryland Merchant*); destination, Virginia.—John Rodd (*Maryland Merchant*); destination, Virginia.—Mary Swetman (*George*); destination, Virginia.—Robert Masters (*Rainbow*); destination, Virginia.—John Pavier; destination, Virginia.

Page 314
John Yarranton; destination, Virginia.—William Reece (*Rainbow*); destination, Virginia.—Jacob Roch; destination, Nevis.—Nathan While; destination, Nevis. —ffrancis Rafe (*Maryland Merchant*); destination, Virginia.—Joane Nickolls; destination, Maryland.—Mary Attwood (*ffellowshipp*); destination, Barbadoes.—Matthew Buttler (*ffrancis and Mary*); destination, Virginia.—John Parsons (*Rainbow*); destination, Virginia.—Thomas Elcock (*Society*); destination, Virginia.—Richard Cox (*Rainbow*); destination, Virginia.—William Cheilds (*Abraham and Isaac*); destination, Nevis.—Sarah ffoord (*Society*); destination, Barbadoes.—Ann Williams (*Dolphin*); destination, Nevis.—Daniel Christon (*Abraham and Isaac*); destination, Nevis.—James Warnum (*Rainbow*); destination, Virginia.—William Batchelor (*Hart*); destination, Nevis.—Ruth Andrews (*Dolphin*); destination, Nevis. —Thomas Pinchen (*Industry*); destination, Barbadoes.—Ann Dempsy (*Rainebowe*); destination, Virginia.—Elizabeth Broadbeard; destination, Virginia.—ffrancis Dew (*Rainebow*); destination, Virginia.

Page 315
William Cheesman; destination, Nevis.—Tristram Davis (*Royall Oake*); destination, Jamaica.—Thomas Johnson (*Rainebow*); destination, Virginia.—William Jones; destination, Barbadoes.—John Ayleworth; destination, Nevis.—Samuel Ockford; destination, Barbadoes and Nevis.—Robert Pemry (*Dolphin*); destination, Nevis.—Ann Prewett (*Dolphin*); destination, Nevis.—Hester Wells (*Dolphin*); destination, Nevis.—Joane Evans (*Dolphin*); destination, Nevis.—Ann Priddie (*Dolphin*); destination, Nevis.—John Prosser (*Gabriell*); destination, Barbadoes.—William Tomkins (*Golden Hart*); destination, Nevis.—Amos Spraggott (*Dolphin*); destination, Virginia.—Robert Bennett (*Dolphin*); destination, Vir-

ginia.—John Powell (*Arthur and Mary*); destination, Nevis.—Hester Harrison (*William and Ann*); destination, Barbadoes.—Abigal Whittwood; destination, Nevis.—Joseph Rowne (*Peter Ketch*); destination, Barbadoes.—Richard Bowden (*Dolphin*); destination, Nevis.—Daniel Rogers (*Dolphin*); destination, Nevis.—Judith Bond (*St. Peter* [?]); destination, Barbadoes.—John Jones (*Hart*); destination, Nevis.—John Willy; destination, Nevis.

Page 316
      Lawrence Tanner (*Olive Branch*); destination, Newfoundland.—William Allen (*Olive Branch*); destination, Newfoundland.—Thomas Boone (*Olive Branch*); destination, Newfoundland.—Enoch Billings (*Hart*); destination, Barbadoes.—William Britten (*Supply*); destination, New England.—Richard Browne (*Saphire Ketch*); destination, New England.—Lettice Jones (*Bristoll ffactor*); destination, Barbadoes.—Thomas Saunders (*Saphire Ketch*); destination, New England.—John Wrentmore; destination, New England.—Nathaniel Thornes (*Supply*); destination, New England.—Peter Coffy (*Jamaica Merchant*); destination, Nevis.—Christopher Talbot (*Benjamin of Boston*); destination, New England.—Thomas Pritchard; destination, New England.—William Price; destination, New England.—Evan Rodrah (*Jamaica Merchant*); destination, Nevis.—William Waple (*William*); destination, Newfoundland.—William Tomkins (*Jamaica Merchant*); destination, Nevis.—Robert Harrison (*Robert and Hester*); destination, Barbadoes.—Gilbert Cooke (*Robert and Hester*); destination, Barbadoes.—John Crookshanke (*Robert and Hester*); destination, Barbadoes.

Page 317
      Edward Poole; destination, Virginia.—William Robinson (*Nevis Merchant*); destination, West Indies or Virginia.—ffrancis ffoord (*Primrose*); destination, Jamaica.—Richard Nicholas (*Primrose*); destination, Jamaica.—Robert Vyne (*Nevis Merchant*); destination, Nevis.—John Beale (*Amity*); destination, Nevis or Jamaica.—Thomas Edwards; destination (no place given).—Philipp Grubb; destination, Jamaica.—John Griffith (*Antego Merchant*); destination, Barbadoes.—Robert Burrell (*Nevis Merchant*); destination, Nevis or Virginia.—Archibald Johnson (*Bristoll ffactor*); destination, Virginia.—Robert Johnson (*Bristoll ffactor*); destination, Virginia.—Morgan Jenkin (*Nevis Merchant*); destination, Nevis.—Arthur Bowen (*Mountserrat Merchant*); destination, Montserrat.—William Dedbridge (*Nevis Merchant*); destination, Virginia.—John Sheppard (*Bristoll ffactor*); destination, Virginia.—John Griffith (*Richard and Ann*); destination, Jamaica.—George White (*Richard and James*); destination, Virginia.—Walter Williams (*Nevis Merchant*); destination, Virginia or Nevis.—Rowland Pytherch (*Richard and James*); destination, Virginia.—William Nicholls (*Bristoll ffactor*); destination, Virginia.

Page 318
      William Jones (*Bristoll ffactor*); destination, Virginia.—Thomas Cornish (*Bristoll ffactor*); destination, Virginia.—William Gouldin (*Bristoll ffactor*); destination, Virginia.—Richard Williams (*Bristoll ffactor*); destination, Virginia.—Charles Clift (*Samuell and Mary*); destination, Virginia.—James Rice (*Bristoll ffactor*); destination, Virginia.—Roger Jones; destination, Virginia or Nevis.—Philipp Waters (*Antego Merchant*); destination, Barbadoes.—Sarah Moody (*Bristoll ffactor*); destination, Virginia.—ffrancis Thomas (*Nevis Merchant*); destination, Virginia.—

Latimer Willmott (*Bristoll ffactor*) ; destination, Virginia.—Robert Camell (*Nevis Merchant*) ; destination, Virginia.—William Philipps (*Bristoll ffactor*) ; destination, Virginia.—Sarah Obryan (*Nevis Merchant*) ; destination, Nevis or Virginia.—Robert Baber (*Bristoll ffactor*) ; destination, Virginia.—Thomas Crispe (*Bristoll ffactor*) ; destination, Virginia.—Richard Jones (*Bristoll ffactor*) ; destination, Virginia.—Ann Bobett (*Bristoll ffactor*) ; destination, Virginia.—Henry Morgan (*Nevis Merchant*) ; destination, Virginia or Nevis.—Joane Ricketts (*Bristoll ffactor*) ; destination, Virginia.—Bridgett Whitethorne (*Bristoll ffactor*) ; destination, Virginia.—John Nicholas (*Bristoll ffactor*) ; destination, Virginia.—William Matthews (*Bristoll ffactor*) ; destination, Virginia.—Joane Gooding (*Bristoll ffactor*) ; destination, Virginia.

Servants to Foreign Plantations

(Scattered Entries : Mar. 27, 1680—June 12, 1686)

~~~~~~

FIRST BOOK

Date	Name	Residence	Ship	Destination
Mar. 27	Thomas Escott		William & Mary	Virginia
29	John David			Jamaica
Apl. 1	John Carouthers		Bristol Merchant	Virginia
	Timothy Burne			Jamaica
19	John Gallaspy		William & Mary	do.
	William Morgan		Bristol Merchant	Barbadoes
	Walter James		do.	do.
	Thomas Pevison		do.	Virginia
26	William Morgan	Keene	do.	do.
May 3	William Barton		William & Mary	Jamaica
	William Inon	Haverford West	Sarah of Bristoll	Nevis
7	Jonathan Gibbons		William & Mary	Jamaica
June 12	John Griffiths	Carmarthen	Comfort	Barbados
18	Richard Britton	Studley	Sarah	Nevis
26	Thomas Jones	Llantrishen	Samuel	Maryland
July 2	Thomas Smart	Co. Glamorgan	do.	Barbados
	Walter Thomas		do.	do.
9	James ffry		do.	Maryland
12	John Williams		Richard & James	Virginia
13	William Webb		Samuel	Maryland
14	David Beynam		Richard & James	Virginia
15	John Price		do.	do.
	Thomas Pondle		do.	do.
19	George Morgan		Samuel	Maryland
22	Andrew Waublyn		do.	Virginia
27	Joseph Westerson		Richard	do.
	Jonathan Wyn			do.
Aug. 2	James Stankliffe		Nevis Merchant	Nevis
3	Thomas Hayford		Samuel	Maryland
	Philip Morgan		do.	do.
4	George Millard	Wotton Underidge	Lamb	Jamaica
	John Harding		Samuel	Virginia

Date		Name	Residence	Ship	Destination
Aug.	10	Richard Williams		Comfort	Virginia
		William Popejoy		Samuel	Maryland
	16	Thomas Gillman		Nevis Merchant	Virginia
	19	Henry ffoote			do.
		George Holmes		Comfort	do.
		Ann Smith		do.	do.
	20	Alicia Wattkins		Richard & James	Maryland
		Joseph Brookes		Samuel	do.
		Peter Burchis		Bristoll ffactor	Virginia
	21	Mary Puttley		Nevis Merchant	Nevis
		Joel Burnhole		do.	
	29	Alexander Mocollock		Arthur & Mary	Barbados
Sept.	1	Robert Lawrence		Bristoll ffactor	Virginia
	10	Richard Roberts		Richard & James	do.
	16	John Thomas		do.	Maryland
		George Barnaby		Nevis Merchant	Nevis or Montserrat
	24	Edward Davis		ffactor	Virginia
		Ann Douding		Richard & James	Maryland
		Thomas Williams		do.	do.
	25	Mary Urlin		Bristoll ffactor	Virginia
	29	Mary Attwood		Richard & James	do.
Oct.	1	William Griffin		ffactor	do.
	4	Thomas Hamond		do.	do.
	6	John ffisher		do.	do.
	7	Tobias ffowler		Bristoll ffactor	do.
	11	Richard Parker		do.	do.
	15	Mary Clarke		ffactor	do.
	20	Anthony Drew		Bristoll ffactor	do.
		Reece Lloyd		ffactor	do.
		Lewis Lloyd		do.	do.
	25	Edward Hulbert		Richard & James	do.
	26	Thomas Merchant		ffactor	do.
Nov.	5	Roger Griffith		Maryland Merchant	Maryland
	10	John Davis		do.	Virginia
		Richard Millard		do.	do.
		George (?) Sanders		do.	do.
		Ann Sanders		do.	do.
	17	John Argos		do.	do.
	19	Ann Browne		do.	do.
		Ann Martyn		do.	do.
Dec.	5	William Tayler		Unicorne	Virginia
	7	Robert Sample		Stephen	do.
		Edward Toms		Resolucon	do.
		Nathaniel Toms		do.	do.
	11	Mary Price		Society	Maryland
		Thomas Ragland		do.	do.
		Samuel Workeman		do.	do.
		John Peirce		Oake	Jamaica

Date	Name	Residence	Ship	Destination
1680–81				
Jan. 7	Phillip Lambert		Society	Virginia

SECOND BOOK

Date	Name	Residence	Ship	Destination
1684				
Apl. 26	Ann Evans		America Merchant	Jamaica
May 8	Arthur Marwood			do.
June 3	John Thomas	Llandaff	Bristoll Merchant	Pennsylvania
6	Thomas Eyre	East Farendon	Rainbow	New England
	William Powell	Caldicott	William & Ann	Nevis
17	Henry Powell	Uske	Amity	Jamaica
	Sarah Neale	Barton	Dragon	do.
June 27	ffrancis Sansom	Browsley	Bristoll Merchant	Virginia or Pennsylvania
30	William Edwards	Oxford	Samuell	Barbados
	William Courtney	Exeter	do.	Jamaica
July 16	Godfry Waterson	Gloucester	Dragon	do.
26	Samuel Pepper	Lyn Regis	do.	do.
28	Roger Price		Bristoll Merchant	
29	Robert Curry	Mary Stoke	Society	Maryland
Aug. 2	John Stevens	London	Samuel	Jamaica
4	Ann Doggett	Bristol	Society	Virginia
	Mary Chandler	Bristol	do.	do.
5	Richard Salisbury	London	do.	Maryland
6	John Whitfeild		Diligence	Barbados
9	George Lloyd	Wiston	Adventure	Virginia
	Daniel Marlow	Coventry	Dragon	Jamaica
11	Jacob Bosley	Chipping Norton	Bristoll Merchant	Pennsylvania
14	Alice Powell	Taunton Deane	Francis & Mary	Virginia
	ffrancis Clarvo	Bristol	Society	Maryland
	Walter Harris	Christchurch	Diligence	Barbadoes
	Ann ffox	London	do.	do.
16	Henry Hart	Bedminster	Society	Virginia
	Silvester Stillingfleet	Pomfrett	Dragon	Jamaica
19	Anthony Swymer		do.	do.
	Edward Pinnick	Seand	Bristoll Merchant	Pennsylvania
	John Pinnick	Seand	do.	do.
	John Evans	Newcastle (Staffs)	New England Merchant	Nevis
21	Mary Jones	St. Brides		Pennsylvania or Virginia
25	William Goldsmith	Falmouth		do. do.
	William Golden	London	Resolucon or Society	Virginia or Maryland
	Richard Athay	Litten	Bristoll Merchant	Pennsylvania
27	William Hall	Levpool (Liverpool)	Samuel	Virginia
28	Richard Day	Shepton Mallet	ffrancis & Mary	do.

Date	Name	Residence	Ship	Destination
Aug. 28	Mary Whitwood	Winscomb		Virginia
	Grace Hardwille	Wedmore		do.
Sept. 1	Samuel Smith	Bristoll	Richard & James	do.
4	Elizabeth Worne	Taunton		do.
5	Margaret Green	Colthall Green Nr. Waltham Abbey		do.
	Thomas Griffin	Llalleston		Jamaica
6	John Mors	Tiddenham		Virginia
8	Richard Sledge	Pensford		do.
	Richard Langford	Icfeild		Jamaica
	Job Cholmley	Whitchurch		do.
	Elizabeth Davis	Worcester	Lamb	do.
	Elizabeth Thomas	Bristoll		do.
	John Bond	Clipsham		do.
12	George Chappell	Allingsey	Abraham & Mary	do.
16	Nathaniel Lawly	Culumiton	Maryland Merchant	Virginia
17	John Morris	Oswestree	Abraham & Mary	Jamaica
Sept. 17	Edward Howell	Oswestree		Jamaica
19	Thomas Garvis	Worcester	Abraham & Mary	Jamaica
23	William Hurd	Shepton Mallett		do.
24	John Pottinger	Sittingbourne	Maryland Merchant	Maryland
25	Ann Thomas	Llany Hangell	Nevis Merchant	Nevis
24	Christopher Allen	Carleton	ffrancis & Mary	Virginia
30	John Kyppen	Sherborne	(Illegible)	do
	Elizabeth Pacie	Almondisbury	Samuel	Jamaica
Oct. 2	Cornelius Hunt	Castle Moreton	Alithea	Maryland
	John Watson	Hamilton	Maryland Merchant	Virginia
4	Bertredge King	Emory	Providence	Jamaica
	Hester Way	Bristoll	Lamb	do
	Jane Jenkins	Tinby	do.	do.
7	William Wheeler	Barton Regis	do.	do
8	Simon Weyford	Wells	Dilligence	Barbados
9	William Hackock	Overseal	Lamb	Jamaica
	John Phelps	Matherntivy	do.	do.
	Thomas Postons	Bowchurch	Martha & Sarah	Barbados
	Ann Sledge	Pensford	Alithea	Virginia
	Elizabeth Moir	Pensford		do.
	Ann Addis	Minehead	Sarah	do.
15	John ffisher	Hirsington	Maryland Merchant	Pennsylvania
	Samuel Veale	Keinsham	do.	do.
	Cæsar Hoskins	Llantverne	do.	do.
16	Christopher Groyn	Abby Door	Comfort	Maryland
	Thomas Williams	do.	do.	do.
	James Williams	do.	do.	do.
18	John Blandford	Shasten	Lamb	Jamaica
20	George Jefferies	North Petherton	Samuel	Nevis

Date	Name	Residence	Ship	Destination
Oct. 24	William Rowde	Oxford	Lamb	Jamaica
	Leonard Symes	St. Olives, Southwark		
	Nicholas Leaverne	Allseston		
	Joane Kerswell	Exeter		Jamaica
	Mary Brewer	Exeter		do.
	Isaac Williams	Landower	Merriland Merchant	Virginia
25	William Bryan	Lawrence Lydiard	Samuel	Jamaica
	Richard Tayler	Court		Virginia
27	Richard Westwood	Old Swinford	Providence	Jamaica
	William Cooke	Llingswinford		do.
	Richard Dally	Wells	Abraham & Mary	Jamaica
	John Kerslake	Exeter	Dilligence	Barbados
	Jeremy Hunt	Brinfeidl	Lamb	do.
	Daniel Baldwyn	Kings County	Ollivetree	do.
	ffrancis Mingo	Gedrington	Providence	Jamaica
	Thomas Webster	Hannam	do.	do.
29	Andrew Jones	Holywell	Olive tree	Barbadoes
	ffrancis Carter	Ilminster	do.	do.
Nov. 3	John Thomas	Week Va-er (in-decipherable)	Lamb	Jamaica
	Ann Crooke	Bristol	Diligence	Barbados
6	Elizabeth King	Stapleton	Lamb	Jamaica
	Sarah Holcomb	Taunton	do.	do.
	Alexander Prichard	Sodbury		Barbados
	Edward Bodman	Westerleigh		do.
	George Myttins	Bath	Lamb	Jamaica
	Joane Russell	Westbury	do.	do.
	James Pound	Munster		Barbadoes
Nov. 12	Mary Powell	Caerlion	Diligence	Barbados
15	John Martin	London	Martha & Sarah	do.
17	Richard Pavy	Abbotts Stoak		do.
	Richard Maunder	Portbury	Dilligence	do.
18	Henry ffonken	(A Dutchman)	Olive tree	do.
19	John Williams	Langattock		do.
27	John Tilbott	Chedder		do.
29	Isaac Williams	Wyke (?)	Olive tree	do.
	John Jestorids	Beominster	Dilligence	do.
30	Elizabeth Driver	Berkley	George	Jamaica
	Richard Marlier	Charleton Kings (?)	Ollivetree	Barbados
Dec. 5	John Male	Haffield	American Merchant	Jamaica
6	Walter Griffith	Llanharvan	America	do.
10	Walter Welsh	Cheltenham	Rose Pink	Barbados
	George Trotter	London	do.	do.
	Mary Trotter, wife of last	London	do.	do.
11	Thomas Orchard	Westerleigh	Ollive Tree	do.

Date	Name	Residence	Ship	Destination
Dec. 16	David Stephens	Co. Salop	Ollive Tree	Barbados
23	William Pierie	Ham	American Merchant	Jamaica
29	Peter Maxy	Syers Newton	do.	do.
29	Thomas West	Taunton	Ollive Tree	Barbados
	Edmond Quayle	Taunton	do.	do.
30	John Ashford	Shepton Mallett	Ollive Tree	do.
1684–85				
Jan. 3	James Webb	Bristoll	Batchellor	do.
5	Moses Lott	St. Georges	do.	do.
6	John Prosser	Ullingick	Ollife Tree	do.
12	Tobey Grey	Busselton		Jamaica
13	George Wilcocks	Chuton Mendipp	George	do.
14	William Cazen	Bedminster		do.
15	Nicholas Huling	Shrewsbury	America Merchant	do.
	Jacobas Iles	Shipton Mallett	Olive tree	Barbados
	Robertus Hordley	Co. Hants	Bachelor	do.
21	Richard Morris	Swansey		Jamaica
22	William Philipp	Llangavelly	Batchellor	Barbados
21	John Harcourt	Bontmore	America Merchant	Jamaica
23	Charles Jefferis	Upton upon Severne	do.	do.
31	Richard Morgan	Penmarke	Olive Tree	Barbados
Feb. 2	Thomas Marchant	Co. Westmurland	America Merchant	Jamaica
3	Henry Evans	Newton Nottidge	do.	do.
4	Nathaniel Cory	Hullington	America	do.
5	Joseph Lokie	Croadmasson	America Merchant	do.
	John Pooler	Evill	do.	do.
	William Margery	Netherbury	do.	do.
	Robert Morgan	Tenby	do.	do.
	John Davis	Bath	do.	do.
6	Joseph Brookes	Gloucester	do.	do.
	Mary Davis	Minehead	do.	do.
	Samuel Jones	Monmoth	Mary	Virginia
	John Sturgis	Shepton Mallett	America Merchant	Jamaica
	Trustrum Chilkin	Spaxell	do.	do.
11	Rebecca Sperin	Bristol	do.	do.
13	Mathew Phillips	Glanelthy	do.	do.
16	John Jenkins	Llanlyntwood	Mary	Virginia
	Charles Edgell	Westharptrey	America	Jamaica
Feb. 16	John Gibbons	Loxley	Mary Pinke	Jamaica
20	Richard Hedon	Landbathurne	Laurell	New England
	William Evans	Bristoll	Mary	Jamaica
	Mary Vick	Berkley	do.	Barbados
21	John Cripps	St. Dunstans in ye West, London	Merchant	Nevis
23	Thomas Davis	Cemmis	Laurell	
25	Thomas Bleakeman	Landininum	Mary	Virginia

Date	Name	Residence	Ship	Destination
Feb. 25	Timothy Yeamans	Truckersell	Mary	Jamaica
	Josias Jeffrys	Bridgenorth	do.	do.
27	Katherine Powell	Layster	Dragon	do.
Mar. 2	Thomas Murry	ffelton	do.	do.
	Thomas Ball	Coldashton	do.	do.
	Thomas Jervis	Durham, co. Gloucs.	do.	do.
4	Jenkin Lloyd	Stradmerrick	do.	do.
5	Daniell Guest	Dudley	Hart	Nevis
9	Arthur Rice	Haverford West	Dragon	Jamaica
	Samuel Plumley	Clapton	do.	do.
11	William Bliss	Pensford	Mary Pinke	do.
13	William Webb	Chepstow	Mary Pink	do.
	Robert Stephens	Bridport	Supply	Newfound-land
14	Charles Shirrey	Yetminster	Jeremy	do.
	Edward Browne	Chipenham	do.	do.
16	John Woods	Gurtontubborod	Mary Pinke	Jamaica
	John Queele	Chepton Sled	do.	do.
19	Anne Jayne	Bristoll	Dragon	do.
20	Judith Lemon	Blagdon	do.	do.
	John Andrews	Landtweed	do.	do.
23	Henry Stone	Wells	Mary William	Barbados
	John Stanly	Pidworthin	do.	do.
1685				
	Edward Isles	Leeds	Samuel & Mary	Jamaica
Mar. 26	David Williams	Llandenny	do.	do.
	John Evans	Winterborne		do.
31	George Ridon	Burnam	Mary	Virginia
	ffrancis Toby	Ueenvoe (?) (Glam)	do.	do.
	John Hastings	Huntspill	Dragon	Jamaica
	James Mackdonnell	Corke	do.	do.
	Katherine Bassett	Padsford	do.	do.
Apl. 1	Ezekiel Jeanes	Taunton	do.	do.
	James Cutler	Taunton	do.	do.
	Frances Sealy	Taunton	do.	do.
11	Edward Morley	Paxford	do.	do.
13	George Cork	Pridden	do.	do.
	John Gyles	Christchurch (Mon.)	do.	do.
	William Adsley	Chatham	do.	do.
14	Charles ffoord	Clippen	do.	do.
16	John Clarke	Tring	do.	do.
18	William Carter	Axbridge		do.
21	Christopher Tayler	ffalmouth	Dragon	do.
24	Thomas Honywell	Bristol	do.	do.
25	Elizabeth Moore	Portescuett	do.	do.
	Mary Warrington	Bristol	do.	do.

N

Date	Name	Residence	Ship	Destination
Apl. 27	Samuell Stirt	Langford	Joseph	Jamaica
	William Beven		do.	do.
30	James White	Corke	Dragon	do.
May 1	James Jones	Davids	do.	do.
	John Tapling	Newport	do.	do.
2	William ffwian	Evill		do.
	Thomas Collins	Bridgewater	Dragon	do.
	Thomas Jayne	Tidenham	do.	do.
May 4	Walter Summers	Preston	Dragon	Jamaica
	Sarah Cribb	Bur	do.	do.
	James Thomas	Halberton	do.	do.
6	Richard Crisp	Chedder	Samuel & Mary	do.
	Sarah Thomas	Salisbury		do.
	Edward Rawlins	Dorsington	Dragon	do.
	John Whoms	frinton	do.	do.
7	Richard Salter	Longley	do.	do.
8	William Luntley	Haverford West	do.	do.
	Meredith Abevan		do.	do.
	Abraham Roome	Bristoll	do.	do.
9	Daniell Lloyd	Leechfeild		do.
	Edward Spooner	Burmingham	Dragon	do.
14	David Jones	Clanorthin	do.	do.
18	Mathew Bagg	Taunton	James & Mary	do.
19	Walter Williams	Abergavenny	Samuel & Mary	do.
	Mary Goodwing	Wrington	do.	do.
	John Cooke	Yarpole	do.	do.
21	John King	Langathen	do.	do.
	Richard Thorne	London	do.	do.
23	Stephen Lewis	Longlewins	do.	do.
25	Robert English	fframpton upon Severne	do.	do.
27	Margarett Pumroy (?)	Wine Caunton	do.	do.
	Treviliam Tayler	Trent	do.	do.
28	Samuel Millicheap	St. Margaretts Clee	do.	do.
30	Cornelius Collins	Sandwich	do.	do.
	Joseph Moore	Burmingham	do.	do.
	Lewis Roberts	St. Tiswells	do.	do.
	Thomas Hill	Sanbidge (Sandbach)	do.	do.
	John Cornish	Taunton	do.	do.
June 1	Griffen Morris	Carmorden	do.	do.
	Charles Elliott	Dublin	do.	do.
	Isaac Wilton	Langoiven	do.	do.
	Walter Reece	Langinney	do.	do.
2	John Deere	Milverton	do.	do.
	Stephen Hide	Somersetshire	do.	do.
	Mary Williams	Bristoll	Joseph	Nevis
	Jane Downe	Little Cheverill	Samuel & Mary	Jamaica

Date	Name	Residence	Ship	Destination
June 2	Griffith Morgan	Langellian	Samuel & Mary	Jamaica
5	John Bleoke (?)	Bristoll	do.	do.
6	Edward Brears	Lester	do.	do.
9	George Masters			do.
10	Susanna Jones	Litton		do.
11	Thomas Burkoxe	Humber		do.
	Eliener, wife of last			do.
	Humphrey Lamb, son of last			do.
	Thomas Browne	Whitchurch		do.
12	Richard Head	Winchester	Samuel & Mary	do.
	Robert Milton	Windsor	do.	do.
	Colon (?) Risdon	Exeter	do.	do.
13	James Watkins	Madly	do.	do.
15	William Payne	Bristoll	do.	do.
	Richard ffall	New England	do.	do.
	ffrancis Dately (?)	Glostester	do.	do.
17	David Williams	Michaell Troy	do.	do.
	Jacob Boyce	The Lea	do.	do.
19	Robert Dickenson	Bristoll	do.	do.
	Thomas Darke	Studdlely	do.	do.
22	William Symons	Cam	do.	do.
	Davies John	Late of Landarvy, now of Cowbridge	do.	do.
June 27	Thomas Harris	Gloucestershire	Samuel & Mary	Jamaica
	James Bishe	Pensford	do.	do.
	Morgan Lewis	Newent		do.
July 1	John Edmonds	Cornwall, co. Monmouth		do.
	John Napp			do.
	John Carter	Bristol		do.
2	Thomas Hilman	Bristol		do.
	George Glasier	Kingston upon Thames		do.
	Israel Batt	Illbishopps		do.
7	William George	Shepton Mallett	Samuel & Mary	do.
	Thomas Britten	Marshfeild		do.
	William Hardwick	Locking		do.
14	Phillipp Smith	Winterborne		do.
	John Mose	Wimborne	Samuel & Mary	do.
16	Richard Dymery	Pursley		do.
18	James Morris	Southbrent		do.
	Thomas Baggs	Chippenham		do.
	John Gunton	Rumerston		do.
20	Richard Jones	Ludport		do.
	William Marsher (?)	Malpas		do.
	John Oxonbourd	Streaten		do.
	William Ellis	Chewstoke		do.

Date		Name	Residence	Ship	Destination
July	21	George Pegg	Epping fforest	Samuel & Mary	Jamaica
		Walter Pitman	Ditchett	do.	do.
		Thomas Drury	Alder Church	do.	do.
		John Dow	Wicke	do.	do.
		Samuel Watkins	Painswick	do.	do.
	22	William Berrey	Newton	do.	do.
		Walter Power	Kenshore		do.
		Thomas Lawrence	Trellickin		do.
		William Stibbins	Dundrey		do.
		Thomas Oakey	Worcester		do.
		ffrancis Lyes	Worcester		do.
	23	Howell Reece	Bowling Grove	Samuel & Mary	do.
		John Evans	Swanzy	do.	do.
		John Jones	Milton		do.
		Robert Jones	Westerley		do.
		William Warner	Worcester		do.
	24	Richard Vickerry	Halberton		do.
		John Gibbs	Worcester		do.
	25	Miles Hennis (?)	Gloucester	Society	Maryland *or* Virginia
		Nathaniell Barnett	Barton Regis		Jamaica
	27	Robert Allen	Trowbridge	Primrose	do.
		Joseph Nash	Worcester	Samuel & Mary	do.
		Joseph Mathews	Manchester	do.	do.
		Katharine Orwell	Christian Malford		do.
		Christopher Harrison	Maxford		do.
	29	Edward Bower	Dursley	Samuel & Mary	do.
		John West	Westerley	do.	do.
		Thomas Phillipps	Phillipps		do.
		Thomas Cox	Peterston	Samuel & Mary	do.
	31	John Lidard	Ruckeley	do.	do.
Aug.	1	Gabriell Waters	Newport	Society	Virginia
		Mary Adams	Thornbury	Primrose	Jamaica
		Jeffery Ellis	Potterne	Samuel & Mary	do.
		William Carter	Conistreet		do.
		John Lodge	Dymacke		do.
Aug.	3	Thomas Barlam	Handmore	Society	Maryland *or* Virginia
		Richard Weekes als. Davis	Shirstone	do.	Virginia
		William Griffith	Carmarthen	Samuel & Mary	Jamaica
	5	William Hill	Ross	do.	do.
		Thomas Browne	Ross	do.	do.
	6	Richard Mitchell	Llanhevett	Providence	do.
		John Dew	Kidlington	do.	do.
		John Saunders	Witchurch		do.
		Thomas Raby	Lowlaytton		do.
	7	William Stathorne	Bristoll	Samuell & Mary	Jamaica
		Thomas Merry	fframpton uppon Severne	Conqueror	Virginia

Date	Name	Residence	Ship	Destination
Aug. 7	John England	fframpton uppon Severne		Virginia
8	Tobias Sprior	Henton	Samuel & Mary	Jamaica
	James Cathen	St. Telom (?)	do.	do.
10	Phillipp Pope	Bristoll	Primrose	do.
	James Goddin	Leominster		do.
	Richard Blower	Handmore		do.
11	Ann Besor	Bristoll	Bristoll Merchant	Virginia
14	Joan Pittman	Bristoll	Samuel & Mary	Jamaica
15	John Raby	Pensford	Great Society	Virginia or Maryland
	Mary Evans	Cardiff	do.	do. do.
	Nathan Eeff (sic)	Uske	do.	Virginia
18	Jenkins Llewellin	Neath	do.	Virginia or Maryland
19	Olliver ffreeman	Bramsgrove	Society	do. do.
	John Bryan	Rochester	Anne	Virginia
20	Elizabeth Nicholls	Bristoll	Patience	Virginia or Maryland
21	Margarett Napp	Brockley	Great Society	do. do.
	Edith Napp	Brockley	do.	do. do.
25	John Roberts	Gloucester	ffactor or Unicorne	Pennsylvania
	ffrances Rayes	Bristoll	Prosperity	Barbados
26	William Tapley	West Chester	Lamb	Jamaica
	Ralph ffalyn	London	New England Merchant	Barbados
	William Raynolls	Uske	Society	Virginia
31	Mary Knowles	St. Philipps	Patience	Virginia or Maryland
Sept. 3	Thomas Thurston	Twineing	ffactor	Pennsylvania
	Owen Morgan	Cardigan		Virginia or Maryland
4	Robert Thomas	Virginia	Lamb	Jamaica
	Katherine Pert	Sandwich	Patience	Virginia
	ffrancis Creech	Devizes	James	do.
8	Randolph Garland	Rolstone	Comfort	Maryland or Virginia
	Margaret Evans	Thornbury	do.	Virginia
9	Elizabeth Williams	Creekhowell	Comfort	Maryland
16	David Miles	Llantrissent	John	Virginia
	Dorothy Price	Carmarthen	do.	do.
	Elizabeth Norton	Cardiff	do.	do.
	Katherine Thomas	Llandedgouth	do.	do.
	Reece Edwards	Llanquidding	do.	do.
	Morgan Llewis	ffagan	do.	do.
18	Sarah Winsloe	Bristoll		do.
19	Thomas Rackes	London	Lamb	do.
	Joseph Morgan	Llandwortis	Unicorne	Pennsylvania
Sept. 19	Benjamin Morgan	Llandwortis	Unicorne	Pennsylvania
	Elizabeth Phillpotts	Bristoll	do.	do.

Date	Name	Residence	Ship	Destination
Sept. 30	Thomas Powell	Ragland	John	Virginia
Oct. 2	Margarett Hartland	Ashlode	Unicorne	do.
	Henry Pearce	Calne	do.	Pennsylvania
3	Benjamin Hickes	Bristoll	Wellcome	Barbados
	Hanna Minchin	Parshore	Maryland Merchant	Virginia
23	William Beard	Defford	do.	do.
	Thomas Tustin	Defford		do.
24	Charles Stone	Elverton	Rose Pink	Nevis
31	William Sanders	Canterbury	Maryland Merchant	Virginia *or* Maryland
	William Bennett	Bridgwater		do. do.
Nov. 9	John Canterbury	Litton	Swallow	Virginia
	Stephen Spear	Chewton	do.	do.
13	Ann Glassingham	St. Mary Redcliff	Maryland Merchant	do.
16	Simon Straw	(Frenchman)	Rose Pinke	Barbados *or* Nevis
23	Luke Eernall (?)	do.	do.	do. do.
26	John James	Nash	Maryland Merchant	Virginia
Dec. 1	William Morgan	Brockway	do.	do.
2	John Muspratt	Claverton	Content	Nevis
	David Jenkins	Swansey	Maryland Merchant	Maryland
	Richard ffrance	Cromwell		do.
	Henry Jones	Whitson	Maryland Merchant	do.
	John Purnell	Russellton	do.	Virginia
7	Edmond Williams	Bristoll	do.	Maryland
	Mary Williams, wife of last	Bristoll	do.	do.
	Sarah Reed	Bristoll	do.	do.
10	Joana Medley	Bridgwater	do.	Virginia
14	William Purnell	Stanton Drew	Rose Pink	Barbados *or* Caribda Islands
30	Richard Morris	Harrow the Hill	ffellowship	Barbados
1685–86				
Jan. 2	Richard Clarke	Winterborne		do.
8	Amy Putman	Bridgwater	ffellowship	do.
19	Nicholas Persons	Lemington	Maryland Merchant	Virginia
Feb. 11	Katherine White	Exeter	Abigaile	Barbados
	David Williams	Kilpetherl		do.
13	Grace Grove	Carleon		do.
15	Thomas Broadripe	Wells	Abigail	do.
Mar. 20	Joseph Bennet	Northampton	Europe	do.
1686				
Mar. 30	Henry Goddard	Whatden	Bossterne Merchant	New England
	John Miles	Whatden	Bostern Merchant	do.
	Susanna, wife of last	Whatden	do.	do.
Apl. 24	John Wilkonson	Hertford	Anna Maria	Jamaica
	Thomas Smallwood	Stone	do.	do.
June 12	Daniel West	Brockenbury	Patience	Montserrat

INDEX